THE WITNESS OF GOD

THE WITNESS OF GOD

The Trinity, Missio Dei, *Karl Barth,*
and the Nature of Christian Community

John G. Flett

Formission Ltd
Rowheath Pavilion
Heath Road
Bournville
Birmingham B30 1HH

FORMISSION

WILLIAM B. EERDMANS PUBLISHING COMPANY
GRAND RAPIDS, MICHIGAN / CAMBRIDGE, U.K.

Published 2010 by

Wm. B. Eerdmans Publishing Co.

2140 Oak Industrial Drive N.E., Grand Rapids, Michigan 49505 /

P.O. Box 163, Cambridge CB3 9PU U.K.

Printed in the United States of America

16 15 14 13 12 11 10   7 6 5 4 3 2 1

Library of Congress Cataloging-in-Publication Data

Flett, John G., 1972-

The witness of God: the Trinity, missio Dei, Karl Barth, and the
nature of Christian community / John G. Flett.

p.   cm.

Includes bibliographical references.

ISBN 978-0-8028-6441-3 (pbk.: alk. paper)

1. Missions — Theory. 2. Barth, Karl, 1886-1968. 3. Trinity.
4. Church.   I. Title.

BV2063.F58 2010

266.001 — dc22

2010006438

www.eerdmans.com

For my friend and mentor
Harold Walter Turner (1911-2002)

Contents

Contents

Preface

Translation is always interpretation as well as translation. One key question raised by this work concerns the widespread omission of mission from Western dogmatic imagination. Specifically, this book examines Karl Barth's thick theological description of mission. Problems develop, however, in that the first supposition comes to dominate the second. The absence of mission as a proper theological category influences how Barth is translated into English. As such, any investigation into his conception of mission raises significant translation issues.

At a perfunctory level, the English edition failed to include the staggering volume of emphases, as indicated by the technique of "S p e r r u n g" contained in *Die kirchliche Dogmatik*. With this omission, one loses much of the dialectical nuance and interplay of Barth's work. What is relevant for this study is that the English often submerges those occasions in the *Church Dogmatics* where heavy emphasis is laid on the missionary nature of Christian existence. Therefore, I have restored all of the italics for emphasis — indeed, all the exclamation points — present in the German. Every italicized word within a passage that I quote from the *Church Dogmatics* occurred in the original; I have not once added any extra emphasis. This procedure was not as simple as locating the corresponding element in the English translation. Barth often emphasized the smaller parts of speech, such as prepositions and conjunctions, which the English entirely omitted. Occasionally the English eliminated an italicized verb or noun, and quite often it produced a sentence structure that accented the incorrect element. In a number of instances I have retranslated the clause or sentence in its entirety and indicated that by placing "rev." after the quotation and before the page citation of the German edition (e.g., rev., *KD* IV/2, 119; *CD* IV/2, 107). All of these references to the *Church Dogmatics* appear in parentheses in the text, and I always include the English (T. & T. Clark) edition for purposes of comparison.

At a material level, by not translating the language Barth uses vis-à-vis mission in a systematic fashion, the English edition misses the identifiable progression in Barth's thinking through each volume. I should add here that the issue is one of "mission," and not simply one of "witness" as associated with the word range *zeugen/bezeugen/Zeuge/Zeugnis*. Where Barth uses the term "mission" early in the *Church Dogmatics*, he has in mind the form of activity typically identified with the nineteenth-century pattern of "foreign missions." Matters change when he introduces the term *Sendung*. Mission gains theological gravitas. While he never relinquishes the term *Sendung*, other terms — for example, *Aufgabe* ("task") and *Auftrag* ("commission") — come to define what Barth means by *Sendung* and, indeed, by *Zeugnis*. Development occurs even within this word set. While the earlier Barth preferred the term *Aufgabe*, the later Barth used *Auftrag*.

The point is, though he is always indicating a function, this is not one that either the community or the Christian may choose to perform. The "task" is not a secondary step besides some other more elemental Christian being or form of piety. The community's "commission" expresses the whole of Christian existence; it is the community's concrete visible form. If the community fails to perform this commission, then she fails to exist as a Christian community. While even German readers fail to refer to Barth's missionary thinking (indicating that the problem is not one of translation alone), inconsistencies within the English translation muddy matters so that the clarity of Barth's thinking on this point never emerges.

A further example of this material problem concerns how the dogmatic weight with which Barth invested certain terms through the *Church Dogmatics* is lost in the third part-volume of the doctrine of reconciliation. An apparent disconnect develops between Barth's earlier and later work, with pronounced effect on the interpretation of his ecclesiology. Three terms are especially pertinent here: *Bestimmung*, *Berufung*, and *Dienst*. First, Barth uses *Bestimmung* in his doctrine of election to describe God's "determination" to be for the human, and the coordinated "determination" of the human for God. A range of other concepts cluster around this central idea, including those of fellowship and participation, and of the relationship of subject to object and active to passive. In the discussion of Christian calling, "ordination" is one of the terms used to translate *Bestimmung*. This not only destroys the link between Christian calling and election, but links calling with an entrenched preconception of ecclesial office. Second, *Berufung* is translated as "vocation." This term bespeaks the special call of an individual within the community to a particular form of Christian existence. By inference, it is proper to the community to distinguish between those Christians with and those without a particular vocation. This problematically obscures Barth's main point in using this language: that calling, active participation in service to Jesus Christ's prophetic office, is the nature of Christian existence. It applies to every member of the community, not to a select few.

Third, after a sustained development of the concept of "service," the English translates the section *Der Dienst der Gemeinde* as "The Ministry of the Community." Though "ministry" is an acceptable translation of *Dienst*, this rendering fails to account for Barth's earlier treatment of "service" and obfuscates his dogmatic point concerning the missionary nature of the Christian community. His point that the Christian community is not a prior institution that then proceeds into the world is lost amidst this range of ecclesiastically freighted terms: "vocation," "ordination," and "ministry."

A final problem concerns pronouns in English. Barth's work sets a variety of actors in motion; this is fundamental to the richness of his work. The problem is, while German differentiates pronouns by reference to the gender of the antecedent noun, the English is often restricted to the neuter pronoun "it." The variety of actors often merges into an "it" morass, and the meaning is lost. Where possible, I have repeated the noun. However, this quickly becomes cumbersome and intrudes on the flow of the text. I decided to use the feminine pronoun to refer to the Christian community (the church), and, when referring to individuals, to use "one" where possible, or to oscillate between masculine and feminine pronouns. The issue is complex given the absolute need for sensitivity towards gender issues. A constitutive element of the following argument rests in affirming that the encounter between God and humanity establishes humanity in its proper dignity. It would be poor theology if such an affirmation were gainsaid by mere literary style.

There is, however, an equally significant theological reason for using the feminine pronoun. Much of this argument concerning the missionary nature of the church includes the critical rejection of the dichotomy between church and mission. The use of a feminine pronoun intends to dis-rupt basic theological assumptions concerning the nature of the church as an institution, and the whole gamut of associations, such as the distinction between clergy and laity and the nature and role of the sacraments, that flow from this assumption. The point is not to make a normative claim concerning gender or gender relations, but to posit the community as a liv-ing and local people sent on her way in service to the world.

These concerns represent some of the conclusions that I have reached after a prolonged and engaged conversation with Darrell L. Guder. The en-tire process of translation, either from previously untranslated materials or from *Die kirchliche Dogmatik,* has been a mutual back and forth — and a period of significant learning. Thus, while an individual author or trans-lator bears final responsibility, this stark attribution does not reflect the profound collegiality central to the kind of translating process of which this work represents an end.

*   *   *

An interdisciplinary work such as this inevitably incurs a double debt of gratitude. With its origins in my Princeton Theological Seminary disserta-tion, it owes much to the supervisory attention of Darrell L. Guder, Bruce L. McCormack, and Daniel L. Migliore. But apart from this already inti-mate relationship, the engaged attention of my *Doktorvater,* Darrell L. Guder, was beyond any reasonable expectation. The entire work would have been significantly less for the absence of this relationship. His, and Judith J. Guder's, willingness to invite my family into his illustrates a be-neficence of spirit that finds expression in his own academic work, which this work hopes to emulate.

Needless to say, many of the main ideas I have formed and sharpened in conversation with my peers. Notable here is the input of Keith Johnson, Peter Kline, Travis McMaken, and Nate Kerr.

Clifford Anderson, curator of special collections at Princeton Theo-logical Seminary, in his former role as director of the Barth Center, ran numerous searches and procured valuable unpublished material. Hans-Anton Drewes, director of the Karl Barth-*Archiv,* directed me, with preci-sion, to unpublished correspondence. Thanks to him and to Dieter Zellweger of the *Nachlaß Kommission* of the Karl Barth-*Archiv* for making these resources available, and for permission to cite them in this work.

Appreciation is due Director Ekkehard Zipser of the *Berliner Missions-gesellschaft*, who liased with Siegfried Knak's daughter, and to Ms. Renate Knak herself, for the gracious permission to cite from her father's correspondence with Barth. My friend Samuel Vogel took a bicycle ride to Leipzig in order to secure a rare article.

In New Zealand, thanks are due John Hitchen for his continued intellectual support and active engagement with my work, and the board of the DeepSight Trust, with its chair, John Kernohan, who supported me throughout. In this regard, I am also indebted to the generosity of Longview Trust, Seong Sik Heo and Joo Yeon Lee, Matthew Robertson, Julian Spinks, and Eric and Annemieke Meinsma.

In being uprooted from friends and family and deposited on the other side of the world, only to have her partner excuse himself much of the time, my wife, Priscilla — and my children, Trinity and Mila — have sacrificed a good deal for this work. This, along with Priscilla's willingness to interrupt her own career, is a prize I cannot hope to repay.

Finally, a profound debt of thanks accrues to Maude Turner, and to my intellectual father, the late Harold W. Turner. His curious mixture of generosity of spirit and intractable drive to excellence ensured an academic sensibility that permits the hearing of a range of voices while cutting through the baggage governing so many discussions and predetermining so many conclusions. He was a missionary in the truest sense of the term, and any relative merit that this work may have is directly proportional to his input.

Acknowledgments

The author gratefully acknowledges receipt of the following:

From the Karl Barth-*Stiftung* (Basel, Switzerland), permission to cite from the following unpublished correspondence: Karl Barth to Karl Hartenstein (10 October 1935); Barth to Siegfried Knak (7 March 1931); Barth to Knak (13 March 1931); Barth to Knak, (13 April 1932); Barth to Werner Koch (26 March 1932); Barth to Julius Richter (9 December 1931).

From Renate Knak, daughter of Siegfried Knak (Berlin, Germany), permission to cite from the following unpublished correspondence between Knak and Barth, dated 9 February 1931; 10 March 1931; 22 March 1931; 24 April 1931; 12 April 1932; 22 April 1932.

From the Reformed Collections at Princeton Theological Seminary, Princeton, NJ, permission to cite the following unpublished documents from the Paul L. Lehmann collection: "Agenda for Commission 1: St. Martin's House, Bernardsville, NJ, January 16 and 27," 1951; "Agenda for Commission on Aim 1: October 27 and 28 at Riverside Church New York City," 1950; Paul Lehmann to John A. Mackay (31 January 1952); Paul Lehmann to Erik W. Nielsen (4 May 1952); "Minutes of the Meeting of Commission 1, October 27 and 28, Riverside Church, New York City," 1950; "Commission on Aim 1: Minutes of the Meeting at St. Martin's House, January 26 and 27," 1951; "Minutes of the Meeting of Commission 1 held at Buck Hill Falls on April 28 and 30," 1951; "Minutes of the Study Conference: Toronto, January 7 and 8," 1952; "Minutes of the Commission on the Missionary Obligation, March 13 and 14," 1953.

Abbreviations

IMC	The International Missionary Council
WCC	The World Council of Churches
CWME	The Commission for World Mission and Evangelism
MSC	The Missionary Structure of the Congregation
Edinburgh 1910	The World Missionary Conference held in Edinburgh, Scotland, 1910
Jerusalem 1928	The International Missionary Council conference held in Jerusalem, Israel, 1928
Tambaram 1938	The International Missionary Council conference held in Tambaram, Madras, India, 1938
Willingen 1952	The International Missionary Council conference held in Willingen, Germany, 1952
Uppsala 1968	Fourth Assembly of the World Council of Churches held in Uppsala, Sweden, 1968
CD	Barth, Karl. *The Church Dogmatics.* 4 vols. in 13 parts. Edinburgh: T. & T. Clark, 1956-69, 1975.
KD	Barth, Karl. *Die kirchliche Dogmatik.* 4 vols. in 13 parts. Munich: Chr. Kaiser, 1932, and Zürich: TVZ, 1938-65.
ChrL	Barth, Karl. *The Christian Life: Church Dogmatics* IV, 4: *Lecture Fragments.* Grand Rapids: Eerdmans, 1981.
rev.	Revised translation (this indicates my own translation of the German in *KD*, distinct from the English translation in the Clark edition [*CD*]).

CHAPTER ONE

Introduction

A *Problem* of God

In 1933, Emil Brunner attributed the surging theological interest in *analogia entis,* natural theology and a so-called point of contact, to Western culture's emerging missionary context.[1] A corrosive secularism and nascent paganism now grew within Christendom's ruins. The church needed to confront these competing accounts of the nature of human history with her own message. Therein lay the problem. However one might define that complex amalgam, Christendom's demise meant the collapse of a long-established connection between the Christian confession and the life of wider society. The mechanisms of the church's response were no longer clear, meaning, lest she fall prey to a "dangerous Chinese Wall mentality," the church had a vital apologetic task of reestablishing a connection with the world.[2]

In Brunner's estimation, reference to missionary methodology provided a solution. With the central question one of the "relationship between the 'natural human' and the word of God," the church had to locate the "point of contact" between the two.[3] This "common imminent possi-

---

1. Emil Brunner, "Die Bedeutung der missionarischen Erfahrung für die Theologie," in *Die deutsche evangelische Heidenmission: Jahrbuch 1933 der vereinigten deutschen Missionskonferenzen* (Hamburg: Selbstverlag der Missionskonferenzen, 1933), p. 8.

2. Emil Brunner, "Die andere Aufgabe der Theologie," *Zwischen den Zeiten* 7 (1929): 274.

3. Emil Brunner, "Die Frage nach dem 'Anknüpfungspunkt' als Problem der Theologie," *Zwischen den Zeiten* 10 (1932): 506.

bility" rests in the sense of guilt shared by all human beings, which itself results from God's general revelation in creation and through the law.[4] To quote Brunner, "[W]hoever thinks as a missionary understands the central significance of this contact — stimulating judgment and penitence — with the double revelation in creation."[5] Mission, in particular, appreciates this position because its very purpose consists of working for this encounter with revelation. The proclamation of the gospel is itself "dependent" on this contact: as it makes humans aware of their fallen condition, so it renders the proclamation of Christ understandable.[6] This gave a positive shape to the church's task. She had to identify those elements within a culture that might be cultivated as positive values fulfilled by the gospel and those that direct the human away from the gospel and thus require disciplining.[7]

Karl Barth's infamous objection made clear that such practical affirmations were not theologically benign. Decisive consequences follow for the doctrine of God. To propose that an independent knowledge of God was both possible and necessary for the relationship between God and humans located the constitution of that relationship external to God himself. This had the pernicious consequence of cleaving God's being from his act. His "being" became generally available to humans apart from his particular act of reconciliation in Jesus Christ. The "criterion of all truth" in the relationship between God and humans was not found in God himself but in the being in which both God and humans participate.[8] Barth's alternative formulation held that God is who he is in his act. "The essence of God which is seen in His revealed name is His being and therefore His act as Father, Son and Holy Spirit."[9] No human action sets the conditions necessary to God's acting; God alone makes himself known.

Not everyone found this response satisfactory. While many admired

---

4. Brunner, "Die Frage," p. 518.

5. Emil Brunner, *Natur und Gnade: zum Gespräch mit Karl Barth,* 2nd ed. (Tübingen: Mohr, 1935), p. ii.

6. Brunner, "Die Frage," p. 530.

7. Brunner, "Die Bedeutung," p. 9.

8. Karl Barth, *The Doctrine of God,* vol. II/1, *The Church Dogmatics* (T. & T. Clark: Edinburgh, 1957), p. 241. Hereafter, references to the *Church Dogmatics* will take the form: Barth, *CD* II/1, 241, followed by the page citation from the German edition, *Kirchliche Dogmatik: KD* II/1, 273.

9. Barth, *CD* II/1, 273; *KD* II/1, 306.

the aesthetic of Barth's dogmatic system, it seemingly provided insufficient resources to address the practical challenges besetting the church.[10] Brunner differentiated his own position from Barth's with this statement: "Barth thinks as a churchman for the church; I think rather as a missionary."[11] This distinction affords an important insight into the nature of the problem. The question of the church's relationship with the world is properly a missionary one. Yet, when it is depicted as a necessary middle point between the church and the world, mission functions as the bridge between the two. In that it prepares the ground for the church's own proper task — the proclamation of the word — mission exists at some distance from the church. It becomes possible, or even normative, to develop theological formulations in particular service to the church without actually engaging the world. This includes sophisticated treatments of divine ontology. The necessities of the church's witness seemingly develop in some contest with the doctrine of God, for dogmatic reference to God's being does not of itself address the nature of the connection between the church and the world.

A simple contention frames this work: the problem of the church's relationship to the world is consequent on treating God's own mission into the world as a second step alongside who he is in himself. With God's movement into his economy ancillary to his being, so the church's own corresponding missionary relationship with the world is ancillary to her being. Some general point of contact external to the church becomes necessary for the task of witness, supplying a positive account of the church's acting in relationship to the world and rendering that witness "intelligible."[12] Mission, as one step removed from the life of the church, facilitates this point of contact both by clearing sufficient cultural space and by repli-

---

10. David Bosch, for example, argues that the dialectical eschatology of the early Barth was "leaving people helpless in the face of the challenges of the modern world." David J. Bosch, *Transforming Mission: Paradigm Shifts in the Theology of Mission* (Maryknoll, NY: Orbis, 1991), p. 503.

11. Emil Brunner, "Toward a Missionary Theology," *Christian Century* 66, no. 27 (1949): 817.

12. Stanley Hauerwas, as one contemporary example, holds that "Christianity is unintelligible without witnesses, that is, without people whose practices exhibit their committed assent to a particular way of structuring the whole." Hauerwas, *With the Grain of the Universe: The Church's Witness and Natural Theology* (Grand Rapids: Brazos, 2001), p. 214.

cating the communal structures basic to the church's actual witness. In other words, this dichotomy between church and mission underlies the problem of the church's relationship with the world. No simple focus on the practical issues solves this problem, for the cleavage of church from mission derives from the cleavage of God's being in his relationship to the world. Specifically, the fullness of God's being is presented without material reference or perhaps even in antithesis to his movement into his economy. The witness of God is, as Barth suggests, "a problem of God," for it is a question of how in anticipation his being in and for himself includes human existence with him.[13] Only in correspondence to God's overcoming of the gap between himself and the world does the church live in her connection with the world.

Missio Dei: The Problem of God in Answer to the Problem of Church and Mission

This book investigates this problem of God through one of the key developments within the theology of mission: *missio Dei.* I use "God's mission" because it recognizes that the question of the church's connection with the world can only be answered by who God is in and for himself. Mission is justified because God is a missionary God. As it works its way out, however, this key theological move seemingly only reinforces the dichotomy between church and mission. It does so because, while the problem presents itself as an issue of the relationship between the church and the world, it is contingent on an account of God's own life whereby his movement into the world is a second step alongside his eternal being. In other words, *missio Dei* theology illustrates well that the cleavage of church from mission derives from a cleavage within God's own life.

Early in the twentieth century, many legitimate criticisms were being issued against the missionary enterprise. World War I and the loss of the claimed spiritual authority of Western civilization, the maturation of the so-called "younger" churches, the West's own encounter with secularism and pluralism, the fierce reactions to colonialism, the growth of indigenous nationalist movements and related resistance of the non-Christian religions to Christian expansion — all challenged the right of cross-

---

13. Barth, *CD* IV/2, 344, 342; *KD* IV/2, 384, 382.

cultural missions to exist. Against these criticisms, *missio Dei* supplied a theological redoubt for the missionary act by placing it within the Trinitarian being of God. This established a critical distance between "mission" and every contingent human form. Following David Bosch's now standard treatment, "mission is not primarily an activity of the church, but an attribute of God. God is a missionary God."[14] The Father sent his Son and Spirit into the world, and this act reveals his "sending" being. He remains active today in reconciling the world to himself and sends his community to participate in this mission. As Libertus Hoedemaker suggests, with *missio Dei*, mission became not "the defense, extension, and expansion of 'the church' or 'Christianity' but participation in the world-relatedness of God himself, in which all historical forms are merely instrumental."[15] The concept allowed theorists to acknowledge the legitimate charges laid against mission, while supplying an inviolate justification for the task itself.

For Bosch, the importance of this "decisive shift," as illustrated by its being "embraced by virtually all Christian persuasions," cannot be doubted.[16] However, such exuberance is just one side of the story. Commentators describe the concept as, at once, "pivotal" and "confused."[17] Reference to the doctrine of the Trinity establishes a requisite formal framework, but "God's mission" fails to draw on this doctrine for its material substance. The resulting vacuity renders *missio Dei* an elastic concept capable of accommodating an ever-expanding range of meanings. For Wolfgang Günther, *missio Dei* functions as a "container term, which is filled differently depending upon each individual author."[18] Tormod Engelsviken regards any consensus the term might supply as "more one of terminology than theological substance."[19] Wilhelm Richebächer illus-

---

14. Bosch, *Transforming Mission*, p. 390.

15. L. A. Hoedemaker, "The People of God and the Ends of the Earth," in *Missiology: An Ecumenical Introduction*, ed. F. J. Verstraelen et al. (Grand Rapids: Eerdmans, 1995), p. 164.

16. Bosch, *Transforming Mission*, pp. 389, 390.

17. Hoedemaker, "The People of God," pp. 171, 165.

18. Wolfgang Günther, "Gott selbst treibt Mission: Das Modell der 'Missio Dei,'" in *Plädoyer für Mission: Beiträge zum Verständnis von Mission heute*, ed. Klaus Schäfer (Hamburg: Evangelische Missionswerk in Deutschland, 1998), p. 56.

19. Tormod Engelsviken, *"Missio Dei*: The Understanding and Misunderstanding of a Theological Concept in European Churches and Missiology," *International Review of Mission* 92, no. 4 (2003): 486.

trates the problem when he observes that *missio Dei* is used by some to "justify the Christocentric definition of all the mission of the church as distinct from religious propaganda, and by others to do just the opposite, i.e., to propound a deity that bears witness to itself in other religions and thereby counters the absolute claims of Christianity."[20]

With such vacillation, in Günther's estimation, the phrase *missio Dei* "blurs more than it clarifies, and thus needs either to be more precisely defined or dropped altogether."[21] Jacques Matthey has called for "a 'moratorium', or at least for the greatest restraint, in the use of classical *Missio Dei* terminology."[22] *Missio Dei* is basic to a theological understanding of mission and dysfunctional to the point of being rejected by those within the field supported by this foundation. What underlies this paradox?

With *missio Dei*, the term "mission," rather than being depicted in flat phenomenological terms, received theological definition. No less a theological authority than Schleiermacher once described mission as "only the pious longing of the stranger for home, the endeavor to carry one's fatherland with one and everywhere to intuit its laws and customs, its higher, more beautiful life."[23] In critical contrast to this dominant assumption, "mission" refers not to the geographical expansion of the Christian faith from the West to the non-Christian world, but to its dogmatic origins, to the activity of the Father in sending his Son and Spirit. God himself has acted and continues to act in redemptive mission. This, for Bosch, is *missio Dei*'s strength. "Our mission has no life of its own: only in the hands of the sending God can it truly be called mission."[24] Mission is not something the church does, dependent on ecclesiastical management and developed according to some notion of the efficient use of resources. It is justified by neither human capacity nor historical accident. Wilhelm Anderson, summarizing the basic thrust, says that "the Church is not the place of origin and goal of the missionary enterprise: the missionary enterprise is the historical happening which embraces the Church and takes it up into its ser-

---

20. Wilhelm Richebächer, "Editorial," *International Review of Mission* 92, no. 4 (2003): 465.

21. Günther, "Gott selbst treibt Mission," p. 56.

22. Jacques Matthey, "Mission als anstößiges Wesensmerkmal der Kirche," *Zeitschrift für Mission* 28, no. 3 (2002): 236 n. 38.

23. Friedrich D. E. Schleiermacher, *On Religion: Speeches to Its Cultured Despisers* (Cambridge: Cambridge University Press, 1996), p. 78.

24. Bosch, *Transforming Mission*, p. 390.

vice."[25] Missions would continue because, while provisional, they originate in — and are sustained by — God's own acting in calling the world to himself. When compared with the phenomenological underpinnings of missions that were normative at the dawn of the twentieth century, *missio Dei* is, in truth, pivotal.

Without any link to a specific act, however, "mission" soon expanded to encompass the entire horizon of divine and human history. Following Stephen Bevans and Roger Schroeder, *missio Dei* is "the very mission of God in creation, redemption and continual sanctification."[26] Every act of God, since God is by nature missionary, is properly described as mission. Mission, when it did not reduce to a vague involvement within the sociopolitical sphere, very soon became a distilled image of the church's general direction within history, with the effect, for Hoedemaker, of providing "theological legitimation to the ecumenical emphasis on the church."[27] Mission was reduced to the being of the church in her mundane operation of word and sacrament, and via an ever-increasing assortment of other practices internal to the church herself. Anything the church did could now be classified as mission. With this, as Stephen Neill famously said, "If everything is mission, nothing is mission."[28] Vsevolod Spiller, for example, makes the following oft-quoted assertion: "Church *as such* is mission."[29] This, on the one hand, is an important Orthodox corrective against the prevailing Protestant reduction of mission to a specialist function undertaken apart from the central life of the congregation. The church is mission because the task belongs to the whole community. On the other hand, Spiller's statement is predicated on a definite understanding of the nature of the church. To continue with Spiller, while mission in its "widest and deepest sense" is the church, "it cannot, in our view, contain the *raison d'être* of the Church."[30] Accenting *mission* would

25. Wilhelm Andersen, *Towards a Theology of Mission: A Study of the Encounter between the Missionary Enterprise and the Church and Its Theology* (London: SCM, 1955), p. 41.

26. Stephen B. Bevans and Roger P. Schroeder, *Constants in Context: A Theology of Mission for Today* (Maryknoll, NY: Orbis, 2004), p. 288.

27. L. A. Hoedemaker, "Mission, Unity and Eschaton: A Triadic Relation," *Reformed World* 50, no. 4 (2000): 176.

28. Stephen Neill, *Creative Tension* (London: Edinburgh House, 1959), p. 81.

29. Vsevolod Spiller, "Missionary Aims and the Russian Orthodox Church," *International Review of Mission* 52, no. 2 (1963): 198.

30. Spiller, "Missionary Aims," p. 203.

erode the "meta-historical pre-establishing of the Church before all ages."[31] The being of the church belongs to eternity, while mission refers to the attitude of this church in a world destined to pass away. The church "is" mission as she is "sacramentally" responsible for the transition between the reconciliation she shares with God and the estrangement from God experienced in the world. Therefore, Engelsviken suggests that "the church has not only a witnessing or participating function in what God is doing in the world, but it has a sacramental or instrumental function, in that the mission of God is carried out in and through the church as its primary focus."[32] This relative justification juxtaposes the missionary act to some more fundamental being of the church, thereby disqualifying it as essential to Christian life and piety.

Missio Dei is a trope. It satisfies an instinct that missionary witness properly belongs to the life of the church without offering any concrete determination of that act. On the fiftieth anniversary of the concept's supposed inception, Matthey made the following sober judgment: "[R]eference to *missio Dei* did not really solve any of the major missiological challenges which shook Protestants from the beginning of the last century."[33] It provided a necessary critical distance between the missionary act and the colonialist project, but it failed to supply that act any alternative form. According to Günther, "with the impending threat of all missions being ejected from the collapsing colonial empires, the *missio Dei* formula came as a relief: 'God's mission, not ours'!"[34] Yet, in that this theological justification seemingly obviated the many legitimate criticisms issued against missionary method, the formula "made it possible very quickly to get on with 'business as usual.'"[35] *Missio Dei* did provide some space for those convinced by the postcolonialist critique to define mission away in terms of church practices such as the Eucharist and in general political involvement. For those organizations that continued with the cross-cultural act, little actually changed by way of practices. As Bosch suggests, "many of the old images live on, almost unchal-

---

31. Spiller, "Missionary Aims," p. 202.

32. Engelsviken, "*Missio Dei*," pp. 485-86.

33. Jacques Matthey, "God's Mission Today: Summary and Conclusions," *International Review of Mission* 92, no. 4 (2003): 581.

34. Wolfgang Günther, "The History and Significance of World Mission Conferences in the 20th Century," *International Review of Mission* 92, no. 4 (2003): 530.

35. Günther, "The History and Significance," p. 530.

lenged."[36] They did so because, with *missio Dei,* they had now received some form of divine validation.

Despite his concerns, Matthey continues that "if we were to lose the reference to *missio Dei,* we would again put the sole responsibility for mission on human shoulders and thereby risk, missiologically speaking, believing that salvation is gained by our own achievements."[37] If mission were only a human activity, reliant on the range of human capacities, then it is untrue and an impediment to the proclamation of the gospel. Bosch supports this conclusion: "The recognition that mission is God's mission represents a crucial breakthrough in respect of the preceding centuries. It is inconceivable that we could again revert to a narrow, ecclesiocentric view of mission."[38] There's the rub. The Copernican turn of *missio Dei* is not something from which the Christian community can depart. Any other conception of the ground, motive, and goal of mission apart from *missio Dei's* Trinitarian location risks investing authority in historical accident and human capacity.

Both the decisive force and fatal flaw of *missio Dei* rests in its relationship to the doctrine of the Trinity. As propounded to date, the concept is deficiently Trinitarian, and the wide range of its contemporary problems is a direct result of this single lack. Reference to the Trinity distanced mission from every particular human act, but, as now a divine attribute, uncertainty arose over the practical transition from divine being to the human missionary act.[39] *Missio Dei's* vacuity emerges at this precise point. Material formulations of God's connection with the world was reduced to the language of "sending," with the effect that his "sending" being included more the particular sendings of the Son and Spirit. *Missio Dei* provides a Trinitarian illusion behind which all manner of non-Trinitarian mediations operate with

---

36. Bosch, *Transforming Mission,* p. 381.
37. Matthey, "God's Mission Today," p. 582.
38. Bosch, *Transforming Mission,* p. 393.
39. Rosin suggests that this inability to indicate any definitive form of human action in relation to God's sending is a result of the "preponderantly passive meaning" the term *missio* had within traditional Trinitarian terminology. The concept "sending" does not of itself hold any material weight when it is removed from its immediate reference to the Son and the Spirit, i.e., when it is deployed in a wider setting to indicate, not only the sending of the church, but also the "sending" of creation as a witness to God. H. H. Rosin, *'Missio Dei': An Examination of the Origin, Contents and Function of the Term in Protestant Missiological Discussion* (Leiden: Interuniversity Institute for Missiological and Ecumenical Research, Department of Missiology, 1972), p. 16.

sanctioned impunity. The Trinitarian formula is pure preamble.[40] This explains how a wide variety of seemingly incongruous positions can all lay claim to the name *missio Dei.*

40. Ecumenical statements affirming the Trinitarian ground of mission illustrate the problem. While Bassham considers the "recognition of the Trinitarian basis of the missionary enterprise" to be the "most significant point of convergence" between ecumenical, Roman Catholic, and evangelical positions, he develops the relationship between the doctrine of the Trinity and missions only minimally. Rodger C. Bassham, "Mission Theology: 1948-1975," *Occasional Bulletin of Missionary Research* 4, no. 2 (1980): 56. The 1986 Orthodox statement on mission, *Go Forth in Peace,* demands "an application of trinitarian theology" for a correct interpretation of mission, and complains that the Trinitarian basis "deserves more attention than it normally receives." "Go Forth in Peace: Orthodox Perspectives on Mission," in *New Directions in Mission and Evangelism 1: Basic Statements 1974-1991,* ed. James A. Scherer and Stephen B. Bevans (Maryknoll, NY: Orbis, 1992), pp. 203-4. Its own articulation, however, simply consists of one short paragraph on the communion nature of the Trinity, leading to a depiction of mission as "the transmission of the life of communion that exists in God." "Go Forth in Peace: Orthodox Perspectives on Mission," p. 204. Reference to existing liturgical and hierarchical structures accomplishes the substantive theological work, with mission noticeable by its absence. In Catholic circles, Eugene L. Smith similarly critiques the role Trinitarian doctrine plays in *Ad Gentes,* arguing that the theological groundwork is "primarily an addition" to a document centrally concerned with questions of "jurisdiction and organization." Eugene L. Smith, "A Response to *Ad Gentes,*" in *The Documents of Vatican II,* ed. Walter M. Abbott (New York: Crossroad, 1989), p. 631. In Evangelical thinking, Engelsviken concurs regarding the Lausanne Covenant, saying that while it "refers to the triune God in the first article, the significance of the Trinity for mission is not spelled out." Tormod Engelsviken, "Convergence or Divergence? The Relationship between Recent Ecumenical and Evangelical Mission Documents," *Swedish Missiological Themes* 89, no. 2 (2001): 202. Once delivered, it remains unclear how the doctrine of the Trinity informs the missionary task, since the resulting forms — both of the missionary act and church order — do not differ from traditional accounts. Even the 2005 Faith and Order paper on "The Nature and Mission of the Church," which sought to unify this split between institution and event by positing the church as both a "Creation of the Word and of the Holy Spirit," omits reference to the Word when expounding on the Trinity. To quote Mary Tanner, "Although the report begins with the church as *creatura verbi* (creation of the word) and *creatura spiritu* (creation of the Spirit), the understanding of the church as *koinonia* remains central in the text. Communion refers to the life of love of the three persons of the Trinity." Mary Tanner, "Ecumenical Theology," in *The Modern Theologians: An Introduction to Christian Theology since 1918,* ed. David Ford and Rachel Muers (Malden, MA: Blackwell, 2005), pp. 562-63. While Tanner makes this observation of the earlier edition, entitled "The Nature and Purpose of the Church," the revised version fails at the same places. The church is defined as *koinonia,* but *koinonia* is itself defined without reference to the missionary movement, the latter only appearing in the document as an act external to the life of the church.

Introduction

Barth and the Origins of *Missio Dei*

Attributing the acknowledged problems of *missio Dei* to a lack of Trinitarian substance runs counter to the overwhelming burden of received history. The original proposal for a Trinitarian basis entered mainstream thinking at the International Missionary Council (IMC) conference held in 1952 at Willingen, Germany. However, the intellectual origins of this shift are attributed to a lecture Karl Barth delivered twenty years earlier, entitled, "Die Theologie und die Mission in der Gegenwart" (theology and mission in the present situation).[41] This is where, it is argued, Barth initiated the connection between missions and the doctrine of the Trinity. Johannes Aagaard, among the earliest to propose this origin, says that "the Willingen conference in 1952 as a whole meant that the approach advocated by Barth already in 1932 was now generally acknowledged. The ground for mission was found in the triune God and His mission."[42]

It is further argued that Karl Hartenstein, as a mission administrator, a student of dialectical theology, and a personal friend of Barth, mediated

41. Karl Barth, "Die Theologie und die Mission in der Gegenwart," *Zwischen den Zeiten* 10, no. 3 (1932): 189-215. Two issues are in play here. First, there is the question of who first related the doctrine of the Trinity to missionary activity. Some Catholic scholars note the work of seventeenth-century Cardinal Pierre de Bérulle. See André Rétif, "Trinité et Mission d'après Bérulle," *Neue Zeitschrift für Missionswissenschaft* 13 (1957): 1-8. A number of Lutheran scholars retroactively attribute *missio Dei* to Martin Luther. While this connection is erroneous, it remains important for understanding how the basic dichotomy of *missio Dei* theology is reinforced by a certain appropriation of Luther's law-gospel distinction within a theocentric framework. See Ingemar Öberg, *Luther and World Mission: A Historical and Systematic Study,* trans. Dean Apel (St. Louis: Concordia, 2007), pp. 3-5 n. 2; James A. Scherer, "The Lutheran Missionary Idea in Historical Perspective," in . . . *That the Gospel may be Sincerely Preached throughout the World: A Lutheran Perspective on Mission and Evangelism in the 20th Century,* ed. James A. Scherer (Stuttgart: Kreuz Verlag, 1982), pp. 1-29. A second issue concerns the term's contemporary development. This is, in the main, ascribed to Barth and Hartenstein. Bonhoeffer is occasionally regarded as an influence, but this more addresses the shape *missio Dei* theology took during the 1960s, with its emphasis on "religionless Christianity." Some attribute the concept to Wilhelm Andersen for his summary of the Willingen conference. Wainwright credits Newbigin with its development due to his penning of Willingen's final statement. Geoffrey Wainwright, *Lesslie Newbigin: A Theological Life* (Oxford: Oxford University Press, 2000), p. 165. Not one of these accounts is satisfactory.

42. Johannes Aagaard, "Some Main Trends in Modern Protestant Missiology," *Studia Theologica* 19 (1965): 252.

the latter's position to Willingen. He is the link between Barth's 1932 lecture and Willingen 1952, and this Trinitarian development constituted the peak of Barth's influence on missiology.[43] By the time of David Bosch's oft-quoted 1991 summary, this genealogy is fixed.[44] The issue is not merely one of historical accuracy. With this history, the evident and lamented problems of *missio Dei* receive precise attribution. The essential dichotomy between God's mission and human activity, which so plagues *missio Dei* theology, is a direct consequence of the concept's dialectical origins. Any constructive solution must first overcome this "Barthian" liability.[45] Such is the unquestioned popular account. But it demands significant revision. A constructive redevelopment of the concept requires, above all, a correct diagnosis of the problem.

In reality, Barth never once used the term *missio Dei,* never wrote the phrase "God is a missionary God," and never articulated a Trinitarian position of the kind expressed at Willingen. No textual evidence indicates that Barth interacted with the missiological discussions that were engaged with his theology. He was well acquainted with Hartenstein, who, as director of the Basel Mission, lived as Barth's neighbor from 1935 to 1939; but nowhere does he refer to Hartenstein's work.[46] Hartenstein, for his part, observes at the beginning of his now famous 1927 lecture, "Was hat die Theologie Karl Barths der Mission zu sagen?" (What does Karl Barth's the-

43. Aagaard says, "While Willingen may be considered the fulfillment of the Barthian beginning from the thirties, it may at the same time be considered the beginning of the end of the Barthian influence as the decisive and unifying force." Aagaard, "Some Main Trends," p. 252.

44. Bosch, *Transforming Mission,* pp. 389-93.

45. As an example of the prevailing confusion, Schreiter erroneously observes that Barth was "one of the first to use the term," and that *"missio Dei* may be coming back with a somewhat modified meaning." This modification consists of "a growing awareness that it is not that we carry out mission, but rather that we participate in what is first and foremost God's work." Robert J. Schreiter, "Epilogue: Mission in the Third Millennium," in *Mission in the Third Millennium,* ed. Robert J. Schreiter (Maryknoll, NY: Orbis, 2001), p. 155. Contra Schreiter, Barth's clearest contribution is precisely an emphasis on God's acting, and his remaining subject in this act. Based on this affirmation, he is, with monotonous regularity, accused of denying the actuality of human agency. In other words, a position with which Barth is castigated has become the new position of *missio Dei,* and the triumph of this *novum* consists in its liberation from these Barthian roots!

46. Barth even invited Hartenstein to use the informal "du" with him because of their "meeting of the minds." Karl Barth to Karl Hartenstein, 10 October 1935, Karl Barth Archive, KBA 9235.289, Basel, Switzerland.

ology say to mission?), that Barth was "not a close friend of missions."[47]
While Hendrik Kraemer, especially via his work at the 1938 IMC Tambaram conference, is regarded as a popularizer of Barth's work, there is no evidence (either in the text of the *Church Dogmatics* or in the form of any correspondence) that Barth interacted with him either.[48]

Barth's most focused development of witness within the *Church Dogmatics* did not appear until seven years after Willingen, but nowhere does he refer to this particular conference. This observation has traction, given that here Barth undertakes his most extended reflection on the ecumenical movement, including a revision of his harsh criticisms of the 1928 IMC Jerusalem and the 1937 "Life and Work" Oxford conferences.[49] When considering Barth's contribution, mission commentators often lament the paucity of reference to missions within the voluminous pages of the *Church Dogmatics,* turning first to the infamous §17 on "The Revelation of God as the Abolition of Religion."[50] Combine this with his rejection of natural

47. Karl Hartenstein, "Was hat die Theologie Karl Barths der Mission zu Sagen?" *Zwischen den Zeiten* 6 (1928): 59.

48. There was at least one occasion of personal contact as Barth, Kraemer, Hoekendijk, and Newbigin were among a select twenty-five theologians who met as part of the advisory commission for the WCC Evanston conference. See Eberhard Busch, *Karl Barth: His Life from Letters and Autobiographical Texts* (Grand Rapids: Eerdmans, 1994), pp. 395-400.

49. Barth, *CD* IV/3.1, 18-38. For Barth's negative comments regarding Jerusalem, see *CD* II/1, 97; *KD* II/1, 107. For an informative survey of Barth's criticisms of Oxford 1937, and of his general relationship with the ecumenical movement, see W. A. Visser 't Hooft, "Karl Barth and the Ecumenical Movement," *Ecumenical Review* 32, no. 2 (1980): 129-51. As an interesting aside, in response to a question concerning the IMC's integration with the WCC, Barth declared: "It is good, in principle. It must be understood that the church is not a church if it is not a missionary church. The church is, as such, a missionary church. Provided this understanding undergirds the union, it is a good thing. Hopefully, it does not mean that mission becomes paralyzed!" Karl Barth, "Gespräche mit Methodisenpredigern, 1961," in *Gespräche, 1959-1962,* ed. Eberhard Busch, *Gesamtausgabe* (Zürich: Theologischer Verlag, 1995), p. 203.

50. Wrogemann, for instance, says that, in the 8,000 pages of the *Kirchliche Dogmatic,* Barth "concerns himself with the theme of mission on only six pages," i.e., *KD* IV/3.2, 1002-7. Henning Wrogemann, *Mission und Religion in der systematischen Theologie der Gegenwart: das Missionsverständnis deutschsprachiger protestantischer Dogmatiker im 20. Jahrhundert* (Göttingen: Vandenhoeck und Ruprecht, 1997), p. 78. Twenty years earlier, Waldron Scott made an identical claim, saying that "within the more than eight thousand pages of his systematic theology Karl Barth devotes a mere four and one-half pages to the specific topic of foreign missions," i.e., *CD* IV/3.2, 874-78. Waldron Scott, *Karl Barth's Theology of Mission* (Downers Grove, IL: InterVarsity, 1978), p. 9.

theology, an assumed necessity for the missionary task, and Barth is mo-
notonously depicted as representative of the position one should avoid.
Reference to Barth hinders mission.

The reception of Barth's 1932 lecture is limited to the lone voice of
Siegfried Knak, director of the Berlin Mission Society from 1921 to 1948,
and to his defense of locating mission methodology in *Volkstum*.[51] No single reference picks up Barth's Trinitarian allusion before Willingen. The
earliest connections occur in 1965, thirteen years after the conference.
Aagaard, as an example, says that Barth "escaped the phenomenological
imprisonment and redefined mission on the basis of the trinitarian theology of the ancient church. Mission is first of all *Missio Dei*, the missio of
the Son and of the Spirit by the Father."[52] Barth certainly denied every
phenomenological ground to mission as inimical to any Christian theology. However, it does not automatically follow that he developed an alternative Trinitarian basis. Nevertheless, by the early 1970s, the connection
between Barth's 1932 lecture, Hartenstein, and Willingen appears settled.[53]

The earliest detailed treatment of Willingen itself, published by Wilhelm
Andersen three years after the conference, only refers to Barth's lecture in a
footnote as one example of the kind of dogmatic interest in missions between the 1928 Jerusalem and 1938 Tambaram conferences.[54] He suggests no
link between Barth's work and Willingen. H. H. Rosin's extended — and to
date the most critical — treatment of *missio Dei* theology (1972) refers to
neither Barth's lecture nor his theology in general. Rather, Rosin quotes an
article by Johannes Dürr, published only months before Willingen, which
says that "the original meaning of the word 'missio' developed in the doctrine of the Trinity and meant the sending of the Son from the bosom of the
Father. It was thus a theological, redemptive-historical term."[55]

51. See Siegfried Knak, "Die Mission und die Theologie in der Gegenwart," *Zwischen den Zeiten* 10, no. 4 (1932): 331-55.

52. Aagaard, "Some Main Trends," p. 244. Wiedenmann makes a similar claim during this period. See Ludwig Wiedenmann, *Mission und Eschatologie: Eine Analyse der neueren deutschen evangelischen Missionstheologie* (Paderborn, Germany: Verlag Bonifacius-Druckerei, 1965), p. 66.

53. See Ludwig Rütti, *Zur Theologie der Mission: kritische Analysen und neue Orientierungen* (Munich: Chr. Kaiser Verlag, 1972), pp. 186-87 n. 143; Anna Marie Aagaard, "Missio Dei in katholischer Sicht," *Evangelische Theologie* 34 (1974): 421.

54. Andersen, *Towards a Theology of Mission*, p. 27 n. 1.

55. Johannes Dürr, "Die Reinigung der Missionsmotive," *Evangelisches Missions-Magazin* 95 (1951): 9 n. 16. He would elsewhere state that "Christmas is for that reason the ac-

Negatively considered, if Barth's 1932 article constituted such a land-
mark, then why did this Trinitarian ground not popularly emerge at the
1938 IMC Tambaram conference — the conference considered most representative of dialectical theology — which was held six years after the lecture
and still a year before the onset of World War II?[56] Hartenstein attended all
of the IMC conferences and authored the main summaries for German au-
diences. If he is responsible for mediating this Barth-derived Trinitarian
position to Willingen, then why did he not propose this earlier than 1952?
What occasioned the appearance of Trinitarian doctrine at this particular
conference? It is difficult to prove an absence, especially given the dominant
status of the received history and the range of theological approaches invested in it. Nevertheless, not a single fragment of textual evidence supports
the connection between Barth's 1932 lecture and Willingen's Trinitarian developments.

Despite the missiological lament concerning Barth's seeming lack of
direct reference to missions, Aagaard described him as "the decisive
Protestant missiologist in this generation."[57] His theological stimulus pro-

---

tual, fundamental 'missio', the mission. The Fathers of the Church were well advised for that
reason in using the Latin expression 'missio' in connection with trinitarian doctrine, for the
sending of the Holy Spirit." Johannes Dürr, "Kirche, Mission und Reich Gottes,"
Evangelisches Missions-Magazin 97 (1953): 137.

56. Bosch does hold that "at the Tambaram meeting of the IMC (1938), a statement of
the German delegation became another catalyst in the development of a new understanding
of mission. The delegation confessed that only 'through a creative act of God His kingdom
will be consummated in the final establishment of a New Heaven and a New Earth.'" Bosch,
Transforming Mission, p. 390. This statement of the German delegation against the perceived
dominance of an American liberalism, which equated the kingdom of God with historical
progress, is considered a pioneering assertion of the eschatological reality of mission. See
John Merle Davis, ed. *The Authority of the Faith,* 7 vols., The Madras Series (London: International Missionary Council, 1939), 1:169-71. Mission, it argued, must emphasize the present
reality of sin and death and the future establishment of the kingdom, since "only this eschatological attitude can prevent the Church from becoming secularized." Davis, *The Authority
of the Faith,* 1:170. Problematically, however, this eschatological statement is predicated on an
affirmation of "distinct orders which God has established and ordained from the beginning
of history," i.e., the "orders of sex and family, nation and races." Davis, ed., *The Authority of
the Faith,* 1:170. Indicative of the confusion basic to *missio Dei,* reference to divine agency is
not of itself sufficient. While it here opposes a coincidence of civilization and mission, this
treatment reinforces an underlying connection between divine agency and givens in creation.

57. Aagaard, "Some Main Trends," p. 238.

vided "the back-bone of the reorientation in Protestant missiology," and further, "practically all aspects of modern Protestant missiology have some relation to the theology of Barth."[58] With his rediscovery of eschatology, to quote Bosch, Barth was the "first clear exponent of a new theological paradigm which broke radically with an Enlightenment approach to theology."[59] Barth destroyed any possibility for grounding mission in simple phenomenological terms, and this clearing certainly assisted mission in securing a theological foundation for the act. It is also accurate to note Hartenstein's constructive debt to Barth on this precise point. According to Kraemer, however, this clearing occurred with the terrifying force of "a purifying storm."[60] Barth's polemic against *Kulturprotestantismus* and the conflation of "German" and "Christian" produced a position that was "artificial, somehow unreal, convulsive and overdone."[61] Such was his rejection of any phenomenological ground that Barth negated even the legitimate role of the human within reconciliation. Kraemer continues that "Barth is consumed, even obsessed, by the desire to suppress the least tendency to minimize or relativize God's activity, and to establish with relentless completeness that human activity or participation is totally nonexistent in the whole story of salvation."[62]

Willem Visser 't Hooft, too, feared that Barth was "in danger of evolving his dualism to the place where no further relation between the saving power of God and the actual situation of this created world can be found."[63] Hoedemaker, reflecting the popular conclusion, says that "reference to the theology of the trinity apparently functions as an instance of the crisis motif in early dialectical theology: Over against God as the real subject of history human activity has no leg of its own on which to stand."[64] *Missio Dei*'s inability to articulate a definite form for the Christian community's missionary activity is an inevitable consequence of its

58. Aagaard, "Some Main Trends," p. 239.
59. Bosch, *Transforming Mission*, p. 390.
60. Hendrik Kraemer, *The Christian Message in a non-Christian World* (London: Harper and Brothers, 1938), p. 131.
61. Hendrik Kraemer, *Religion and the Christian Faith* (Philadelphia: Westminster, 1956), p. 192.
62. Kraemer, *Religion and the Christian Faith*, p. 192.
63. Quoted by Werner Ustorf, *Sailing on the Next Tide: Missions, Missiology, and the Third Reich* (Frankfurt am Main: Peter Lang, 2000), p. 105.
64. Hoedemaker, "The People of God and the Ends of the Earth," p. 163.

Barthian origins. Therefore, Aagaard complains that Barth's "hypostatical missiology" stimulated "empty concepts, ideas, generalization without roots. It may be a help in theologizing but it does not help much in practice."[65] Barth's emphasis on divine agency did afford a necessary critical disjunction between missions and the colonialist enterprise, but other voices, most notably those of Brunner and Gogarten, were enlisted when it came to the positive reformulation of the missionary act.[66]

A history of direct lineage between Barth and *missio Dei* misidentifies the insufficient Trinitarianism that so plagues the concept. Attributing the concept's evident difficulties to a supposed dialectical disjunction between divine and human agency disguises the concept's ground within competing theologies of creation. While such a position stands in clear contrast to Barth's own, given the basic assumption that any constructive development in *missio Dei* must first overcome his influence, much of the contemporary debate remains blinkered to Barth's potential contribution. Apart from reference to its supposed Barthian origins, no account of *missio Dei* or of a Trinitarian grounding to mission treats his work in a substantive way. Any resources here for the theology of mission, and especially for clarifying *missio Dei* theology, remain fallow.

A Trinitarian Proposal

The problem of *missio Dei* is finally one of an undue breach between who God is in himself and who he is in his economy. While it uses the doctrine of the Trinity for the critical purpose of distancing mission from the colo-

---

65. Johannes Aagaard, "Church — What is Your Mission Today?" *Spirituality in East and West* 15 (2002) [journal on-line]; available at http://www.dci.dk; accessed 8 July 2008.

66. As Ustorf suggests, "Barth's cleansing of the missionary message from 'liberalism' and 'civilization' was happily accepted, but as soon as it came to questions of method and *Volkstum,* Emil Brunner (1889-1966) and Fredrich Gogarten (1887-1967) were the preferred theological sources." Ustorf, *Sailing on the Next Tide,* p. 22. Though Hartenstein is considered to have taken Barth's theology to Willingen, correspondence between him and Brunner demonstrates that during this period he identified more with Brunner than with Barth. Gerold Schwarz, *Mission, Gemeinde und Ökumene in der Theologie Karl Hartensteins* (Stuttgart: Calwer Verlag, 1980), p. 63. This holds true also for Kraemer. See Libertus A. Hoedemaker, "Hendrik Kraemer 1888-1965: Biblical Realism Applied to Mission," in *Mission Legacies: Biographical Studies of Leaders of the Modern Missionary Movement,* ed. Gerald H. Anderson et al. (Maryknoll, NY: Orbis Books, 1994), pp. 511-14.

nialist endeavor, its use of "sending" to connect God with the world only focuses on a range of mediating entities external to who God is in and for himself. Reference to God's "sending" nature supplied a Trinitarian façade but abstracted the act from the particular sendings of the Son and Spirit. God's being became generally available, and this provides the base material for the missionary task. The irony is that, where a Trinitarian theology of mission should address this problem of the gap between God and the world, *missio Dei* accomplishes the opposite: it establishes the gap and posits the missionary task as the means for overcoming it.[67] That this occurs, however, is not the result of the prior methodological move of locating the justification for mission within God's own life. The difficulties of *missio Dei* are derivative in nature: they manifest a larger problem within Trinitarian theology, as it concerns the nature of God's own coming into the world. One can enter this issue through the contemporary discussion on divine ontology and the nature of Christian community with respect to Arius, Augustine, and the Cappadocians.

Arius, Augustine, and the Cappadocians

Though history judges his position to be heretical, Arius wrote with the positive intention of protecting Jesus Christ's status as the mediator between God and humanity. He worked under a given assumption concerning the nature of divinity: nothing sent by God can itself be God. As the Son was sent by the Father, so he was a dependent and subordinate entity. It is precisely in this subordination that Jesus Christ bridges the unbridgeable gulf between God and his creation.[68] He constitutes the necessary middle point between divinity and humanity, establishing the means by which the human might approach God.

---

67. As John F. Hoffmeyer suggests, "the divine missions of Word and Spirit are not the bridging of a gap between a divine realm and a creaturely realm, between invulnerable being and vulnerable becoming, between timelessness and time. . . . If the church's mission is participation in the mission of the triune God, then the church's mission is also not to get God into the world. Unfortunately, the church's thinking about its mission has often been shaped by gap-bridging models." Hoffmeyer, "The Missional Trinity," *Dialog* 40, no. 2 (2001): 109.

68. See Rowan Williams, *Arius: Heresy and Tradition*, rev. ed. (Grand Rapids: Eerdmans, 2002), pp. 175-77.

In opposition to Arius, Nicaea addressed the question of Jesus' divinity. He is "Light of Light, very God of very God, begotten, not made, being of one substance with the Father." However, the nature of the defense seemed to ratify the prevailing philosophical assumption. As divinity receded into eternity, so it did not include his actual movement into the world as necessary to a theological account of who God is in and for himself. Good reasons exist for taking this position, not the least of which is avoiding lazy connections of an immanentist variety that threaten God's freedom and, with that, the veracity of his promise. But it is not without its consequences. Augustine's doctrine of the Trinity is understood as illustrative of the problem. He protects the divinity of the Son and Spirit by ascribing the economy only epistemological significance: "[A]nd just as being born means for the Son his being from the Father, so his being sent means his being known to be from him. And just as for the Holy Spirit his being the gift of God means his proceeding from the Father, so his being sent means his being known to proceed from him."[69] One finds here a basic juxtaposition whereby ontology is resolved within God's immanent life, alongside which the economy is merely a temporal replication of this eternal reality for the specific purpose of revealing it to humanity.[70] God's movement into his economy is a second step alongside who he is from all eternity.

69. Augustine, *De Trinitate*, trans. Edmund Hill, vol. 1/5 (Brooklyn: New City, 1991), p. 174.

70. Aquinas would reinforce this distinction between the processions and the missions. Q. 43, Art. 1, Obj. 1 begins with the affirmation that "a divine person cannot be properly sent. For one who is sent is less than the sender." In his reply, Aquinas agrees that "mission implies inferiority in the one sent, when it means procession from the sender as principle." The sending within God, as such, "means only procession of origin." Protecting the divinity of Christ requires this ontological distinction from the economy. In Art. 2, Obj. 3, Aquinas asks the same question from an alternate angle: "Mission implies procession. But the procession of the divine persons is eternal. Therefore mission is eternal." To this he responds, "*mission* and *giving* have only a temporal significance in God; but *generation* and *inspiration* are exclusively eternal." This is the case because "a thing is sent that it may be in something else, and is given that it may be possessed." However, if one intrudes on this notion of human possession of the divine and the resulting ecclesiology, this concern to protect the aseity of God dissipates, for God remains subject in the economy. See Thomas Aquinas, *Summa Theologica*, trans. Fathers of the English Dominican Province, 5 vols. (Westminster, MD: Christian Classics, 1981), 1:219-20.

Augustine and the Unknowable God

A litany of theologians, such as Karl Rahner, Jürgen Moltmann, Catherine Mowry LaCugna, and Colin Gunton, attribute Augustine's position to a prior Neo-Platonic metaphysic.[71] For Gunton, Augustine's emphasis on Jesus' divinity against the Arian detractors and his "neoplatonic assumptions of the material order's incapacity to be really and truly the bearer of divinity" results in an account of the Trinity abstracted from the economy of salvation. Augustine, in effect, undermines the reality of God's being in the economy, with the consequence that his revelation as Father, Son, and Spirit becomes merely a formal identification.[72] God's threeness applies only to the economy as an epistemological pointer back to the one God. "The true being of God *underlies* the threeness of the persons."[73] This modalistic distance between who the one God is in himself and who he is in his economy assumes finally that it does not belong to God's being to reveal himself. For Rahner, Augustine's Trinity is a being "absolutely locked up within itself," only entering the world by way of a "strange paradox."[74] God is unknowable and has to somehow contravene his own being in order to make himself known.

Such a position, it is claimed, must be overcome for the sake of the church's witness in the modern world.[75] The only connection Augustine could form between the life of the church and the being of God was via an analogy "between the inner structure of the human mind and the inner being of God."[76] This so-called psychological analogy forms in clear corre-

71. For Colin Gunton, "what has to be examined is not simply his statement of doctrine but the underlying presupposition which gives the doctrine the shape it has." Gunton, *The Promise of Trinitarian Theology*, 2nd ed. (London: T. & T. Clark, 2003), p. 32. Here Augustine allowed the "insidious return of a Hellenism in which being is not communion, but something underlying it." Gunton, *The Promise*, p. 10.

72. Gunton, *The Promise*, p. 32.

73. Gunton, *The Promise*, p. 42.

74. Karl Rahner, *The Trinity*, trans. Joseph Donceel (New York: Crossroad, 1997), p. 18.

75. See Gunton, *The Promise*, pp. 15-29. Bringing in the issue of Christendom, Gunton elsewhere states that this is a question of the "nature and mission of the church in the modern world. At a time when the church has lost its old and assured place in society, it can depend only on the source of its being in the gospel." Gunton, "The Community of the Church in Communion with God," in *The Church in the Reformed Tradition: Discussion Papers Prepared by a Working Party of the European Committee*, ed. Colin E. Gunton, Réamonn Páraic, and Alan P. F. Sell (Geneva: WARC, 1995), p. 40.

76. Gunton, *The Promise*, p. 45.

spondence to the epistemological status of God's economy. But, with God's true being at some distance from his economy, this analogy can only be realized as a "choice between this world and the next, rather than seeking a realization of the next in the materiality of the present."[77] The human becomes oriented to this God-beyond-the-economy, and the resulting ecclesiology conceives "the being of the church as in some sense *anterior* to the concrete historical relationships of the visible community."[78]

The church belongs in eternity with God, and her act in history consists of conforming to that eternal being. In practical terms, an invisible church becomes ontologically prior to the visible historical reality, meaning that those institutions that identify the church in history, such as the clergy, constitute her actual being.[79] The church is the institution. This, by extension, denudes the life of *community* as essential to the Christian faith, and means that the church's witness in the world consists, not of this reconciled community's life, but of replicating and maintaining the purity of the institution.

The verity of this diagnosis has undergone vigorous challenge. Augustinian scholarship rejects as outdated the setting of his thought within a Neo-Platonic framework.[80] Instead, his work is "pro-Nicene" in nature and "polemical" in tone.[81] Augustine's argument counters the false ac-

---

77. Gunton, *The Promise*, p. 50; see also David Bosch's lament regarding the deleterious effect of Augustine's position on mission practice during the Middle Ages in Bosch, *Transforming Mission*, pp. 214-26.

78. Gunton, *The Promise*, p. 74.

79. Gunton, *The Promise*, pp. 59-60, 74.

80. Michel René Barnes, for example, argues against the viability of "neoplatonism as a historical phenomenon," for such a "location fails to reflect the doctrinal content of the texts it is supposed to explain." Barnes, "Rereading Augustine's Theology of the Trinity," in *The Trinity: An Interdisciplinary Symposium on the Trinity,* ed. Stephen T. Davis, Daniel Kendall, and Gerald O'Collins (Oxford: Oxford University Press, 1999), p. 153. Much of the erroneous reading of Augustine is attributed to an artificial distinction between a Greek and a Latin position first articulated in Olivier du Roy, *L'Intelligence de la foi en la Trinité selon saint Augustin* (Paris: Études augustiniennes, 1966). Rowan Williams maintains that it is du Roy who presents "Augustine's trinitarian thought as monist and essentialist, a scheme in which the economy of salvation plays relatively little part." Quoted in Michel René Barnes, "Augustine in Contemporary Trinitarian Theology," *Theological Studies* 56 (1995): 244 n. 33.

81. Barnes argues that Augustine's position in Books II to IV of *De Trinitate* "is a polemically charged argument, designed to combat a false 'economy of the Trinity.'" Barnes, "Augustine in Contemporary," p. 247. This polemic applies equally to Augustine's use of the designation "Arian," for opponents of "a theology identified with Nicaea were reduced to, or

count of the economy as posited by the Homoians: "[T]he Son's role as revealer of the Father means that the Son cannot be God as the Father is God."[82] Because Augustine is countering this economy, he cannot himself be guilty of a similar de-divinizing of Jesus Christ. Given that the material consequence of his supposed formal philosophical structure is modalism, defenders focus on the Trinitarian substance of God's life *in se*. Augustine does not limit God's threeness to his economy; God the Father, the Son, and the Spirit is in himself from all eternity. Lewis Ayres concludes that "the charge that Augustine's theology describes the divine essence as prior to the divine persons, or as the source of the persons, is unwarranted."[83]

The defense is generally convincing: the highlighted issue is not the result of a Neo-Platonic metaphysics. However, in defenders' focusing on Trinitarian ontology, they leave untouched the precipitating concern of attributing only *epistemological* status to the economy. Or, instead, they confirm this to be the significance of the economy. Michel René Barnes defends Augustine's position by arguing for "the epistemic character of the Incarnation as the decisive revelation of the Trinity."[84] As God is known to be triune in the economy, so he is triune in himself. There is no need to give the economy any ontological weight. To suggest so, in Ayres's estimation, is a result of — and dismissed as — an unwarranted Hegelianism.[85] It is not a "real" theological problem, but one bequeathed to modern theology through its dalliances with post-Enlightenment philosophy. A reengagement with Augustine's position will enable contemporary theology to escape this backwater.

Augustine's defenders do not develop a corresponding ecclesiology, but the second stage of the argument against him — that his doctrine of the Trinity lacks a satisfactory analogy in the economy of salvation — does re-

---

identified as, followers of Arius and holders of his theology." Barnes, "Rereading Augustine's Theology," p. 166 n. 35.

82. Michel René Barnes, "The Visible Christ and the Invisible Trinity: MT. 5:8 in Augustine's Trinitarian Theology of 400," *Modern Theology* 19, no. 3 (2003): 330.

83. Lewis Ayres, "The Fundamental Grammar of Augustine's Trinitarian Theology," in *Augustine and His Critics: Essays in Honour of Gerald Bonner,* ed. Gerald Bonner, Robert Dodaro, and George Lawless (London: Routledge, 2000), p. 68.

84. Barnes, "Rereading Augustine's Theology," p. 175.

85. See, e.g., Ayres's polemical chapter entitled "In Spite of Hegel, Fire, and Sword," in *Nicaea and Its Legacy: An Approach to Fourth-Century Trinitarian Theology* (Oxford: Oxford University Press, 2004), pp. 384-429. Barnes and Ayres both maintain that much modern theology is captured by the Enlightenment and modern categories, and this explains the misreading of Augustine. See Barnes, "Rereading Augustine's Theology," p. 175.

quire some account of the resulting form of the community. One notable contribution is Daniel Williams's relativization of the clerical imperialism assumed as basic to the monolithic "Constantinian" ecclesiological pattern. The "Constantinian fall" thesis perceives the church's alignment with the structures of social power "as the beginning of its corruption and a degeneration from its original apostolic character to a position of temporal supremacy, necessarily involving the accretion of unbiblical practices and the misalignment of the true faith."[86] For Williams, such a position fails the test of history. Nicene theology never functioned in this way. Removing this menace of institutional hierarchy creates space for Ayres's positive argument that "pro-Nicene theology is best understood as a theological culture."[87] There is a "central imaginative, doctrinal matrix of pro-Nicene theologies as that which was intentionally aimed at shaping the Christian *habitus*."[88]

Augustine's doctrine of the Trinity is a product of that economy and aims at its stimulation. With reference to Matthew 5:8, Barnes highlights Augustine's development of a "relationship between faith and the vision of divinity as epistemological events in the immediate life of the believer."[89] His refutation of the Homoians begins where they do, with an "unflinching" affirmation of "the necessarily invisible character of divinity."[90] The Son is not a direct revelation of divinity, for his divinity is not available to general human perception. Faith leads to "seeing" God in his form of a servant. This "seeing" is not "knowledge," but the act of contemplation; the very invisibility of God draws the Christian to "his or her proper end, namely, delight in the vision of God the Trinity."[91] The resulting ecclesiology, as Ayres argues, shapes a theological culture, developed through "interrelated conceptions of the Christian *habitus* — of the Christian imaginative universe — and of a collection of intellectual practices seen as consonant with that *habitus*."[92] All of this aims at nurturing and drawing the community into this contemplative existence.

---

86. Daniel H. Williams, "Constantine, Nicaea and the 'Fall' of the Church," in *Christian Origins: Theology, Rhetoric, and Community,* ed. Lewis Ayres and Gareth Jones (London: Routledge, 1998), p. 119.

87. Ayres, *Nicaea and Its Legacy,* p. 83.

88. Ayres, *Nicaea and Its Legacy,* p. 278.

89. Barnes, "The Visible Christ," pp. 342-43.

90. Barnes, "The Visible Christ," p. 335.

91. Barnes, "The Visible Christ," p. 330.

92. Ayres, *Nicaea and Its Legacy,* p. 275.

While these potential theological resources accrue here for contemporary ecclesiologies that are concerned with the kinds of eucharistic practices basic to the formation of *habitus,* such an account becomes highly problematic when considered from the perspective of mission. Gregory Robertson notes that Eusebius of Caesarea, in his *Demonstratio Evangelica,* posits "two distinct forms of Christian existence: the first is the call to separation and to overcoming the world for those who would be perfect, while the second is for those who remain in the world yet to whom is attributed a 'secondary grade of piety.'"[93] This derivative piety occurred with a special missionary dispensation: it consists of "giving such help as such require, so that all men, whether Greeks or barbarians, have their part in the coming of salvation, and profit by the teaching of the Gospel."[94]

The act of communicating the gospel is itself contrary to the "perfect" nature of Christian existence. Reducing God's economy to only epistemological status directs Christian being toward a God whose perfection lies beyond his coming in the economy. The contemplative life is the true form of Christian being. However, such a declension at this point tends toward ecclesial forms that reduce the task of proclaiming the gospel to cultural propaganda. Perfection in this life demands the imaginative universe and practices basic to forming this *habitus* and culture. As Ayres suggests, the culture itself includes within it "a mode or a particular practice of handing on" that reflects the patterns of thought basic to this culture.[95] With such structures now necessary to Christian being, the transmission of the gospel consists of their replication, with Christian witness flowing as a derivative out of and pointing back to this life.

The Cappadocian "Ontological Innovation"

A popular response to Augustine's supposed legacy draws on the "ontological innovation" of the Cappadocians.[96] As Father, Son, and Spirit, God's

---

93. Gregory Alan Robertson, "'Vivit! Regnat! Triumphat!' The Prophetic Office of Jesus Christ, the Christian life, and the Mission of the Church in Karl Barth's *Church Dogmatics* IV/3" (Th.D. diss., Wycliffe College and the University of Toronto, 2003), p. 261.

94. Eusebius of Caesarea, *The Proof of the Gospel: Being the Demonstratio Evangelica of Eusebius of Caesarea,* trans. W. J. Ferrar, 2 vols. (Grand Rapids: Baker, 1981), 1:50.

95. Ayres, *Nicaea and Its Legacy,* p. 275.

96. Gunton, *The Promise of Trinitarian Theology,* p. 9 (page references from this source that follow appear in parentheses in the text).

being in and for himself is communion. Modalism is impossible with this position, for "there is no 'being' of God other than this dynamic of persons in relation" (Gunton, p. 10). There is no hidden God behind the God we see in the economy, no three Gods in creation and one God in eternity. God acts in his economy as he is in himself. A clear analogical extension of divine ontology into ecclesiology follows: the church forms "on the analogy of the Trinity's interpersonal relationships" (p. 51). In contrast to the eschatological dualism and consequent institutionalism that he identifies in Augustine's ecclesiology, Colin Gunton holds that "the actual relations of concrete historical persons constitute the sole — or primary — being of the church, just as the hypostases in relation constitute the being of God" (p. 74). The church is called to "echo" in time the communion that is God's life in eternity: she is "called to be a being of persons-in-relation which receives [her] character as communion by virtue of [her] relation to God and so is enabled to reflect something of that being in the world" (p. 12). This life in community both addresses the corrosive effects of modernity and is itself eloquent as it witnesses to the truth of reconciliation.

This position has a twofold strength. First, the connection between the church and the world ceases to be external to the gospel in which the church finds her being. The church, as John Milbank has argued, cannot speak into the world subject to some "ultimate organizing logic."[97] When this occurs, the church serves alternate authorities and propagates alternate messages. While reference to mission history displays the travail of such a course, it is increasingly evident that this problem belongs to Western ecclesiologies.[98] The event of reconciliation must itself establish the nature and form of the church's relationship in and to the world. Second, this concentration on the church's community life delineates a concrete account of the nature of Christian witness and the consequent role of church practices. A particular definition of the church's "visibility" develops, whereby the community is seen as the community of God's reconciliation as she lives in active doxological correspondence to God's own life of communion as "enabled by the Spirit to order [her] life to where that reconciliation takes place in time, that is to say, to the life, death and resurrec-

97. John Milbank, *Theology and Social Theory: Beyond Secular Reason* (Cambridge, MA: Blackwell, 1990), p. 1.

98. See, e.g., Reinhard Hütter, "The Church as 'Public': Dogma, Practices and the Holy Spirit," *Pro Ecclesia* 3, no. 3 (1994): 344-61.

tion of Jesus" (Gunton, p. 81). This emphasis constitutes an important corrective to the perennial Protestant temptation to treat that life as simply
"apparatus" for the act of proclamation.[99] Elements, such as worship, baptism, and the Lord's Supper become of central importance as "temporal
ways of orienting the community to the being of God" (p. 20). Via these
"sacraments of incorporation and *koinonia*," the Spirit "incorporates people into Christ and in the same action brings them into and maintains
them in community with one another" (p. 82). No longer is recourse to an
external monotheistic natural theology required; the life of the community itself bears the evangelistic load.

Given that the precipitating problem is one of connection to the world
for the sake of witness, proponents of this position are clear in repudiating
an inward-turning church. "The concrete means by which the church becomes an echo of the life of the Godhead are all such as to direct the
church away from self-glorification to the source of its life in the creative
and recreative presence of God to the world" (p. 81). Life in communion
does not lead to sectarianism — that much is clear. The community is
called to witness to the reconciliation of the world by living reconciled
lives. But a problem emerges when this external witness is defined in terms
of a proper focus on the internal practices that, by the Spirit, draw the
community together as a distinctive fellowship. Christian witness proceeds
as a gestalt out of this life of communion. For Robert Jenson, as the church
lives in communion with the triune life, so she becomes "a distinctive, even
'countercultural' community," and this marks the church as a "missionary
community."[100] Christian witness takes the practical form of an ever-
intensified internal focus, which instills the kind of visible character distinguishing the church as a holy people.[101]

Aside from this account of Christian visibility, no mention is made
of the church's external movement into the world. This absence is under-

99. As Webster suggests, "Much modern Protestant theology and church life has been
vitiated by the dualist assumption that the church's social form is simple externality and so
indifferent, merely the apparatus for the proclamation of the Word." John B. Webster, *Confessing God: Essays in Christian Dogmatics II* (Edinburgh: T. & T. Clark, 2005), p. 154.

100. Robert W. Jenson, *Systematic Theology II: The Works of God* (New York: Oxford
University Press, 1999), p. 187.

101. See Stanley Hauerwas, "Worship, Evangelism, Ethics: On Eliminating the 'And,'" in
A Better Hope: Resources for a Church Confronting Capitalism, Democracy, and Postmodernity
(Grand Rapids: Brazos, 2000), pp. 155-61.

standable: the divine ontology underlying this image of communion militates against it. Gunton's defining Trinitarian insight is that the "central concept is that of shared being: the persons do not simply enter into relations with one another, but are constituted by one another in the relations."[102] Such is the nature of God's own being. Extending this ontology into the church leads to an account of communion defined primarily in terms of creating and strengthening the relationships within the community. A particular treatment of Christian edification follows. Gunton seeks "an articulation of the faith for its own sake as the faith of the worshipping community." It is by the "internal orientation of theology" that the "believing community" is enabled to live according to the truth in which she exists. Any failure to develop such an account amounts to a failure to define the very being of the church. A second task forms alongside this primary one: elucidating the faith to those external to this communion, the "missionary function" (Gunton, *Promise*, p. 7). Worship as a value in its own right becomes contrasted with, and so prioritized over, the act of external movement into the world. The "communion" that is the church's being exists apart from the missionary task, and the external act in no way defines the nature of that communion or the worship life of that community.[103]

While this position does not subject the missionary act to any theological attention, it nevertheless spawns a definite missionary method. As God

---

102. Colin E. Gunton, *The One, The Three, and The Many: God, Creation, and the Culture of Modernity* (Cambridge: Cambridge University Press, 1993), p. 214.

103. In his examination of missionary ecclesiology since Vatican II, Stephen Bevans creates a contrast between "communion" and "communion-in-mission" ecclesiologies. With communion ecclesiologies, that this "communion is *missionary* is immediately stated," but not so clearly stated that "mission is *constitutive* of that communion." Stephen B. Bevans, "Ecclesiology Since Vatican II: From a Church with a Mission to a Missionary Church," *Verbum SVD* 46, no. 1 (2005): 43. A further example, one based in the "mission of the Trinity," maintains that "communion is the ultimate end, not mission." While this communion is contrasted with "introspection or fellowship among ourselves," this outward turning only takes the liturgical form of a "dismissal." Nothing more is said of how the church as a communion acts in the world. Andy Crouch, "The Mission of the Trinity: An Interview with Simon Chan," *Christianity Today* 51, no. 6 (2007): 48. This position holds true across the theological spectrum. See, e.g., the evangelical John Piper's influential popular books, which justify the missionary task by dichotomizing between mission and worship, and thus from the life of the community. John Piper, *Let the Nations Be Glad! The Supremacy of God in Missions,* 2nd ed. (Grand Rapids: Baker Academic, 2003).

connects with the world through the economy of his being-in-communion, so the church connects with the world in her being-as-communion. Of this approach, Nicholas Healy observes that "the identities of the world and the church are perforce essentially the same at base. The only difference between them can be that the church more visibly realizes the primary reality than do other religions and ways of life."[104] Mission again forms as the task of cultivating that point of contact that is external to the life of the church herself. Because witness flows out of this fellowship, the external missionary act consists of transplanting those practices and habits that build up this community, including confessions, hymnody, dress, church order, hierarchy, and so forth.[105] The complaints made against Christian missions during the early part of the twentieth century are unanimous in labeling such mission method propaganda.[106] Defining the nature of Christian communion in internal terms and investing the burden of witness in that communion makes this method inevitable.

Observing this link with propagandistic missionary methods invites Arius and Augustine back into the discussion. It is certainly true that the originating christological controversies struggled with how God is one and yet is three in this economy, and that this precipitating concern frames a good deal of the contemporary discussion. That is, the neo-Cappadocian response to Augustine focuses on his supposed reduction of God's Trini-

104. Nicholas M. Healy, "Communion Ecclesiology: A Cautionary Note," *Pro Ecclesia* 4, no. 4 (1995): 446.

105. Jenson, for example, argues — based on an overt recognition of the church's missionary context! — that enculturation into the church's inner culture, which is "in fact thicker and more specific than any national or ethnic culture" and, due to the accidental path of Christianity's expansion, predominantly Western in form, is necessary for Christian catechesis. Robert W. Jenson, "Catechesis for Our Time," in *Marks of the Body of Christ,* ed. Carl E. Braaten and Robert W. Jenson (Grand Rapids: Eerdmans, 1999), pp. 144-45.

106. While it has become common currency to identify the Eucharist as the missionary center of the church, certain inconsistencies remain. Note here Bosch's treatment of Orthodox ecclesiology and the reduction of eschatological expectation, which drove the missionary existence of the early church, to the liturgy, and the concomitant reduction of the church to an institution of salvation. The resulting missionary method, Bosch says, "was hardly mission in the Pauline sense; rather, it was Christian propaganda." Bosch, *Transforming Mission,* p. 201. This is not some facile criticism against word and sacrament, or against the idea that these are properly missionary events. It is an observation that when missionary language is used with regard to an ecclesial ontology in which the church is a preexistent entity, the resulting method looks very much like the transplantation of a culture as necessary to Christian life and witness, i.e., propaganda.

tarian character to his economy. However, there is another way of approaching this matter: the question is whether the neo-Cappadocian response overcomes the base assumption that God's perfection precludes the act of sending as essential to his being. God might be three in himself, but is the nature of his communion understood in terms of his sending into his economy? While God's external mission proceeds as a natural overflow of his being and reveals this being to humanity, to quote Stephen Holmes, are the sendings of the Son and Spirit merely "anomalous events, not expressions of who God most fundamentally is in his eternal life"?[107] This would seem to remain the key assumption governing both the neo-Cappadocian and Augustinian responses.

Gunton acknowledges the centrality of the economic actions of Christ and the Spirit given their close relationship "to the question of the status of the events from which the church originated" (*Promise*, p. 70).[108] But this is of itself insufficient. "If we wish to say something of what kind of sociality the church is we must move from a discussion of the relation of christology to pneumatology to an enquiry into what it is that makes the church what it is. And that first necessitates a move from the economic to the immanent trinity" (p. 70). The distinction between the economic and immanent Trinity is not itself the problem. In what follows I will argue that such a distinction remains necessary for the missionary act. At issue is, though the ontology of the Cappadocians moves the form of Christ's life as revealed in the economy back into the life of God, an absolute account of his being occurs without reference to his economy. Indeed, one must look beyond this economy. The corresponding ecclesiology confirms that this is true. As God moves into the world through an overflow of his otherwise defined perfection, so the church's witness proceeds as an overflow of her otherwise defined life of communion. This communion exists before

107. Stephen R. Holmes, "Trinitarian Missiology: Towards a Theology of God as Missionary," *International Journal of Systematic Theology* 8, no. 1 (2006): 79.

108. One should note here that, while Gunton is careful to posit this movement as one from the ontic to the ontological, other social Trinitarians are guilty of the same disjunction with which they charge Augustine. Stanley Grenz, for example, holds that "any truly helpful explication of the doctrine of the Trinity must give epistemological priority to the presence of the Trinitarian members in the divine economy but reserve ontological primacy for the dynamic of their relationality within the triune life." Stanley J. Grenz, *Rediscovering the Triune God: The Trinity in Contemporary Theology* (Minneapolis: Fortress, 2004), p. 222.

and apart from the community's movement into the world; the movement is incidental to the being.

Barth, the Trinity, and the Missionary Community

A revised *missio Dei* theology must address this wider problem of God, of the God who in himself transitions the gap between himself and his creation. Only in answer to this does a solution to binary opposition of the church from mission, so deleterious to both the life of the church and to her relationship to the world, present itself. As God is a missionary God, so his community is a missionary community.

This book is composed of two distinguishable parts. The first is a diagnostic investigation into the origins of *missio Dei* in an attempt to precisely describe the concept and its attendant problems. The second part develops a constructive proposal using the work of Karl Barth. Given the absence of mission from the volume of secondary literature dealing with Barth's theology, one could be forgiven for thinking that this is a category absent from his thinking. But that is simply not the case. References to the missionary task emerge at the most decisive points throughout the *Church Dogmatics,* and one must ask how it is possible to overlook such references. While a number of answers may be given, not the least of which is the ambiguous status of theology within secular universities, the answer to this egregious blind spot seems simple: mission is not understood to be a matter of first-order theological reflection.[109] This is an immediate consequence of approaches to the Trinity that reduce the economy to secondary significance.

109. A number of reasons may be given to explain this absence, including defining Christendom as the abrogation of the missionary endeavor to political authorities. Thus Shenk's statement that "the Christendom model of the church may be characterized as *church without mission.*" Wilbert R. Shenk, *Write the Vision: The Church Renewed* (Valley Forge, PA: Trinity Press International, 1995), p. 35. This is not to suggest the absence of missionary activity, but to observe that the act became external to the life of the church and to her theological reflection, a distinction now enshrined within the dominant proportion of the tradition. A more immediate example is given by Brian Stanley, who notes the apologetic origins within Chinese Marxism of the complaint against Christian missions and the general acceptance of this position within Western scholarship — including the theological disciplines. See Brian Stanley, *The Bible and the Flag: Protestant Missions and British Imperialism in the Nineteenth and Twentieth Centuries* (Leicester, UK: Apollos, 1990), pp. 29-30.

One argument underlying this work is that a significant number of theological problems are a result of the omission of mission from the dogmatic horizon. My extensive treatment of Barth is, in one sense, for the purpose of exegeting the explicit missionary material in his work. In another and perhaps more important sense, however, it is for the purpose of demonstrating how our theology ignores mission as part of its core focus. Ignoring it in Barth is an illustration of how theology dismisses it from its wider project, with all the concomitant consequences for the church, its life of worship, and its being in and for the world.

Though his constructive treatment of mission fails to appear within secondary literature, for Barth the Christian community is nothing other than a missionary community. The language of "mission" is no mere rhetorical device.

> The community is alive there, and only there, where she is engaged in recruitment and when she strives for this recruitment especially in the apparently darkest areas of the world: in places where the gospel is still completely unknown or completely rejected, *in medio inimicorum.* The community is as such a missionary community, or she is not the Christian community. (rev., *KD* III/4, 578; *CD* III/4, 504-5)

Dire consequences follow for failing to so live:

> [T]he community which has not existed in the interim period as a *missionary* community as such, whose witness has not been *invitational* and *persuasive* according to the measure of her power, with the return and final revelation of her Lord will be banished into the darkness, where there can be only wailing and gnashing of teeth instead of the promised banquet. (rev., *KD* III/2, 610; *CD* III/2, 507)

These stark statements result from Barth's construal of divine and human fellowship. That human relationship with God takes this missionary form is precisely a consequence of the doctrine of the Trinity.

In the context of the missionary command of Matthew 28, Barth proposes a suggestive logic. The words "Father," "Son," and "Holy Spirit" are terms "for the enumeration of the *dimensions* of the one name of God . . . for the *expansion* of the one name, work, and word of God" (*CD* IV/4, 96-97; *KD* IV/4, 106). This Trinitarian identification expresses the movement of God from his immanent being into his economy. The focus here is not

31

— that is, not yet — one of how God's being is also his becoming. The point is that this Trinitarian self-expansion forms a corresponding human action. The names Father, Son, and Holy Spirit are found "in the context of the command to do mission. In objective terms, mission is *expansion* of the reality and truth of Jesus Christ. This definition is the *tertium comparationis* between mission and the *expansion* of the designation of the one name of God — that name is not just christological! — into a trinitarian one" (rev., *KD* IV/4, 106; *CD* IV/4, 97).[110]

Mission is the act accompanying God's own self-enumeration. Barth even ascribes the origins of trinitarian theology to *"missionary* theology" (*CD* IV/4, 100; *KD* IV/4, 110). The trinitarian formula is "a confession which follows the transition of the message of salvation from Israel to the Gentiles, which may even anticipate this transition, but which certainly confirms and explains it" (rev., *KD* IV/4, 110; *CD* IV/4, 100). This universal expansion of salvation narrates the triune being of God. Again, this reference to mission is no idle rhetoric. "'Mission' . . . is here concrete: it is the reaching out of salvation and its revelation beyond the borders of Israel into the nations, that step in which the Messiah of Israel discloses Himself as the Savior of the world" (*CD* IV/4, 97; *KD* IV/4, 106)[111] The doctrine of the Trinity demands a corresponding missionary form, and this confirms the reality of God's becoming being.

The nature of missionary expansion is not to be conceived in flat geographical terms; it corresponds to the nature of God's own becoming existence. Just as God transitions the gap between himself and his creation, so active participation in the missionary existence of the Christian community is the form of human fellowship with the divine. No human act

110. My thanks to Karlfried Froehlich for his assistance in translating this section.

111. It is important to note here a similar account suggested by Robert Jenson. He illustrates how many of the issues previously examined, such as that of God's hiddenness, inform a "trinitarian logic," which is "the structure of the church's historical existence, as authoritatively described in the New Testament." This is evident in "both fundamental churchly realities: the mission and the Lord's Supper." Robert W. Jenson, *The Triune Identity: God According to the Gospel* (Philadelphia: Fortress, 1982), p. 28. Jenson locates the missionary act within the "trinitarian time-pattern" of being blown on by the Spirit, serving Jesus Christ to carry the promises of the Father (p. 31). This framework connects the church with Israel, for it is a continuation of "God's own eschatological act to unite humankind" (p. 30). The "triune shape of Christian mission was immediately given by its claim to be Israel's eschatological mission," and the doctrine of the Trinity developed in resistance to the trend toward divinization as Christianity encountered Hellenism (p. 34).

bridges that gap: mission does not complete an only partially achieved reconciliation between God and humanity. Nor does a proper emphasis on the disjunction between the divine and the human devalue the human activity. God is perfect and complete in himself in such a way that his becoming in the economy belongs to his being from all eternity. It is because it belongs to God's own life that mission describes the nature of Christian fellowship. As God's being includes his movement into the economy within it, so his being does not cease to become with the completion of the act of reconciliation. The opposite is true. It is in this way that the resurrection, as the confirmation of the nature of God's being from all eternity, brings human beings into a like missionary existence. As the one action of God, his community is impelled by the gathering action of the Spirit to go into the world, following her preceding living Lord as a secondary subject.

This apostolic existence is the Christian community's concrete existence, that is, the being of the church and her act coincide in such a way that her community existence anticipates her calling in the world, and her act is the actualization of her being. One consequence of mission's distillation from the life of the church is its reduction to a peculiar occupation undertaken by spiritual elites alongside which the community lives a nonmissionary existence. A disjunction forms between the act of proclamation and the life of the community. Rethinking the nature of the community in light of this missionary existence means that Christian fellowship takes a particular form. "What can His name, work and word be now, after the Easter revelation of the old covenant confirmed in the new, but the divine self-attestation which is echoed in the witness of the one people of the last time, the community of Jews and Gentiles?" (*CD* IV/4, 97; *KD* IV/4, 106). This includes a particular determination of the community's life of worship and the nature of her edification. For if God is by nature missionary, then the proper worship of this God must assume a corresponding missionary form. Christian witness is not some overflow of an otherwise intact fellowship. It is a life given for the sake of the world.

As the nature of God's own communion is one of becoming, so the communion of his community declares the divine communion as it lives in the movement of reconciliation to those who would be God's enemies. The resulting community is one for which the "middle wall of partition" is no longer in effect (Eph. 2:14). Such a community is a missionary community. It is the nature of human fellowship with God that corresponds to Christ's completion of his act and to the act of the Spirit in calling and sending the community to follow her risen Lord into the world. This "intimate and necessary connection" between Jesus Christ and his community "would obviously snap if she tried to exist otherwise than in this imitative and serving participation in His mission to the world" (rev., *KD* IV/3.2, 906; *CD* IV/3.2, 792). Mission is not a second step in addition to some other more proper being of the church, because, as the living one, God's relationship to the world belongs to his eternal being. The Christian community is, as such, a missionary community, or she is not a community that lives in fellowship with the triune God as he lives his own proper life.

CHAPTER TWO

The Problem That Is Missio Dei

Introduction

What is *missio Dei?* Given its significance and the extent of its popular usage, this is a surprisingly difficult question to answer. It can, at one level, be
simply stated: the missionary act is grounded in, and flows from, the very
nature of the triune God. Drawing on the Johannine "Great Commission"
(John 20:19-23), the Father's sending of the Son includes the second movement of the Son sending his church in the peace of the Spirit. Push deeper
than this, however, and it becomes evident that *missio Dei* lacks coherence.
Significant ambiguity surrounds axiomatic phrases such as "God is a missionary God," "the church is missionary by her very nature," and "the
church participates in God's mission." The paucity of primary sources only
exacerbates this ambiguity. Few authors reflect on the underlying theological issues. Most introduce the concept by citing from the few seminal texts;
but, apart from these oft-repeated forms, little substantive development
has occurred.[1]

---

1. The most commonly referred to sources include: Karl Hartenstein, "Theologische
Besinnung," in *Mission zwischen Gestern und Morgen*, ed. Walter Freytag (Stuttgart: Evang.
Missionsverlag, 1952), pp. 51-72; H. H. Rosin, *'Missio Dei': An Examination of the Origin,
Contents and Function of the Term in Protestant Missiological Discussion* (Leiden:
Interuniversity Institute for Missiological and Ecumenical Research, Department of
Missiology, 1972); Georg F. Vicedom, *Missio Dei: Einführung in eine Theologie der Mission*
(Munich: Chr. Kaiser Verlag, 1958); Norman Goodall, ed., *Missions under the Cross* (London:
Edinburgh House, 1953).

who is the agent of mission. 40

Missio Dei's genesis as a response to the prolonged interrogation of mission's motives, methods, and goals helps explain this deficient theological development. It is not, in the first instance, a constructive concept; rather, it serves a critical function. Grounding mission in the doctrine of the Trinity distances the Western missionary enterprise from every colonialist association. While key, this Trinitarian position was but one theological reaction to the colonialist challenge. Other developments, notably the eschatological orientation to the kingdom of God and the missionary nature of the church, were already in process. The language of *missio Dei* provides a rubric for these three theological affirmations, but in so doing it hides the fact that the eschatological orientation and the missionary ecclesiology developed independently of Trinity doctrine. *Missio Dei* claims to provide a Trinitarian framework for concepts that do not draw on that doctrine. The apparent logical homogeny of the concept submerges often radically discordant positions. This produces a range of positions consolidated under the designation *missio Dei*, which, when placed alongside each other, exist in irreconcilable tension.

The proposed critical reconstruction of *missio Dei* requires significant preparatory work. Foremost, it requires a clear definition of the problem. In this chapter I survey the three constitutive elements of *missio Dei* and their purported interrelationship, and my intent is to delineate the concept's actual functioning.

Sent by a Missionary God

"Sending"

Treatments of the "missionary God" focus on his "sending" *(missio)* nature: the Father sends his Son, the Father and Son send the Spirit. That is, the phrase "God is a missionary God" reduces to "God is a sending God." For Anna Marie Aagaard, "the mission of God is *missio*," that is, "God has a mission, a sending to the world, but God is also in himself sending, the triune God, who as Son and Holy Spirit is sent into the world."[2] The economic "sendings" of the Son and the Spirit reveal a God who is missionary in his

2. Anna Marie Aagaard, "Missio Dei in katholischer Sicht," *Evangelische Theologie* 34 (1974): 422.

life *in se.* To be sent implies a sender, so "sending" refers to God's initiative in the missionary enterprise. Georg Vicedom holds that "*missio Dei* means first of all that mission is God's work. He is the lord, the commissioner, the owner, the one who accomplishes the task. He is the acting subject of mission. If we attribute mission to God in this way, it is withdrawn from every human whim."[3] As an action of God, mission is only wrongly attributed to political, economic, and cultural machinations. These elements will necessarily intrude, but they do not determine missionary activity. David Bosch, too, considers the prime contribution of *missio Dei* theology to be the "conviction that neither the church nor any other human agent can ever be considered the author or bearer of mission."[4] Only as God uses the church as an instrument of his own missionary activity can the church's act be properly considered mission. A focus on "sending" both critically distances the human act from alternate authorities and affords it an inviolate authority.

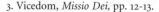

While many treat this as a later development, the term "sending" holds an esteemed place within traditional mission theory. Warneck used it as the cornerstone of his pioneering work, which dominated missionary thinking from 1870 to the crisis occasioned by World War I. According to Hartenstein, Warneck constructed a "doctrine of mission under the two main thoughts of the foundation and direction of this activity that he called sending."[5] Significantly, he grounded this activity in the doctrine of God, "in the certainty that the origin of mission lies in *God,* is rooted not only in all subjective missionary obedience, but the whole objective *existence* of mission."[6] The church's origins resided in God's sending of his Son, and in the Son's sending of his apostles. This is the objective basis of all missionary activity. Since mission originates in God, the onus falls on the Christian community to maintain and propagate missions according to God's will. The church must send missionaries to the end of the world

3. Vicedom, *Missio Dei*, pp. 12-13.

4. David J. Bosch, *Transforming Mission: Paradigm Shifts in Theology of Mission* (Maryknoll, NY: Orbis, 1991), p. 392.

5. Karl Hartenstein, *Die Mission als theologisches Problem: Beiträge zum grundsätzlichen Verständnis der Mission* (Berlin: Furche Verlag, 1932), pp. 11-12.

6. Gustav Warneck, *Evangelische Missionslehre: ein missionstheoretischer Versuch,* 2nd ed., vol. 3.2 (Gotha: Friedrich Andreas Perthes, 1905), p. 69. See also P. T. Forsyth's 1908 description of each member of the Trinity as "missionary," and consequently the church as missionary. P. T. Forsyth, "The Greatest Creditors The Greatest Debtors," in *Missions in State and Church: Sermons and Addresses* (New York: A. C. Armstrong and Son, 1908), pp. 270-71.

and to the end of time. Warneck held, according to Dürr, that "mission *is* sending, the sending out of the missionaries from our churches into the whole world, and by this the expansion of Christianity among the peoples." Mission is the "spreading activity of the church."[7]

"Sending," by this account, is a phenomenological category. Therefore, while the concept remains central for missions, Dürr observes that it must undergo a process of purification due to its Eurocentric and geographical connotations. Though theologically grounded in God, the human act of "sending" succumbed to the colonialist agenda by being framed in terms of geographical expansion. Two conclusions follow: first, an emphasis on "sending" does not of itself safeguard mission against horizontalization, against an occupation with ecclesial agency that may result in a pragmatic definition of mission; second, while reference to "sending" uses references to the doctrine of God, it does not necessarily result in any material consideration of God's agency.

Missio Dei links the missionary act with God via this sending language, but confusion arises over this issue of agency. Following 2 Corinthians 5:20, we can say that God makes appeals through his ambassadors. But does this mean that divine agency consists of that initial act, the economy of which is then handed over to human mediators? What is the relationship between God's divine act of sending and those sent by him? Even a brief survey demonstrates the matter's muddled nature.

First, some exponents of *missio Dei* theology emphasize God's sending initiative to the negation of human agency. Paul Aring, for example, says that "we have no reason to articulate God. In the final analysis '*Missio Dei*' means this: God articulates himself without the way to him having to be prepared by missionary or any other type of effort."[8] Jesus' once-for-all completion of reconciliation has achieved everything the missionary act proposes. Missions achieve nothing, neither establishing the ground for, nor substantively contributing to, God's act.

Second, Anna Marie Aagaard, though she affirms that "all mission is *missio Dei*," denies the correlated affirmation that "God alone is the agent of all mission." Her objection centers on the issue of human agency. In-

7. Johannes Dürr, "Die Reinigung der Missionsmotive," *Evangelisches Missions-Magazin* 95 (1951): 2.

8. Paul Gerhard Aring, *Kirche als Ereignis: ein Beitrag zur Neuorientierung der Missionstheologie* (Neukirchen-Vluyn: Neukirchener Verlag, 1971), p. 88.

vesting missionary agency in God alone emphasizes "the distance between God and man," so that "human mission can never be anything other than a sharing in the signs of God's own *missio* which God himself establishes." The logic is simple: Locating missions within the triune God removed them from any compromise with improper political motives, but this critical function so distanced divine from human agency that the latter disappeared from view. Aagaard responds by coordinating divine and human activity. *Missio Dei* bespeaks "a *common* history of God and man which can take place *both* when and where the Holy Spirit wills *and* when and where the people of God which confesses Christ takes seriously its mission."[9] God's mission occurs where the Spirit is at work, and where the church engages in missionary activity.

Third, if one extreme attributes sending to God alone, the other develops sending without reference to God. Dürr says:

> Mission is sending! The church sends her messengers in order to proclaim the gospel of Jesus Christ among non-Christian peoples, gather the community through the Word, and cooperate in the construction of independent churches. By this sending commission the church lives; it belongs to her authentic nature. The church that stops sending, stops being church.[10]

God's own act and his consequent missionary command established a pattern of sending as central to the Christian faith. Nothing more need be said. The church now bears the responsibility of "the primary agent of the mission of God."[11] Reference to *missio Dei*, in this third option, functions primarily as an apologia aimed at a church that treats the missionary act as only of derivative significance.

While it is possible to distinguish these notions of agency, most treatments of *missio Dei* blend all three — with peculiar dogmatic effect. Reference to the Trinity distinguishes the divine from the human, and so supplies a necessary critical distance between "mission" and its compro-

9. Anna Marie Aagaard, "Missiones Dei: A Contribution to the Discussion on the Concept of Mission," in *The Gospel and the Ambiguity of the Church*, ed. Vilmos Vajta (Philadelphia: Fortress, 1974), p. 82.

10. Johannes Dürr, "Sendung: einige Fragen und Erwägungen," *Evangelisches Missions-Magazin* 98 (1954): 146.

11. Christopher J. H. Wright, *The Mission of God* (Downers Grove, IL: InterVarsity, 2006), p. 27.

mised historical forms. The material significance of the doctrine for missions rests in the language of "sending." This provides the mediating step between the missionary *being* of God and the church's *act:* that is, it *bridges* the Trinitarian grounding of missions to the ecclesiastical activity. However, this formal connection is materially vacuous. For Paulo Suess, "*missio Dei* is the theological concept that allows us to speak of both — the presence and transcendence of God." It connects the being of God with his acts in history, and this "draws our attention to the question of the mediating divine presence."[12] *Missio Dei,* while it claims a focus on divine agency, actually focuses on entities that mediate between the divine and the human, entities Johannes Aagaard terms "theandric realities, God-human acts in history."[13] As will become clear, these "theandric realities" include a vast range of phenomena. As an orthodox example of the problem, Vicedom says that "the church, by the Spirit, is privileged to act in God's place even as God acted with his Son. . . . The church now carries out the sending, and by this the *missio Dei* becomes visible to the world."[14]

The church takes up God's mission, becoming its visible embodiment as she engages in the task of being sent into the world. Without immediate reference to the action of God, "sending" becomes an inviolate divine justification for human actions. Thus it is only a formal justification. Other forces, be those expansionist desires or ideal political forms, substantiate the actual motive, method, and goal of this act. God's sending initiative validates a range of mediating entities that lie beyond God himself, but that connect his intention for reconciliation with its actuality. Material accounts of these mediating agents turn to doctrines other than that of the Trinity, most notably those of creation and of a universal spirit.

The Trinity's Manifold Sendings

"Sending" links the Trinitarian ground of mission with the church's act, but what forms qualify as "Trinitarian" sendings? *Missio,* in contrast to the

12. Paulo Suess, "*Missio Dei* and the Project of Jesus: The Poor and the 'Other' as Mediators of the Kingdom of God and Protagonists of the Churches," *International Review of Mission* 92, no. 4 (2003): 552.

13. Johannes Aagaard, "Mission After Uppsala 1968," in *Crucial Issues in Mission Today,* ed. Gerald H. Anderson and Thomas F. Stransky (New York: Paulist, 1974), p. 19.

14. Vicedom, *Missio Dei,* p. 64.

processio ad intra, originally described the *ad extra* movement of the Son and the Spirit, the sending of Jesus Christ into history in the power of the Spirit. *Missio Dei,* based as it is on John 20:21, adds to the Father's sending of the Son, the Son's sending of the church into the world. By way of the relationship between the economic and immanent Trinity, this evident connection to the economic sendings means that the missionary activity of the church becomes linked to the being of God. Participation in God's mission equates to human participation in God's divine life. *Missio Dei* is, in this sense, extra-Trinitarian, while claiming some grounding in divine ontology for these extra-Trinitarian acts. Moltmann's observation that the terms "sending" (πέμπειν) and "sending forth" (ἐξαποστέλλειν) encompass "the whole appearance, history and meaning of Christ in the light of God" might provide one explanation.[15] Insofar as the Christian community participates in Christ's history, she participates in the life and thus the sending of the Trinity. While this validates mission, it affords no criteria for differentiating between the sendings constitutive of God's triune being and the range of other sendings incorporated by *missio Dei* theology. How does *missio Dei* apply the designation "Trinitarian" to historical sendings that are not immediately related to the economic sendings of the Son and the Spirit?

Georg Vicedom, popularizer of the term *missio Dei* and considered its orthodox representative, argues that the scriptural use of the term "sending" refers to the "epitome of the work and working God, so that the whole of redemptive history presents itself as a history of the *Missio Dei.*" Vicedom posits something he terms the *missio Dei specialis,* primarily the Trinitarian sendings of the Son and the Spirit, but inclusive of the sendings of the prophets and apostles. It is possible, however, to defer reference to these special sendings and still locate "many places in which a *Missio Dei* is described," such as the sending of "even impersonal realities" by which God "acts directly upon the world."[16] Vicedom's position thus contains a second form of the *missio Dei* that is described by Jan-Martin Berentsen as the *"missio Dei generalis,"* the universal work of God based in creation.[17]

15. Jürgen Moltmann, *The Church in the Power of the Spirit: A Contribution to Messianic Ecclesiology* (Minneapolis: Fortress, 1993), p. 53.

16. Vicedom, *Missio Dei,* p. 15.

17. Quoted by Tormod Engelsviken, *"Missio Dei:* The Understanding and Misunderstanding of a Theological Concept in European Churches and Missiology," *International Review of Mission* 92, no. 4 (2003): 484.

"Sending," by this measure, becomes abstracted from the particular event of the atonement. While Vicedom prioritizes the special sending of Jesus Christ, this event becomes one special instance within a universal genus. God is a missionary God because he sends a variety of emissaries to communicate his message, the ultimate expression of which is his Son and Spirit.

Hoekendijk, often depicted as the radicalizer of a supposed orthodox *missio Dei* position, has much in common with Vicedom. The phrase "mission is a predicate of God" indicates God's "all-encompassing sending-economy: sending His angels, prophets, word, Messiah, Son, Spirit, apostles, Church, etc."[18] Like Vicedom, Hoekendijk understands "sending" as an expansive category that governs God's relationship to his creation. The classical location of *"missio"* as a descriptor of divine ontology breaks from God's own particular act. His missionary activity is fuller and more representative of his nature than can be told by simply referring to the Father's sending the Son and the Spirit. To quote Anna Marie Aagaard, "the mission which is God cannot be identified with the sending of the Son and of the Holy Spirit in history; it is a feature of the nature and activity of God." It is true of every act of God in history. She continues that *"the many sendings (missions)* — including those of the Son and the Spirit — *are signs which God uses to demonstrate the identity of his acts with his nature.* That God is the God of mission, therefore, means that mission is the determining factor of God's nature and acts. In God, being and acting cannot be separated."[19] While God's being and act should not be separated, this method of coordination abstracts the "act" from its material location within the Son and Spirit. Birkeli says: "Mission is a predicate of God. God is a missionary God. . . . *Missio Dei* is active in the whole of history, and it consists of God's addressing himself to the whole world, both in and outside of the church. Through the events of history God leads the world."[20] The act of "sending" is located within history. According to

18. J. C. Hoekendijk, "Notes on the Meaning of Mission(-ary)," in *Planning for Mission: Working Papers on the New Quest for Missionary Communities,* ed. Thomas Wieser (New York: U.S. Conference for the WCC, 1966), p. 41.

19. Anna Marie Aagaard, "Missiones Dei," p. 81. Johannes Aagaard also maintains that "God's acts reveal his essence: God is the *missio.*" Johannes Aagaard, "Trends in Missiological Thinking during the Sixties," *International Review of Mission* 62, no. 1 (1973): 15.

20. Quoted by Anna Marie Aagaard, "Missio Dei in katholischer Sicht," p. 421.

Hoekendijk, Jesus Christ's resurrection established this "messianic pattern" to be repeated.[21]

Manecke observes that, for both Vicedom and Hoekendijk, Jesus establishes the fullness of sending by providing every instance of sending with its meaning and goal. However, "the trinitarian derivation of mission means no more than the fact *that* mission occurs. What occurs in mission is grounded in other ways." This is correct. "Sending," located in an abstract account of triune *being,* provides a formal justification of missions, while the defining substance of the act draws on other authorities. This problem has a retroactive effect. The material definition of "sending" comes to define the nature of God himself and of his act in the world. Mission becomes "a hidden but controlling assumption, not only of the doctrine of the Trinity, but also of the doctrine of reconciliation."[22]

A dichotomy develops between the particular person and work of Jesus Christ, and the universal being of the Trinity. Even the notorious 1968 Uppsala assembly warned that "there is a real danger lest the blanket phrase *missio Dei,* which is meant to establish the divine initiative, is used so vaguely that it includes the whole action of God throughout time and space, as though, if he chose, God might have accomplished the renewal of man without Jesus Christ."[23] One no longer works from christology to the Trinity, but the doctrine of the Trinity, grounded in an abstracted notion of sending for which the movement of history constitutes the act, informs christology. A breach develops between God's being and his act. This position moves toward modalism, for the unity of God rests in this abstract "sending," while the actions of Son and the Spirit merely signify this prior identity. With this abstraction of God's being the nature of connection be-

---

21. Hoekendijk, "Notes on the Meaning of Mission(-ary)," p. 41. See also the WCC Department on Studies in Evangelism, *The Church for Others, and the Church for the World: A Quest for Structures for Missionary Congregations* (Geneva: WCC, 1967), pp. 13-14. Vicedom's position is, however, unstable, and easily reduces to Hoekendijk's. There is, at this level of fundamental theology, no discernible difference between the two — an observation that apparently surprised Vicedom. See Rosin, '*Missio Dei*,' p. 25.

22. Dieter Manecke, *Mission als Zeugendienst: Karl Barths theologische Begründung der Mission im Gegenüber zu den Entwürfen von Walter Holsten, Walter Freytag und Joh. Christiaan Hoekendijk* (Wuppertal, Germany: Rolf Brockhaus Verlag, 1972), pp. 187-88 n. 18.

23. "Section II of the Fourth Assembly of the WCC, Uppsala, 1968," *Ecumenical Review* 21, no. 4 (1969): 364.

tween himself and the world, attention fell on those mediating entities constitutive of the divine and human relationship.

The Trinity as Initiator and Completer

If the above account of "sending" distances Trinity doctrine from its ground in the atonement, a second approach establishes Jesus' particular sending as the basis of the church's contemporary mission. Wilhelm Andersen argues that the "two sentences, 'Mission is *missio Dei*' and 'The Cross of Jesus Christ is the center of mission,' belong indissolubly together. They mutually explain and interpret each other. If the second sentence does not follow the first, there exists the danger of making a timeless speculation out of the truth of *missio Dei*."[24] This christological emphasis set *missio Dei* within an eschatological framework. For Margull, missionary activity is "nothing other than the obedient participation in the mission of God moving towards the end. Mission is an eschatological occurrence. Incarnation means sending."[25] In becoming human, Jesus began an event that awaits fulfillment in the *parousia*. The Christian community's missionary activity is her obedient response during the interim period. It is a provisional continuation of Jesus' own mission. While this position avoids the above problematic consequences for divine ontology, it proves guilty of omitting reference to the divine economy. This account of *missio Dei* creates space for the human missionary act by emphasizing the future return of Jesus Christ to the detriment of his present acting.

According to Hoekendijk, the legitimate fear of a reductionist *terminus ad quem* position (mission defined according to a phenomenological goal) drove this *terminus a quo* position (mission defined according to its origins in the Christ event). Mission is not colonialism: it does not consist of "being en route to the parts of our maps that are colored differently." Mission is true because it belongs to the very heart of the gospel: God sent his Son and Spirit to reconcile the world to himself. Therefore, Hoekendijk agrees that the "point of departure is God himself. He is behind every act

---

24. Wilhelm Andersen, "Further Toward a Theology of Mission," in *The Theology of the Christian Mission*, ed. Gerald H. Anderson (New York: McGraw-Hill, 1961), p. 303.

25. Hans Jochen Margull, "Sammlung und Sendung: Zur Frage von Kirche und Mission," *Evangelische Missions-Zeitschrift* 16, no. 3 (1959): 73.

of mission as the authorizer and authenticator. . . . We are agreed on this: the church is never the subject of mission, but at most a partner in the *Missio Dei.*" Every variety of *missio Dei* agrees on this single point. But stopping here encourages a twofold problem.

First, by only attending to God's initiative in mission it is impossible to "arrive at an adequate definition of what one has traditionally understood as 'mission.'"[26] Initiation, ipso facto, never gets beyond the point of departure. For Hoekendijk, this results in a deus ex machina approach to missions. While *missio Dei* theology attempts to address "traditional anthropocentric" conceptions of mission, it merely refers back to "God's prevenient initiative, merely a theocentric preface to an unaltered anthropo- or ecclesio-centric text; God is recognized in an almost deistic fashion as the great Inventor and Inaugurator of the Mission, who has since withdrawn and left the accomplishment of the Mission to His ground personnel."[27] The Christ event initiates missionary activity, but its accomplishment rests in the actions of the Christian community. The church's mission, in other words, continues as an activity of administrative economy. *Missio Dei* theology did not require the church to think through the implications of God's triune being for mission. It provided sufficient theological justification for missions to continue much as they had done.[28]

Second, reference to Jesus Christ's future return developed as a counterbalance to this problem of initiation. Rosin grants Hoekendijk's point: "'*Missio Dei*' can certainly not mean: a starting shot — and then history,

---

26. J. C. Hoekendijk, *Kirche und Volk in der deutschen Missionswissenschaft* (Munich: Chr. Kaiser Verlag, 1967), pp. 335-36.

27. Hoekendijk, "Notes on the Meaning of Mission(-ary)," p. 41.

28. For Wilhelm Andersen, "God did not cease to participate in the missionary enterprise with the sending of His Son once for all in the flesh. He did not make a beginning, which must then be carried forward by human efforts; He did not lay down a pattern, after which men were to develop their missionary enterprises. With the sending of the Holy Spirit — who proceeds from the Father and the Son — He has made it evident that He retains the missionary enterprise in His own hands and does not surrender it to any human authority." Andersen, *Towards a Theology of Mission: A Study of the Encounter between the Missionary Enterprise and the Church and Its Theology* (London: SCM, 1955), p. 47. While it seemingly addresses all the key concerns, a statement such as this provides a theological gloss for traditional accounts of church and mission. If one can attribute divine agency — the key safeguard against the colonialist complaint — to the action of the Spirit, especially in word and sacrament, then the precipitating cause is addressed. Therefore, much of the problem lies in developing this theological question according to a contingency. Only a partial answer resulted.

respectively, church history, begins." Christ's mission does not simply run into the historical existence of the church. Mission cannot only be, as per the postcolonialist complaint, the transplantation of particular cultural communities. It is not, because, for Rosin, "the sending God as such is also He who comes."[29] The eschatological reality of Christ's return validates the church's missionary activity during this interim period. This fails to address the key problem. It supplies insufficient resources for overcoming the concrete deficits within mission methodolgy as highlighted by postcolonialism, because it offers no critical standard for the missionary act here and now.

The greatest temptation for mission, according to Hoekendijk, consists in "the ever-recurring attempt to re-ba'alize God; the conspiracy to make Him again the residential god of a well-defined locality; which may be a continent *(corpus christianum?),* a nation *(Volkskirche?)* or a more restricted residential area (parish?)."[30] Conceiving of God in residential terms drives geographical conceptions of mission. We can carry God across boundaries because we can carry God: that is, revelation rests within the church's walls. Emphasis on God's initiative and *parousia* alone, though it alleviates the immediate challenges besetting mission, fails to address their underlying cause. It may even reinforce this cause by so investing missionary responsibility in the church that she considers herself the chosen vessel for continuing the mission begun by the Son. Vicedom illustrates Hoekendijk's basic concern when he says that "the community becomes the bearer of the revelation in the world. She possesses something that others do not have."[31]

This stimulates the kind of superiority that underlies imperialism and distances the church from true solidarity with the world. Thus the "Missionary Structure of the Congregation" (MSC) notes the "danger of confining God's activity to the Church — his activity in the world being no more than that of the Church itself — so God is refashioned in the image of a residential deity and the world is left apparently bereft of the divine presence, which is enshrined within and reserved exclusively for the Church."[32] Without a sufficient account of God's present acting, mission

29. Rosin, 'Missio Dei,' p. 33.
30. Hoekendijk, "Notes on the Meaning of Mission(-ary)," p. 42.
31. Vicedom, *Missio Dei,* p. 97.
32. WCC Department on Studies in Evangelism, *The Church for Others,* p. 17.

collapses into the kind of theological problem so manifestly illustrated by the illegitimate liaison between Western colonialism and the missionary endeavor.

A correlate of this temptation toward domestication is the failure to provide "an adequate definition of the *totality* of what is happening in the world at God's command and initiative (and thus happening in the church)."[33] The divine bracketing of Jesus Christ's past acting and future return, for Johannes Aagaard, succeeded only in reinforcing the fundamental division between divine and human agency. "The future had a meaning. And the past had its meaning, because in the acts of Christ the decisive things had already happened."[34] This present time, however, "somehow lost its meaning. It became a 'pause', an interim, a *provisorium*, which only had its meaning from the past and from the future."[35] Only in the mission of the church does contemporary history have any meaning. Creating space for the missionary act by emphasizing God's act in initiation and completion effectively bracketed out his ongoing activity. The mission of the church holds history open, forestalling final judgment by perpetuating this limbo between God's past and future. Ironically, those missionary accounts that linked God's sending to the event of the Son developed a justification for the act predicated on God's necessary absence. His return would mean the final judgment and the end of history.

The Trinitarian Problem

J. Andrew Kirk's affirmation that "to speak about the *missio Dei* is to indicate, without any qualification, the *missio Trinitatis*" indicates the popular notion that Trinity doctrine underlies *missio Dei* theology.[36] No such necessary connection exists. For Hoedemaker, though *missio Dei* theology established a broader theological basis for mission, "this effect is free from any direct connection of the term with the theology of the trinity. It arises especially from the fact that in *missio Dei* one hears more notes than in a

33. Hoekendijk, *Kirche und Volk*, p. 336.

34. Johannes Aagaard, "Some Main Trends in Modern Protestant Missiology," *Studia Theologica* 19 (1965): 243-44.

35. Aagaard, "Some Main Trends," 243-44.

36. J. Andrew Kirk, *What Is Mission? Theological Explorations* (London: Darton, Longman and Todd, 1999), p. 27.

christological or ecclesiological narrowing of mission: Notes from creation theology and pneumatology are included."[37] One can doubt neither the biblical provenance of the term "sending" nor the potential link this establishes between the missionary act and the doctrine of the Trinity.[38] Problems emerge in the way "sending" provided merely a Trinitarian façade, behind which a range of alternate doctrines informed the material content of *missio Dei*.[39] "Sending" is susceptible to manipulation by a range of agendas, which were not conditioned by the doctrine of the Trinity but become ratified by its authority.

Missio Dei, for Johannes Aagaard, "resulted in a very formalistic

37. L. A. Hoedemaker, "The People of God and the Ends of the Earth," in *Missiology: An Ecumenical Introduction*, ed. F. J. Verstraelen et al. (Grand Rapids: Eerdmans, 1995), p. 165. John Bolt and Richard Muller, too, observe that, *missio Dei* theology contains a variety of "collateral assertions," which are "not at all clear and are potentially quite mischievous." Bolt and Muller, "Does the Church Today Need a New 'Mission Paradigm'?" *Calvin Theological Journal* 31 (1996): 204.

38. See, for example, John D. Harvey, "Mission in Jesus' Teaching," in *Mission in the New Testament: An Evangelical Approach*, ed. William J. Larkin and Joel F. Williams (Maryknoll, NY: Orbis, 1998), pp. 31-39. Frances M. DuBose highlights something of the problem. He observes that "those who are the recipients of God's salvific sending become the instruments of that sending. This is more than a missional mandate however; it is a missional compulsion which emanates from the very impulse of Christian existence itself. Moreover, it relates ultimately to the divine impulse which sent the Son from the bosom of the Father." DuBose, *God Who Sends: A Fresh Quest for Biblical Mission* (Nashville: Broadman, 1983), p. 68. This encapsulates much of the spirit of the recent "missional" discussion. Bosch, however, expresses caution for two reasons. First, "it is unwarranted to single out the verb 'send' as *the* key verb in scripture. . . . [T]he word 'send' is a very common word in *any* language. Does DuBose then not erect an enormous superstructure on a somewhat incidental word?" Second, interpreting Scripture in terms of this single idea means that sending becomes "the essence not only of *mission* but of the entire theology of scripture. Mission is referred to as 'the very work of God'. It becomes an over-arching concept that threatens to swallow up everything." David J. Bosch, "Mission in Biblical Perspective: A Review Essay," *International Review of Mission* 74 (1985): 533-34. This astute observation illustrates key flaws within *missio Dei*: "sending" lacks substance and yet comes to have a determinative effect on the doctrine of God.

39. Jack Shepherd observes that "conservative evangelicals readily consent" to the idea that God "is the source of the sending activity and is continuously involved in it." However, the interesting element here is the accompanying reasoning: Evangelicals improperly separate creation from redemption. Thus, though the affirmation centers on God's sending activity, its force concerns the doctrine of creation. Jack F. Shepherd, "The Missionary Objective: Total World Evangelization," in *Protestant Crosscurrents in Mission: The Ecumenical-Conservative Encounter*, ed. Norman A. Horner (Nashville: Abingdon, 1968), p. 109.

missiology. Mission tends more and more to become an empty term, which can be filled out by anything."[40] "Sending" failed to refer to the particular actions of the Father, Son, or Spirit, becoming a metaphor indicative of an abstract dynamic vaguely constitutive of the life of the Trinity. God is a sending God. For Matthey, this direct connection between divine sending and the life of the church encourages "transposing our own ideal conceptions of just or inclusive community into the doctrine of the Trinity."[41] Aagaard furthers this basic point. Without any determining criteria, everything the human does can become "identified with the historical *missio* of God, unqualifiedly and indiscriminately. In this way all secular activities can get a kind of divine sanction — and support — again indiscriminately and unqualifiedly."[42] Thus, while the critical edge of the doctrine of the Trinity distances the missionary task from Western culture, "sending" positively encourages other accidental authorities to take the place vacated by the West. This is what occurred during the 1960s with the coordination of *missio Dei* and communism, secularization, humanization, and so on. Reference to the Trinity simply reinforced the key cultural narratives of the period.

40. Johannes Aagaard, "Church, What Is Your Mission? — Today," *Update* 3, no. 3/4 (1979): 7.

41. Jacques Matthey, "Mission als anstößiges Wesensmerkmal der Kirche," *Zeitschrift für Mission* 28, no. 3 (2002): 236-37. He further laments how "some theologies seem to fall into the temptation of transferring to God politically correct and relevant visions of the ideal community, church or society." Jacques Matthey, "Reconciliation, *Missio Dei* and the Church's Mission," in *Mission — Violence and Reconciliation: Papers Read at the Biennial Conference of the British and Irish Association for Mission Studies at the University of Edinburgh, June 2003*, ed. Howard Mellor and Timothy Yates (Sheffield, UK: Cliff College Publishing, 2004), p. 122. But Matthey continues: "I now accept the case for keeping the reference to *missio Dei*, but under the condition that it be delinked from particularist (or universalist) political theories and social analyses." Mission must be formulated apart from every accidental authority, and *missio Dei* theology remains central for this single reason. Matthey's own preference includes using *missio Dei* as "a metaphor for God's love and presence, God's unconditional accessibility," balanced with an affirmation of "God's unavailability." Matthey, "Reconciliation, *Missio Dei*," pp. 118, 121. However, as the substance of this position rests in "metaphor," it fails at the same point as do previous accounts.

42. Johannes Aagaard, "Mission After Uppsala 1968," p. 17. This must be recognized as a general temptation, and it makes the emphasis on God's subjectivity all the more significant. Bosch suggests that "whoever we are, we are tempted to incarcerate the *missio Dei* in the narrow confines of our own predilections, thereby of necessity reverting to one-sidedness and reductionism." Bosch, *Transforming Mission*, p. 512.

Such a position prompted something of a backlash against the Trinitarian grounding for missions. Hoedemaker does not want to deny "the basic perspective that the church is 'sent,'" but he does seek a position in which "the concept of *missio* has somewhat receded in the background, or at least no longer occupies a key position."[43] Matthey, more strongly, disavows "any more precise description of inner-trinitarian *processiones*, as was often attempted in past and present times. Who are we to know the inner life of God?"[44] This lament indicates, first, that *missio Dei*'s appropriation of the doctrine of the Trinity concentrated at the level of ontology, and second, it did so without any theological method for moving into the economic Trinity. Carl Braaten, summarizing the general instinct, observes that "it is because of the very close connection, indeed, some kind of identification of the immanent and the economic trinity, that the trinity becomes a source and model for our thinking about the church, its unity and mission."[45] This illustrates the issue well. To acknowledge the relationship between the act and being of God in the vague language of "some kind of identification" is not sufficiently robust to indicate how that identification might then inform the missionary activity of the Christian community. To overcome this problem, missiologists modified the basic insight that God was *in himself* missionary to say that God *had* a mission.[46] The problem of *missio Dei*, in other words, became identified with its key methodological move rather than with its deficient Trinitarianism.

43. Hoedemaker, "The People of God and the Ends of the Earth," p. 171. Christopher Wright agrees. He is "dissatisfied with accounts of mission" that only emphasize the "dynamic of sending or being sent," because "if we define *mission* only in 'sending' terms we necessarily exclude from our inventory of relevant resources many other aspects of biblical teaching that directly or indirectly affect our understanding of God's mission and the practice of our own." Wright, *The Mission of God*, p. 23.

44. Matthey, "Reconciliation, *Missio Dei*," pp. 121-22.

45. Carl E. Braaten, "The Triune God: The Source and Model of Christian Unity and Mission," *Missiology* 18, no. 4 (1990): 416.

46. So dominant is this revision in certain circles that it seems to be forgotten history that the main talk was of God's missionary nature. As an example of this "ecumenical amnesia," Holmes holds that "ecumenical theology will happily talk of the *missio Dei*, the mission of God, but seems reluctant to accept 'missionary' as a possible attribute of God. God *has a mission*, but *is not missionary*, or so the rhetoric of ecumenical theology would seem to imply." Stephen R. Holmes, "Trinitarian Missiology: Towards a Theology of God as Missionary," *International Journal of Systematic Theology* 8, no. 1 (2006): 72.

Oriented to the Kingdom of God

While most often identified with the doctrine of the Trinity, *missio Dei* theology is a blend of three elements, the second of which is an orientation to the kingdom of God.[47] *Missio Dei* theology deposed the church from her position as the goal of missionary activity. For Andersen, "the final and real goal of the *missio Dei* . . . is not the Church, but the establishment of God's kingdom, to which the Church as *ecclesia viatorum* is on its way."[48] The church fails to understand herself if she does not understand herself in terms of this fundamental relationship between the kingdom of God and the world. Or, as Hoedemaker suggests, "eschatology precedes ecclesiology."[49] The world loved by God is the object of his mission, and its final reconciliation is coincidental with the final revelation of the kingdom of God. Traditional missionary goals, such as individual conversion and planting churches, are not improper, but they are reductionist when considered against the fullness of God's kingdom. Conversion applies to the whole of life, including social and cultural institutions.[50]

Again, missions wielded this eschatological reference as a weapon against the improper liaison between colonialism and missions. Conceiving missions against the backdrop of God's in-breaking kingdom relativized

47. The complex variety of eschatological positions lies beyond the immediate scope of this study and is well summarized elsewhere. For a full treatment, see Ludwig Wiedenmann, *Mission und Eschatologie: Eine Analyse der neueren deutschen evangelischen Missionstheologie* (Paderborn, Germany: Verlag Bonifacius-Druckerei, 1965). For a summary account, see Bosch, *Transforming Mission*, pp. 498-510.

48. Andersen, "Further Toward a Theology of Mission," p. 304.

49. L. A. Hoedemaker, "Die Welt als Theologisches Problem: Kritischer Rückblick auf die Niederländische Theologie des Apostolates," *Zeitschrift für Dialektische Theologie* 2, no. 1 (2004): 9.

50. This was affirmed as early as the 1928 IMC Jerusalem conference. Oliver Chase Quick, summarizing the "Jerusalem Message," says that "it is a fatal error to consider the church's missionary task too much in terms of space, as though it involved only the asserting of Christ's claim over all people or all lands. It involves the asserting of that claim over all life. No aspect or department of human life, political, economic, scientific or aesthetic, any more than the secret thought of the individual's heart, can be exempt from, or allowed 'to contract out' of, the Gospel's claim." This conception developed in reaction to an overidentification with the Christian message and geographical expansion. Instead, "the mission field has no geographical limits and is not to be spatially conceived." Quick, "The Jerusalem Meeting and the Christian Message," *International Review of Mission* 17, no. 4 (1928): 453.

their necessary cultural location. For Lamin Sanneh, "the historical missions were side-effects of the *missio Dei,* and without that correlation Western missions propagated an ethnocentric view of Christianity."[51] Conceiving mission within an eschatological framework distances that community from the partial and provisional expressions of the gospel; it frees her to recognize the necessarily cultural location of her faith. As Verkuyl argues, "We represent a living Messiah who is enroute to the final revealing of his kingdom. . . . The danger of trying to annex Christ to one's own ends remains ever present, and therefore we must continue to strip off those myths and dreams in which he has been wrapped."[52] The kingdom orientation of the Christian community must itself be active. It is only as one engages with different particular expressions of the gospel that one's own partial cultural expressions can be identified and broken open. No particular expression of the gospel is normative for the whole. No particular language is the sacred language; every language can communicate God. Planted churches are not called to mirror the institutions of the West. Every culture can express the gospel in indigenous forms, and, by doing so, engages the church universal's understanding of the person and work of Jesus Christ.

A consensus formed on this position: the church is not the kingdom of God; the kingdom is wider than the church. God acts in and apart from the church and calls her to participate in this wider activity. Matters become confused, however, with how God's kingdom relates to the world, on the one hand, and how God's work in the world relates to his work in and through the church, on the other. The question is interpreted as one of procedure. If the problem of colonialism is the problem of the church propagating a particular cultural form of the gospel, then one solution emphasizes the world as the stage of God's acting. God acts in the world before acting through the church, thereby rendering partial every particular expression of the gospel.

Hoekendijk initiated this line of questioning when he argued against a "church-centric" approach in the early 1950s. The church is neither at the beginning nor at the end of mission. The proper order is "kingdom-gospel-Apostolate-world"; the world and the kingdom "belong together." The

---

51. Lamin Sanneh, "The Horizontal and the Vertical in Mission: An African Perspective," *International Bulletin of Missionary Research* 7, no. 4 (1983): 170.

52. Johannes Verkuyl, "The Kingdom of God as the Goal of the Missio Dei," *International Review of Mission* 68 (1979): 170.

world is the realm of God's acting in which he establishes signs of the kingdom. The gospel and the apostolate also belong together since "in the *apostolate* God continues to struggle with the world for the sake of the world." Through this apostolate, the subject of which is "the Apostle Jesus (Heb. 3:1)," the "Gospel comes to 'fulfillment.'" [53] For the church to follow Christ, she must be active in the world. The later study on the "Missionary Structure of the Congregation" simplified this logic, stating that "the old sequence of God — Church — world" falsifies "the biblical account of the way God works in the world: it leads one to think that God always initiates change from inside out, from inside the Church to the 'outsiders' in the world."[54] The church does not bear God's mission as a possession that can be picked up in the West and deposited in the East. The actual order is "God — world — Church" because "the events reported in the Bible are worldly events"; they are not sacred acts "apart from the world."[55] This visibility counters one improper condition underlying missionary superiority: the church is not the bearer of a secret knowledge, the sole interpreter of a hidden history. Yet, if mission is the Christian community enlisting in God's revolutionary acting in the world, it first becomes necessary to identify where God is acting. This, to quote Pachuau, is *missio Dei*'s "most serious drawback," for it lends itself to projection, becoming more a gauge of the values of those identifying God's acting in history.[56]

Divergent Forms?

Two apparently contrasting emphases developed from this discussion: first, God acts through the church, which mediates his reconciliation to the

---

53. J. C. Hoekendijk, "The Church in Missionary Thinking," *International Review of Mission* 41 (1952): 333. Hoedemaker observes that "*missio Dei* sees mission as part of an encompassing, overarching action of God in which 'world' and 'kingdom' are held together." L. A. Hoedemaker, "Mission, Unity and Eschaton: A Triadic Relation," *Reformed World* 50, no. 4 (2000): 175.

54. WCC Department on Studies in Evangelism, *The Church for Others*, p. 17.

55. WCC Department on Studies in Evangelism, *The Church for Others*, p. 69.

56. Lalsangkima Pachuau, "Missiology in a Pluralistic World: The Place of Mission Study in Theological Education," *International Review of Mission* 89, no. 4 (2000): 543. Bolt and Muller agree: this task is "too unnuanced and unclear." Bolt and Muller, "Does the Church Today Need a New 'Mission Paradigm'?" p. 206.

world; second, God acts in the world and calls the church to participate in this act. Interpreters identify these positions, which Matthey terms the "classical" and the "ecumenical," as competing forms of *missio Dei* theology.[57] The classical approach affirms that "God is in mission through creation, and the sending of the Son and the Spirit to enable the church to witness in the world."[58] It simply holds these two affirmations in tension: mission is an act of God in creation and in the atonement. It is larger than the church and oriented toward the world, and the church is the prime conduit through which God works. Mission, by this account, looks very much like the church in the faithful operation of the word and sacraments, alongside which the external movement is a necessary, but secondary, step. The ecumenical approach, by contrast, to quote Harvey Cox, affirms that "God is first of all present in political events, in revolutions, upheavals, invasions, defeats," since "it is the world, the political world and not the church, which is the arena of God's renewing and liberating activity."[59] God's missionary act is undertaken within the range of political and social movements that are breaking down and building up history as it progresses toward the kingdom of God. The related status of the church is ambiguous at best.[60] Fol-

57. Jacques Matthey, "Missiology in the World Council of Churches: Update," *International Review of Mission* 90, no. 4 (2001): 429-30. This formalizes a distinction present at the very inception of *missio Dei* theology. Kramm, for example, speaks of the *heilsgeschichtlich-ekklesiologische* (redemptive historical-ecclesiological) interpretation associated with Barth, Hartenstein, and Vicedom, and a *geschichtlich-eschatologische* (historical-eschatological) interpretation, associated with Hoekendijk and Aring. Thomas Kramm, *Analyse und Bewährung theologischer Modelle zur Begründung der Mission* (Aachen, Germany: Missio Aktuell Verlag, 1979), pp. 185-92.

58. Matthey, "Missiology in the WCC," p. 429.

59. Harvey G. Cox, *God's Revolution and Man's Responsibility* (Valley Forge, PA: Judson, 1965), pp. 23, 25.

60. While identified with developments in the 1960s, a qualified version of this approach persists today. Wickeri, for instance, regards as "no longer tenable" the position that "the church was the chosen instrument for the world, and that the church embraced the work of Christ whose message was universal as it spread to the ends of the earth." He favors an emphasis "on Christian particularity set in a trinitarian framework for ecumenical mission." Philip L. Wickeri, "Mission from the Margins: The *Missio Dei* in the Crisis of World Christianity," *International Review of Mission* 93, no. 2 (2004): 191-92. This "Trinitarian" language requires some decoding: every human community worships a departicularized universal divinity, pluriform in manifestation, mediated by particular instances of the diverse economy, guided by a ubiquitous spirit present as a given in creation, common, but not reducible to any single community. The particularity of the Christian community derives

lowing Matthey's summary, her "mission is to discern the signs of the times and joining God (or Christ) where God is active to transform the world towards shalom."[61] The missionary act is that of enlisting in those revolutionary historical processes through which God is establishing his kingdom.

That one can distinguish these two positions is not in doubt. Its formal nature, however, hides more than it reveals. First, the language of "classical" suggests that the "ecumenical" position is a later divergence from an established original view. No such pristine position exists. *Missio Dei* theology underwent two concentrated periods of development: at Willingen in 1952, and in the study on the "Missionary Structure of the Congregation" (MSC), from 1961 to 1968. The distinction implies that the classical position appeared at Willingen and the ecumenical position during the later study. The core issue this formal distinction highlights (the issue of whether God works first in the world or first through the church) appeared at *missio Dei*'s very inception. The aforementioned Hoekendijk essay was one of Willingen's preparatory documents. According to Bosch, Hartenstein used the term *missio Dei* in reference to the Willingen conference in order "to protect mission against secularization and horizontalization, and to reserve it exclusively for God."[62] Hartenstein, in other words, asserts it in opposition to the trends that emerged at Willingen. Despite the temporal priority of its nomenclature, the classical position is a reaction to the tendencies of the ecumenical position.

Second, the language of divergence disguises the identical Trinitarian base from which the two positions proceed. An oft-quoted statement by Scherer maintains that the MSC study produced

---

from its peculiar allegiance to the life and message of the person Jesus Christ. It is the particularity of one instance within a general framework populated by multiple particularities. Reference to the *Missio Dei*, for Wickeri, "emphasizes the radical activity of God in history. . . . God's work in all cultures was seen to be part of salvation-history, and something that challenged all human institutions and provoked a crisis in the church and its mission." He continues that "the church is active alongside other movements which anticipate God's reign, for the *missio Dei* sees all the ways in which God is involved in the world, not just the evangelistic mission of the church" (p. 187). Participation in God's mission is defined as solidarity with the marginalized of the world, and cooperation with diverse religious traditions as we together further the reign of God over the whole of creation. However, the substance of religion — of every religion — drops away as the particularity of each does not contribute to this variety of God's acting in the world.

61. Matthey, "Missiology in the WCC," p. 429.
62. Bosch, *Transforming Mission*, p. 392.

. . . a radically different and fundamentally nontrinitarian understanding of Missio Dei. This new view was actually a secular reworking of the trinitarian Missio Dei concept. God was seen to be working out the divine purpose in the midst of the world through immanent, intramundane historical forces, above all secularization. The trinitarian Missio Dei view was replaced by a theory concerning the transformation of the world and of history, not through evangelization and church-planting, but by means of a divinely guided immanent historical process, somewhat analogous to the deistic views of the Enlightenment.[63]

By this account, the doctrine of the Trinity distinguishes the classical position from the ecumenical. Yet, according to Wilhelm Richebächer, "Hoekendijk and his colleagues spoke almost exclusively of mission as a movement within the Trinity."[64] Scherer may reject the kind of trinitarianism articulated by Hoekendijk, but what alternative does the supposed classical position express? As seen above, Vicedom, representative of the classical position, and Hoekendijk, representative of the ecumenical position, delineate similar accounts of God's manifold sendings. For Johannes Aagaard, "the political theology of the sixties has genuine roots back in Willingen."[65] While that is correct, it is necessary to extend his point: the Trinitarianism of Willingen is the Trinitarianism of the ecumenical position, and the classical position is a more traditional focus on the institutions of the church retrofitted with this account. No satisfactory original position exists to which *missio Dei* theology can return. The problem is not that one is Trinitarian and the other is not; the problem is that both draw on an identical and insufficient Trinitarianism. The formal distinction, in other words, disguises their shared and basic flaw.

Matthey suggests the recent arrival of a "balanced position" that could be interpreted as "a 'third' trend of *missio Dei* theologies."[66] These ecu-

---

63. James A. Scherer, "Church, Kingdom and *Missio Dei:* Lutheran and Orthodox Corrections to Recent Ecumenical Mission Theology," in *The Good News of the Kingdom: Mission Theology for the Third Millennium,* ed. Charles van Engen et al. (Maryknoll, NY: Orbis, 1993), pp. 85-86.

64. Wilhelm Richebächer, "*Missio Dei:* The Basis of Mission Theology or a Wrong Path?" *International Review of Mission* 92, no. 4 (2003): 591.

65. Aagaard, "Trends in Missiological Thinking during the Sixties," p. 23.

66. Matthey, "Missiology in the World Council of Churches: Update," p. 430.

menical statements attempt to include both emphases on the universality of God's mission and on the role of the church in that mission.[67] This only reinforces our central contention: that the eschatological orientation to the kingdom of God snags on the issue of distinguishing and relating divine and human agency. *Missio Dei* theology forces treatments either to emphasize the divine acting in opposition to the human or to formulate an account of human agency via ecclesiology or creation. The dichotomy is irreconcilable, and the proposed solution lies in placing the two affirmations side by side. The contrary positions, while divergent regarding the place of mission and the role of the church, suffer from the identical problem of relating the Trinitarian basis of mission to the church's activity.

The Completion of Reconciliation

The link the ecumenical position forms between the kingdom and history results from an emphasis on the objective completion of reconciliation.[68] Jesus' death and resurrection completed, once and for all, the reconciliation of the world. With this, the ecumenical position concludes that "the world is already a redeemed world so that, whether men discern their true condition or not, and even if they deny it, they are still the heirs of God's redemption."[69] The completion of reconciliation means its *subjective* completion; all of creation is already saved. For the classical position, this indicates mission's demise; for the ecumenical, this means mission's natural terminus.

Barth, according to the classical position, bears responsibility for the

67. See, e.g., "Mission and Evangelism in Unity Today," *International Review of Mission* 88, no. 1/2 (1999): 109-27.

68. Sundermeier correctly describes it as "false" to understand the "ecumenical" position "as an offspring of Barthian theology." However, he continues that "Barth's theology of mission does share two weaknesses with this latter theology: the difference between law and gospel is blurred, and the inner-trinitarian distinction between God the creator and God the reconciler is reduced to mere verbal distinction." This is incorrect, but Sundermeier continues that, with this, Jesus' work becomes universalized and true irrespective of individual adherence, and "this conviction leaps out of every sentence" of the "ecumenical" position. Theo Sundermeier, "Theology of Mission," in *Dictionary of Mission: Theology, History, Perspectives,* ed. Karl Müller et al. (Maryknoll, NY: Orbis, 1997), pp. 435-36.

69. World Council of Churches Department on Studies in Evangelism, *A Theological Reflection on the Work of Evangelism* (Geneva: WCC, 1963), p. 7.

denuding of the church that is evident within the ecumenical position. Since reconciliation is objectively true for all, according to Krusche, the church does not possess an "ontic otherness." The church is no different from the world. "To the contrary, they are precisely therein united, in that they are reconciled through the same reconciler and form the new mankind — the peculiarity of the Church is rather that it *knows* all this." The Christian community only possesses a "cognitive head-start."[70] The ecumenical advocates agree: "This head start is its distance from the world."[71] The church must not conceive of herself as possessing any kind of ontic otherness since this prompts the attitude of presumptive superiority underlying imperialism. The goal of mission, according to the MSC, "is not something that can be objectified and set apart. It is not the *plus* that the *haves* can distribute to the *have-nots,* nor is it an internal condition (peace of mind) that some can enjoy in isolation."[72] The Christian community's cognitive head start obliges her to witness to the reconciliation of the world by participating in God's revolutionary acts in history and, by so doing, to call the world to become what it already is. Krusche rejects this position because "the statement that all men already belong to the new creation could also mean — and it must almost necessarily be understood as meaning — that all are beyond danger because there is no judgment."[73] Reducing the temporal actuality of reconciliation to knowledge retards the missionary impetus, for it destroys any need for conversion and thus any need for the church as the mother of the faithful. The church ceases to be a

---

70. Werner Krusche, "Parish Structure — A Hindrance to Mission? A Survey and Evaluation of the Ecumenical Discussion on the Structures of the Missionary Congregation," in *Sources for Change: Searching for Flexible Church Structures,* ed. Herbert T. Neve (Geneva: World Council of Churches, 1968), pp. 60-61. For von Balthasar, this focus on reconciliation's completion makes the basis of the church identical to that of the wider creation. As such, "Barth was forced to stress this relativization of the Church — even to the point where the Church would completely merge into the world. But he was likewise forced to proceed rather cautiously on this score, because otherwise the necessity of the Church would disappear from view entirely." This is, of course, what happened with the MSC, against which Krusche is writing. Hans Urs von Balthasar, *The Theology of Karl Barth: Exposition and Interpretation* (San Francisco, CA: Ignatius, 1992), p. 245.

71. Thomas Wieser, ed., *Planning for Mission: Working Papers on the New Quest for Missionary Communities* (New York: U.S. Conference for the World Council of Churches, 1966), p. 81.

72. WCC Department on Studies in Evangelism, *The Church for Others,* p. 14.

73. Krusche, "Parish Structure," p. 82.

necessary organ of God's activity. Barth seemingly confirms this with his statement that "it is only with regard to its knowing this new reality that the world is dependent upon the community," and, as such, "the world would not necessarily be lost if there were no church."[74] This, for Donald Bloesch, is "the Barthian error" and results in a de facto doctrine of *apokatastasis.*[75]

The "ecumenical" position, for its part, is equally dissatisfied with Barth's position. According to Aring, Barth falls to the allure of the traditional God — church — world pattern.[76] Aring quotes Barth to the effect that "the goal, toward which the real church is on the way and in motion, is the revelation of the *sanctification of the whole human world* that has already occurred *de iure* in Jesus Christ." Though affirming the de jure reconciliation of humanity, Barth's failure rests in his refusal to locate this as a given of the new creation; that is, he affirms the church in her peculiar task of witness. The Christian community, in this interim age, is "as a people to whom that lifting up and setting upright, that sanctification has happened not only *de iure* but also *de facto,* and which she is now to *present* to all other people as a witness, the sanctification in Jesus Christ that has already happened to them and to all people as well."[77] As will become clear, the de jure, or objective, completion of reconciliation in Jesus Christ demands the corresponding historical form of the witnessing community in the de facto, or subjective, completion of reconciliation in the power of the Holy Spirit. Aring remains unsatisfied with this procedure, for here "the world is not finally taken seriously as the place and appointed partner in God's reconciling action." He continues that this "seductive" Trinitarian formulation "assigns to the church this second step location over against the world," and thus "demotes the world ideologically as a place of decay, of not-yet-being-reconciled, in which everything depends upon the initiative, the activity, the solidarity, the mission of the church and of Christians,

---

74. Barth, rev., *KD* IV/3.2, 946; *CD* IV/3.2, 826.

75. Donald G. Bloesch, *The Evangelical Renaissance* (Grand Rapids: Eerdmans, 1973), p. 98. Barth, by contrast, says that "nowhere does the New Testament say that the world is saved, or can we say that without doing violence to the New Testament. We can say only that the election of Jesus Christ has taken place on behalf of the world, i.e., in order that there may be this event in and to the world through Him" (*CD* II/2, 423; *KD* II/2, 468). For Barth's position on *apokatastasis,* see *CD* IV/3.1, 477-78; *KD* IV/3.1, 549-51.

76. Aring, *Kirche als Ereignis,* pp. 63-64.

77. Barth, rev., *KD* IV/2, 702; *CD* IV/2, 620.

in order that the *missio Dei* might become an event within this world and it might then *become* the saved and reconciled world of God."[78] According to Aring, Barth conceives of a necessary place for the church as the form provisionally mandated by reconciliation, and this unduly prioritizes the church.

Instead, Aring argues that the world requires no missionary activity "in order to become what it already is since Easter: the reconciled world of God."[79] Mission is redundant because God completed his mission in the man Jesus Christ. The subjective appropriation of reconciliation may be an ongoing event as human society grows toward what it already is, but appropriation is an inevitable consequence of historical movement. Hoekendijk, too, maintains that "the structures in the world have been made Christian . . . these matters are part of history. They have been transformed into public events on the road to the final cosmic liberation."[80] Reconciliation's completion is historically available and evident in the forces of secularization, humanization, and urbanization. Therefore, Aring concludes, "New possibilities emerge for the revival of allegedly overcome 'natural theologies.'"[81] God's subjectivity turns full circle: he acts according to his messianic pattern of sending, which is necessarily discernible in historical progress, and this clears the ground for a revitalized natural theology.

This bifurcated appropriation of Barth's position demonstrates that the respective concerns of the "classical" and "ecumenical" positions do not flow as a logical necessity from his thinking, that is, he cannot negate and overemphasize the church at the same time. Barth does use epistemic language to describe both human fellowship with God and the motive and task of Christian mission. As an example of the latter, the "contrast of the *knowledge* in the community and the terrible *ignorance* in the world is the *motive,* and its bridging is the *problem* of the original Christian mission." The knowledge at stake here is one of universal judgment, not of universal reconciliation. "This reality compels mission."[82] Mission is a necessity be-

78. Aring, *Kirche als Ereignis,* p. 65.

79. Aring, *Kirche als Ereignis,* p. 28.

80. J. C. Hoekendijk, "Feier der Befreiung: Was ist Mission?" in *Kontexte 4,* ed. H. J. Schultz (Stuttgart, Berlin, 1967), p. 131. Quoted by Richebächer, "*Missio Dei:* The Basis of Mission Theology or a Wrong Path?" p. 591.

81. Aring, *Kirche als Ereignis,* p. 24.

82. Barth, rev., *KD* III/2, 738; *CD* III/2, 607.

cause the reality it expresses is precisely that — a reality. It distinguishes the Christian message from other propagandistic messages, such as moral or philosophical beliefs, and from a form of proclamation based in humanistic impulses and a dead sense of duty.

Missionary by Her Very Nature

Affirming that the church is missionary by her very nature is the third constitutive element of *missio Dei* theology. For Darrell Guder, such a position is a "dominant consensus" of the global church.[83] While certainly true at the level of ecumenical pronouncement, this consensus receives little treatment within systematic accounts of the church. Popular imagination turns to *Ad Gentes* as initiating this now axiomatic position: "The Church on earth is by its very nature missionary since, according to the plan of the Father, it has its origin in the mission of the Son and the Holy Spirit."[84] In actuality, it begins much earlier. Reference to the concept's genealogy elucidates the complexity of the issue, including its lack of reference to the doctrine of the Trinity and the set opposition between the "being" of the church and her "act" of mission underlying the concept.

Mission as a Function of the Church

The issue of the relationship between the institution of the church and missions arises at the turn of the twentieth century: during this period, volunteer parachurch agencies bore the main missionary responsibility within Protestant denominations. Andersen notes that

> . . . the missionary enterprise regarded itself as a separate institution concerned with Christian operations overseas within, on the fringe of, in certain cases even outside, the existing Christian bodies; and, in ac-

83. Darrell L. Guder, *The Continuing Conversion of the Church* (Grand Rapids: Eerdmans, 2000), p. 20. For a rare opposing opinion, Bolt and Muller describe the language of the "mission-shaped church" as "vacuous." See Bolt and Muller, "Does the Church Today Need a New 'Mission Paradigm'?" p. 208.

84. Austin Flannery, *Vatican Council II: The Conciliar and Post Conciliar Documents*, rev. ed. (Northport, NY: Costello, 1996), 1:814.

cordance with this understanding of its nature, it developed its own independent organizational structure within or alongside of the organized Churches.[85]

Churches and missionary societies were distinctive entities. Missions occurred apart from the church. While the church could not exist without worship, the same did not hold for missionary activity. A church could exist without reference to mission. Worship was an act demanded of all the faithful; mission was the exclusive responsibility of special individuals called and equipped for the task. This essential distinction produced a relationship whereby mission existed as a derivative function of a pre-existent church. This practical question merely manifested a deeper theological problem. To quote Jüngel, the "theological distortion in missionary *practice*" was consequent on a "*theoretical* gap in the *doctrine* of the church."[86] Volunteer missionary societies developed because the ecclesiologies of the period proved insufficient for the missionary task.[87] The disjunction of church from mission does not merely devalue mission with respect to the life of the community; it indicates that the church misconceives herself. She is too static, that is, not oriented to the purpose for which she exists.[88]

85. Andersen, *Towards a Theology of Mission*, p. 15. Bosch confirms that "another factor responsible for the present embarrassment in the field of mission is that the modern missionary enterprise was born and bred outside the church. . . . [W]hen the missionary flame was eventually kindled, it burned on the fringes of the institutional church, frequently meeting with passionate resistance from the official church." David J. Bosch, "Theological Education in Missionary Perspective," *Missiology* 10, no. 1 (1982): 17.

86. Eberhard Jüngel, "To Tell the World about God: The Task for the Mission of the Church on the Threshold of the Third Millennium," *International Review of Mission* 89, no. 1 (2000): 205.

87. Andrew Walls observes that "it suddenly became clear that there were things — and not small things, but big things, things like the evangelization of the world — which were beyond the capacities of these splendid systems of gospel truth." Walls, "Missionary Societies and the Fortunate Subversion of the Church," in *The Missionary Movement in Christian History: Studies in the Transmission of Faith* (Maryknoll, NY: Orbis, 1996), p. 247.

88. Stephen Neill, for example, laments that ecclesiologies have all "been constructed in light of a static concept of the Church as something given, something which already exists. . . . As far as I know, no one has yet set to work to think out the theology of the Church in terms of the one thing for which it exists," i.e., mission. Stephen Neill, *Creative Tension* (London: Edinburgh House, 1959), p. 111. Johannes Blaauw, during the period of Vatican II, observes that "outside the existing missionary movement, the conviction that the Church is

Somewhat counterintuitively, the postcolonial depiction of the Christian faith challenged this disjunction. This derivative relationship of mission to church established the church both as the beginning and as the end of mission: missions, of necessity, consisted of replicating these particular denominational and cultural forms. In 1905, Martin Kähler, by way of response, formulated a distinction between mission and propaganda. He warned against treating a secularized gospel — a particular expression of gospel embedded within a local environment — as the whole gospel. While necessary, this contextualized gospel belongs to a "partial church" and is something that the church owns and manages.[89] Propaganda occurs when those who "think that in bringing their particular Christianity, they are bringing Christianity itself, and thus the gospel itself."[90] The gospel is, by default, identified with a definite historical and cultural form, and mission is successful as it translocates that particular manifestation. In this context,

> ... there is no substantial difference between whether one propagates a churchly Christianity, a confessional, institutional morality, or some non-church modern faith. One just expands what is already one's own. Here competition with other religions and worldviews automatically re-

---

a missionary Church or it is no Church is accepted by the great majority. The centuries-old ecclesiology which remained so static is now gradually being replaced by a more dynamic one which is both eschatological and missionary." Blauw, *The Missionary Nature of the Church: A Survey of the Biblical Theology of Mission* (New York: McGraw-Hill, 1962). While this may be true of the period since Vatican II, such an affirmation finds no confirmation in the great body of theological reflection.

89. Bavinck, for example, defines *Corpus Christianum* as "the idea of the necessity not only of the gospel but also of the cultural garment with which the gospel is clothed in our own civilization." J. H. Bavinck, "Theology and Mission," *Free University Quarterly* 8 (1962): 61-62.

90. Martin Kähler, *Schriften zu Christologie und Mission: Gesamtausgabe der Schriften zur Mission*, ed. Heinzgünter Frohnes (Munich: Chr. Kaiser Verlag, 1971), p. 115. Bosch summarizes the problem in this way: "Propaganda is always the spreading of 'Christianity', that means: the gospel plus culture; the gospel plus confessionalism; the gospel plus a set of moral codes; the gospel plus some feeling of ethnical superiority, always resulting in reproducing exact replicas of the sending church." He goes on to say that "the problem is that those whom we may describe as 'propagandists' themselves aim at nothing but spreading the *gospel*." This positive intention — and the related blindness toward the actual effects — is itself a defining characteristic of propaganda. David J. Bosch, "Systematic Theology and Mission: The Voice of an Early Pioneer," *Theologia Evangelica* 5, no. 3 (1972): 183.

sults. It is a matter of human acquisitions and formations only. One proselytizes, i.e., makes repetitions of oneself.[91]

The distinction between church and mission reduced the missionary task to the replication of ecclesiastical forms, prompting a competitive relationship between Christianity and other faiths and among different forms of Christian expression. The problem was not missions per se, but a failure of the church to understand her purpose. Kähler argues that because the proclamation of the word was the concern of the church, mission was the concern of the church. Beyond every other possible authorization for her existence — such as the presence of a Christian culture, a religious institution, or historical circumstance — the church lives "on the charter of her church-grounding preaching, and of the extension of the service of the Word defined by that preaching."[92] Kähler concludes — in 1899! — that "there is no mission without church, and mission is always an expression of the church," and "as there is no mission without church, so there is no church without mission."[93] The church is, by nature, a missionary community.

Attention to this missionary nature disrupted the drive toward domestication that occurs when the gospel becomes identified with a cultural context. Thus Kähler famously asserts that the "earliest mission became the mother of theology because it attacked the existing culture."[94] This

91. Kähler, *Schriften zu Christologie und Mission*, p. 114.

92. Kähler, *Schriften zu Christologie und Mission*, p. 156. This kind of thinking also surfaced at Edinburgh in 1910. Gairdner regarded recognizing the "existence of a *non-contributing Church*" and that "Christendom is not yet missionary" to be among Edinburgh's most significant discoveries. One delegate called for the "Church of the living God [to] arise as a great Missionary Society," and the realization of this "ideal" was the "grand problem." Gairdner responded to this observation by saying that "it is, indeed, a sign of an unnatural state of things that it should be called an 'ideal' at all: in the very nature of the case, it should be an essential part not of the ideal but of the actual definition of the Church." W. H. T. Gairdner, *Echoes from Edinburgh, 1910: An Account and Interpretation of the World Missionary Conference* (New York: Fleming Revell, 1910), pp. 240-41.

93. Kähler, *Schriften zu Christologie und Mission*, p. 78. For a summary of Kähler's position, see Erich Krüger, *Wesen und Aufgabe der Missionstheologie* (Wuppertal-Barmen: Verlag der Rheinischen Missions-Gesellschaft, 1960), pp. 44-47; Henning Wrogemann, *Mission und Religion in der systematischen Theologie der Gegenwart: Das Missionsverständnis deutschsprachiger protestantischer Dogmatiker im 20. Jahrhundert* (Göttingen: Vandenhoeck and Ruprecht, 1997), pp. 23-36.

94. Kähler, *Schriften zu Christologie und Mission*, p. 190.

analysis, reinforced by the post–World War I rediscovery of eschatology, dominated the intellectual reconstruction of the missionary task within German mission circles during the early part of the twentieth century.[95] To think of the church from the perspective of the "end" was to think of the church in terms of her purpose.

The marked successes of the Western missionary enterprise, coordinated with the failure of Western civilization evident in World War I, established a second historical condition leading to the discovery of the church's missionary nature.[96] Once missions had established Christian communities, what relationship did these younger churches have to the older sending churches? Complex infrastructure, paternalism, and fears concerning the leadership capacity of "native" Christians made it difficult for Western missions to relinquish governing control. World War II proved a boon in this regard. As missionaries found themselves interned, indigenous leadership assumed control over these "orphaned" missions. These historic missions became recognized as churches in their own right. The two world wars equally alerted missionary leadership to the ineffectiveness of Christianity in the "sending" countries of the West. As Hartenstein suggests, "We have learned in these last years to think differently about the superiority of European culture. Every heathen throws our own words back into our faces."[97] Missions could no longer draw on some imagined Western superiority. Indeed, they discovered a mission field in their own backyard. Geographical terms were no longer adequate to frame the missionary enterprise. Mission became something true for every church regardless of the particular location. The church does not have a mission, she *is* missionary.

95. For Hoekendijk, Kähler's distinction between propaganda and missions constituted "a judgment over so much that promoted itself as 'mission' in those years." However, since he was writing before World War I, few of Kähler's contemporaries understood this aphorism. With the sweeping away of the culture of optimism, "the new German missiology begins a cleansing process, which Kähler's conceptual scheme (mission-propaganda) initiates." Hoekendijk, *Kirche und Volk in der deutschen Missionswissenschaft*, p. 43.

96. For a treatment of this issue and the "crisis" it stimulated within missions, see Hendrik Kraemer, "Mission im Wandel der Völkerwelt," in *Der Auftrag der Kirche in der modernen Welt: Festgabe zum siebzigsten Geburtstag von Emil Brunner*, ed. Peter Vogelsanger (Zürich: Zwingli Verlag, 1959), pp. 291-307.

97. Karl Hartenstein, "Was hat die Theologie Karl Barths der Mission zu Sagen?" *Zwischen den Zeiten* 6 (1928): 66.

Johannes C. Hoekendijk

These historical factors coincided with an analogous examination of the relationship between gospel and culture, embodied especially in the criticisms issued against cultural Protestantism. The resulting "crisis" stimulated such statements as Brunner's 1931 affirmation: "The church exists by mission, just as a fire exists by burning."[98] For Kraemer, the church "ought to be a bearer of witness to God and His decisive creative and redeeming acts and purposes. To become conscious of its apostolic character is for the Church the surest way to take hold of its real essence and substance."[99] Hartenstein, summarizing the findings of Tambaram 1938, notes that "whoever says church, says mission. Or conversely: whoever says mission, says church."[100] While such statements might suggest the completed coordination of church and mission, existing ecclesiologies simply absorbed the theological language. The default distinction of church from mission remained intact. For the church to be missionary meant that it had to "be the church."[101] The Western church had bequeathed much of her social re-

98. Emil Brunner, *The Word and the World* (London: SCM, 1931), p. 108.

99. Hendrik Kraemer, *The Christian Message in a non-Christian World* (London: Harper and Brothers, 1938), p. 2.

100. Karl Hartenstein, "Was haben wir von Tambaram zu lernen?" in *Das Wunder der Kirche unter den Völkern der Erde: Bericht über Weltmissions-Konferenz in Tambaram,* ed. Martin Schlunk (Stuttgart: Evangelischer Missionsverlag, 1939), p. 194.

101. The watchword "let the church be the church," against which the charge of "ecclesiocentrism" was laid, became the hallmark cry of the 1937 Life and Work Oxford conference, and it underwent prolonged criticism during the 1950s. See John A. Mackay, *Ecumenics: The Science of the Church Universal* (Englewood Cliffs, NJ: Prentice-Hall, 1964), pp. 3-10. The missionary intent behind this phrase is especially interesting given the reappearance of the idea within the work of Hauerwas. "The first social ethical task of the church is to be the church — the servant community." Stanley Hauerwas, *The Peaceable Kingdom: A Primer in Christian Ethics* (Notre Dame, IN: University of Notre Dame Press, 1983), p. 99. This 1983 statement, of course, follows John Howard Yoder's 1972 position that "the church's calling is to be the conscience and the servant within human society," which itself draws directly on Oxford's architect, J. H. Oldham, albeit with qualification, as well as the phrase "let the church be the church." John Howard Yoder, *The Politics of Jesus: Vicit Agnus Noster,* 2nd ed. (Grand Rapids: Eerdmans, 1994), pp. 155, 150. Hauerwas's argument, in other words, shadows Oxford's logic: the church has become too complicit with her surrounding culture, and she must repudiate this undue liaison by living according to her own agenda and in developing her own cultural forms. He does this without referring to the criticisms issued against this "church-centric" approach to mission theology during the 1950s.

sponsibility to the state. Now, against the acids eroding Western civilization, the church needed to become a community characterized by a different way of life. Only this would engender "a reconstruction of our whole outlook, and a reorientation of our fundamental attitudes."[102] We should not underestimate the missionary intent of such a position, but it was precisely this intent that reduced the missionary act into the church. This notion of community, defined as it was within an existing Christian culture, located the distinctiveness of the gospel in established ecclesial practices. The church was, therefore, missionary as she focused attention on her internal life. In other words, such a focus became a necessary prerequisite for any external activity. J. C. Hoekendijk soon subjected this dominant "church-centric" approach to vigorous criticism, the ramifications of which were to direct ecumenical mission thinking for the next two decades and beyond.

Driven by the post–World War II reaction against *völkisch* approaches, Hoekendijk sought to rid mission method of every semblance of propaganda. The problem, for Hoekendijk, was that normative Reformation-era ecclesiologies inevitably produced such a mission method for two reasons: first, mission aimed at establishing Christendom; second, it did so because the ecclesiastical forms posited by the Reformers presupposed Christendom as the normative social condition. Christendom afforded a long-established base community structure, and it was natural to expect both the continuation of the structure and its establishment in other contexts as a logical outworking of the gospel. Presupposing this social condition allowed the Reformers not to develop a "full doctrine of the Church." They did not require one, nor was this their purpose. They sought "not to create new communities, but to reform those already in existence." The missionary duty took the form of Christianization, the purification of the faith. Only when "the presupposed foundation of Christendom sank away" did this "reduced ecclesiology" come into relief.[103] While Christendom's de-

---

102. W. A. Visser 't Hooft and Joseph H. Oldham, *The Church and Its Function in Society* (Chicago: Willett, Clark, 1937), p. 14. For an examination of the missionary intent of this position, see John G. Flett, "From Jerusalem to Oxford: Mission as the Foundation and Goal of Ecumenical Social Thought," *International Bulletin of Missionary Research* 27, no. 1 (2003): 17-22.

103. J. C. Hoekendijk, "The Call to Evangelism," *International Review of Mission* 39 (1950): 164. Lesslie Newbigin summarizes the general logic, saying that "to be convinced on biblical and theological grounds that the Church not only has a missionary task but is itself

mise provided clear motivation for the evangelistic task, the underlying deficient ecclesiology, predicated as it was on a community structure, meant that mission-as-Christianization required first the establishment of a culture. One had to re-create Christendom — not its political structures but its fundamental link between religion and culture and evangelism.

For Hoekendijk, it is those churches that formed in protest against gathering the church under the conditions of establishment that prove the point. The Pietists and the Methodists "realized that individualism completely lacked the spiritual setting for their work. Yet they continued as if they still lived in Christendom. They tried to isolate individuals and assemble them in an island of the saved, floating on a flood of perdition." Conversion alone was insufficient: conversion first required enculturation. Mission method demanded a Christianized life as a necessary precondition. It made no difference whether this life was conceived — following a church polity based in a state or cultural church — in broad civilizational terms, or — following a church polity based in a gathered or believers' church — in narrow congregational terms. Hoekendijk concludes that "the call to evangelism is often little else than a call to restore 'Christendom', the *'Corpus Christianum'*, as a solid, well-integrated cultural complex, directed and dominated by the Church."[104] This vision informed the motive, method, and goal of mission. This bequeathed the contemporary church an impotent basis and an impossible missionary task derived from — and orientated toward — this impotent basis.

Mission required this cultural structure as basic to its method, but it also furnished its goal. Related to "an ideology of Christendom," the missionary act extended the church. Evangelistic outreach is "the repetition of the Church on a larger scale."[105] Missionary activity planted churches. "Mission and Church are not conceived of as being coexistent, but rather as consecutive entities. The Church is the ultimate object of the Mission

---

the form of God's mission ('As the Father sent me so send I you') was to be driven to acknowledge that congregations as we know them are not structured for mission. They reflect the assumptions of the Christendom era that the whole of society is already baptized and therefore within the Church. They invite people to come out of the world into the Church: they do not themselves go into the world as those who are sent by God." Newbigin, "Recent Thinking on Christian Beliefs: VIII. Mission and Missions," *The Expository Times* 88, no. 9 (1977): 261.

104. Hoekendijk, "The Call to Evangelism," pp. 163-64.
105. Hoekendijk, "The Call to Evangelism," p. 164.

and takes its place."[106] Missions paved "the road from the Church to the Church. It is the outgoing activity of one church — it can remain as it was before — to a place in the world where again a church is planted. In principle, the task of missions is completed as soon as this church exists."[107] The process is "first the Mission, then the Church-free-from-the-Mission."[108]

Hoekendijk continues that "it is common to think of evangelism, to think of the apostolate, as a function of the Church. *Credo ecclesiam apostolicam* is often interpreted as: 'I believe in the Church, which has an apostolic function." The church was engaged in "churchification." The missionary message became that of a preparatory cultural form through which the gospel was expressed as a way of life.[109] Moreover, mission dis-

---

106. Hoekendijk, "The Church in Missionary Thinking," p. 326.

107. Hoekendijk, "The Call to Evangelism," p. 170.

108. Hoekendijk, "The Church in Missionary Thinking," p. 327.

109. Hoekendijk, "The Call to Evangelism," pp. 170-71. Hoekendijk's lament is far from mere caricature. Robert Jenson's conception of catechetical practices provides a good illustration of the problem. This topic is of utmost importance for two reasons: first, Christendom's demise means that church and Western culture are undergoing a separation; second, the church's mission within this context means that the church must not adapt her own "culture to seekers, but seekers to the church's culture." Robert W. Jenson, "Catechesis for Our Time," in *Marks of the Body of Christ*, ed. Carl E. Braaten and Robert W. Jenson (Grand Rapids: Eerdmans, 1999), p. 145. This is a missionary method that opposes any attempt by the church — often validated using the language of "evangelism" — to "maintain its cultural position by minimizing the differences, that is, by minimizing its own character as church" (Jenson, p. 142). The missionary context demands that the church attend to her proper culture. This takes a definite form. "The church, like every living community, has her own interior culture, built up during the centuries of her history. That is, the acts of proclamation and baptism and Eucharist are in fact embedded in a continuous tradition of ritual and diction and music and iconography and interpretation, which constitutes a churchly culture in fact thicker and more specific than any national or ethnic culture." Jenson willingly acknowledges the Western character of this culture. "If the church's first missionary successes had taken her more south than west, her music and architecture and diction and so on would surely have developed differently" (p. 144). This contingency within a missionary context means that the church is not "permitted simply to shuck off chant and chorale, or the crucifix, or architecture that encloses us in a biblical story, or ministerial clothing that recalls that of ancient Rome and Constantinople, and so on and on." Catechesis takes the form of "music training and art appreciation and language instruction, for the *church's* music and art and in the language of Canaan." Jenson even lends this approach divine justification: teaching individuals how to "live in the fellowship of the church" is nothing less than initiating them into the "eternal fellowship of the triune God" (pp. 144-45). This is a clear example of how theological systems would benefit from direct reference to mission theology and history.

appears when that culture has been established as not itself essential to that culture. The missionary act does not itself bear the evangelistic message; it transfers the fundamental building blocks of a culture, in preparation for the evangelistic message that results as a byproduct of that culture. Any conception of mission for which the church and her replication held a logical priority inevitably prioritized particular cultural histories and resulted in transplanted cultural churches. This conceptual dichotomy of mission from church is one enduring legacy of Reformation-era ecclesiologies.

Hoekendijk's constructive proposal begins with the affirmation that "Church-centric missionary thinking is bound to go astray, because it revolves around an illegitimate centre."[110] The *plantatio ecclesiae* cannot be "the end of evangelism"; this stimulates a "too static view of the Church as a closed and definite entity."[111] Mission serves the world, not the church, and it should focus on the dynamic of the coming kingdom and the world's rejection of that kingdom. Hoekendijk understands this to mean that "the Church has no other existence than in *actu Christi,* that is in *actu Apostoli.*" The church, as an institutional form of the gospel, "has no fixed place at all in this context, it happens in so far as it actually proclaims the kingdom to the world." Hoekendijk continues that "the *nature* of the Church can be sufficiently defined by its *function.*"[112] The church exists only as she participates in Christ's apostolic activity.

This is where matters become complicated. Mission theorists affirm that union with Christ occurs only insofar as the church participates in his mission to the world. It remains unclear, however, what this means for the church as an identifiable historical entity. Hoekendijk's criticism of the link between evangelism and "community" resulted in the denuding of the community. Mission became the pursuit of shalom in the world, with the church, to quote the MSC, "a *postscript,* that is, added to the world for the purpose of pointing to and celebrating both Christ's presence and God's ultimate redemption of the whole world."[113] In practical terms, this made the church, for Scherer, "virtually dispensable as an

---

110. Hoekendijk, "The Church in Missionary Thinking," p. 332.

111. Hoekendijk, "The Call to Evangelism," p. 171.

112. Hoekendijk, "The Church in Missionary Thinking," p. 334.

113. Evangelism, *The Church for Others,* p. 70. For a general summary of this position and a preliminary reaction, see Markus Barth, "What Is the Gospel?" *International Review of Mission* 53, no. 4 (1964): 441-48.

agent of divine mission, and in some cases even a hindrance."[114] Mission occurred in deliberate distinction to the life of the Christian community. The community, as a community, contributed nothing to the missionary task. It could not contribute because this, according to Hoekendijk, would only result in propagandistic missionary methods.[115]

While he properly decries the terminus of mission in the church, Hoekendijk proves guilty of the same dichotomy; he simply inverts the emphasis: a mission-centric approach replaces a church-centric approach. Of this Newbigin observes, "An unchurchly mission is as much a monstrosity as an unmissionary Church." In reaction to Hoekendijk, Newbigin maintains that the church can only witness to the kingdom of God if her life is "a *real* foretaste of it, a real participation in the life of God Himself." Newbigin agrees that positing a church without mission "involves a radical contradiction of the truth of the Church's being," and that "no recovery of the true wholeness of the Church's nature is possible without a recovery of its radically missionary character." Yet, this occurs insofar as the means of missionary witness is congruous with its end; that is, the witness to the reconcilia-

114. Scherer, "Church, Kingdom and *Missio Dei*," p. 85. This would lead to Newbigin's lament that "we had a missiology that found God's redeeming action almost everywhere except in the preaching of the Gospel. It was a sad period." Lesslie Newbigin, "Reply to Konrad Raiser," *International Bulletin of Missionary Research* 18, no. 2 (1994): 52.

115. Hoekendijk contrasts the missionary act with the institutional life of the Christian community via the language of "event," and he claims to develop on Barth at this decisive point. Hoekendijk, "The Church in Missionary Thinking," 334 n. 2. Hoekendijk draws this position from a subsection of the *Church Dogmatics* entitled "The Active Life." See Barth, *CD* III/4, 470-521. There is, of course, a question of how faithfully Hoekendijk follows Barth. For Rossel, "the definition of Mission as the step of the Church beyond itself that is profoundly necessary because it belongs to its very being brings Barth's teaching close to the recent concept of *The Church for Others.*" Jacques Rossel, "From a Theology of Crisis to a Theology of Revolution? Karl Barth, Mission and Missions," *Ecumenical Review* 21, no. 2 (1969): 208-9. This cannot be doubted. With his "event" language, Barth appeared more to align himself with Hoekendijk's school than with mediatorial conceptions of the church's mission. Like Aring, however, Johannes de Jong maintains that Barth remained locked in a churchly paradigm. Hoekendijk moved into realms Barth left unexplored: questions of "the shape of the community in the post-Constantinian age and in the stormily surfacing global society, the church as shape of the *Missio Dei*, the sending of the world, the relationship of the proclamation of the word to the Pantomime of salvation." Johannes Marie de Jong, "Ist Barth überholt?" in *Theologie zwischen Gestern und Morgen: Interpretationen und Anfragen zum Werk Karl Barths,* ed. Wilhelm Dantine and Kurt Lüthi (Munich: Chr. Kaiser Verlag, 1968), p. 46.

tion in Christ demands an actual reconciled fellowship with Christ. "This life in Christ," Newbigin continues, "is not merely the instrument of the apostolic mission," it is equally the "eschatological end and purpose of reconciliation."[116]

The Being of the Church versus the Act of Mission

It is clear that affirmations of the church's missionary nature continue to trade on the dichotomy between church and mission. Emphasis accomplishes the substantial theological work: Does one prioritize church over mission, or vice versa? As Newbigin suggests, "We have corrupted the word 'Church' (and distorted the life of the churches) by constantly using it in a non-missionary sense."[117] A secondary observation concerns the lack of any theological connection between the rhetorical affirmations concerning the church's missionary nature and the doctrine of the Trinity.[118] The connectors relating church and mission are constructed more of historical accident than of theological substance. Acknowledging the church's missionary essence establishes sufficient cultural dissonance for the church to refrain from identifying her peculiar historical and cultural form as the normative expression of the gospel, and to encourage diverse forms of the gospel as vital expressions of the church universal. Quoting Andrew Kirk, as a representative example, "the Church is by nature missionary to the extent that, if it ceases to be missionary, it has not just failed in one of its

116. J. E. Lesslie Newbigin, *The Household of God: Lectures on the Nature of the Church* (London: SCM, 1953), pp. 147-48.

117. J. E. Lesslie Newbigin, *One Body, One Gospel, One World: The Christian Mission Today* (London: IMC, 1958), p. 42.

118. This holds true for the coincidental development in Catholic theology. Henri de Lubac argues for the missionary nature of the church in his "The Theological Foundation of the Missions," first published in 1941, with a second part delivered after the fall of Nazi Germany in 1946. He says that, "in missionary activity, what is at issue is not merely the extension of the Church but her very existence." Henri de Lubac, *Theology in History*, trans. Anne Englund Nash (San Francisco: Ignatius, 1996), p. 387. The church is by nature missionary, and, given the ontological location, this receives some connection with the doctrine of the Trinity. But with this development, too, Gianfranco Coffele observes that "de Lubac does not fully develop his trinitarian language, at least *ex professo et in extensor*, in his thinking on the missions." Coffele, "De Lubac and the Theological Foundation of the Missions," *Communio* 23 (1996): 773.

tasks, it has ceased being Church."[119] If she relinquishes her missionary existence, the church becomes mere contingency. She submits to that natural desire of all institutions to become content with the status quo, locating her identity in the givens of local language, rituals, customs, stories, history, and even in her ethnicity.

Noting this critical intent, however, establishes a point of intersection for the otherwise independent conceptions of the missionary nature of the church and the Trinitarian grounding of mission. Both developments distance missionary activity from every justification based in historical accident, including particular expressions of the gospel. Solutions tend either to posit mission only in terms of the church's institutions, or to posit church only in terms of the missionary dynamic. The critical function of Trinitarian doctrine separates God's missionary activity from the mundane act of cross-cultural mission. The church participates in God's mission, and, as Rosin suggests, participation constitutes a deliberate distinction over against "identification."[120] This safeguarded the practical act, that is, the justification for missions lay in an act of God, not in historical accident.

Yet the missionary church cannot think of her own mission as being *the* mission. Thus, according to Aagaard, "the church can never be Lord over her own mission and place the authorization for mission in question. To do so would be to place her own existence in question."[121] Mission ceases to be something properly identified with the act of the church, even while mission is viewed as the church's essential act. Mission is something the Christian community must receive in order to be, and any attempt to seize control of this act threatens her being. Since the original import of the now axiomatic "missionary nature of the church" resides in its critical capacity, any attempt to resolve its underlying disjunctions results in this impossible logic.

In terms of missionary practice, this irresolvable predicate tension prompted the return to old patterns of thought. The disjunction of God's mission from the church's mission necessitated a concept of the *missio ecclesiae* to counterbalance the *missio Dei*.[122] As Matthey suggests, "There

---

119. Kirk, *What Is Mission?* p. 30.

120. Rosin, '*Missio Dei*,' p. 30.

121. Aagaard, "Missio Dei in katholischer Sicht," p. 423.

122. This tension emerges immediately post-Willingen, with Hartenstein's observation that "the '*Missio ecclesiae*' comes from the '*Missio Dei*' alone." Hartenstein, "Theologische Besinnung," p. 62.

is an almost unbridgeable tension between the concepts of *missio Dei* and *missio ecclesiae*."[123] Because God's mission exists at a distance from the church's mission, and because the church passively receives the justification for her missionary act via God's act, the church can only put herself in a position of missionary movement in the expectation of God's faithfulness within human confusion. This logic effectively reinforced the traditional functional conception of missions. Aagaard observes that in the attempt "to reinterpret mission as the mission of the church," the missionary task "was still defined from those things labeled as mission."[124] *Missio Dei* functions as a theological preamble, supplying all the necessary caveats and thereby validating traditional accounts of the missionary task.

Bosch, reflecting the current state of the debate, regards the tension between participatory and mediatory approaches as "fundamentally irreconcilable."[125] The language of reconciliation here suggests an adversarial relationship. Where Hoekendijk, according to Anderson, held that "the church is simply the mission,"[126] Kirk now describes the statement that "the church is mission" as "an overstatement of an important emphasis." Mission may well describe the church's activities in the world, but it cannot encompass every activity of the church, or the whole of God's acting in the world.[127] The axiomatic "the church is missionary by her very nature" collapses back into the church as a worshiping community with a missionary function. The contrast remains that of church versus mission, the church's internal liturgical and sacramental function versus her external evangelistic function.

123. Matthey, "Missiology in the World Council of Churches: Update," p. 430.

124. Aagaard, "Church, What Is Your Mission? — Today," p. 1.

125. Bosch, *Transforming Mission,* p. 381.

126. See Andersen, *Towards a Theology of Mission,* p. 54.

127. J. Andrew Kirk, "Missio Dei; Missio Ecclesiae," in *Contemporary Issues in Mission,* ed. J. Andrew Kirk (Birmingham, UK: Selly Oak Colleges, 1994), p. 2. Evangelicals would later return to a functional definition of mission, as this theological approach tended to negate the actual task of cross-cultural missions. Shepherd, writing in 1968, denies that mission is "a kind of involuntary reflex that comes from being a partaker of life in the Spirit as a member of the body of Christ." Christians who are not missionaries have not ceased to be Christian, but have simply "failed to fulfill the function for which the new nature in Christ has been given them." He concludes: ". . . not that the church *is* mission but that the church *has* a mission." Shepherd, "The Missionary Objective: Total World Evangelization," p. 119. While Shepherd affirms that God "is the source of the sending activity and is continuously involved in it," he continues that "not all the work of God, nor of his church, nor of the Christian, is mission" (pp. 110, 109).

This kind of contrast, however, prioritizes the internal function: it assumes that, while "worship" characterizes Christian existence for eternity, the missionary act ceases with the *eschaton*. Moltmann, for example, maintains that while the three marks of one, holy, and catholic will "continue in eternity, and are also the characteristics of the church when it is glorified in the kingdom, the apostolic mission will come to an end when it is fulfilled." Apostolicity is "not an eschatological term, but a term related to the *eschaton*, because it is not a characteristic of the *eschaton* itself."[128] The missionary act ceases with Christ's return; sin, and thus the need for conversion, will not be a part of postconsummation human existence. The act of mission cannot be the being of the church, because that act is temporal and the being of the church is eternal. This has driven contemporary ecclesiologies into a preoccupation with church practices, and especially with communion. While such approaches affirm the category of "witness," this is defined without singular reference to the external missionary act as the intentional form of this practice. This dominant theological supposition is grounded in a phenomenological — that is, nontheological — account of missionary activity. Mission *is* that activity of sending missionaries from the Christian West to the non-Christian world.

Theology, in other words, has abrogated its proper duty when it comes to the question of mission. No doubt this evangelistic mission will end with the *eschaton*, but, if mission is an attribute of God, then it bespeaks something of God's nature and of reconciled human existence with God.

128. Moltmann, *The Church in the Power*, p. 357. Such sentiments, of course, are not limited to systematicians. For Wilbert Shenk, "the *missio Dei* will be consummated in the *eschaton;* but in the interim the *eschaton* infuses the messianic community with hope and power as it continues its witness amid opposition and suffering." Wilbert R. Shenk, "The Mission Dynamic," in *Mission in Bold Humility: David Bosch's Work Considered*, ed. W. A. Saayman and J. J. Kritzinger (Maryknoll, NY: Orbis, 1996), p. 93. O'Grady holds an alternative view: mission is an eschatological ideal, fully present only in Christ, but toward which the church moves. "Apostolicity is not an 'essential' feature of the present-day Church in the sense that it is a perfect gift given to the Church, to be preserved and 'stored up' for the *parousia*. The Church's apostolicity is a perfect reality only in the risen Christ and in the *eschaton*. In this time between, on its way from the *Christus solus* to the *Christus totus*, the Church must continually strive to realize ever more perfectly its apostolicity or mission, and so build itself up to the measure of the stature of the fullness of Christ (Eph. 4:12-13, 15-16)." Colm O'Grady, *The Church in Catholic Theology: Dialogue with Karl Barth* (Washington, DC: Corpus, 1969), p. 311.

As Holmes suggests, one consequence of maintaining that "God is missionary *in se*" is that "the divine mission cannot ever come to an end. There must, therefore, be an eschatological continuation of God's mission. For all eternity, the Father will continue to send his Son and Spirit to bring peace and joy to creation."[129] This suggests that the unequal weighting of worship and mission at the heart of the problem may be theologically improper and, at the very least, deserving of greater attention. *Missio Dei*'s insufficient Trinitarianism has not encouraged constructive thinking in this direction. Its critical deployment of Trinitarian doctrine establishes the above range of disjunctions, but the positive potential of the doctrine for properly coordinating elements like church and mission remains untapped.

The Problem of *Missio Dei*

Missio Dei is a Rorschach test. It encourages projection, revealing our own predilections rather than informing and directing our responses. Though fifty years have passed since its inception, Scherer laments that "we are in the midst of a transition" and "have not yet fully grasped the meaning of a move toward the kingdom orientation, which closely correlates with the trinitarian *Missio Dei* viewpoint."[130] This is correct and consequent on the fundamental confusion undergirding the concept. *Missio Dei*, with its critical necessity, flawed Trinitarian basis, complex range, and lack of cohesion, conspires to create a concept that mires any constructive potential in a bog of elasticity.

Though it coordinates three constitutive elements, such coordination remains at a superficial level. The doctrine of the Trinity plays only a negative role, distancing mission from improper alignments with accidental human authorities. This afforded a needed corrective to the phenomenological approach to mission so compromised by the colonialist endeavor, and established a theological means for distancing a local church from her host culture, that is, identifying her as a missionary community. The critical emphasis of *missio Dei* theology is attributed to a dialectical disjunction of the divine and the human and regarded as something to be

129. Holmes, "Trinitarian Missiology: Towards a Theology of God as Missionary," p. 89.
130. Scherer, "Church, Kingdom and *Missio Dei*," p. 82.

overcome for any positive account of the missionary act. An emphasis on creation accomplishes this by reinstating many of the improper liaisons eschewed by Trinity doctrine — while retaining a Trinitarian façade. This permits the projection of ideal accounts of human community or political movements onto the doctrine of the Trinity, or it reinforces mediatorial accounts of the church's being as the necessary opposite to this political position. Paradoxically, while the doctrine of the Trinity is counted as the Copernican heart of *missio Dei* theology, in actuality it holds no constructive place in that theology.

The two other elements of *missio Dei* theology — the orientation to the kingdom of God and the missionary nature of the church — developed independently from the doctrine of the Trinity. The same critical challenges drove the development, and this contingency allows for their coordination under the *missio Dei* rubric. However, this move submerges the actual location of the problem. It presumes an intact doctrine of the Trinity and attributes any resulting issues to eschatological or ecclesiological trajectories associated with the orthodox/liberal divide. This presumption is the key error. Despite its Trinitarian language, *missio Dei* never escapes an anthropological grounding for missions. This is the dominant cause of its contemporary problems.

CHAPTER THREE

German Missions and Dialectical Theology, 1928-1933

Introduction

Popular accounts of *missio Dei* trace its origins to a 1932 lecture delivered by Karl Barth that was entitled "Die Theologie und die Mission in der Gegenwart" (theology and mission in the present situation).[1] The grounding for mission established here, some have argued, informs the developments at the IMC conference held at Willingen in 1952. By implication, the evident problems of *missio Dei* can be attributed to these "Barthian" roots. I will challenge this dominant historical view. While dialectically informed motifs emerge, no direct path connects Barth's lecture with the Trinitarian grounding for mission established at Willingen. His own engagement with the theme of mission during the early 1930s is another instance of his battle against the hyphen connecting Christianity and *Volkstum*.[2] German mission theorists, drawing on a "Lutheran" con-

---

1. Karl Barth, "Die Theologie und die Mission in der Gegenwart," *Zwischen den Zeiten* 10, no. 3 (1932): 189-215.

2. I leave the concept *Volk* untranslated because it is without a satisfactory English equivalent. However, there is an equally substantive reason for doing so. While missionary theories centered on the concept of *Volk* seek indigenous forms of the gospel, this Germanic concept determines what counts as indigenous. It is a concept drawn from the "German" experience, and for which the German expression *Volk* is the greatest illustration. *Volk*, as defined by Gensichen, is "the sum total of social and environmental relationships, constituted both by ties of blood and by the sharing of common ground, by *Blut* [blood] and *Boden* [soil]." Hans-Werner Gensichen, "German Protestant Missions," in *Missionary*

78

ception of the orders of creation, presupposed a necessary link between cultural forms and the reception of the gospel.

This natural grounding for mission established the mode of human agency necessary to missionary proclamation. Through the repristination of primal ties, through the proper application of the law, and by the humanizing institutions of schools and hospitals, missionaries stimulated prior conditions essential for the reception of the Word. By destroying this natural link, Barth's critics contend, he not only stymies the missionary act but denies the seminal processes of missionary translation: that is, Barth's criticisms of natural theology result in the "paralysis of mission." With the removal of this "Lutheran" grounding, Barth consigned missionary activity to the only alternative missionary strategy, the imperialist Anglo-American method and its equation of mission with the imposition of Western civilization.

In this chapter I address the German mission theorists' appropriation of dialectical theology between 1928 and 1933. This is not an arbitrary selection: a definite corpus of mission literature examines dialectical theology during this period. The 1928 IMC Jerusalem conference prompted German missiologists to use the critical standard of dialectical theology against an Anglo-American approach located in prewar liberalism. Hitler's ascendance to power in 1933 cut this budding dialogue short. This milieu, occupied with questions of *Volkstum,* precluded any reception — positive or negative — of Barth's 1932 essay. German mission administrators, under critical pressure from nationalist political forces, proved unable to relinquish this emphasis for fear of relinquishing the activity of mission. *Volkstum* established some affinity between missions and the political climate. Remove this common ground, and

Ideologies in the Imperialist Era, 1880-1920, ed. Torben Christensen and William R. Hutchison (Århus, Denmark: Aros, 1982), p. 187. Because the term developed in reaction to French superiority during the Napoleonic era, and thus prior to any unified German state, the concept *Volk* was "infinitely vaguer and at the same time much more powerful than 'citizenship.'" Identity is, as such, not located in political institutions, but in blood and a shared history. David J. Bosch, *Transforming Mission: Paradigm Shifts in Theology of Mission* (Maryknoll, NY: Orbis, 1991), p. 299. For more on the relationship between *Volk* and its application in mission, see Richard V. Pierard, "*Völkisch* Thought and Christian Missions in Early Twentieth Century Germany," in *Essays in Religious Studies for Andrew Walls,* ed. James Thrower (Aberdeen, Scotland: Department of Religious Studies, University of Aberdeen, 1986), pp. 138-40.

the political authorities might have suppressed the already struggling missionary endeavor.[3]

Despite the received history, the divorce between Barth's 1932 work and Willingen is so evident that the following discussion appears almost incidental to any consideration of *missio Dei* theology. However, this history is not benign; it bears two substantive theological consequences. First, Barth's supposed influence, especially his Trinitarian disjunction of the divine from the human, is the single deleterious cause to which *missio Dei* theology's contemporary problems are attributed. This is simply not the case. Second, though no Trinitarian connection emerges, this period nevertheless contributes substantively to *missio Dei* theology. The kind of connection with creation urged by German missions becomes confirmed by *missio Dei* theology.

Imperialism and Christianization

Wolfgang Günther is correct that "Barth's influence on German mission was hardly noticeable before the Jerusalem conference."[4] Good reasons exist for this absence. Julius Richter, Gustav Warneck's successor, could claim, in the standard reference work *Die Religion in Geschichte und*

---

3. German missions during this period had to fight for their continued existence. On the one hand, they were in a state of "crisis" due to practical factors, such as the lack of financing and Versailles's annexing of colonial territories, which were only deepened under National Socialist control. On the other hand, the kind of *völkisch* thinking that valorized "Germanness" held that "each race had its own religion based on its own primal revelation that was impossible to replace." Karla Poewe, "The Spell of National Socialism: The Berlin Mission's Opposition to, and Compromise with, the *Völkisch* Movement and National Socialism: Knak, Braun, Weichert," in *Mission und Gewalt*, ed. Ulrich van der Heyden, Jürgen Becher, and Holger Stoecker (Stuttgart: Franz Steiner Verlag, 2000), p. 267 n. 5. Christianity was considered unsuitable to the "racial history and mental capacities" of indigenous peoples. Karl Hartenstein, "The Outlook for German Missions," *World Dominion* 13 (1953): 159. Conversion became impossible and mission unnecessary. This general climate forced mission administrators into some compromises, leading, as Poewe suggests, to the exploitation of "cultural organismic thinking in order to survive." Karla Poewe, "Liberalism, German Missionaries, and National Socialism," in *Mission und Macht im Wandel politischer Orientierungen*, ed. Ulrich van der Heyden and Holger Stoecker (Stuttgart: Franz Steiner Verlag, 2005), p. 634.

4. Wolfgang Günther, *Von Edinburgh nach Mexico City: die ekklesiologischen Bemühungen der Weltmissionskonferenzen, 1910-1963* (Stuttgart: Evangelischer Missionsverlag, 1970), p. 45.

Gegenwart as late as 1930, that "the spread of mission occurs everywhere today parallel with the expansion of the white race, partly in the form of colonial subjugation, partly by economic exploitation and the spread of western culture. Mission is indissolubly connected with both."[5] Dialectical theology opposed such entanglements as a clear consequence of the decadence characteristic of cultural Protestantism. Yet it is precisely this negating stance that attracts German missions to dialectical theology as an ally in its struggle against the supposed "accommodationism" of Anglo-American missions.

Stephen Neill describes the 1928 IMC Jerusalem conference as "the nadir of the modern missionary movement."[6] Whether or not this is the case is open to debate. Nevertheless, it would be affirmed by the German delegates to Jerusalem, who perceived in the preparatory work a persistent theological liberalism, heavy dependence on the social gospel, an atmosphere of religious relativism, a general disregard for evangelistic missions, and a syncretistic link between Western civilization and the kingdom of God. Karl Heim, summarizing this animus, notes the concern that they, "as representatives of the old biblical gospel, would face a crushing majority of others for whom the kingdom of God means nothing more than the League of Nations, democracy, and the overcoming of militarism and capitalism."[7] They opposed Jerusalem's "compromise" as a legacy of prewar liberalism and Anglo-American ignorance of the decisive theological debates then raging on the European continent. This justified fear, however, was simply an eruptive manifestation of a preexisting fissure.

American mission methodology was, to German thinking, imperialist in nature. This dissatisfaction is evident as early as 1888, and further antagonized by the popular appropriation of the phrase "the evangelization of the world in this generation."[8] German missions detected here a syncretistic

---

5. Julius Richter, "Mission: Evangelische Mission," in *Die Religion in Geschichte und Gegenwart: Handwörterbuch im gemeinverständlicher Darstellung,* ed. Hermann Gunkel and Leopold Zscharnack (Tübingen: J. C. B. Mohr, 1930), p. 43.

6. Neill continues that "this was the moment at which liberal theology exercised its most fatal influence on missionary thinking, the lowest valley out of which the missionary movement has ever since been trying to make its way." Stephen Neill, *The Unfinished Task* (London: Edinburgh House, 1957), p. 151.

7. Karl Heim, "Die Tagung des erweiterten internationalen Missionsrats in Jerusalem," *Evangelisches Missions-Magazin* 72 (1928): 161-62.

8. See, e.g., Gustav Warneck, "The Mutual Relations of Evangelical Missionary Soci-

mixture of the Christian faith with American culture. "Americanism," as this method became known, referred to the human capacity to bring about the kingdom of God, according to William Hutchison, via "a certain busy-bodied optimism" and "with little more than consultative assistance from the Deity." Hutchison continues that "activism connoted, practically, a quantitative habit of mind, excessive individualism, and some form of imperialism." Here the "activist stood as the religious representative of what the American culture as a whole was commonly perceived to be."[9] A particular form of the gospel, one located in American culture, had become normative for mission methodology.

Heinrich Frick, writing in 1922, maintained that, via their dominance within the world mission conferences, the Americans had secularized mission, reducing it to mere propaganda.[10] Frick even proposed a link between the 1910 World Missionary Conference held in Edinburgh and the treaty conference held at Versailles.[11] "In their innermost meaning, these apparently antagonistic phenomena belong together, because in retrospect one sees that they are products of the same spirit: namely, of the Americanism in modern evangelical missions."[12] The watchword, Hutchison concludes,

---

eties to One Another," in *Report of the Centenary Conference on the Protestant Missions of the World, London, 1888*, ed. James Johnston (London: James Nisbet, 1888), pp. 431-37; see also Gustav Warneck, "Die moderne Weltevangelismus-theorie," *Allgemeine Missions-Zeitschrift* 24 (1897): 305-25.

9. William R. Hutchison, "American Missionary Ideologies: 'Activism' as Theory, Practice and Stereotype," in *Continuity and Discontinuity in Church History*, ed. F. Forrester Church and Timothy George (Leiden: Brill, 1979), p. 351. Hutchison continues that "an overwhelming sense of the rightness, glory and providentiality of their own Christian civilization made it nearly impossible for these American theorists to stifle the cultural and national elements in their message. As theory, and even as a kind of 'proclamation,' American activism was surely a reality." Hutchison, "American Missionary Ideologies," p. 355.

10. See Heinrich Frick, *Die evangelische Mission: Ursprung, Geschichte, Ziel* (Bonn: K. Schroeder, 1922), pp. 352-429. Quoted by Hutchison, "American Missionary Ideologies," p. 352.

11. See William R. Hutchison, *Errand to the World: American Protestant Thought and Foreign Missions* (Chicago: University of Chicago Press, 1987), p. 136.

12. Frick, *Die evangelische Mission*, p. 392. Quoted by Hutchison, *Errand to the World*, p. 136. Hartenstein makes a similar point, declaring that the First World War endangered the existence of German missions and that "the notorious §438" of the treaty of Versailles documented "the collapse of the so-called 'Edinburgh pattern' of mission." See Karl Hartenstein, "Botschafter an Christi Statt," in *Botschafter an Christi Statt: von Wesen und Werk deutscher Missionsarbeit*, ed. Martin Schlunk (Gütersloh, Germany: Bertelsmann, 1932), p. 1.

really meant "the evangelization of the world by and for Anglo-American culture."[13] Whether or not this was true, the decisive point is that German missiologists held this position to be true, stimulating, in turn, a blinkered valorization of their own mission method.[14]

Mainline German missions advocated the method of Christianization.[15] According to Warneck, "the greatest of all mission problems" was "the implantation of Christianity into the foreign soil of heathen nations in such a way that it takes root like a native plant and grows to be a native tree." An independent Christianity will only grow where the faith has become naturalized. This process requires the Christianization of the local language, customs, and social ties. If the "national and popular customs" are destroyed, "Christianity will never become a national and social power."[16] Two dangers are to be avoided: first, a narrow pietism, and second, "a confounding of Christianisation with Europeanisation or Americanisation."[17] This second danger perpetuates Christianity's foreignness, and it introduces the corrosive acids of Western civilization, the individualism of which was antithetical to the communal nature of the body of Christ. In other words, this approach contained an implicit evaluation of Germany's peculiar contribution to missions. Warneck maintains that "it is a special charisma of the Germans to respect foreign nationali-

13. Hutchison, *Errand to the World*, p. 136.

14. This fear persisted even during the Nazi period. Ustorf, quoting minutes taken in 1943, notes how "it was one of the main worries of the Missionsrat that this ecumenical support might lead to a 'western' takeover of German mission work, or at least, to the 'americanisation' of it by introducing 'gospel-unfriendly' and 'syncretistic' tendencies, like forms of higher education and democracy." Werner Ustorf, "The Documents that Reappeared: The Minute-Books of Council and Federation of German Protestant Missions 1924-1949," in *Mission Matters*, ed. Lynne Price, Juan Sepúlveda, and Graeme Smith (Frankfurt am Main: Peter Lang, 1997), p. 75.

15. German missions, of course, were not themselves immune to the temptation of imperialism. Bosch provides an example with reference to the "Allgemeiner Evangelisch-Protestantischer Missionsverein," the stated purpose of which was to "spread Western Christian religion, morals and culture among non-Christian peoples, always linking these with already existing 'elements of truth' in the religions of those peoples." David J. Bosch, "Systematic Theology and Mission: The Voice of an Early Pioneer," *Theologia Evangelica* 5, no. 3 (1972): 175.

16. Gustav Warneck, "Thoughts on the Missionary Century," *Missionary Review of the World* 23, no. 6 (1900): 415-16.

17. Gustav Warneck, *Outline of a History of Protestant Missions from the Reformation to the Present Time*, ed. George Robson, 3rd ed. (New York: Fleming Revell, 1906), p. 404.

ties and thus to enter selflessly, without prejudice and with consideration, into the peculiar qualities of other peoples."[18] This, he continues, is "especially a German charisma, while the English and American nature accommodates itself with difficulty."[19] Such charisma required that missionaries concentrate also on their own cultural particularities. "If the missionary is no longer capable of appreciating his own *Volkstum*, he cannot be expected to appreciate the foreign *Volkstum* which he is supposed to cultivate in his converts."[20] The preoccupation with *Volk* was the determining characteristic of German mission methodology, and it stood juxtaposed to the Anglo-American approach. German missions could not relinquish its *völkisch* focus without also relinquishing its identity, which was impossible in the aftermath of World War I and the Treaty of Versailles, as well as during the rise of National Socialism. This unresolved tension fed into the Jerusalem conference, and after the conference it determined how German missions wielded the sword of dialectical theology.

Though they resisted Jerusalem's syncretistic trajectory, the very dominance of a horizontalized approach to missions had a significant effect on German mission thinking. According to Hoekendijk, "the disillusionment and barely veiled defeatism of Jerusalem prompted a new and anxious questioning concerning the possibility and truth of mission."[21] Missions were fighting for their own survival. Hartenstein, with reference to Jerusalem and *Re-Thinking Missions*, observes that "by far the greatest Protestant mission movement, which proceeds from America, stands in dire danger of losing its commission in favor of a secular reform movement of an ethical nature."[22] German missions turned to dialectical theology in its search for possible resources.

18. Quoted by Hans-Werner Gensichen, "Evangelisieren und Zivilisieren: Motive deutscher protestantischer Mission in der imperialistischen Epoche," *Zeitschrift für Missionswissenschaft und Religionswissenschaft* 67, no. 4 (1983): 188. This perception was long entrenched within the German mission's self-characterization. Gensichen says of Zinzendorf that he "seems to have been the first to describe the Germans as 'a people which adapts itself to all nations, loves them all and tends to accommodate itself to their ways, disregarding or even neglecting for their sake its own way. That is why it is so well suited for the apostolate'" (p. 188).

19. Warneck, *A History of Protestant Missions*, p. 404.

20. Warneck, quoted by Gensichen, "Evangelisieren und Zivilisieren," p. 188.

21. J. C. Hoekendijk, *Kirche und Volk in der deutschen Missionswissenschaft* (Munich: Chr. Kaiser Verlag, 1967), p. 123.

22. Karl Hartenstein, *Die Mission als theologisches Problem: Beiträge zum grundsätzlichen Verständnis der Mission* (Berlin: Furche Verlag, 1932), pp. 16-17.

Barth's own criticism of Jerusalem took two forms. Most well known is his rejection of "all sorts of natural theologies for the purpose of linking the Christian Gospel to the heathen situation."[23] His second criticism concerned the ease with which the Christian faith could be "adapted" to reinforce "the divinity of 'race, people, nation.'" Contra Jerusalem's devotion to "the 'values' of the non-Christian religions," the Christian response, Barth argues, must be mission. Humanity did not require propaganda, "which deals with human 'needs' and adapts itself to them, but mission which tells man to his face, that he misunderstands his own deep 'needs.'"[24] While questions of natural theology and propaganda were essentially related in Barth's thinking, German missions differentiated them. On the one hand, they gratefully received dialectical theology's criticisms of propaganda; the Anglo-American syncretism, missions which had adapted Christianity and divinized the nation, provided the prime target.[25] On the other hand, however, they remained deaf to any suggestion that a focus on *Volk* constituted a Germanic domestication of the Christian gospel.

The Missionary Reception of Dialectical Theology

Mission theorists approached dialectical theology with a great deal of suspicion. Dialectical theology showed no interest in the topic of missions. This silence and its pronounced rejection of all forms of cultural accommodationism stimulated the perception that it opposed all missionary activity.[26] For Devaranne, "one encounters a cold reception toward mission on the part of the crisis theologians, who bring criticism, sitting in judgment over mission in such a way that it paralyzes and totally sets aside mission's motives, methods, and goals."[27] Karl Jäger extends the point. Dialec-

---

23. Barth, *CD* II/1, 97; *KD* II/1, 107.

24. Karl Barth, "Questions which 'Christianity' Must Face," *The Student World* 25, no. 1 (1932): 96-98.

25. Adolf Keller, *Karl Barth and Christian Unity: The Influence of the Barthian Movement upon the Churches of the World,* trans. Werner Petersmann and Manfred Manrodt (New York: Macmillan Company, 1933), p. 247.

26. Ludwig Wiedenmann, *Mission und Eschatologie: Eine Analyse der neueren deutschen evangelischen Missionstheologie* (Paderborn, Germany: Verlag Bonifacius-Druckerei, 1965), p. 56.

27. T. Devaranne, "Theologie der Krisis und Mission: Theorie und Praxis," *Zeitschrift für Missionskunde und Religionswissenschaft* 46, no. 1 (1931): 25.

tical theology "exercises the sharpest possible critique of mission, tantamount to questioning its very right to exist."[28] Though such a negative perception remained dominant, it was tempered by a general acknowledgment that missions required some reorientation. Dialectical theology functioned, in this regard, as "the signal buoys at the edges of the narrow channel, which protect us from straying."[29]

It behooved missions, for W. Brachmann, to create bridges between itself and dialectical theology "to prevent it from falling into the continual temptation of confusing its ethical activism with the gospel."[30] Dialectical theology rejected every form of accommodationism that the Germans perceived as basic to the Anglo-American mission method. As Vernier notes, "mission is neither the spreading of the social or cultural advantages of the accidental forms of Christianity, nor the preaching of a social gospel."[31] Devaranne, too, declares that with dialectical theology "the final judgment breaks in over the age of national, colonial and cultural motivations for mission, so that one can never accuse [mission] of having made an invasion out of a crusade."[32]

Dialectical theology, however, proved difficult to control. Its critical judgments extended beyond the confines carefully demarcated by German missions, questioning missionary practices as well as motives. According to Adolf Keller, it entered the debate "like a dissolving ferment." On the one hand, this provided "a welcome reinforcement to European missions in their critical discussion with American missions." On the other hand, precisely in this questioning of accommodationism, dialectical theology questioned the dominant method of medical and pedagogical missions. This was tantamount to denying "occidental Christianity the moral and religious right to carry on missions."[33] Dialectical theology "paralyzes the will to do mission," or so ran the popular perception.[34]

28. Karl Jäger, "Die Neubesinnung der evangelischen Mission auf ihre Motive, Methoden und Ziele," *Evangelische Missions-Magazin* 77 (1933): 204.

29. G. Simon, "Die gegenwärtige theologische Kritik an der Mission," *Jahrbuch der Theologischen Schule Bethel* 3 (1932): 209.

30. W. Brachmann, "Theologie der Krisis und Mission," *Zeitschrift für Missionskunde und Religionswissenschaft* 45, no. 10 (1930): 309.

31. J. Vernier, "La théologie de Barth et les Missions," *Le Monde non chrétien* 1 (1931): 81.

32. Devaranne, "Theologie der Krisis," p. 24.

33. Adolf Keller, *Karl Barth and Christian Unity*, pp. 240-42.

34. According to Schwarz, Visser 't Hooft, himself later popularly identified as a student

Of course, the topic of "religion" dominated mission's reception of dialectical theology. Continental thinking generally acknowledged, illustrated by its strong reaction to Jerusalem, that the Christian religion did not constitute the zenith of a universal religious value system. Christianity was unique among religions, and its message was superior.[35] Dialectical theology's failure in this regard was a consequence of academic theology's formal nature and its distance from the actual missionary context. With this theology, in Adolf Köberle's estimation, "one *sits* in one's house elated over the exclusive possession of one's flawless teachings and, in the process, forgets to *go* into the world."[36] Barth's "higher rationalism" was too categorical, simplistic, formal, removed from the mission field, and counter to the reality of mission experience.[37] For all its revolutionary characteristics, it clung to a "provincial, nationalistic and confessional Christianity."[38] Siegfried Knak suggests, by comparison, that no one who sees the beauty of the cultural life of the non-Christian world would doubt that God is at work there.[39] In other words, the Western nature of dialectical theology manifested itself in its denial of synergism. Received wisdom assumed, to quote Martin Richter, that "the goal of religion is not the demarcation, but the blending of humans with the divine."[40] Though the forms required breaking and reformulation, the blending occasioned by personal piety, cultural aesthetic, and natural social relationships provided essential base material through which the missionary could facilitate indigenous reception of the Christian gospel. According to Vernier, it was typical to approach world religions "with the aim of knowing if they, by themselves, contained certain elements of truth that the missionary

---

of Barth, wrote to Hartenstein expressing his fear that Barth's theology denied the will to do mission. Gerold Schwarz, *Mission, Gemeinde und Ökumene in der Theologie Karl Hartensteins* (Stuttgart: Calwer Verlag, 1980), p. 30 n. 5.

35. Heinrich Frick, "Is a Conviction of the Superiority of His Message Essential to the Missionary?" *International Review of Mission* 15, no. 4 (1926): 625-46.

36. Adolf Köberle, "Die Neubesinnung auf den Missionsgedanken in der Theologie der Gegenwart," *Neue Allgemeine Missions-Zeitschrift* 7, nos. 11-12 (1930): 323.

37. Brachmann, "Theologie der Krisis und Mission," p. 299.

38. Keller, *Karl Barth and Christian Unity*, p. 246.

39. Siegfried Knak, "Missionsmotive und Missionsmethode unter der Fragestellung der dialektischen Theologie," in *Botschafter an Christi Statt: von Wesen und Werk deutscher Missionsarbeit*, ed. Martin Schlunk (Gütersloh: Bertelsmann, 1932), p. 70.

40. Martin Richter, "Dialektische Theologie und Mission," *Allgemeine Missions-Zeitschrift* 5 (1928): 233.

would be grateful to simply develop."[41] Dialectical theology "paralyzes" mission precisely because it interrupts this kind of activity. Because God remains subject in his self-revelation, Christian mission cannot be an activity that massages religious, cultural, social, political, or legislative contexts so as to manufacture a natural path from common life to religious commitment.

These complaints, familiar even today, did not occur in abstraction. They included a basic assumption concerning the kind of influence culture exerts over the entrance of the gospel, and thus a specific conception of what constitutes a theology capable of adapting beyond Western origins. Walter Marx, for instance, observes: "I am afraid that a missionary with a consistently dialectical attitude of mind would hardly be understood on African soil." Dialectical theology, as a product of Europe's cultural, historical, and political developments, cannot be transferred to less evolved cultures. In reference to the Bantu, Marx says that "they stand at the beginning of a development beyond which we in Europe have already moved. The proclamation which they require at their present stage of development must bear another character from that which the Word of God speaks into the European context." He suggests that, like Israel, the Bantu "first require an education by the law before they can grasp the gospel." Where dialectic theology is "pure, purest gospel," Marx experienced "daily with pain that our black Christians want to have the 'law' — and, indeed, need it."[42]

The implied racism there and the contemporary repudiation of such a position threatens to disguise the theological bridge Marx forms between the notion of cultural development and the law. The law disciplines the basic orders of creation, including religious occupation, cultivating them to a level of maturity suitable for the reception of the gospel. While Marx's formulation may lack sophistication, it was typical within Lutheran mission thinking. Beyerhaus observes of Gutmann, to whom we shall turn, that "only Luther's Church can send out missions," as only these churches properly coordinate the Word and creation.[43]

---

41. Vernier, "La théologie de Barth et les Missions," p. 88.

42. Walter Marx, "Mission und dialektische Theologie: Mission und Volkstum," *Neue Allgemeine Missions-Zeitschrift* 10, no. 7 (1933): 227-28.

43. Peter Beyerhaus and Henry Lefever, *The Responsible Church and the Foreign Mission* (Grand Rapids: Eerdmans, 1964), p. 50.

Point of Contact and Point of Connection

This point requires the introduction of a conceptual distinction between a "point of contact" and a "point of connection." Though the Barth-Brunner debate made notorious the term *Anknüpfungspunkt,* this idea of a "point of contact" was already common in both German and English mission literature.[44] The problem is that this singular term contains two conflated

44. Given *Anknüpfungspunkt*'s prominence within twentieth-century theology, it is surprising that no detailed history of the formal concept exists. Despite the constant reference to Acts 17 and Mars Hill, no discussion examines the decidedly non-first-century theological and philosophical underpinnings of the contemporary discussion. General theological examinations of the term's origins fail to refer to the primary missionary material. The debate is often framed in terms of the Barth-and-Brunner debate. Two assumptions follow: first, this discussion unfolds under the category of "theological prolegomena." While mission discussions do not use such a formal designation, for the purposes of this study, doing so establishes a clear entrance point for the doctrine of the Trinity. Second, Brunner validates his own approach using the language of "missionary" against Barth's recourse to "theology." This fateful dichotomy means that examinations of the concept suppose the priority of the dogmatic debate and consequently frame their discussion without due investigation into the concept's missionary context. See, e.g., George R. Sumner, *The First and the Last: The Claim of Jesus Christ and the Claims of Other Religious Traditions* (Grand Rapids: Eerdmans, 2004), pp. 134-39.

The best available account of the concept's origins is Siegfried Jacob, *Das Problem der Anknüpfung für das Wort Gottes in der deutschen evangelischen Missionsliteratur der Nachkriegszeit* (Gütersloh: C. Bertelsmann, 1935). This, as the title suggests, is merely an examination of the use of the concept in the mission literature of the period. While it does not assist the investigation into historical origins, it does illustrate well the extent of the debate before Brunner's contribution. According to Jacob, mission methodologies are necessarily derivative since — as illustrated by how the "Pietist," "religious history," and the "cultural propaganda" methods developed — they form after identifying the perceived "point of connection" between the human and the gospel. This "point" is both theological (e.g., the Pietists' sense of individual conversion located that point within the conscience and directed attention to this organ), and cultural (e.g., the religious history approach, favored by the mainline Germans, sought basic conceptual connections with traditional religions that might smooth the transition to a new religion).

For Warneck, Paul's approach at the Areopagus constituted a "typical model of the missionary point of connection." Jacob, *Das Problem der Anknüpfung,* p. 41. He held, first, that conversion requires argument, and the best way to argue is by using the indigenous resources as a "content rich missionary textbook" as this provides a mediating presentation of the gospel. Second, life with the indigenous audience allows for a ready identification of their basic religious need and a demonstration that only the Christian faith truly meets this need. See Gustav Warneck, *Evangelische Missionslehre: ein missionstheoretischer Versuch,* 2nd

senses. First, "point of contact" refers to the simple and necessary process of listening and responding to the questions of one's audience. Such an approach neither expects those hearing the message to assume the mission-

---

ed. (Gotha: Friedrich Andreas Perthes, 1905), 3.2: 95. In other words, the point is not that the Athenians had a true knowledge of God, but that argumentation at this level, while still confrontational, i.e., calling for conversion, is preferable to that of an imperialistic attitude. This affirmation occurs in deliberate reaction to the sharp negative polemic of the Anglo-Americans against indigenous religions.

Jongeneel argues that Schleiermacher first coined the term, and Kähler applied it to the missionary context. Jan A. B. Jongeneel, "Anknüpfungspunkt," in *Die Religion in Geschichte und Gegenwart: Handwörterbuch für Theologie und Religionswissenschaft,* ed. Hans Dieter Betz et al. (Tübingen: Mohr Siebeck, 1998), pp. 507-8. An electronic search of Schleiermacher's complete works demonstrates that he does not once use the term in a way that is consonant with its usage in missions during the mid-nineteenth and early twentieth centuries. One might argue that Schleiermacher's advocacy of "the feeling of absolute dependence" reflects a "point of connection" position *in nuce.* The closest he comes to any semblance of this formal kind of "point of connection" occurs when he notes the Hebrews' rejection of a "religious point of connection capable of development," and its coordination with their rejection of polytheism. Friedrich D. E. Schleiermacher, *Schriften,* ed. Andreas Arndt (Deutscher Klassiker Verlag, 1996), p. 969. Schleiermacher's position vis-à-vis *Anknüpfungspunkt* is, as such, wholly negative.

A more promising early use of *Anknüpfungspunkt,* one that aligns with the "Lutheran" position of the early part of the twentieth century, is identified by Barth himself. In reference to Georg Calixt of Helmstedt (1586-1656), Barth quotes W. Gass to the effect that "revelation does not need to force itself into its rightful place; there is within the entirety of the Spirit's activity a place which it must occupy, points of connection which it must grasp, indicators which strengthen the consciousness of its truth . . . both kinds of intellectual appropriation [reason and revelation] exist according to divine order beside each other." W. Gass, *Geschichte der protestantischen Dogmatik: in ihrem Zusammenhange mit Theologie überhaupt,* 4 vols. (Berlin: G. Reimer, 1854), 2:88, quoted in Barth, CD I/2, 557; KD I/2, 619. This quote — Gass writing in 1854 and Calixt in 1613 — contains all the elements essential to the German missionary stance of the early twentieth century: first, a suspicion of any overwhelming entrance into history by revelation; second, the depiction of a reserved place within creation for that revelation; third, the notion that, when it follows the path laid out for it, revelation strengthens an already given knowledge of the divine; and, fourth, this relationship between revelation and natural knowledge is part of, and thus subject to, a greater divine order, which is indicative of a split between God's act and being. Due to the diffuse history of the "point of connection" concept, and the lack of any evidence that mission theorists of the nineteenth century were aware of this debate, one cannot make too much of this fact. However, given Calixt's Lutheran credentials and his role in the "syncretistic controversy," which aimed at Lutheran unification with Rome via the Apostles' Creed, one can sense something of the rationale that develops when issues of the theological relationship between law and gospel, interreligious and cross-cultural encounter, and power intersect.

aries' own questions, nor mandates the necessity of particular imported cultural expressions of the gospel. It also assumes that, in becoming Christian, those converts have the responsibility of converting their own environment rather than assuming the missionaries' culture. The second sense, which I will call the "point of connection," includes the more problematic element of establishing or massaging cultural conduits as a necessary precondition for receiving the gospel. The "point of connection" accentuated human agency and established the form of the missionary task. To quote Kraemer, this question is twisted by

> . . . the secret conviction that a surer grasp of points of [connection] would ensure a greater and easier missionary result. This conviction has, properly understood, much truth in it; but it has, of course, the same tendency as all human instruments, to induce us to entertain a delusive trust in these points of contact as the real *agents* of missionary results in the sense of previously unbelieving people coming to believe in Christ.[45]

Knak, by way of example and in express opposition to those who suppose that mission work begins with the proclamation of Christ, says that "missionary experience has taught them that the preaching of the Cross of Christ can only be properly understood if all sorts of preliminary conditions are first created — as God Himself used centuries of preparation before He set up the Cross of Christ as a pulpit for the whole world from which the summons resounded 'Be ye reconciled to God.'"[46] It is this concept of missionary activity, this notion of creating preliminary conditions for a more or less fertile ground for the reception of the gospel, that underlay German mission strategy. With the common conflation of these two senses, if one criticized an approach predicated on an improper "point of

---

45. Hendrik Kraemer, *The Christian Message in a non-Christian World* (London: Harper and Brothers, 1938), p. 132.

46. Siegfried Knak, "The Characteristics of German Evangelical Missions in Theory and Practice," in *Evangelism*, ed. John Merle Davis and Kenneth G. Grubb, The Madras Series (New York: International Missionary Council, 1939), p. 314. Mott, as an Anglo-American example from 1905, notes that the "value of medical, educational, literary, and all other forms of missionary activity, is measured by the extent to which they prepare the way for the Gospel message, promote its acceptance, manifest its spirit and benefits, multiply points of contact with human souls and increase the number and efficiency of those who preach Christ." Quoted by Hutchison, *Errand to the World*, p. 120.

connection," one perforce criticized the mundane "point of contact" and with it the very possibility of missionary translation. Either one supported a "point of connection" or one paralyzed missionary activity. Either one supported theologically sanctioned accommodations, or one forced missionary activity into the kind of imperialist approach typified by Anglo-American missions.

Missions used the critical edge of dialectical theology to cut away the unwanted cultural baggage evident at Jerusalem. With Barth's austere rejection of "points of connection" long sanctioned by missionary experience, he failed to provide an alternative basis for the missionary act. On these questions, mission turned to Brunner as one who brought the critical edge of dialectical theology, but who also emphasized the lessons of missionary experience and the propriety of missionary method located in natural conditions. As a preliminary conclusion, Günther argues that "German mission, to the extent that it was defined by Pietism and Gustav Warneck — which with few exceptions was true of it in its entirety — evaded an encounter with dialectical theology by ignoring its own philosophical assumptions."[47] Mission's failure to expose its fundamental assumptions to critical questioning precluded the reception of dialectical theology's positive reconstruction.

Paul Schütz and the 'No' of Dialectical Theology

A single author and a single book bear the responsibility for the fear engendered by dialectical theology: Paul Schütz and his 1930 book entitled *Zwischen Nil und Kaukasus* (Between the Nile and the Caucasus).[48] As Hoekendijk suggests, "for an extended period one had dreaded 'a paralysis of the will to do mission' generated by dialectic theology. Schütz was considered exemplary of this position."[49] Schütz's importance is twofold. First, while extreme, he exemplifies dialectical theology's preoccupation with

---

47. Günther, *Von Edinburgh nach Mexico City*, p. 48.

48. Paul Schütz, *Zwischen Nil und Kaukasus: ein Reisebericht zur religionspolitischen Lage im Orient* (Munich: Chr. Kaiser Verlag, 1930); see also Paul Schütz, "Heidnisch und Christlich: Versuch einer Bestimmung der Begriffe vom Menschen her," *Orient und Occident* 2 (1929): 3-28; Paul Schütz, "Der politisch religiöse Synkretismus und seine Entstehung aus dem Geist der Renaissance," *Orient und Occident* 5 (1930): 1-19.

49. Hoekendijk, *Kirche und Volk in der deutschen Missionswissenschaft*, p. 124.

the state of *Western* theology. If Western values drove the missionary enterprise, how had cultural Protestantism misshaped missionary method? Second, though authors such as Brachmann and Schlunk have noted the distance between Schütz and Barth, Schütz represents the default dialectical position.[50] He frames the missiological reception of Barth. For instance, Keller incorrectly ascribes to Barth the position that Western Christianity "should not be permitted to do mission work at all, for it has only too evidently betrayed to the world its original message."[51] It was actually Schütz who held this position, and it prompted a vigorous reaction from the mission establishment.

Schütz was the pastor of a small parish when, for a brief period between 1926 and 1928, he served as the mission director of a small mission to the Islamic Near East.[52] In 1928 he undertook a journey to Egypt, Palestine, Syria, Iraq, Iran, and the Russian border, and his *Zwischen Nil und Kaukasus* describes this experience. The logic of his argument is as simple as it is epigrammatic.

First, mission is — and remains — a foreign enterprise. The Western missionary's foreignness is a demonic wall, and though invisible, it "always hastened in advance of us and scoffed at every attempt to climb over it" (p. 6). Many missionaries "finally settled *in front of* the wall, saying to themselves that the soil under their feet was nevertheless the soil of the Orient, performing their task there as well as they could see it, and perhaps finally believing they were, in fact, within the *'interior'* of the land, *behind* the wall" (p. 6). This belief was misguided: the demonic wall persists. Its permanence was, in part, due to the way the missions clustered around the

---

50. For some responses to Schütz, see, W. Brachmann, "Theologie der Krisis und Mission: Theorie und Praxis," *Zeitschrift für Missionskunde und Religionswissenschaft* 46, no. 1 (1931): 30; Martin Schlunk, "Die Mission im Feuer der Kritik," *Neue Allgemeine Missions-Zeitschrift* 10, no. 8 (1933): 258-59; Jäger, "Die Neubesinnung der evangelischen Mission auf ihre Motive, Methoden und Ziele," pp. 205-19; Heinrich Balz, "Berliner Missionstheologie und Karl Barth: Aneignung und Widerspruch," in *450 Jahre Evangelische Theologie in Berlin*, ed. Gerhard Besier and Christof Gestrich (Göttingen: Vandenhoeck und Ruprecht, 1989), p. 421; Karl Hartenstein, "Krisis der Mission?" *Die Furche* 17 (1931): 201-7.

51. Keller, *Karl Barth and Christian Unity*, p. 242.

52. For some brief biographies of Schütz, see, Hans-Werner Gensichen, "Schütz, Paul," in *Biographical Dictionary of Christian Missions*, ed. Gerald H. Anderson (Grand Rapids: Eerdmans, 1998), p. 605; Hans-Werner Gensichen, "Zur Orient- und Missionserfahrung von Paul Schütz," *Zeitschrift für Missionswissenschaft und Religionswissenschaft* 77, no. 2 (1993): 152-59.

bases of Western influence. This expressed the Western missionaries' unease as they experience their own foreignness. It was also an issue of control. As the home country paid missionary salaries, so a "foreign" influence determined the action of the missionary. A second and more significant reason concerns the local maintenance of the wall through the constant refrain of "baksheesh."[53] The expectation of financial support perpetuates the distance. If the missionary were to become a local, then he or she would only have access to local resources. It behooved the indigenous population to perpetuate Christianity's foreignness because it maintained these economic lines.

Second, the missionary recognizes this foreignness and attempts to bridge it via humanitarian means. The demonic wall precludes direct contact, and so mission entered through the side entrance as invited to do so by the cry of "baksheesh." Mission took the form of cultural diffusion through the operation of these medical and educational missions, and was assisted to do so by the structures of politics and civilization. Protestant missions even made a virtue of this failure, propagating it as the right and necessary missionary method. The problem is that, with these "gifts," Western missions simply reinforced the propagation of Western civilization throughout the Middle East (pp. 192-93).

Third, with diffusion now the default missionary method, mission had become wholly secularized. Schütz asks: "Is not our mission universalism a very worldly, enlightened, secular affair?"(p. 59). Activism is the essence of enlightenment, manifesting itself as technology, construction, theory, obedience to oneself, to an ideal, to civil security. "We are 'driven' to do mission. Drivenness is at work here. A natural force, religious in form, proliferates here as expansion within the similar drivenness of our time" (p. 54).[54] The missionary fascination with action is nothing more

53. Gensichen notes how one mission doctor objected to Schütz's characterization, not on condition that it was false, but because it was insulting. Gensichen, "Zur Orient- und Missionserfahrung von Paul Schütz," p. 156.

54. Reinhold Niebuhr, writing in 1927, similarly interrupts the link between missions and nature, thus reconceiving even the West in missionary terms. "Our business is no longer merely to Christianize the nominally non-Christian world but to Christianize the world which is nominally Christian. Western civilization, you see, has become a missionary territory, and it is our business to expatriate ourselves not only from America but from the world and to learn again what those simple words mean, 'Be ye not conformed to this world, but be ye rather transformed by the renewing of your mind.' . . . We have prided ourselves upon

than an infatuation with nature. "Action is nature. It is drivenness" (p. 245). In language reminiscent of Nietzsche, Schütz says, "Action is not the overcoming of nature, but only super-nature" (p. 246). This oblation to an Enlightenment zeitgeist demonstrates the essentially unconverted nature of the missionary, and the mode of missions reflects its own degradation. Schütz outlines the process as "the dissolution of the church into religion, the dissolution of religion into the secular spirit of the age, and the dissolution of the spirit of the age into the chaos of self-glorifying 'earth' (the machine, the gold, the blood!)" (p. 230).[55] These signs "indicate the greatest danger for mission, namely, that it has lost itself" (p. 191). He continues that "the determination of the church in the chaos of the time is thoroughly political" (p. 246). Missions have become base, and with this, a "political marionette" (p. 220). Akin to the role religion plays in Germany, missions supply the "moral ideology" for the political, social, and worldview interests of its Western masters. Here mission is "entirely in its element," and "either willingly or unwillingly, 'Caesar's hunting dog'" (pp. 229, 196). It is merely one political factor among many.

Fourth, now secularized, mission ceases to be a possibility. To quote Devaranne, in "the motherland of mission we discover a putrefaction similar to that outside."[56] If the forms of Western civilization define the message, then mission only propagates Western apostasy. No spiritual effect can result from the moribund state of Christendom, since, as Wiedenmann suggests, "this neo-heathen secularism was worse than the old heathenism."[57] The civilizing process created walls against the missionary endeavor because it introduced a secularism that had become inoculated against the gospel in the way indigenous religion had not. Devaranne, summarizing Schütz's position, says that "at home, on every street, Christ is pronounced dead, while out there the missionaries announce a twilight of the idols of the heathen world!"[58] In actuality, the true mission field is that of the West.

---

conquering nature. What we did was to arm nature — the nature in us, and as we discover that this world of man is just a part of nature and that some of its historic incidents are just the fight of herds, one with an other, we realize that the price that we pay for fellowship with a good God is complete disassociation from that kind of a world. Of course, that means the Cross." Reinhold Niebuhr, "Our World's Denial of God," *Intercollegian* 44 (1927): 130.

55. See also Simon, "Die gegenwärtige theologische Kritik an der Mission," p. 190.
56. Devaranne, "Theologie der Krisis," p. 27.
57. Wiedenmann, *Mission und Eschatologie*, p. 57.
58. Devaranne, "Theologie der Krisis," p. 27.

Western missions, insofar as they neglect the only field without the demonic wall of foreignness, are forms of cowardice and desertion. Schütz
asks, "Did I not flee with this age into the mountains, into the exposure of
the periphery, and away from the dense distress at the center?" (p. 190). The
overwhelming need of the West prompts the missionary to flee to a place in
the sun where she can proclaim an idealized gospel and delude herself with
a romanticized memory.

Schütz concludes that "the house of the church is burning. We resem-
ble a lunatic wanting to store his harvest in a burning barn" (p. 195). The
Western church is aflame, and this already determines the failure of her
mission. The time of missions is past, and mission administrators know
this. Schütz, by contrast, proposes that "prophecy leads the church along
the path of passion" (p. 245). Passion opposes the strength of nature that so
afflicts missions. Passion is not suffering; it is an action that persists and
endures. "Passion is the breakthrough of history. It is the breaking through
into the second creation. Passion is sacred history in the midst of secular
action" (p. 245). Schütz links this eschatological approach to God's own
mode of acting in the world. In passion resides

> . . . the strength to receive a determination from outside. In it is the
> strength of obedience. Passion is the divine form of acting in history.
> Passion is the divine form of existence in the world. To be the Word in
> the flesh. Likewise, the *mission* of the church in the world is passion, it is
> sending into the midst of the wolves. It is participation in God's exis-
> tence in the world. (p. 245)

Following the mode of Christ's incarnation leading to his crucifixion, missions had to surrender the power of nature for a power external to human
history. Schütz does not ground missions in the doctrine of God. He does,
however, juxtapose natural methods available to human control with "participation in God's existence in the world." This indicates well the eschatological trend initiated by dialectical theology.

Condemnation of Schütz's position appeared with apoplectic fervor.
While some acknowledged, to quote Jäger, that Schütz's "accusation has a
kernel of truth," all energetically resisted his apparent negation of foreign
mission.[59] The identification of mission with a single approach meant that

---

59. Jäger, "Die Neubesinnung der evangelischen Mission auf ihre Motive, Methoden
und Ziele," p. 217.

any criticism of that approach constituted a condemnation of mission it-self.[60] Even Devaranne, who, based on his own experience in China, af-firmed mission's devolution into mere mechanics, concluded that Schütz's position is "a *caustic solution* of a diffluent kind, dissolving away not only putrid flesh, but also healthy."[61] Of all the responders, Hartenstein was the most constructive. The key problem lay with Schütz's own improper geo-graphical framing of mission, as a movement from West to East. If mission was only geographical, then it was only imperialist.

Hartenstein, himself shaped by dialectical theology, responded that the Great Commission "resounds in a community that has become cold, in the midst of a completely secularized world governed by the demonic." Unbelief is always the context of mission. Nevertheless, the command to mission "resounds with apodictic certainty," because it is Jesus Christ him-self who, as the victor, struggles for his universal dominion.[62] The author-ity to undertake mission lies not in the authority of the individual or the community, but in the action of God. This, of course, shares some affinity with Schütz's own position. The difference is that Schütz's geographical approach places the merit of the missionary message in the authenticity of its Western expression. His criticisms of the secular nature of Western Christianity can be reversed. If Western Christianity performs the gospel, then, presumably, missions become justified. Missions remain located in human capacity and faithfulness.

Knak's response indicates more the general reaction. He allows for the necessary corrective of dialectical theology, but laments that this critical mindset results in a lack of pastoral love. An emphasis on the prophetic alone is inadequate for missionary engagement. Pastoral love is necessary for a per-son of foreign, that is, Western, race occupying an imposed leadership posi-tion to demonstrate the truth of the gospel. Schütz's criticisms of missionary activism translate, for Knak, into a default quietist or passive approach. Pasto-ral love demands action. Knak also acknowledges that the colonial era intro-duced certain tones at odds with the missionary task, but he maintains that German missions resisted the more egregious excesses of this temptation.[63]

---

60. As Bosch suggests, it was precisely "the inadequate foundation and ambiguous mo-tivation of the missionary enterprise" that blinkered mission supporters to Schütz's chal-lenge. Bosch, *Transforming Mission*, p. 6.

61. Devaranne, "Theologie der Krisis," p. 28.

62. Hartenstein, "Krisis der Mission?" p. 206.

63. Siegfried Knak, *Zwischen Nil und Tafelbai: eine Studie über Evangelium, Volkstum*

Medical missions and the influencing of national governments remained "necessary because without them the foreign peoples would not be able to recognize that the message of God's saving love is seriously meant."[64] Mission "cannot withdraw from these 'cultural works,' because without them the proclamation of the gospel would become simply incomprehensible."[65] These activities "prepare the inward capacity to receive the divine word and to assist new converts in their independent comprehension of the biblical word."[66] Again, if one rejects a "point of connection," then one rejects mission.

Knak illustrates the persistent inability of German missiologists to connect the criticisms issued against the propagandistic approach of Anglo-American missions to their own structurally similar approach. German missions, in a very real sense, could not make this connection. As Poewe argues, National Socialism believed that imperialism and internationalism had defeated Germany in World War I; thus, for its own survival, it was vital that missions distanced itself from these trends.[67] Dialectical theology served this purpose. The key distinction remained that of establishing a homogenous universal civilization versus sanctifying the particular character of the native peoples. Dialectical theology's warnings against the human possession of the gospel did not apply to this question of context because this emphasis was itself theologically ratified by reference to a particular account of the relationship between law and gospel located in the Lutheranism basic to German identity.

---

und Zivilisation, am Beispiel der Missionsprobleme unter den Bantu (Berlin: Heimatdienst-Verlag, 1931), p. vii.

64. Knak, "Missionsmotive und Missionsmethode," p. 79. Against Schütz's criticisms that the state schools led to the infiltration by Western culture, Simon asks whether the Egyptian state schools, which are Moslem in nature, would not have done the same thing. Christian mission is, as such, justified in employing this method to protect against Moslem influence. G. Simon also suggests that any "evaluation of the activity of the mission doctors and their hospitals must be based on the way they create for us the platform which allows us to bring the gospel to the people." This approach, though in reaction to Schütz, seems entirely to confirm his position. See Simon, "Die gegenwärtige theologische Kritik an der Mission," pp. 184, 182.

65. Knak, "Missionsmotive und Missionsmethode," p. 79.

66. Knak, "Missionsmotive und Missionsmethode," p. 79.

67. Poewe, "The Spell of National Socialism," p. 271.

Bruno Gutmann and the Missiological Drift into National Socialism

If Schütz was the dialectical antagonist, then Gutmann was the Lutheran protagonist. Building on the tradition of Warneck and the "German" approach to missions, Gutmann was, to quote Pierard, "the most significant exponent of the relationship between church and *Volk* in German missiology."[68] His work, while contested, established a baseline from which other missiologists responded to Barth. For our purposes, Gutmann's position permitted a positive connection between mission theory and the political ideology of National Socialism. It is this missiological reflection of the general theological context that provides the immediate framework for Barth's 1932 lecture — and prohibits any reception of his position.

Western civilization, for Gutmann, constituted the greatest disruption to the propagation of Christianity in the non-Western world. The "civilizing" process of the West, imbued as it was with an atomistic view of life, only succeeded in destroying the key social relationships found within traditional societies. Spiritual ties become secularized through the application of material values, as, to quote Beyerhaus, "money becomes a substitute for brother and neighbor, dehumanizing and dissolving all mutual obligations."[69] Gutmann held that the dissolution of "the common bonds of the native" makes these primitive societies "susceptible to all the germs which assist the decomposition of our soulless civilization," the most notable of which is the "emasculating illusion of the independent individual soul."[70] Destroying these ties, because it destroyed their childlike innocence, had the secondary effect of immunizing the indigenous population against Christianity. This general problem occurred as much in the Anglo-American approach as it did in Pietism, with the latter's disruptive conception of baptism and comparatively sectarian ecclesiology. Nor, in addressing this problem, did Gutmann employ dialectical theology, the one-sided

---

68. Pierard, "Völkish Thought and Christian Missions," p. 143. Knak says of Gutmann that he is "among those who have helped to mold the form of the German Protestant missions of today." Knak, "Characteristics of German Evangelical Missions," p. 315.

69. Quoted by Ernst Jäschke, "Bruno Gutmann 1876-1966: Building on Clan, Neighborhood and Age Groups," in *Mission Legacies: Biographical Studies of Leaders of the Modern Missionary Movement,* ed. Gerald H. Anderson et al. (Maryknoll, NY: Orbis, 1994), p. 177.

70. Bruno Gutmann, *Gemeindeaufbau aus dem Evangelium: Grundsätzliches für Mission und Heimatkirche* (Leipzig: Evangelische Lutherisch Mission, 1925), pp. 136, 15.

nature of which created a disjunction between God and the individual that appeared very much like the erosion of civilization.

Gutmann's alternative proposal sought an indigenous Christianity rooted in the *Volkstum* of the people. Three main characteristics frame this position.[71] First, God has left a permanent witness to himself in creation, especially in the "primordial ties."[72] These elements of "the fabric of being" reveal the "order of creation," rendering them universally valid across time and determinative for every human relationship and community. They were, according to Jäschke, "the absolute basis of true Christian life."[73] Gutmann emphasized three ties in particular: that of the *clan,* based on blood relationships *(Blut);* that of the *neighborhood,* a relationship of mutual assistance shared by those living from the same soil *(Boden);* and that of *age groups,* which establishes bonds of hierarchy within the tribe and an organization for war and peace.[74] These were necessary for humanization, and without them, according to Beyerhaus, "an individual convert is deprived of social relations essential to his full self-realization."[75] Gutmann's own experience among tribal peoples informed his thinking.

Timothy Yates indicates how later commentators, such as J. V. Taylor and John Mbiti, with such statements as "I am, because we are," affirm Gutmann's basic conviction that "what you are, you are only through connectedness."[76] Civilization severs the people from their organic roots, and thus mission, to quote Simon, must prioritize the "ethical-sociological task to halt the fragmentation of the *Volk.*"[77] Second, these primary social relationships provide the necessary points of contact through which God reveals himself to, and dwells with, humanity.[78] Gutmann says that "both

71. This summary follows Gensichen, "German Protestant Missions," pp. 186-87.

72. For a discussion of Gutmann's key term, *"urtümliche Bindungen,"* see J. C. Winter, *Bruno Gutmann, 1876-1966: A German Approach to Social Anthropology* (Oxford: Clarendon, 1979), pp. 6-7.

73. Jäschke, "Bruno Gutmann 1876-1966," p. 176.

74. See Per Hassing, "Bruno Gutmann of Kilimanjaro: Setting the Record Straight," *Missiology* 7, no. 4 (1979): 425-27.

75. Beyerhaus and Lefever, *The Responsible Church and the Foreign Mission,* p. 50.

76. Timothy Yates, *Christian Mission in the Twentieth Century* (Cambridge: Cambridge University Press, 1994), p. 41. Quoting Gutmann, *Gemeindeaufbau aus dem Evangelium,* p. 15.

77. Simon, "Die gegenwärtige theologische Kritik," p. 176.

78. According to Knak, Gutmann is misunderstood if one fails to read this emphasis through two other lenses: first, "the whole social life of the African tribes lies under the influence of sin, in the grip of daemonic forces," and second, "no one can become a Christian

— the church and the primordial ties — are divine creations, an immediacy related to each other, and represent, with such relatedness, the fullness of God's immanence in the world of human beings."[79] Without these ties, one cannot properly understand the kingdom of God even "if he takes the centre of the divine revelation through Christ as his point of contact."[80] These ties frame revelation, providing the form through which revelation lives and is known. Third, so framed, the church is now a *Volkskirche*. She is not an imported foreign structure that calls individuals out of their self-constituting social relationships, but a new independent and self-sustaining community that elevates the primordial ties into the new creation, and by this means becomes fully indigenous.[81]

Missions, Volkstum, *and Nazism*

Gutmann's work remains important simply because of the debt contemporary theologies of contextualization owe to his insights.[82] By positing a Germanic perspective as normative for the missionary task, however, he established some correlation between mission method and Nazi ideology. While mission administrators did not necessarily affirm Nazism, many influential missiologists did affirm *völkisch* thinking as integral to the contextual nature of German missionary method.[83] For Hoekendijk, while

---

without taking a personal decision." Knak, "Characteristics of German Evangelical Missions," p. 318. Gensichen, too, suggests that Gutmann would reject the accusation that this position represents an undue focus on the first article. Only the coming of Christ fulfills and validates these ties. Gensichen, "German Protestant Missions," p. 187. At issue, however, is the notion that God cannot work apart from these ties, that human activity cultivates the necessary preliminary conditions for the proclamation of the gospel, and that this activity constitutes the whole of the missionary act.

79. Gutmann, *Gemeindeaufbau*, p. 15.

80. Gutmann, *Gemeindeaufbau*, p. 159.

81. Gensichen, "German Protestant Missions," p. 187.

82. In Neill's estimation, "On many essential matters Gutmann was right; missionaries and colonial authorities alike have often paid too little attention to the background of native thought, to those presuppositions which do not readily find expression in speech, but nevertheless colour and determine the whole of life." Stephen Neill, *Colonialism and Christian Missions* (New York: McGraw-Hill, 1966), p. 401.

83. Certain missionaries did identify with National Socialism. Schlunk, chair of the Missionary Council from 1924 to 1946, described himself in 1939 as "a dedicated Nazi." Werner Ustorf, " 'Survival of the Fittest': German Protestant Missions, Nazism and Neocolo-

some individuals raised alarm bells concerning National Socialism's conception of *Volk,* others acknowledged its legitimacy.[84] A focus on *Volkstum* was, perforce, a focus on context, and it bled into that Germanic contextualization that was Nazism. Any criticism of this compromised connection amounted to a denial of mission proper.

While sharing certain key ideas with National Socialism, Gutmann seemingly opposed it. As Gensichen suggests, "Gutmann can hardly be charged with applying [the terms *Blut* and *Boden*] in order to justify German political claims, let alone colonial imperialism. He had been thoroughly disillusioned by the realities of European power politics and all its consequences, nationally and internationally."[85] He sought indigenous, not colonial, churches, to encourage the native *Volk,* not transplant a Germanic one. Given that the kingdom of God was present within the primordial social ties, Gutmann was critical of futurist eschatologies, especially of those that linked the kingdom of God to the historical progression of civilization.[86] The terminus of Gutmann's position consisted in returning to an original state. Salvation corresponds to the repristination of the orders of creation, through which God's immanence flows. Of this position, Hassing maintains that "the Gospel does not move forward to its consummation in the kingdom of God, but moves back into primeval ties which seem to be static, unchangeable."[87] Herein lay the problem, for it sanctioned *völkisch* thinking via a general ap-

---

nialism, 1933-1945," *Journal of Religion in Africa* 28, no. 1 (1988): 97. Christian Keyßer became a member of the Nazi party, and he considered Nazism to be the fulfillment of his concept of mission. Pierard, "Völkish Thought and Christian Missions," pp. 144-45. He would name Hitler a confederate against the corrosive influence of individualism, declaring, "Today, thank God, National Socialism rules." Quoted by Yates, *Christian Mission in the Twentieth Century,* p. 54. Hartenstein, who before 1933 regarded Hitler and Rosenberg to be "irreconcilable opponents of the Christian church," after 1933 hoped that, in Hitler, Germany had found a true leader capable of restoring German spirit and strength, and inaugurating a new period of German history. In Hartenstein's case, this hope swiftly dissipated. Karl Rennstich, "Hartenstein als Direktor der Basler Mission," in *Karl Hartenstein: Leben in weltweitem Horizont,* ed. Fritz Lamparter (Bonn: Verlag für Kultur und Wissenschaft, 1995), pp. 44-45. Freytag, too, was compromised. Gensichen observes that "the Freytag whom I knew, and to whom I owe so much, is actually somebody other than the one who appears to have existed between 1933 and 1945." Quoted by Werner Ustorf, *Sailing on the Next Tide: Missions, Missiology, and the Third Reich* (Frankfurt am Main: Peter Lang, 2000), p. 12.

84. Hoekendijk, *Kirche und Volk,* p. 303.
85. Gensichen, "German Protestant Missions," p. 187.
86. Beyerhaus and Lefever, *The Responsible Church and the Foreign Mission,* p. 51.
87. Hassing, "Bruno Gutmann of Kilimanjaro," p. 432.

preciation of the orders of creation and of the law/gospel distinction. This position mandates an uncritical appreciation of history.

Hoekendijk and Kraemer both note Gutmann's debt to Romanticism, a certain principle of social organization, and Western superiority.[88] Gensichen argues that, while Gutmann sought to indigenize the gospel, his "own particular system of indigenization" reflected a cultural conservatism that amounted to "German nationalism in disguise."[89] Building on the anti-Americanism of German missiology, Gutmann's approach promoted an "affinity with the system."[90] The conservative and traditional elements of a particular history became representative of the culture, which, in turn, became a necessary expression of indigenous Christian existence. This social conservatism, according to Gensichen, brought German cultural pride "back with a vengeance, for it was this peculiar method of indigenization which was elevated as evidence of German superiority — an illusion which in some circles survived even the shock of war."[91] Even in defending Gutmann, Jäschke notes that, while it may not have been his intention, Gutmann's ideas "received wider circulation" when Rosenberg's writings were declared to be "the official world-view of National Socialism."[92] Putting it more strongly still, Schärer declares that Gutmann's "völkisch-religiösen" myth "differs neither from Rosenberg nor Stapel in principle."[93]

88. Hoekendijk says: "One can describe the methodology of mission as it developed in Germany between the two world wars (in which mission ideology found its clearest expression) as the product of a scant century of unclear missiology — with all those now transparent rationalizations of only half-digested morsels of Romanticism and Historicism, and all this combined with an expressly 'bourgeois' view of humanity and society and, naturally, not lacking a proper shot of western — or simply national — superiority consciousness ('the charism of German mission'!)." Hoekendijk, *Kirche und Volk*, p. 303. Kraemer concurs, saying that "Gutmann, in our opinion, errs in another direction, by conceiving the tribal life-structures and patterns as 'creational orders,' that is to say, as divinely sanctioned structures. Clan, tribe, people, nation, etc., are forms and spheres of life that are direct consequences of God's will. This is romanticism fortified by the weight of metaphysical reasoning." Kraemer, *The Christian Message*, p. 340.

89. Gensichen, "German Protestant Missions," p. 188.

90. Werner Ustorf, "Anti-Americanism in German Missiology," *Mission Studies* 6, no. 1 (1989): 25.

91. Gensichen, "Evangelisieren und Zivilisieren," p. 268.

92. Ernst Jäschke, *Bruno Gutmann: His Life, His Thought, and His Work: An Early Attempt at a Theology in an African Context* (Erlangen: Verlag der Evangelische Lutheran Mission, 1985), p. 313.

93. Hans Schärer, "Die Begründung der Mission in der katholischen und evangelischen

Knak illustrates well the affinity. While certain tendencies within Nazism needed to be biblically confronted, the focus on *Volkstum* learned on the mission field foreshadowed and reinforced the developments in the Third Reich.[94] In an article entitled "Mission and Church in the Third Reich," Knak says that "it is mission itself (in any event German mission, like all missionary work growing out of the German Reformation) that can here teach us to recognize with persuasive force the significance of the *Volkstum* for humanity and history." Long before the advent of National Socialism, says Knak, missions had known the "value of the *völkisch* distinctive," and the Third Reich only wanted to "protect" the German distinctiveness. Based on this experience, missions "can grant the church a good conscience for saying a *joyful* yes to the intentions of the Third Reich."[95]

Missionswissenschaft," *Theologische Studien* 16 (1944): 37. Hoekendijk recommends that "one [pay] attention to the circles that gave Gutmann warm applause. Certain political groups excitedly followed his work, assuming that they had found therein support in the fight against 'democracy.'" Hoekendijk, *Kirche und Volk*, p. 173.

94. Siegfried Knak to Karl Barth, 22 March 1931, Karl Barth Archive (KBA) 9331.189, Basel, Switzerland. Ironically, because the Berlin mission joined the Confessing Church, Poewe notes that "Knak was considered an enemy of the state, suffered searches, interrogation, and was banned from [public speaking]." Poewe, "The Spell of National Socialism," p. 271.

95. Siegfried Knak, "Mission und Kirche im Dritten Reich," in *Das Buch der deutschen Weltmission*, ed. Julius Richter (Gotha: Leopold Klotz Verlag, 1935), pp. 242-43. Elsewhere Knak states the principle "that *the national character of heathen peoples should not be obliterated by the preaching of the Gospel*, has done much to win over ecclesiastical circles to the idea of the national Socialist State, which also lays stress on the *preservation of national characteristics*." Siegfried Knak, "The New Germany and Foreign Missions, 7.11.1933" (Geneva: International Missionary Council Archives 1910-1961, Microfiche 264011.4, World Council of Churches), p. 3. Knak was not alone in this judgment. According to Ustorf, Freytag maintained "that part of the 'deepest blessing' resulting from overseas mission was its impact for the Christians at home, particularly in the area of race and *Volk*." Ustorf, *Sailing on the Next Tide*, p. 171. Gogarten too formed identical connections among mission experience, Gutmann and Knak, and an approach to the evangelization of the West based in *völkisch* methodology. He, for example, affirms Gutmann's fear that the focus on the individual is of greater danger than an emphasis on the *Volk*, for "we recognize the *Volk* and *Volkstum* as an excellent gift in which God proves to us that he is our creator." Friedrich Gogarten, "Schöpfung und Volkstum: Vortrag, gehalten auf der Berliner Missionswoche, am 3. Oktober 1932," *Zwischen den Zeiten* 10 (1932): 504. He further says that "it is a strange fact that the question of *Volkstum* presses us, coincidentally, on the mission field and in our own historical situation." Gogarten, "Schöpfung und Volkstum," p. 481.

The official "guidelines" of the German Christian Faith Movement, published on June

This reference to mission method served not merely to confirm the Nazi state; it reflected a positive evangelistic intent.

In the national revolution of 1933, God had presented Germany with an opportunity for reestablishing Christendom. Because missionary method held that the gospel flowed through cultural ties, and this flow could be encouraged by repristinating these ties, it follows — since the Third Reich sought "to form the German *Volkstum*" — that National Socialism would assist with the reevangelization of Germany.[96] As Ustorf suggests, the ambiguous approach of missions to Nazi ideology is a consequence of the "widespread conviction that Nazism would help missions achieve their goal."[97] The normative missionary methodology of *Volk*, via the medium of Nazism, could now be applied to the home church. Knak is even willing for Nazism to take the lead: he says that, "if the state lays claim to the powers of the church, then it does so in name of the *Volkstum*, and here the church finds the starting point for her yes to the totalitarian claims of the state."[98] This gentle logic constitutes the immediate backdrop to Barth's 1932 lecture.

"Theology and Mission in the Present Situation"

The earliest record of Barth's dealing with missions consists of a 1910 catechesis class, where he affirmed its role in bringing "European culture to the

6, 1932, use this logic to justify its racial position. Guideline 7 states that "German foreign mission, on the ground of its experience, has for a long time, told the German people to 'Keep your race pure,' and said to us that faith in Christ does not destroy race, but rather deepens and sanctifies it." The "Richtlinien der Glaubensbewegung 'Deutsche Christen' 1932/1933" are reprinted in Heiko Augustinus Oberman, Adolf Martin Ritter, and Hans-Walter Krumwiede, *Kirchen- und Theologiegeschichte in Quellen*, vol. IV/2 (Neukirchen-Vluyn: Neukirchener Verlag, 1977), pp. 117-21. For an examination of the link between Bruno Gutmann's mission method and the German Christians, see "Die Volksnomoslehre in der Missionstheologie, vornehmlich dargestellt an den Schriften Bruno Gutmanns," in Wolfgang Tilgner, *Volksnomostheologie und Schöpfungsglaube: ein Beitrag zur Geschichte des Kirchenkampfes*, ed. Kurt Dietrich Schmidt, vol. 16, Arbeiten zur Geschichte des Kirchenkampfes (Göttingen: Vandenhoeck und Ruprecht, 1966), pp. 212-17.

96. Knak, "Mission und Kirche im Dritten Reich," pp. 242-43.

97. Ustorf, "The Documents that Reappeared," pp. 70-71.

98. Siegfried Knak, "Totalitätsanspruch des Staates und der Totalitätsanspruch Gottes an die Völker," *Neue Allgemeine Missions-Zeitschrift* 10, no. 12 (1933): 406. He continues that "the church can and must answer Hitler's state with a fundamental and wholehearted yes." Knak, "Totalitätsanspruch," p. 407.

heathens," that is, bringing technology and education for the purposes of humanization. Human unity meant that the "goods of culture must become common to all." And he concludes, "culture, *therefore* Christianity."[99] In other words, before writing the *Römerbrief,* Barth understood mission as a civilizing task. By 1932, the combination of this and his prior understanding of mission that was seemingly confirmed by the above link between mission method, *Volkstum,* and Nazism, the whole missionary enterprise may have seemed anathema to Barth — a living manifestation of *Kulturprotestantismus.* However, following the furor instigated by Schütz, Julius Richter invited Barth to deliver the annual lecture at the Brandenburg mission conference as a way of clarifying the disjunction between Hartenstein's positive evaluation of Barth's contribution and Schütz's dialectical denial of the missionary enterprise. Richter further proposed that Siegfried Knak respond, accompanied by an open discussion.[100] Barth accepted the invitation, noting that "neither Hartenstein nor Schütz are my 'students.' I see, however, that one has the right to request a statement from me about the situation created by the contrasting views of these two people."[101]

Whatever the constructive potential of Barth's lecture, it is evident that the above prehistory precluded its reception — positive or negative. In terms of the development of *missio Dei,* despite the acclaim of recent history, this lecture remains a historical addendum. Barth developed his posi-

99. Karl Barth, "Evangelische Missionskunde," in *Vorträge und kleinere Arbeiten II: 1909-1914,* ed. Hans-Anton Drewes and Hinrich Stovestandt, *Gesamtausgabe* (Zürich: Theologischer Verlag Zürich, 1910), p. 62.

100. Julius Richter to Karl Barth, 3 December 1931, Karl Barth Archive, KBA 9331.629, Basel, Switzerland.

101. Karl Barth to Julius Richter, 9 December 1931, Karl Barth Archive, KBA 9231.393, Basel, Switzerland. Two weeks before the lecture, Barth acknowledges his ignorance of the missionary enterprise, and his need to hastily "appropriate some real knowledge" of the subject. Karl Barth to Werner Koch (Basel, Switzerland: Karl Barth Archive, 26 March 1932, KBA 9232.116). John Hart argues that Barth, in his 1932 lecture, "took on Brunner and the 'point-of-contact' (anonymously but clearly)." While Brunner may well have hovered in the background, such conjecture requires challenging for one dominant reason: systematic treatments of the Barth-Brunner discussion concerning natural theology never address the buttress Brunner uses to stabilize his position. It is not that Barth responded to the question of "theology and mission" while preoccupied with his own dogmatic questions, but that Brunner's position proceeds out of the same missionary milieu criticized by Barth. John W. Hart, *Karl Barth vs. Emil Brunner: The Formation and Dissolution of a Theological Alliance, 1916-1936* (New York: Peter Lang, 2001), p. 138 n. 68.

tion in deliberate contrast to the emphasis on *Volkstum*. The dominant fear that a rejection of this German missiological "charism" would paralyze mission predetermines its historical marginalization. In terms of content, certain themes, such as the emphasis on God's subjectivity, clearly emerge as part of *missio Dei*. However, this lecture does not encourage a Trinitarian position, simply because Barth does not himself draw on the doctrine of the Trinity in any overt way. Barth structures his lecture around four central missionary themes: the mission motive, mission recruitment, the task of mission, and the mission sermon.

The Mission Motive

Reference to its motive justified mission as "an essential function of the church and an irreplaceable expression of the vitality of Christianity."[102] The fact that mission required justification was not in doubt. The question was one of authority, and locating mission within a range of accidental historical, economic, and cultural motivations constituted self-justification. Barth, while he resists Schütz's terminal conclusions, agrees that the "undeniable origins of mission in the Jesuits and the Pietists" established a clear warning against overestimating mission motives. One cannot ground mission in "some system of Christian truth and morality," or in a "'point of connection' that the Word of God will and must find among its heathen hearers." This leads to the empty motivation of "a powerful 'will for mission' as the tangible product" (p. 199). Grounding mission in these human capacities, no matter how apparent the claim, draws on an authority not grounded in obedience, for this demands the negation of all false justifications.

Mission as a work of faith is an "unprotected endeavor" (p. 193). The ground of its existence is not visible to all, and what is visible often appears complicit with a range of improper compromises. Mission has, at times, functioned as "an instrument of religious or cultural propaganda or even of economic power politics," and it cannot protect itself against this suspicion (p. 194). All human motives can be contested, and mission "neither stands nor falls with its proffered and vulnerable motives"; mission "ulti-

---

102. Barth, "Die Theologie und die Mission in der Gegenwart," p. 203. Quotes in English from this lecture are from an unpublished translation by Darrell L. Guder; the page numbers refer to the German original.

mately cannot justify itself at all." It "must place its hope in its *being* justified as an act of obedience" (pp. 204-5). This passivity is due to the location of the true motive for mission within the prior act, will, and command of the living Lord. Mission possesses no internal justification. Only as God justifies it does mission continue to exist.

Barth reinforces his point by referring to the fierce missionary outcry that accompanied Schütz's challenge to its motives. If the missionary motive were located in the will of the living Lord, challenges to that motive would not stimulate that kind of aggressive reaction. Only when mission "rejects all possible self-justification and relies upon the justification that it can only receive" will it receive "its real and effective justification." Barth acknowledges that this redirection unsettles the human activity, but only here does mission find "its factual preservation"(p. 205). It is in this context of distancing missionary justification from any accidental historical grounding that Barth asks the now famous rhetorical question:

> [M]ust not the most faithful, the most convinced missionary think seriously about the fact that the concept *'missio'* in the ancient church was a term from the doctrine of the Trinity, the designation of the divine self-sending, the sending of the Son and of the Holy Spirit into the world? (p. 204)

This incidental reference offers no developed account of the doctrine of the Trinity, or of God's "sending" nature. His key emphasis is on the freedom of God against every human attempt to possess him. Nor do any authors after Barth take this up. As opposed to the received history of *missio Dei,* this relocation of missionary justification becomes a key element in the missionary *suspicion* of Barth. For Knak, his refusal "to identify the divine revealing activity with the speech and actions of the missionaries . . . may have an inhibiting effect upon all missionary activity."[103] Knak's own reference to the Trinity reinforces missionary activism in deliberate contrast to Schültz's emphasis on passion. The triune God is love, and love motivates the missionary to sink into the local con-

---

103. Knak, "Characteristics of German Evangelical Missions," p. 340. This fear had some justification. Hoekendijk notes how "a gap emerged between mission and theology on the home front, a discrepancy between motive and method. The crisis shifted. The significant question became how the 'pure' motives might now be put into practice. Here theology generally left one in the lurch." Hoekendijk, *Kirche und Volk,* pp. 125-26.

text.[104] "Love simply cannot present itself to me other than through action!"[105] Missionary activism is necessary for making the gospel comprehensible, for preparing the ground and so assisting the reception of the gospel. In other words, this is in diametrical opposition to Barth's main point, for such "passivity" led to the paralysis of the will to do mission.

Recruitment for Mission

The second section addresses the recruitment for mission. When the justification of mission rests in human activism, recruitment occurs via published reports and congregational lectures. Missionaries present stories of success and failure designed to stimulate energy for missionary work. Such methods posit mission more as an instance of works-righteousness, the reserve of an elite few, than as an obedient response of the community to God's call. Mission occurs at a fundamental distance from the community, and calls the congregation to mission in a manner at odds with the way it is called to be a Christian community. As mission describes the church herself, so the call to missionary activity must align with the call constitutive of the church's being. This very early construal of the church's missionary nature stems from Barth's interpretation of Christian existence as continual dependence on God's call. The church is "a human community *called* to the act of mission" (p. 207). Her specifically missionary activity is a form of confession directed to those "not yet" within the church, to those who have "not yet" made their confession visible, through repentance, confession, and baptism. This "not yet," however, does not only denote those outside the Christian community; the church is herself "a church of heathens," which is "still and frequently very unconverted" (pp. 190, 196). Mission is an extension of the church as each member is "constantly thrust back to that 'not yet' stance over against the message, repentance, and baptism." Barth thus affirms that "*all* activity of the church is mission, even if it is not expressly called that." The particular missionary act serves the church by revealing the nature of her existence as repetition by "risking beginnings with people who are not members"

---

104. Siegfried Knak, "Die Mission und die Theologie in der Gegenwart," *Zwischen den Zeiten* 10, no. 4 (1932): 349.

105. Knak, "Die Mission und die Theologie," p. 352.

(p. 190). This movement of mission is one of solidarity shared between the heathen outside and the heathen inside, and constitutes a necessary part of the church's universal confession. Barth concludes that "the community of heathen Christians should recognize themselves and actively engage themselves as what they essentially are: a missionary community!" (p. 207).

The Task of Mission

From Barth's perspective, three accounts of the mission task dominate modern European mission history: the Pietistic, the Anglo-American, and Gutmann's "genuinely Lutheran" version (p. 208). The Pietistic approach treats conversion as a process of inner transformation, a process with a definite starting point. For the missionary, this process is behind him; for the heathen, this process is before her. The Anglo-American approach understands conversion to be "the adoption of a new moral structure," and proclamation to be the task of leading the heathen into this Christian culture or civilization. Gutmann's approach understands conversion to be that process of awakening the heathen to the natural *telos* of one's social context. The task of the missionary is the "calling of the heathen to himself and thus to God" (p. 208). Barth makes two points in response. First, he does not disqualify any one of these approaches: all three contain elements of truth, and the true task of mission, he suggests, resides "somewhere in the middle." Missionaries must remain open as the task will disclose itself "little by little and day by day" (p. 212). This openness occurs as one relinquishes allegiance to any particular system. Barth seeks an approach where each view becomes "an honest and unavoidable but subordinate corollary of missionary action" (p. 209). The missionary must await the call of God and his justification of missions, while being focused on developing forms suitable for the task at hand.

Second, these three approaches, though they are considered divergent, share a unified foundation: the doctrine of creation. The Pietistic position ends, so to speak, with conversion. As to what occurs after conversion, it draws on the other two approaches. This leaves the "contrasting" positions of the Anglo-American and the German. However, Barth calls this assumed contrast into question. The Anglo-American approach "can lay claim to the same concept of creation, with some slight variations, to which we too turn to formulate our allegedly pure antithesis against it" (p. 210). Barth finds the Anglo-American failings paralleled in Gutmann: the operative metaphor of organization versus that of organism; the transformation of human societies through Christian civilization versus that of Christianization; the appreciation of human will through humanitarianism versus those of social structures; and the fact that both coordinate Christ and a unified humanity in the one Adam. He concludes that one "might have justifiable reservations about the shape and application" of the Anglo-American approach, but one cannot condemn it on theological grounds "here in Lutheran Germany" (p. 210).

These two positions can be differentiated on "inner-humanitarian," but not theological grounds. Barth continues that "the truly ingenious Gutmann literature" reads "as one long variation on the entrancing song of the serpent, 'Grace does not tolerate but supplements and perfects nature'" (p. 211).[106] Since it is the location of the missionary task within natural theology that results in the propagandistic prioritization of human experience, both the Anglo-American and the German positions secularize mission. Secularism means that "Christ is absorbed into some conception of Christ and disappears, and what then remains is human" (p. 211). What matters if this human is civilized or primitive? The missionary focus shifts from "the one essential and dominant figure whose concretion is revelation itself, to whom Scripture testifies," to the initiation of a new system, "a special historical form of the gospel" either in a European, an Asiatic, or an African form (p. 214).[107]

---

106. Jäschke maintains that, "if Karl Barth saw in Gutmann's contribution 'that ancient serpent' raising its head, it was a carry-over of his own experience with a heretical and degenerate nationalism." But this is precisely the point: far from mere legacy, some continuity exists between Gutmann's position and Nazi ideology: the logic of natural theology opens a breach that goes both ways. Jäschke, *Bruno Gutmann*, p. 244. For an examination of Barth's criticisms of Gutmann, see Yates, *Christian Mission in the Twentieth Century*, pp. 49-53.

107. Barth elsewhere argues that the church readopted the missionary task when the Christian faith began to view itself as "a better foundation for philosophy and morality, as a better satisfaction of ultimate needs." It became inevitable, with "the sending Church . . . herself seeking her strength at a different point from where it could be found," that mission would suffer. "The debate whether the aim of the mission was the representing of an Americo-European or the founding of an autochthonous African and Asiatic Christianity, could not help towards a solution of the hidden difficulty that either way the main concern was the 'glory' of this or that Christianity in its relation to the needs and postulates of the human" (*CD* I/2, 336; *KD* I/2, 368).

The Mission Sermon

Barth concludes with a reflection on how the missionary clarifies the gospel to her hearers. What givens can the missionary draw on? Can the missionary use local names for God? Barth answers that no European theologian can prescribe what the missionary must do. This is the missionary's responsibility, and only the missionary's theology can determine the content of her sermon. Translating the message for the sake of communication is a necessity, and it occurs in the midst of a conglomeration of practical, pedagogical, psychological, *völkisch*, and religious reasoning. If the missionary approaches this task understanding the subordination of language to the superordination of Scripture, then "he can claim all the freedom he needs at that subordinate level." The missionary "will 'connect' — how should he not connect since all language is a process of 'connecting' — to the entire life situation of his hearers, which includes their religion." The issue, for Barth, is not whether the missionary theologically *should* translate the gospel using the resources — including religious resources — at hand. The issue is that one translates the *gospel,* and that one does not identify the gospel with some partial and derivative version. Missionary translation is necessary and proper, but this does not result in "a theory of a 'point of connection,' a natural revelation that precedes the revelation" (p. 214).

Siegfried Knak and the Missionary Reception

Bonhoeffer's recollection of the resulting Barth-Knak "discussion" affords a pithy summary of its general reception. Knak's formal rebuttal "conveyed the tone of the heated discussion and full extent of nationalist animosity against the dialectic thinkers."[108] After a long silence, "Knak started by asking where, in Barth's view, the difference lay between Swiss and Prussian national feeling."[109] This response came as a surprise to Barth, who wrote

108. Eberhard Bethge and Victoria Barnett, *Dietrich Bonhoeffer: A Biography,* rev. ed. (Minneapolis: Fortress, 2000), p. 177. Knak's response was not actually based on Barth's own text, as he failed to receive the lecture in advance. See Siegfried Knak to Karl Barth (Basel: Karl Barth Archive, 12 April 1932, KBA 9232.183). Knak's response to Barth was published as "Die Mission und die Theologie in der Gegenwart" (see n. 104).

109. Bethge and Barnett, *Dietrich Bonhoeffer,* p. 177.

to Knak expressing his personal embarrassment over Knak's lecture. If Knak's response was representative of "the view of the leading circles in German mission," then Barth had received "a clear and complete rejection by those circles."[110] Barth should not have been surprised. He and Knak had corresponded previously, and the general tenor of their correspondence illustrates well both the central questions underlying his lecture and the impossibility of its reception.

Knak first contacted Barth in the aftermath of the latter's lecture "Die Not der evangelischen Kirche" (The Emergency of the Protestant Church), which he delivered in Berlin on January 31, 1931. In that lecture Barth spoke against "the hyphen between Christianity and *Volkstum*, Protestant and German." The German people needed "the existence of a *Protestant* and *not* a *German*-Protestant church."[111] That this was the entry point is telling in itself. Knak reacts strongly, warning that, while there may be some warrant in critiquing hyphenated Christianity, one cannot do so superficially. "The Swiss, apparently, have no internal connection with the matter when they speak of this difficult problem of Christianity and *Volkstum*, of Christianity and nation." Slighting what every German knows to be true prompts them to ignore Barth's positive contribution. With his failure to

110. Karl Barth to Siegfried Knak, 13 April 1932, Karl Barth Archive, KBA 9232.131, Basel, Switzerland. Between March 1931 and April 1932, Knak and Barth exchanged a series of nine letters. The first six expressly deal with the German focus on context, and the final three concern Knak's reaction to Barth's lecture. Knak initiates both discussions, but the second discussion begins with an apology from Knak. He admits that he reacted too violently to Barth's presentation for fear that this position might encourage the kind of paralysis for mission that he had previously witnessed among the church's youth. The series of letters ends on a discordant note, and this conclusion deeply affected Knak. In a final letter, written more than twenty years later — encouraged by a positive greeting from Barth via a mutual friend — Knak notes the many nights he had lain awake thinking of his own conduct with regard to Barth, his shame over his earlier position, and his wish for Barth's continued strength in his work on the *Church Dogmatics*. Siegfried Knak to Karl Barth, 15 April 1954, Karl Barth Archive, KBA 9354.215, Basel, Switzerland. Ustorf observes that, when other German mission administrators were seeking a rapprochement with the wider mission community after World War II by denying any involvement with National Socialism, Knak proved more contritely forthright. See Ustorf, *Sailing on the Next Tide*, pp. 242-56. My thanks to Renate Knak, Siegfried Knak's daughter, for permission to quote from this unpublished correspondence, and to Juliette Appold for transliterating the final letter from the original handwritten text.

111. Karl Barth, "Die Not der evangelischen Kirche," *Zwischen den Zeiten* 9, no. 2 (1931): 115-16.

take "seriously one's belonging to the *Volkstum* as a gift of God, and therefore as God's task," Barth "will talk past the conscience of German Christians."[112] Barth's "no" merely incited the youth to reject mission, a classic instance of dialectical theology's paralyzing of mission.

Barth responds by agreeing that the issue is not a superficial one. This "constant emergence of the terms 'Christian' and 'German'" must be met with "a straightforward and sharply protesting 'no.'"[113] The issue has nothing to do with being either Swiss or Chinese, but with human disdain for God. On this point, Knak and his friends encounter Barth as their opponent and rebutter. This led Knak to question whether Barth did justice to the reality of Prussian national sentiment. Prussians are not idolaters; they "never place the concepts 'Christian' and 'German' side by side as equivalents." *Volkstum* is part of temporal human existence and is, as such, transitory, but this does not render it incidental to one's Christianity. He says:

> We do not consider our belonging to the German *Volk* to be a coincidence, not as something which perhaps has nothing to do with our Christianity, as something which might be easily set on the line of "time," while what is truly Christian belongs on the line of "eternity." Rather, for us, our belonging to the German *Volk* is the place where we have to represent, to realize, our biblical Christianity.[114]

Volkstum is the location of God's call, the framework within which individuals articulate their faith. Hyphenated Christianity simply points to the necessarily contextual nature of every Christian expression. Given that creation is itself a gift of God, "the fact that we are Germans is something made by God, and we may never regard anything made by God with indifference. The first condition of our earthly life . . . is that we are Germans."[115] Apart from the reality of mundane physiological existence,

112. Siegfried Knak to Karl Barth, 9 February 1931, Karl Barth Archive, KBA 9331.082, Basel, Switzerland.

113. Karl Barth to Siegfried Knak, 7 March 1931, Karl Barth Archive, KBA 9231.088, Basel, Switzerland.

114. Siegfried Knak to Karl Barth, 10 March 1931, Karl Barth Archive, KBA 9331.159, Basel, Switzerland.

115. Knak to Barth, 10 March 1931, KBA 9331.159. A clear example of this position is found in the closing resolution of the First National Assembly in Berlin, held in April 1933. It stated: "God has created me a German. Germanism is a gift of God; God desires that I battle for my Germanism. . . . The church is, for a German, a communion of believers that is duty

which is true of the newest infant, context defines the human person.[116] Every aspect of human existence is interpreted through *Volkstum*. Even individuality cannot be understood apart from the *Volk*, because one cannot grow to maturity apart from this nursery.

Cross-cultural experience affirms the validation of context. Barth's failure to take Germanness seriously is

> ... something we German mission workers cannot participate in. This is because we have learned, much too strongly, on the mission fields, how serious the fact needs to be taken that someone is Chinese, or that someone is born as a Bausto or a Papuan. Those are God-given conditions, which, according to our convictions, the gospel does not seek to place under the light of a quantité négligeable, but rather seeks to effectuate toward their ultimate consequences. For where the creator has planted the seed he also seeks to bring it to completion.[117]

One cannot denude national characteristics because, if we do that, the gospel will never take root in this new territory. Knak even declares that "we are committing a capital crime if we educate the African to be the imitator of the European, instead of helping him to develop his distinctive characteristic."[118] Mission cannot impose a culture; it must assist the flourishing of native culture. God speaks through a culture's social structures, and the preservation of this distinctiveness is a holy duty. It is not a matter of "building bridges, where only the miracle of divine grace has its right." Only God is the one who speaks into the human condition. One must, nevertheless, ground mission in the preexisting social structures because it is not possible for the gospel to be understood by "the heathens without the possibility of a harmony between the revelation of Christ, which newly approaches him, and the revelation, which had already sought him."[119]

---

bound to battle for a Christian Germany." Ernst Christian Helmreich, *The German Churches Under Hitler: Background, Struggle, and Epilogue* (Detroit: Wayne State University Press, 1979), p. 133.

116. Knak would later confirm this position, declaring that "from the first instant of my *mental* life, I make use of the inheritance of my *Volkstum*, because I cannot think a thought without the language of my *Volk*." Siegfried Knak to Karl Barth, 22 March 1931, Karl Barth Archive, KBA 9331.189, Basel, Switzerland.

117. Knak to Barth, 10 March 1931, KBA 9331.159.

118. Knak to Barth, 22 March 1931, KBA 9331.189.

119. Knak, "Die Mission und die Theologie," p. 343.

The process of harmonization constitutes the path through which God has spoken and will speak.

Knak held this position in accordance with the standard missionary method. Schlunk, for example, observes:

> [W]e have recognized that for a church, as she forms here on earth as an imperfect realization of the kingdom of God, two formative powers must always and necessarily coalesce: first, the confession in which the faith of the church members expresses itself, and second, the community of the blood or of the *Volk* which through the faith that gathers them in the same confession becomes the church.[120]

Race and nationality are secondary "constitutive elements for building the church."[121] While subject to an ordering principle, these two givens function as necessary preconditions for the gospel. God is active in the culture before the arrival of the missionary, evident in the way a mother loves her child, and in the respect of the young for their elders. Though mission circles may too quickly determine "family, tribe, and *Volk*" to be "realities of creation," they remain of "drastic significance for all future mission practice."[122]

As Schärer suggests, "the entirety of mission methodology and mission practice is determined by this double grounding for mission."[123] Any denial of this double grounding amounts to a denial of missionary translation. For Knak, the act of exegesis is itself an instance of translating the message "into the conceptual world of any particular time period, of different cultural and national spheres . . . into the language of here and now."[124] Is such an approach, he asks, "a compromise with the human nature of the heathen listeners, or is it the correct way of bringing them first of all to a consciousness of their own need"? Is this process "a betrayal of the message or wise pedagogy"?[125] By so conflating hyphenated Christianity with a mundane account of translation, Knak concludes that Barth's

120. Schlunk, "Die Mission im Feuer der Kritik," p. 263.

121. Schlunk, "Die Mission im Feuer der Kritik," p. 264.

122. Knak, "Die Mission und die Theologie," p. 345.

123. Schärer, "Die Begründung der Mission," p. 33. He continues that the affinity between Gutmann and National Socialist ideology represents "the ripe fruits" of the "double grounding for mission" in revelation and anthropology.

124. Knak, "Die Mission und die Theologie," p. 339.

125. Knak, "Missionsmotive und Missionsmethode," p. 68.

position lacks the capacity to connect with the context and thus stymies the missionary act. As himself a theologian and not a practitioner, Barth cannot understand what is actually occurring. It may not be his intent, but Barth's theology subjects missions to strong criticism both at home and abroad. Knak formed this judgment concerning the paralyzing effect of Barth's theology on the basis of experiences with promising young candidates for missionary service who gave up their training after reading dialectical theology.

For Barth, the necessarily contextual nature of Christian faith and the need for missionary translation are not at issue. He concurs with Knak that "the *Volkstum* into which someone is born belongs to the divinely intended creative substance of one's existence, and that this component of his existence will certainly form one enduring component of the command of God that has laid claim upon him."[126] One speaks out of a context, but, Barth asks, "Do you believe really that the divine meaning and the divine right of *Volkstum* is undervalued, if it is seen in its relativity — not only in relation to God, but also concretely in its relation to everything that is otherwise a reality and commandment of creation?" Why is it necessary to coordinate gospel to the arbitrary category of *Volkstum*? Could not sexuality fulfill the same function? Though Knak claims not to idolize *Volkstum,* by asserting its primacy within created human reality, has he not "secretly idolized this moment"? Does the missionary task really require this hyphen? Barth acknowledges the common accusation that his position paralyzes mission, and in response inquires whether "it really is the churchly practice as such away from which one sees the young people retreating, or not much more either a certain type of grounding of this praxis, or a certain form in which it has been practiced by its exponents up until now."

This basic differentiation between missions as such, its motive, and its method, seems an obvious one. With the hyphen functioning as the shibboleth of orthodoxy, however, these three categories become mutually dependent.[127] The grounding of mission in *Volkstum* leads to the method of Christianization, and together these define the whole of the missionary

126. All quotations in this paragraph are from Barth's letter to Siegfried Knak, 13 March 1931, Karl Barth Archive, KBA 9231.101, Basel, Switzerland.

127. This point had already been made by Barth in his lecture on "The Emergency of the Protestant Church," stating that "this hyphen has become today the actual criterion of church orthodoxy." Barth, "Die Not der evangelischen Kirche," p. 115.

task. A challenge to this totalizing logic at any point amounts to a denial of the possibility of missions.

The categorical nature of Knak's assessment means that Barth's benign acknowledgment of *Volkstum* as the necessary context of Christian expression renders him an automatic confederate against the Anglo-American position. The key threat is as follows:

> The drive to make everything uniform spreads itself all over the earth on the wings of technology and industry. Its latent meaning is that of subjugating humankind under Mammon and the machine. This movement derives its ideological superstructure from the Anglo-Saxon ideals of a democracy built upon the over-exaggeration of the value of the personality, and the identification of civilization with Christianity, out of which the purpose emerges of "elevating the world" to the Kingdom of God with the help of these two powers.[128]

In terms of mission strategy, this approach is evident in the "Englishman's" desire to "educate" the native, that is, to make the native like the educator. Because this type of accommodationism is "the *farthest* thing" from Barth's position, Knak intuits that the German struggle against the Anglo-American trend within the global mission conferences "corresponds much more to the view of the kingdom of God, revelation and the gospel represented, among other things, by dialectic theology, than the international efforts to shift the nationalistic into the background." The German approach differs in wanting to bring the native to hear the message expecting that the Spirit will create something completely different. It is necessary for the missionary to show the native that "God does not speak to him first through mission, but *has* spoken for a very long time in various forms of primal knowledge, primal human impressions which his fathers bequeathed to him." Knak notes his strengthening impression that

> . . . the special tasks of *German* Christianity lie in this direction — particularly insofar as its spiritual nursery is to be sought in Wittenberg. If, in opposition to this, our consciousness of the distinctive character of our people diminishes, then that means a further victory for the will to

128. Siegfried Knak to Karl Barth, 22 March 1931, Karl Barth Archive, KBA 9331.189, Basel, Switzerland. Unless otherwise noted, the rest of the quotations in this section are from this letter.

make everything uniform behind which I see the hubris of modern humanity, who would make itself master of the world and still convince itself that it is "building the kingdom of God" — a particularly fatal idiom, for me, from the vocabulary of mission.

Again, there emerges here the assumed link between the affirmation of the peculiar "German" ethnic or cultural contribution, and the origins of this contribution within the theological nursery of Wittenberg. If one discredits the particular German preoccupation with context, one immediately attacks the theological core of the Protestant Reformation and presents those chaotic forces that attack the primal revelation in creation with a further victory. Either support the Germanic missionary charism, or support forces destructive to the gospel.

> The ideas of freedom in the sense of the emancipation, of equality in the sense of the democracy, of fraternity in the sense of the termination of all national and race differences within this world age, are, for us, human attempts to replace divine legislation with one's own. If you sense in us a certain passionate rejection of internationalism, then its cause is located in the resentment against the attempts of humans to put themselves in the place of God, not in *völkisch* arrogance.

The emphasis on *Volk* is itself a theological impulse, and the desire to reject internationalism is a natural correlate of this theological position. Yet this theological judgment is insulated from criticism by reference to the very centrality of context.

> What is the larger danger today: that we turn our nation into an idol, or that we are submerged by the floods of internationalism and are Americanized or bolshevized? . . . I believe that only that person who, from youth on, has experienced German history in the past and present and in one's own internal development, can have any instinct as to where the greater danger for us might be. It is only for that reason that it is not irrelevant for me whether the criticism of our attitude comes from an empire German or a Swiss.

This is the lodestone. The German mission's need to define itself against the Anglo-American position, especially as this reflects a real political threat to German culture and identity, promotes an identification of the process of contextualization with German Christianity. Denying the hyphen meant denying this distinctive contribution, and with it a theological account of contextualization itself. For Knak, the hyphen does not, as Barth suggests, indicate the secularization of Christianity; it opposes the secularization attendant to the Anglo-American position. Either we accept the reality of contextualization — and the concomitant theological baggage — or we follow the imperialist route. Knak, accordingly, rejects Barth's thesis that the difference between Gutmann and the Anglo-American position is inner-humanitarian and not theological.[129]

Writing in 1938, at the high point of Nazi Germany, Knak would even affirm that "the influence of the dialectical theology upon the pure proclamation of the word is compatible with a protecting attitude towards the existing *Volkstum* and with the true idea of the *Volkskirche* as the historical goal of the missionary undertaking."[130] Even if Barth had explicitly developed a Trinitarian position, such a statement exemplifies the intractability of the German charism and the concomitant ability to deflect and reformulate all criticisms, treating them as theological confirmations of its original position. The battle was precisely that of a secular (Anglo-American) versus a biblical (German) approach to mission. Mission was the cultivation of the ground in preparation for God to speak. To deny this preparation was to deny the essential missionary act. It was, in other words, impossible for German missions to receive Barth's 1932 lecture.

Barth's 1932 Lecture and *Missio Dei* Theology

Apart from the barest passing reference by Schick and Schlunk, no other author during the intervening period leading to Willingen examined Barth's 1932 essay.[131] Günther concludes that "K. Barth's lecture to the Brandenburg Mission Conference in 1932 and S. Knak's answer resulted in no real change. The common struggle against the 3rd Reich soon overlaid the theological contrast."[132] The political revolution of 1933, occurring less

129. Knak, "Die Mission und die Theologie in der Gegenwart," p. 353.
130. Knak, "Characteristics of German Evangelical Missions," p. 355.
131. See Schlunk, "Die Mission im Feuer der Kritik," p. 259; E. Schick, "Wortverkündigung — Bekenntnis — Zeugnis," *Evangelisches Missions-Magazin* 77 (1933): 131.
132. Günther, *Von Edinburgh nach Mexico City*, p. 47.

than a year after Barth's lecture, is a clear mitigating factor, but it does not explain the dearth of extended treatments and the evident silence from authors such as Barth's confederate, Karl Hartenstein. Knak stands alone, and his response shadows the general trends of German mission: the rejection of the internationalism and syncretism of the Anglo-American position; the affirmation of German mission's charism with its language of *Volkstum*; the fear of a popular appropriation of Schütz; and the grounding of mission within preexisting social structures understood as part of the orders of creation, all theologically reinforced by reference to the law.

One can appreciate how the constructive potential of Barth's 1932 lecture became identified as a key theological turning point. Bosch is correct to maintain that the developments associated with the term *missio Dei* "would be difficult to imagine without the stimulus of Barth."[133] His reorientation of Protestant theology during the twentieth century inevitably bled into missions. Writing in 1941, Schlunk noted the "stimulus" of "crisis theology" for missionary thinking, especially on the question of "adaptation *versus* building on a people's past" — a comparison illustrative of the basic confusion within missions concerning dialectical theology. He notes appreciatively Barth's argument that "heathenism can be found quite as easily within as without the Church: that we are all heathen — missionaries and pastors too." This includes the related conviction that "mission represents an essential function of the church's life."[134] Schlunk continues, however, that by the late 1930s, dialectical theology had been "decisively rejected."[135] Mission theorists, at best, only engage in an ad hoc appropriation of certain dialectical themes. For Günther, "as a rule, Barth's system was not usually adopted as a whole, but served as quarry for one's own theological construction," with the "very many lines of Barth's thought becoming common property."[136]

German mission's preoccupation with its particular approach to

133. David J. Bosch, *Witness to the World: The Christian Mission in Theological Perspective* (London: Marshall, Morgan and Scott, 1980), p. 167.

134. Martin Schlunk, "Theology and Missions in Germany in Recent Years," *International Review of Mission* 27, no. 3 (1938): 464-67.

135. Martin Schlunk, "German Missionary Literature Since 1939," *International Review of Mission* 30, no. 4 (1941): 546.

136. Günther, *Von Edinburgh nach Mexico City*, pp. 79, 82. Aagaard, too, maintains that Barth provided "a general pattern of thinking." Johannes Aagaard, "Some Main Trends in Modern Protestant Missiology," *Studia Theologica* 19 (1965): 252.

indigenization blinded it to any potential within Barth's dogmatic framework for a thick theological account of mission. As Ustorf suggests, "the German missiologists' theological manoeuvring between a theological . . . and an anthropological . . . point of departure produced missiological ambivalence (either-or theology) and ended with the victory of anthropology."[137] These appropriated elements were reframed according to the theological substructure of natural theology, using the dogmatic guise of the law and the orders of creation.

Barth's 1932 lecture does not ground missions in the doctrine of the Trinity. His emphasis on God's subjectivity is a direct consequence of his understanding of the doctrine, but he does not develop a positive account of the Trinity's missionary economy. He never articulates something similar to the central *missio Dei* affirmation that "God is a missionary God." The eventual Trinitarian grounding of mission as articulated at Willingen 1952 affirms creation and culture as central to mission, and it does so in overt opposition to a christological emphasis. Barth's attempt to dislocate mission from creation is precisely the approach against which *missio Dei* theology reacts.

137. Ustorf, *Sailing on the Next Tide*, p. 24.

CHAPTER FOUR

Tributaries to the IMC Willingen Conference, 1952

Introduction

In this chapter I will examine the origins of the Trinitarian grounding of mission as articulated at the IMC conference held in Willingen, Germany, in 1952. Conventional history holds that Hartenstein brought Barth's 1932 position to Willingen. But it is clear that Barth, while he placed the justification for mission apart from any accidental grounding, did not develop a positive Trinitarian theology of mission. Neither did any mission theorist of the period understand his contribution in Trinitarian terms. Thus the question shifts to this one: Did Hartenstein, either building on Barth or independently of him, introduce Trinitarian doctrine to missions? He did not. He did originate the phrase *missio Dei,* and he drew enduring dialectical themes into mission thinking, including an emphasis on God remaining subject in his act. But he did not expressly ground mission in the Trinity. His position developed to address a particular concern. *Missio Dei* constitutes an apologia for the church's missionary activity during a period of crisis. It is the church's assumption of Christ's mission in this interim period between the ascension and the *parousia.*

The Trinitarian thrust actually originates in a preparatory document for the Willingen conference entitled "Why Missions?" The development of this document was chaired by Paul Lehmann and informed by H. Richard Niebuhr, and the study uses the doctrine of the Trinity as a foil against a "Unitarianism of the Son." This overemphasized christology, only reinforced by Barth's putative christomonism, was identified as the heretical root underlying propagandistic forms of mission method. *Missio Dei*'s Trinitarian deficiencies are a direct legacy of this study and its underlying abstraction of God's being from his economy. After Willingen, Hartenstein's *missio Dei* position is retrofitted with the doctrine of the Trinity, and, drawing as it does on a traditional account of the church, it came to be espoused as the "classical" alternative to the prior position articulated by Lehmann and Hoekendijk. However, this only succeeds in submerging the *missio Dei*'s Trinitarian deficiencies, causing commentators to locate the resulting problems in the areas of eschatology or ecclesiology.

Karl Hartenstein: Originator of *Missio Dei*

One should not underestimate Hartenstein's legacy within the theology of mission. Jacques Rossel maintains that "theology, on the western European scene, was dominated by Karl Barth, Emil Brunner, and Karl Hartenstein."[1] While it is somewhat hyperbolic, this statement contains an important truth. Where German mission administrators and theorists were preoccupied with issues of *Volkstum* and Christianization, Hartenstein shifted the material of missiological reflection from sociology to biblical exegesis.[2] According to Rossel, he was "the first continental mission leader to confront the pious and conservative mission supporters with a theology that broke away from so many of their cherished shibboleths."[3] Hartenstein's pioneering work included a positive theological account of the missionary task. The question is whether he drew on Barth for this theological reconstruction, and whether this resulted in a Trinitarian grounding of missions of the type seen at Willingen.

1. From the foreword to Hermann Witschi, *Geschichte der Basler Mission 1920-1940*, vol. 5 (Basel: Basileia Verlag, 1970), p. 7.
2. J. C. Hoekendijk, *Kirche und Volk in der deutschen Missionswissenschaft* (Munich: Chr. Kaiser Verlag, 1967), p. 124.
3. Jacques Rossel, "From a Theology of Crisis to a Theology of Revolution? Karl Barth, Mission and Missions," *Ecumenical Review* 21, no. 2 (1969): 204.

"What Does Karl Barth's Theology Have to Say to Mission?"

Hartenstein's popular association with Barth begins with a lecture he delivered in 1927, which was entitled "Was hat die Theologie Karl Barths der Mission zu sagen?" (What does Karl Barth's theology say to mission?)[4] In contrast to Schütz, Hartenstein was as an engaged member of the missionary movement: he served as director of the Basel Mission from 1926 to 1939. With the onset of World War II, he returned to Germany to become the prelate of Stuttgart, a position he held until his premature death mere weeks after Willingen.[5] His unique appreciation of both missions and Barth included a degree of social stigma. Freytag notes that, for the old heads of the mission council, "a Barth student who strongly advocated mission appeared to be nothing other than a contradiction."[6] Nevertheless, Hartenstein understood that mission theory needed radical rethinking, and, according to Rossel, "foresaw that Barth's new emphasis contained the seed of this renewal."[7] Delivered prior to Jerusalem 1928, and thus prior to the wider discussion between missions and dialectical theology, Hartenstein's lecture examines Barth's positive potential for mission theory.

For Hartenstein, revelation is "the personal act of God," the "real and concrete act of God in history."[8] Divine agency distances missionary activity from every improper liaison. The missionary speaks of the "*gospel* and *not* of Christian *culture*." The world needs salvation, whereas the transmission of cultural forms only leads nations to "the higher planes of life." Mission cannot be "the dissemination of human words, goals and ideals," of things humans have "in their own religious possession" (p. 66). Mission method must, as such, "reject all political protection, every attempt to put

---

4. Karl Hartenstein, "Was hat die Theologie Karl Barths der Mission zu sagen?" *Zwischen den Zeiten* 6 (1928): 59-83. Quotations in English from this lecture are from an unpublished translation by Darrell L. Guder; the page numbers refer to the German original.

5. Hartenstein was a decorated World War I field artillery officer, earning both a second- and first-class Iron Cross. In 1918, he personally received from Kaiser Wilhelm II the Knight's Cross of the Royal Hohenzollern House Order with Swords. See Söhnen Hermann and Markus Hartenstein, "Der Lebensgang," in *Karl Hartenstein: ein Leben für Kirche und Mission,* ed. Wolfgang Metzger (Stuttgart: Evangelischer Missionsverlag, 1953), pp. 16-24.

6. Walter Freytag, "Mitglied im Deutschen Evangelischen Missionsrat und Missionstag und bei den Tagungen der Ökumene," in Metzger, *Karl Hartenstein: ein Leben,* p. 296.

7. Rossel, "From a Theology of Crisis to a Theology of Revolution?" p. 204.

8. Hartenstein, "Was hat die Theologie Karl Barths der Mission zu sagen?" pp. 61, 65. The remainder of the quotations in this section are taken from this essay.

it at the disposal of cultural aims" (p. 70). This rejection of propaganda includes within it a critical stance toward "religion." A qualitative distance
exists between God and humanity. Religion is the human attempt to overcome this gulf and build a direct bridge between humanity and God. "The
one who says religion is saying pious ego" (p. 71). This critique applies
equally to the Christian religion, which, as one religion among others, is
"to be surrendered." Mission cannot construct an "essence of religion" behind all religions, which is then identified with Christianity. Nor can it
consider Christianity the zenith of a religious evolution. Mission must
"avoid at all costs the spreading of the Christian religion" (p. 72). It cannot
serve the general human religious drive.

Underpinning these developments is Hartenstein's emphasis — remarkable for being delivered in 1927 — on God's bearing of the missionary
act. "The first mission history, the book of Acts, knows that all mission is a
continuation of the life of Christ, an act of the Lord. The Lord remains the
subject in all mission" (p. 66). This spills over into how the church must
understand herself. "The Lord as the One who speaks is the One who
drives mission, not we, but also not without us" (p. 67). The task of mission is witness, with the kingdom of God the goal. If humanity were the
goal, then the missionary would be guilty of an implied superiority: mission would consist of the attempt to elevate the heathen to the missionary's own social level (p. 70). The church lives in humility and obedience
and must recognize the "fluid boundaries" between herself and heathenism (p. 81). "True fellowship arises only out of the soil of the kingdom. . . .
The final word of mission is not the converted heathen as convert, not the
heathen-Christian church as church, but rather both in relation to the
kingdom." Her role is that of a "sign and a pointer to this coming kingdom
of God" (p. 70). This orientation foreshadows by twenty-five years what
Bosch considers one of the major triumphs at Willingen in 1952.[9]

This lecture, in clear distinction to the *völkisch* emphasis of Hartenstein's contemporaries, establishes key thrusts of what would become
missio Dei theology. God is the agent of mission. Neither the church nor
mission holds the priority; both are called to the kingdom of God. The
church is a missionary community. It is not difficult to form a link between Barth, Hartenstein, and Willingen based on such statements. But

---

9. David J. Bosch, *Transforming Mission: Paradigm Shifts in Theology of Mission* (Maryknoll, NY: Orbis, 1991), p. 370.

this 1927 treatment was the furthest Hartenstein was to follow Barth. Though Barth exerted an intellectual influence throughout Hartenstein's career, the work of Emil Brunner, Karl Heim, and Oscar Cullmann soon surpassed Barth's contribution to his thinking.[10]

Barth's Missionary Inadequacies

During the early 1930s, Hartenstein reinterpreted these foundational dialectical themes in light of his Swabian heritage. He did this, as Gerold Schwarz suggests, because, in 1927, Hartenstein "was not yet questioning Karl Barth's position, but rather permitted mission to be questioned by the challenge of dialectic theology."[11] The wounds that had been inflicted on the mission method were his central concern, and he identified Barth as a salve. The more Hartenstein came to "actual missiological questions, the less he found the 'Barthian formulas' sufficient, and the more he stressed 'the right and significance of Pietism in the context of our mission work and the church.'"[12] Barth cleared the improper connections that had developed between missionary activity and propaganda. For the positive redevelopment of the missionary task, Hartenstein turned to other sources, and especially the "eschatological thinking of the Württemberg patriarchs."[13]

For Witschi, the political occurrences of 1933 initiated this shift. He maintains that Hartenstein "rejected the political consequences of dialectic theology" because the method of "open resistance against anti-Christian powers" did not correlate with the Christian community's call to suffering.[14] Hartenstein needed a variety of theological support against the Nazi challenge that Barth's theology failed to provide.[15] Christian activists

10. See Karl Hartenstein, "Der Beitrag der Theologie zu den missionarischen Problemen der Gegenwart," *Evangelische Missions-Magazin* 82 (1938): 69-83.

11. Gerold Schwarz, *Mission, Gemeinde und Ökumene in der Theologie Karl Hartensteins* (Stuttgart: Calwer Verlag, 1980), p. 43. The following paragraphs draw on Schwarz's research.

12. Schwarz, *Mission, Gemeinde und Ökumene*, p. 64. The quoted portions are from a circular letter (dated 16 July 1938) from Hartenstein to missionaries in India associated with the Basel Mission.

13. Witschi, *Geschichte der Basler Mission*, p. 65.

14. Witschi, *Geschichte der Basler Mission*, p. 65.

15. Schwarz, *Mission, Gemeinde und Ökumene*, p. 60.

require an alternative grounding for ethics, and Barth's singularly anti-*Volkstum* position removed the material ground of ethical reflection. According to Schwarz, Hartenstein regarded "the sharply antithetical position of the early Barth toward anthropocentric thinking [as] too barren and one-dimensional."[16] This is reinforced by a letter Hartenstein wrote to Visser 't Hooft: "I have for some months experienced a strong internal churning, asking myself whether the first article of creation is not, to date, short changed in dialectical theology. I believe that we must find more positive answers to all the questions of the body, of *Volkstum*, of marriage etc., than Barth has given us to date."[17]

The issue for mission theorists was whether Barth's theology offered constructive solutions, or whether his relativization of *Volkstum* led to a concomitant wholesale negation of missionary translation. This led Hartenstein to the work of Emil Brunner, who understood his own position on natural theology to be drawn from missionary experience. In one letter to his "dear friend" Hartenstein, Brunner characterized his work, *Mensch im Widerspruch* (Man in Revolt), as "missionary through and through."[18] Brunner allowed Hartenstein to retain the critical element of dialectical theology, while he drew on both his Pietistic roots and the cultural dalliances common within traditional missionary thinking.

For Siegfried Knak, while he avoids an improper emphasis on "creation and the historical development of the orders of creation," Hartenstein retains the concept of *Volksordnungen*.[19] This is clear from his

16. Gerold Schwarz, "Karl Hartenstein 1894-1954: Missions with a Focus on 'The End,'" in *Mission Legacies: Biographical Studies of Leaders of the Modern Missionary Movement*, ed. Gerald H. Anderson et al. (Maryknoll, NY: Orbis, 1994), p. 593.

17. Quoted by Schwarz, *Mission, Gemeinde und Ökumene*, p. 59. For an example of his turn toward a missiology grounded in "ethical" questions, see Karl Hartenstein, "Versuch einer missionarischen Ethik," *Evangelisches Missions-Magazin* 79 (1935): 1-10, 33-44, 65-72.

18. Schwarz, *Mission, Gemeinde und Ökumene*, p. 63. In terms of Hartenstein's debt to Brunner, Schwarz states that "Hartenstein's missionary effort to identify the vertical dimension of the revelation of God, as an active and transformative force, on the horizontal level in the multiform complexities of human life, moves him into the theological company of Emil Brunner, which expanded into a personal friendship. The chief denominator of Hartenstein and Brunner's theological approach was the missionary character of their thinking." Schwarz, *Mission, Gemeinde und Ökumene*, p. 63.

19. Siegfried Knak, "Ökumenischer Dienst in der Missionswissenschaft," in *Theologia Viatorum II: Jahrbuch der Kirchlichen Hochschule Berlin*, ed. Walter Delius (Berlin: Walter De Gruyter, 1950), pp. 167, 170.

1935 article "Mission and the Cultural Question: Adaptation or Revolution," in which he refers appreciatively to both Keyßer and Gutmann.[20] Mission is subject to two temptations. First, it works for success via "secure methods," that is, formulating strategies according to givens in local cultures that will produce direct successes.[21] This is the negative connection broken on the anvil of Barth's theology. Second, it treats as mutually exclusive the two approaches of adaptation and revolution. The missionary has an either/or choice: either there is historical, cultural, and religious continuity, or these things are discontinuous. Hartenstein, while he prioritizes revolution, affirms both, for the question remains "how far God bestows His Word upon the natural, national and cultural forms of the peoples, and in how far the task of adaptation is thereby set to missions."[22]

Against the imperialism associated with the Anglo-American approach, Hartenstein cautions: "Do not be misled by the claim that the gospel might destroy the *Volk*-orders. It destroys paganism, but it respects custom, sanctifies language, and purifies *Volkstum*."[23] This basic position is to be affirmed. Insofar as culture is basic to human existence, it is converted along with the whole person and the community. The question is whether this context has the capacity to promote or derogate the conversion process. Here Hartenstein follows the basic position of German missions: "The Gospel is a breaking-up, a revolutionizing force," but the "original ties" are "revealed ordinances of God, the destruction of which would mean the slow disintegration of the tribes and people." These social relations "are so indispensable for one another that really living community arises only where the Body of Christ and the body of the people are in a mysterious way bound up with one another."[24] While Hartenstein avoids the double grounding for mission affirmed by his contemporaries, the nature of the missionary task demands some "mysterious" account of God's working through these given conduits. Hartenstein considers the sub-

20. Karl Hartenstein, "Mission und die kulturelle Frage: Anpassung oder Umbruch," *Evangelisches Missions-Magazin* 79 (1935): 350-67. Reprinted as Karl Hartenstein, "Adaptation or Revolution," *The Student World* 28, no. 4 (1935): 308-27.

21. Hartenstein, "Adaptation or Revolution," p. 308.

22. Hartenstein, "Adaptation or Revolution," pp. 309-10.

23. Karl Hartenstein, *Warum Mission? Eine Antwort an die deutsche evangelische Jugend,* vol. 4, *Mission und Gemeinde: Das Zeugnis der Mission in der Kirche der Gegenwart* (Stuttgart: Evang. Missionsverlag, 1935), p. 15.

24. Hartenstein, "Adaptation or Revolution," pp. 315, 326, 321.

stance of the practical act, in other words, apart from his theological assertion of divine agency.

Hartenstein's work in the early thirties reoriented mission thinking for
the next twenty-five years. When compared to the contemporary mainline
German mission theorists, he cleared a path between key dialectical themes
and the theology of mission. His emphases on the primacy of the Word
shifted the focus from a phenomenological to an exegetical basis; missionary
forms were themselves secondary to the acting Word. With this position intact throughout his career, Hartenstein never totally broke from Barth. As
Schwarz suggests, "the dialectical tension of Barth's theology remained a
'dominant factor' for Hartenstein, who retained its critical function as a corrective for church and mission." However, he dissolved this "tension in the
'tonic' of a salvation-historical biblical Pietism."[25] Hartenstein infrequently
refers to Barth and typically only in reference to his section on the *Aufhebung*
of religion. His Tübingen dissertation under Karl Heim, "Die Mission als
theologisches Problem" (Mission as a Theological Problem), often considered
exemplary of his dialectical approach to missions, does not treat Barth. Only
once does he refer to Barth's 1932 essay with regard to the notion that the
church is a community of heathen Christians, and nowhere does he note the
Trinitarian allusion.[26] Though typically associated with Barth, Hartenstein
even traces his emphasis on God as acting subject to Zinzendorf and
Warneck.[27] Any thick sense that Hartenstein mediated Barth to Willingen
must either be subjected to strict qualification or rejected outright.

The Origin of Missio Dei

The Pietist eschatology of his Swabian heritage dominated Hartenstein's
constructive missionary formulation. Freytag, suggesting that this ap-

---

25. Schwarz, *Mission, Gemeinde und Ökumene*, p. 63.

26. Karl Hartenstein, *Die Mission als theologisches Problem: Beiträge zum grundsätzlichen Verständnis der Mission* (Berlin: Furche Verlag, 1932), p. 159 n. 5.

27. For example, "'In Christ's stead' is how this service is done, as representative service,
designating not only the eschatological limitedness of this service, but also its nature as the
'continuous action of God' (Zinzendorf)." Hartenstein, *Mission als theologisches Problem*, p. 31.
Schwarz, too, says that "Hartenstein employed Zinzendorf's slogan that mission is the 'continuous action of God,' and placed it in God's plan of salvation as the 'continuation of the "actio
dei" in view of the salvation of the world.'" Schwarz, *Mission, Gemeinde und Ökumene*, p. 129.

proach was present *in nuce* in 1927, says that "the eschatological existence of the community between the resurrection and Jesus' return, her life in the tension between the arrived and coming kingdom of God, mission as sign and commission in God's plan of salvation, is at the centre of his missionary thinking."[28] Mission is grounded in the sending of the Son and in the expectation of his return. The completion of reconciliation, as evidenced by the ascension, establishes the new time of mission.[29] Mission is rightly distanced from the kinds of phenomenological positions associated with the dominant Warneck tradition, while being confirmed as the action that supplies the meaning of this interim period. Since it belongs to the essence of the church, every Christian is responsible for the missionary task. In 1934, Hartenstein designated this approach *missio Dei.*

The first contemporary usage of *missio Dei* comes in his essay "Wozu nötigt die Finanzlage der Mission," which dealt with the financing of missions, the critical issue underlying the German missionary crisis.[30] There Hartenstein says: "The decisive question for mission is the question of substance, not the question of finance. Mission stands and falls with the reality and truth of the living *Christ,* with his word and with his mission. If he is there — and he *is* there — mission will be there" (p. 217). Mission is not an accidental consequence of surfeit; it exists because Christ lives. Hartenstein continues:

> [M]ission today is called to examine itself in every way and always anew before God, to determine whether it is what it ought to be: *missio Dei,* the sending of God, that is the sending which Christ the Lord commands to the Apostles: "As the Father has sent me, so I send you" — and the response to the call passed along by the apostles to the church of all times on the basis of its Word: "Go into all the world." (p. 217)

This original use of the term draws on the missionary text of John 20:21: Christ, in his own sentness, commands the sending of the Christian com-

---

28. Walter Freytag, "Karl Hartenstein zum Gedenken," *Evangelische Missions Zeitschrift* 10, no. 1 (1953): 2-3.

29. Dorothea R. Killus, "Mission und Heilsgeschichte nach Hartenstein," in *Karl Hartenstein: Leben in weltweitem Horizont,* ed. Fritz Lamparter (Bonn: Verlag für Kultur und Wissenschaft, 1995), p. 113.

30. Karl Hartenstein, "Wozu nötigt die Finanzlage der Mission," *Evangelisches Missions-Magazin* 79 (1934): 217-29.

munity. "The primary or decisive element with which Protestant mission stands and falls is the Lord of the mission, and the call of the living Lord to his community to serve the world" (p. 217). This establishes the church's missionary existence, for it issues the mandate to proclaim "with authority." Authority, for Hartenstein, is located in the action of the Son and Spirit. First, "the message announced by us is the living Word of God." The authority is that of Christ himself. Second,

> ... this authority is "handed over" to us, handed over to the laborers and maids of the Lord, who is the Word, and who daily places their witness in his name on their lips and in their hearts. The question of authority is therefore the question of the *Spirit,* the Holy Spirit through whom the Lord wills to equip his messengers, and without whom the mission remains a noisy gong or a clanging symbol. (p. 217)

While this twofold emphasis might suggest a satisfactory account of God's present act, this is not Hartenstein's intent. It is the community as the recipient of this authority that is the acting subject. "Mission stands or falls with the complete and unconditional *yes of faith*" (pp. 217-18). It is an activity for which the church bears responsibility and cannot relinquish, for this is the task given her by the Lord and linked to her reception of the Spirit. "Mission is the decisive sign of her life, and the expression of her God-given existence" (p. 218). *Missio Dei* develops as an apologia for the missionary existence of the Christian community.

Though he does not use the phrase *missio Dei* in this sequence of quotations, the above position follows Hartenstein's early position. In a 1932 article entitled "Ambassadors in Christ's Stead," he says that "the 'I' of genuine mission, as well as of every genuine Christian proclamation, is the 'I' of God. ... Accordingly, mission is, in essence, withdrawn from every mere human activity, marked and declared as God's will and deed, as uncompromising reference to God's revelation."[31] Reference to divine agency lifts the missionary act beyond improper accidental liaisons. Mission is not, contra the 1928 IMC Jerusalem conference, the "call to participate, in a

31. Karl Hartenstein, "Botschafter an Christi Statt," in *Botschafter an Christi Statt: von Wesen und Werk deutscher Missionsarbeit,* ed. Martin Schlunk (Gütersloh: Bertelsmann, 1932), p. 5. This essay is a section from Hartenstein's dissertation entitled "The Question of the Subject, Object, Means and Goal of Mission." Hartenstein, *Mission als theologisches Problem,* pp. 32-39.

transformative manner, in the political, economic, social and racial questions of this world."[32] After clearing this ground, the church's missionary sending, which is "first and foremost an activity of God," is "rooted in the sending of Christ into the world."[33] This christological emphasis forces the church into her missionary agency, becoming the basic form of discipleship. Drawing on 2 Corinthians 5:20, Hartenstein concludes that "'*we* are now ambassadors in Christ's place.' This 'we' of the Apostle testifies that this mission is insolubly bound to calling, sending, with the service of this Word. Thus, with regard to the question of the 'I' of mission, one must add, through the mouth of the ambassador, 'in Christ's place.'"[34] The missionary is Christ's instrument, operating in his place. God remains the "Lord of missions," but in the interim period between the ascension and the *parousia*, his lordship is that of an ascended general over his ground forces. Mission, thus, becomes an imperative.

A Preliminary Reaction

This connection between the act of God and the human response coincidently distances mission from the charges of propaganda and establishes it as essential for Christian existence. Hartenstein's Zinzendorf-derived emphasis on mission as the "continuous action of God" propels the response of a missionary community: God sends his community in this period between the twin events of ascension and *parousia*. While he uses the language of sending, and links the acting of Son and Spirit with mission, Hartenstein does not himself identify this position as Trinitarian.[35] However, might it qualify as an *in nuce* Trinitarian position? "Much missionary theory and practice," says John Webster, is predicated on a flawed understanding of Jesus' perfection, assuming that the space in

32. Hartenstein, "Botschafter an Christi Statt," p. 7.

33. Karl Hartenstein, "The Theology of the Word and Missions," *International Review of Mission* 20, no. 2 (1931): 214, 218.

34. Hartenstein, "Botschafter an Christi Statt," p. 5.

35. For an expressly Trinitarian examination, see Karl Hartenstein, "Die trinitarische Verkündigung in der Welt der Religionen," in *Die deutsche evangelische Heidenmission: Jahrbuch der vereinigten deutschen Missionskonferenzen* (Selbstverlag der Missionskonferenzen, 1939), pp. 3-13. Nothing in the essay even approximates the Trinitarianism associated with *missio Dei*, nor does Hartenstein use the language of *missio Dei* in this context.

which the church undertakes its mission is one in which Jesus' perfection is not operative." Christ appears to have "resigned his office and transferred it to the missionary community."[36] Hartenstein falls into this temptation. His apologia for the church's missionary activity is predicated on this "transfer" of Christ's own missionary act. It is the church, in her faithful operation of word and sacrament, that mediates Christ to the world. Despite his reference to God's subjectivity, the community is the locus of missionary agency. Failure at this point illustrates the deficient Trinitarian basis of Hartenstein's position.

Barth develops an especially pertinent treatment of such an account with his depiction of the three forms of the one *parousia*: the commencement in the Easter event, the interim impartation of the Holy Spirit, and the definitive return of Christ (*CD* IV/3.1, 346-47; *KD* IV/3.1, 399-401). Missionary existence is a test of genuine faith. One "is a Christian only insofar as one is obedient to this calling to be a witness, as one is a messenger of Jesus Christ" (rev., *KD* IV/3.1, 397; *CD* IV/3.1, 344). In an exegetical treatment of the parable of the talents (Matt. 25:14-30), Barth notes that the Lord has "appointed his community the trustee and administrator of his properties," that is, the community is "entrusted with his Gospel and his Spirit" (rev., *KD* III/2, 609; *CD* III/2, 506). This strong language refers to the church's calling to operate in accordance with the nature of resources given her. "The same Word she has heard seeks new hearers: the community should not hear it without passing it on. The same Spirit that is given to her seeks new dwellings and new witnesses; the community should be so obedient to it that its witness creates new dwellings and awakens new witnesses" (rev., *KD* III/2, 610; *CD* III/2, 506). Such is the meaning of this interim form of the *parousia*, between Easter and the final consummation. Failure to exist as a *"missionary* community" demonstrates the bankruptcy of that "Christian" community, and such a community will be "banished into the darkness" on Christ's return (rev., *KD* III/2, 610; *CD* III/2, 507).

---

36. John B. Webster, "'Eloquent and Radiant': The Prophetic Office of Christ and the Mission of the Church," in *Barth's Moral Theology: Human Action in Barth's Thought* (Grand Rapids: Eerdmans, 1998), p. 148. Webster continues that "much church life is predicated on the assumption that God is only real, present and active in so far as the church's moral action or spirituality or proclamation make him so. Not only is this a (covert or explicit) denial of the resurrection; it is a miserable burdening of the church with a load which it cannot hope to support." John B. Webster, "The Church as Witnessing Community," *Scottish Bulletin of Evangelical Theology* 21, no. 1 (2003): 31.

The missionary existence of the Christian community is the necessary form of her relationship to the Son and the Spirit during this interim period. Barth thus affirms two key assertions made by Hartenstein: the eschatological meaning and structure of the current period, and the missionary nature of Christian existence.

However, Barth differs on one significant point: "[T]his interim period is not the period of an empty absence of the Lord" (rev., *KD* III/2, 610; *CD* III/2, 507). While Hartenstein repeatedly grounds his conception of mission in the resurrected Christ, he emphasizes the first and last forms to the detriment of the interim form of the *parousia*. Though such a position certainly affirms Jesus Christ's ongoing work in this contemporary sphere of history, this forms only as a light which shines down upon us. In this way his act is "omitted, by-passed, or passed over, so that it constitutes a kind of vacuum in the centre of this event. In this vacuum, *remoto Christo,* occurs all the Christian and non-Christian activity of our given creaturely freedom" (rev., *KD* IV/3.1, 400; *CD* IV/3.1, 346). Hartenstein's apologetic purpose requires this vacuum as supplying the impetus behind the church's missionary responsibility; mission does not occur as a consequence of historical accident, but because Jesus Christ has handed his missionary task over to his messengers. Christ's absence propels the church's task.

Barth describes such a position this way: while Christians may rejoice in the triumphant return of the exalted Lord, Christ's "life and act here, among us, *pauses;* He is *not* personally himself actively here and at work; He does not directly prove, attest, or operate as He is; but rather has, until further notice, abandoned the exertion of His function in favor of — the *Christian person*" (rev., *KD* IV/3.1, 401; *CD* IV/3.1, 347). The dominant emphasis in this approach is "the complex of those positive and critical *conditions* given for human being, but seriously and ultimately the subject existing under these conditions: simply put, the *person*" (rev., *KD* IV/3.1, 400-401; *CD* IV/3.1, 347). This, in Hartenstein's case, manifests itself in his need to use an approach — albeit modified — to the orders of creation as determinative for missionary methodology, for this supplies the necessary connection between the missionary act and the world.

Freytag says in his 1953 eulogy that "*missio Dei,* in the double sense of the sending of the Son by the Father and of the disciples by the Son, stood at the center of his understanding of the Word by which [Hartenstein] lived."[37]

---

37. Freytag, "Karl Hartenstein zum Gedenken," p. 1.

This "double sense," the transference of missionary responsibility from the Son to the church, is the impetus of *missio Dei* theology in its original form. Hartenstein sought to convince the church of her responsibility when the dearth of practical support for mission threatened the endeavor. Hartenstein's remarkable contribution should not be underestimated, but he neither intended to develop a Trinitarian grounding for the missionary act nor succeeded in doing so.

3. The North American Report: "Why Missions?"

The first five decades of the twentieth century took its toll on the missionary movement. Though the 1928 Jerusalem conference was contentious, Freytag observes that "missions had problems, but they were not a problem themselves."[38] The priority of Western missions and traditional patterns of missionary activity retained the initiative. After World War II, this initiative, located as it was in a perception of cultural authority, was wrested from Western hands, as became decisively apparent with the expulsion of Western missionaries from China. The so-called China-shock propelled Anglo-American missions into the kind of existential crisis previously experienced by German missions during the Versailles period. Despite the prolonged period of criticism, institutional longevity had helped maintain the colonialist pattern of missionary expansion. With China, this pattern suffered its final and, according to Newbigin, "complete extinction."[39] With much of the missionary movement invested in this pattern, at least functionally if not theologically, the destruction of the pattern seemingly threatened missions themselves. According to Max Warren, it inspired "a loss of certainty about the whole missionary enterprise, a loss of any sense of direction, a loss of confidence in the whole method of Mission."[40] T. V. Phillip extends the point, observing that "many felt that the

38. Walter Freytag, "Changes in the Patterns of Western Missions," in *The Ghana Assembly of the International Missionary Council, 28 December 1957 to 8 January 1958: Selected papers, with an essay on the role of the IMC,* ed. Ronald Kenneth Orchard (London: Edinburgh House, 1958), p. 138.

39. J. E. Lesslie Newbigin, "Mission to Six Continents," in *The Ecumenical Advance: A History of the Ecumenical Movement, 1948-1968,* ed. Harold E. Fey (London: SPCK, 1970), p. 177.

40. Max A. Warren, *Challenge and Response: Six Studies in Missionary Opportunity* (New York: Morehouse-Barlow, 1959), p. 131.

Western foreign missionary enterprise was coming to an end."[41] Even for those who did not consider this a terminal interruption, it certainly signified the end of a mission "epoch."[42]

An "orgy of self-criticism" resulted, an era obsessed with the failings of Western missions.[43] Freytag's preliminary contribution to Willingen, for example, surveyed four different methods before concluding that "there is one thing from which they have all in common failed to protect themselves: they all strayed into the torrent of the propagation of western civilization."[44] The historical context demanded a radical rethinking of the missionary act to distance it from this confederacy with power politics and provide a surer theological foundation. To this end, the IMC set "The Missionary Obligation of the Church" as the theme for its 1952 conference, with the intention of developing a constructive biblical and theological basis for missions.[45] In addition to the two reports commissioned by the IMC, which became known as the "Dutch" and the "American" reports, a general call produced a number of constructive studies.[46] Numerous historical treatments of Willingen already exist, so my investigation will examine the particular contribution of the "American report."

Missions and the Doctrine of the Trinity

The commission responsible for the American report was charged with the first aim of the Willingen study: "To restate the universal missionary obli-

41. T. V. Phillip, "Ecumenical Discussion on the Relation between Church and Mission from 1938-1952," in *A Vision for Man: Essays on Faith, Theology and Society*, ed. Samuel Amirtham (Madras, India: Christian Literature Society, 1978), p. 212.

42. Hendrik Kraemer, "Mission im Wandel der Völkerwelt," in *Der Auftrag der Kirche in der modernen Welt: Festgabe zum siebzigsten Geburtstag von Emil Brunner*, ed. Peter Vogelsanger (Zürich: Zwingli Verlag, 1959), p. 294.

43. Max A. Warren, "The Christian Mission and the Cross," in *Missions under the Cross*, ed. Norman Goodall (London: Edinburgh House, 1953), p. 27.

44. Walter Freytag, "The Meaning and Purpose of the Christian Mission," *International Review of Mission* 39, no. 2 (1950): 156.

45. T. V. Phillip, *Edinburgh to Salvador: Twentieth Century Ecumenical Missiology, A Historical Study of the Ecumenical Discussions on Mission* (Delhi: CSS and ISPCK, 1999), p. 46.

46. For the Dutch report, see "The Biblical Foundations of Foreign Missions," 1952, International Missionary Council Archives 1910-1961, Microfiche 264007.10 (Geneva: WCC, 1952).

gation of the Church (i) as grounded in the eternal Gospel, and (ii) in relation to the present historical situation."[47] Chaired by Paul Lehmann, it is this study that locates the missionary act in the doctrine of the Trinity. The final report, "Why Missions?" begins with a section entitled "The Christian Mission and the Triune God." It holds that "the missionary obligation of the Church is grounded in the outgoing activity of God, whereby, as Creator, Redeemer, Governor and Guide, God establishes and includes the world and men within His fulfilling purposes and fellowship."[48] Already at the 1950 annual meeting of the Division of Foreign Missions, Lehmann noted that "one of the real points where the missionary obligation had to be thought through concerned the Church's faith in the Triune God."[49] The minutes of this meeting record F. W. Dillistone's call for a theology of mission that needed to

> . . . witness to a missionary god [sic] who sends forth his missionary son in missionary spirit. . . . The biblical God is not abstract, unknown; but he is a God who calls, who redeems, who enters historical process. The Christ of the Christian faith is not primarily a Christ-idea, attractive and appealing, a divine logos, the divine rational principle of all existence. He is not even an event in time which eludes our categories, but he is rather a saviour, a seeker of the lost, a lifter of the fallen. The Holy Spirit of the Christian faith is not an abstract, super-rational life force, or an esprit des corps but primarily the perpetuator and the witnesser to Christ. It is preeminently the missionary spirit.[50]

47. Of the five proposed aims, Norman Goodall, then secretary of the IMC, attached "particular importance" to the first aim. For a list of the five aims and an introduction to the study, see Norman Goodall, "First Principles," *International Review of Mission* 39, no. 3 (1950): 257-62.

48. For the American report, see "Why Missions? Report of Commission I on the Biblical and Theological Basis of Missions," 1952, Paul L. Lehmann Collection, Special Collections (Princeton Theological Seminary, Box 41.2, Princeton, NJ). Though Willingen considered making the document available, "Why Missions?" was never formally published and remains in manuscript form. An abridged version, minus some of the more contentious elements, appeared in Paul Lehmann, "The Missionary Obligation of the Church," *Theology Today* 9, no. 1 (1952): 20-38.

49. Theodore F. Romig, "Minutes of the Study Conference: Toronto, January 7-8, 1952," p. 3. Paul L. Lehmann Collection, Special Collections (Princeton Theological Seminary, Box 41.2, Princeton, NJ).

50. "Minutes of the Sectional Discussion Group 'A': 'The Gospel and the Commission,'" 1950, pp. 2-3, International Missionary Council Archives 1910-1961, Microfiche

While noteworthy from its historical perspective, Lehmann's observation might suggest that his commission met with an overtly Trinitarian intention. The minutes do not reflect this. The key focus is one of the pattern of God's acting in history, and reference to the Trinity provided a theological medium for this prior concern.[51] God acts in judgment and redemption in the revolutionary movements of the period, especially within communism.

The commission's discussion began with the question of "the difference between a relevant and an irrelevant mission in the world" ("Why Missions?" p. 3). What form does the Christian faith assume when it ventures into the world? Theodore Gill, in his popular rendition of the report, notes epigrammatically: "Two documents lie behind the new effort to understand the missionary obligation. One is the New Testament; the other, your morning newspaper."[52] Christology tells us that "the communication and implementation in the world of the reality of God in Jesus Christ is a dynamic, not a static responsibility" ("Why Missions?" pp. 2-3). The Christian life must embody a corresponding dynamism, for it follows both "the way Jesus Christ is related to and at work in the world" and "the revolutionary approach to life and thought made by the Apostles and their followers" (p. 3). As individuals and communities participate in this existence, they "outthink and outlive their contemporaries in giving meaning and motivation to culture" (p. 3).

Mission, by extension, becomes "a creative enterprise of word and deed in the formation and the transformation of individual lives and of cultural and social patterns."[53] The report is constructed around this cul-

---

260033.9 (Geneva: WCC, 1950). See also F. W. Dillistone, "The Dispensation of the Spirit," in *Missions under the Cross*, ed. Goodall, pp. 82-83. Likewise, Eugene Smith, in his closing address, notes that reference to God's triune nature leads to two points. First, "truth in its ultimate form is not propositional, but personal." Second, "truth, being personal, is real not so much in being as in relationship." Eugene L. Smith, "The Challenge of the Future," 1950, p. 1, International Missionary Council Archives 1910-1961, Microfiche 260033.9 (Geneva: WCC, 1950).

51. Such a conclusion is borne out by reference to this same commission's post-Willingen discussions, which ignore Willingen's Trinitarian affirmation and focuses instead on time and history. See Theodore F. Romig, "Minutes of the Commission on the Missionary Obligation, March 13-14," 1953, Paul L. Lehmann Collection, Special Collections (Princeton Theological Seminary, Box 41.1, Princeton, NJ).

52. Theodore Gill, "Christian Missions: Whence and Wither?" 1952, p. 2, International Missionary Council Archives 1910-1961, Microfiche 264007.6 (Geneva: WCC, 1952).

53. Lehmann, "The Missionary Obligation of the Church," p. 22.

tural center point. As Jesus Christ sets people on the path to dynamic living, "the lordship of the living Christ" provides the "point of departure for the missionary activity of the Church" (p. 3). With success in the cultural sphere as the end of the Christian dynamic, "an exclusive concentration upon Jesus Christ is, however, not enough" (p. 3). A theological account of the church's missionary obligation required a shift "from vigorous Christo-centricity to thoroughgoing trinitarianism" (p. 6).[54]

Not all members accepted the juxtaposition. Lehmann reports that "the more vigorous 'Christocentrics' among us urged that we begin by preaching Christ."[55] An emphasis on the Trinity, nevertheless, "prevailed"; culture as the proper realm of missionary activity held the priority.[56] Proceeding from an appreciation of the "reconciling action of the triune God" changes the missionary task from "an ingenious secretarial maneuvering of the territorial and financial expansion of the mission and its efficient administration" to a "creative enterprise of word and deed in the formation and the transformation of individual lives and of cultural and social patterns" ("Why Missions?" p. 6). This precluded the traditional missionary task of planting churches, for "a copy of a copy is bound to be pretty bad, especially if the copy's copy is a reflection in a distorting mirror" (p. 32). Traditional missionary readings of the Great Commission, due precisely to a christological overemphasis, had failed to link "the explicit mandate of Jesus, the Lord, with the triune name of God" (p. 3).[57] With a

54. Lehmann says that, "although we began with rooting the missionary obligation in the lordship of Christ, we found that this simple Christological starting point was not enough and that unless we started with the full apostolic confession of the Trinity we were not doing full justice to the Gospel and to the mind of the churches." "Minutes of the Study Conference: Toronto, January 7-8," 1952, p. 3, Paul L. Lehmann Collection, Special Collections (Princeton Theological Seminary, Box 41.2, Princeton, NJ). However, of this general trend, as Berkouwer suggests, "the characterization 'from vigorous Christo-centricity to thoroughgoing trinitarianism' as 'the direction of missionary theology' is meaningful only starting from a wrongly understood christocentrism." G. C. Berkouwer, *Studies in Dogmatics: The Church*, trans. James E. Davison, vol. 18 (Grand Rapids: Eerdmans, 1976), p. 395 n. 11.

55. "Minutes of the Study Conference: Toronto, January 7-8," p. 3.

56. "Minutes of the Study Conference: Toronto, January 7-8," p. 3.

57. This coordination of Trinitarian doctrine with culture follows the conclusion of Cochrane's *Christianity and Classical Culture,* and his depiction of the original culture-creating function of the doctrine. See Lehmann, "The Missionary Obligation of the Church," p. 22. The report draws a parallel between the social instability of the Greco-Roman world and the world at the end of the Second World War. It states that "the ground

proper Trinitarian reading, the missionary duty was not one of saving souls but one of "the sensitive and total response of the Church to what the triune God has done and is doing in the world" (p. 6). The debt of later constructions of *missio Dei* to this is clear. Saving souls is only a "peripheral" goal, because it is driven by ecclesiastical competition and "the arrogance of spiritual security" (p. 6). This violates "the missionary obligation by abandoning the individual to frustrating isolation from his social and cultural matrix" (p. 6).[58] God's subjectivity in reconciling the world to himself is here distanced from church institutions and placed in the world, that is, in culture-creating sociopolitical revolutions.

Acknowledging the priority of God's triune acting in culture "exposes the heretical root" nourishing the emphasis on conversion — that root being a "Unitarianism of the Son" (pp. 6-7). This position follows the work of H. Richard Niebuhr, who, in his presentation to the commission, characterized his theological standpoint as "Trinitarian, that is to say it is neither Christocentric, nor spiritualistic nor creativistic but all of these at once. In this sense it seeks to be theocentric."[59] This contribution developed into his 1946 article — quoted extensively in the report — entitled "The Doctrine of the Trinity and the Unity of the Church."[60] Niebuhr regards Unitarianism, which he defines as an overemphasis on the actions of one member of the Trinity to the detriment of the other two, as commonplace throughout Christian history. It manifests itself, in terms of the Father, by overemphasizing creation and natural theology, in terms of the Son, through individualistic piety, and in terms of the Spirit, as mysticism and immanentism.

The church, Niebuhr argues "must undertake to correct the overemphasis and partialities . . . not by means of a new over-emphasis but by means of a synthesized formula in which all the partial insights and con-

---

and the framework of what the Church has to say in the world are the same and the cultural alternatives to Christianity in the modern world — humanism and syncretism, polytheism and totalitarianism — run back to strangely similar anticipations in the Gnosticism and Stoicism, the Mysteries and the Caesarism of the Hellenistic world." "Why Missions?" p. 4.

58. The presence of such language is already suggestive of how German missions became attracted to Willingen's Trinitarianism.

59. This was later published as H. Richard Niebuhr, "An Attempt at a Theological Analysis of Missionary Motivation," *Occasional Bulletin of Missionary Research* 14, no. 1 (1963): 1.

60. H. Richard Niebuhr, "The Doctrine of the Trinity and the Unity of the Church," *Theology Today* 3, no. 3 (1946): 371-84. Such is its seeming significance that it was republished under the title "Theological Unitarianisms" in *Theology Today* 40, no. 2 (1983): 150-57.

victions are combined."[61] An exclusive focus on Christ militates against connecting him to "the Creator of nature and Governor of history as well as to the Spirit immanent in creation and in the Christian Christ."[62] In its most extreme form, this ethical dualism leads to "an ontological bifurcation of reality," with a material realm opposed to Christ, and a spiritual realm guided by Christ.[63] The lack of a robust Trinitarianism, in other words, prompts an undue emphasis on the transcendent over against nature and history. This domesticates Christ and isolates individuals from their cultural matrix by focusing the effective power of the gospel on the soul and on institutions designed to care for the soul. The report posits the Trinitarian formula as

> . . . a corrective to the idea that Jesus is just "my pal" and to the tendency of the average minister to form a mental image of God indistinguishable from himself. The Trinitarian concept of God implies that men can, indeed, find God, for He is at work moulding and shaping the stability of the world in Christ, and enlightening and regenerating by his Holy Spirit. The Trinitarian doctrine lifts me out of my isolation, puts me in a global dimension, and says: "Get going in this direction."[64]

Trinitarian doctrine provides a defense against charges of propaganda and imperialism as these are the result of an improper christological emphasis that expresses itself in an easy identification of Christ with domestic structures. The present acting of the triune God propels Christians into an engaged life, abandoning the safe shelters of the church for culture as witnesses to the in-breaking reign of God.[65]

It is evident that the juxtaposition of christocentrism and Trinitarianism, with its accompanying warning against "a new over-emphasis," occurred as a reaction to Barth. Newbigin reinforces this conclusion, recollecting that

61. Niebuhr, "The Doctrine of the Trinity and the Unity of the Church," p. 383.
62. H. Richard Niebuhr, *Christ and Culture* (New York: Harper, 1951), pp. 80-81.
63. Niebuhr, *Christ and Culture*, p. 81.
64. "Minutes of the Study Conference: Toronto, January 7-8," p. 3.
65. John Howard Yoder would complain of this position that Niebuhr attributes "to the World that intrinsic ontological dignity which neither the New Testament nor history allows it to claim. We must affirm the reality of the world, but not by ascribing to it the right to the place it usurps." Yoder, "The Otherness of the Church," *The Mennonite Quarterly Review* 35, no. 4 (1961): 294.

... for a long time, the World Council of Churches was criticized by some people as being too christo-monist or christo-centric. The most formidable theological proponent of that criticism was H. Richard Niebuhr who continually accused the WCC during its early years, when its theology was very much dominated by Karl Barth, of being too christo-centric.[66]

That is to say, Barth's theology too narrowly demarcated legitimate experiences of God. This was not an uncommon perception. Wilhelm Andersen, summarizing the Lutheran version of Willingen, articulates a similar position. In 1935, the shift to christocentrism was vital for the "rejection of very dangerous forms of a natural theology."[67] However, continuing with this project after the event renders "Barth's Christological concentration" susceptible to the charge of "Christomonism."[68] It is "the particular theological task of our day to take care that the christological concentration in Church and theology given by God in the time between the two world wars does not lead to a Christomonism ... but to a Trinitarian structure of thought." The defining characteristic of this is an evident progression "from creation by reconciliation to the new creation." While Andersen praises the *Church Dogmatics* for being "nothing other than an exultation of the divine Trinity," Barth's treatment of law and gospel reveals a deficient Trinitarianism. His positing of "a single covenant between God and humanity prompts the question of whether the differentiated character of this covenant emerges clearly enough." Other covenants and the shades of the law indicate different experiences, which the doctrine of the Trinity encompasses in a way christology alone cannot. One can only understand the covenant in Jesus Christ "if

66. Newbigin continues this way: "I think there can be good and bad reasons behind this criticism of a so-called christo-centric or christo-monist stance. The good reason, of course, is that we must never think of Jesus apart from the whole Trinitarian doctrine of God, and if I found Richard Niebuhr more clearly committed to a Trinitarian view of God I would feel more sympathetic to his criticism." J. E. Lesslie Newbigin, *Come Holy Spirit — Renew the Whole Creation* (Birmingham, UK: Selly Oaks College, 1990), p. 3. Yoder also describes Niebuhr's position as "modalistic trinitarianism." John Howard Yoder, "Sacrament as Social Process: Christ the Transformer of Culture," in *The Royal Priesthood: Essays Ecclesiological and Ecumenical,* ed. John Howard Yoder and Michael Cartwright (Grand Rapids: Eerdmans, 1994), p. 371 n. 14.

67. Wilhelm Andersen, *Das wirkende Wort: Theologische Berichte über die Vollversammlung des Lutherischen Weltbundes Hannover 1952* (Munich: Evangelischer Presseverband für Bayern, 1953), p. 62.

68. Andersen, *Das wirkende Wort,* p. 68.

one considers the threefold reality of the self revealing God."[69] Though the American report does not enlist the concept of the law, the two positions agree that Barth's christocentrism closes the space necessary to an adequate theology of the new creation and, by extension, that a revised Trinitarian position allows for other varieties of religious experience.

This leads to two clear and related conclusions. First, the report, Günther argues, perceived the theological roots of increasing Christian irrelevance in world affairs to lie in dialectical theology and the dichotomy it established between the divine and the human.[70] Whether the report developed its argument in this reactive sense is difficult to substantiate, but Günther highlights an important facet of the basic logic: the Trinitarianism of *missio Dei* theology developed, not in continuity with, but in direct opposition to Barth. His christocentrism separates the Christian community from the new creation by way of an ontological bifurcation of reality, and that is only surmounted by reference to the Trinity. Second, while the report develops an important emphasis on the church's missionary nature, it nonetheless denudes the church as a consequence — albeit unintended — of juxtaposing christology and the Trinity. Christocentrism led to an undue distinction between redemptive history and simple history. As the guardian of this redemptive history, the church came to focus on herself, thereby defining conversion as a process managed by an ecclesiastical structure that isolated individuals from their necessary cultural matrix.[71]

69. Andersen, *Das wirkende Wort*, pp. 73-74. The translation is by Andersen himself. See Wilhelm Andersen, "Dr. Kraemer's Contribution to the Understanding of the Nature of Revelation," *International Review of Mission* 46, no. 4 (1957): 369.

70. Günther says that "in this the Americans saw a retreat from the world — an accusation which had accompanied dialectical theology from its inception, and by no means from the American side alone." Wolfgang Günther, *Von Edinburgh nach Mexico City: die ekklesiologischen Bemühungen der Weltmissionskonferenzen, 1910-1963* (Stuttgart: Evangelischer Missionsverlag, 1970), p. 101.

71. For example, upon reading the preparatory material circulated prior to Willingen, including the contributions of Hartenstein, Freytag, Warren, and Hoekendijk, Lehmann wrote that "I was a little oppressed by the feeling that the Church was talking to itself in blissful innocence of the very great likelihood that what the Church was saying would not only not convince the world, but would make no sense to the world. In a word, the papers bear out Hoekendijk's challenge. If this should happen at Willingen, it would be disastrous." Paul Lehmann to Erik W. Nielsen, 4 May 1952 (Paul L. Lehmann Collection, Special Collections (Princeton Theological Seminary, Box 41.4, Princeton, NJ). This was a prescient comment in light of what did occur.

Trinity doctrine resists this domestication by forcing the Christian community into culture as the proper sphere of God's activity. The church's self-occupation required a reorientation to the world through an emphasis on the historical dynamic produced by God's triune acting.

The Strategy of God's Contemporaneity

One early objection noted that the shift from christology to Trinitarianism "led us from Jesus whom we know to a vague 'action of the Triune God' which we know only vaguely." Lehmann replied that the report does not expound Trinity doctrine "on the basis of a theological formula," but certain sections "form a kind of commentary on the action of the Triune God."[72] The report establishes a pattern it terms "The Strategy of God's Contemporaneity" as the means by which the Trinitarian grounding of mission finds expression ("Why Missions?" p. 8). Trinitarian theology focuses the "light of the gospel upon historical and social change that every present situation may be understood in terms of the strategy — not of its own but of God's contemporaneity" (p. 19). After the resurrection, the gospel stimulates a dynamic, a mandate; it does not stabilize, but revolutionizes.

This pattern of breaking down and building up is the contemporary form of the triune God's act; and identifying God's act with this pattern enabled a direct connection between historical progression and mission.[73] For Lehmann, "it is misleading to speak of the history of missions for there is a juxtaposition of missions and history." He continues that "the concept of mission and time forbids us to think in terms of the expansion of the mission, because every situation is pregnant with God's time."[74] Mission is history. A revolution is underway as "the old age, before the resurrection," is overcome by "the new age, following it" ("Why Missions?" p. 14). Historical change is not a good in itself, but is "God's way of pressing home his plans for the fulfillment of His purposes." It is "the instrument of God's new order" in that change "breaks through and breaks down the self-justifying pat-

---

72. "Minutes of the Study Conference: Toronto, January 7-8," p. 4.

73. "Minutes of the Study Conference: Toronto, January 7-8," p. 9.

74. Theodore F. Romig, "Minutes of the Study Commission in the Theological Basis of the Mission, November 20-22," 1953, p. 2-3, International Missionary Council Archives 1910-1961, Microfiche 261126.8 (Geneva: WCC, 1953).

terns and pretensions of the old order" (p. 18). With social and political revolution the most radical instance of change, the report, quoting Victor Hugo, notes the "significance of revolution as the vehicle of cosmic order and purpose" for accounts of the "context of the gospel story and the missionary proclamation of the triune God." Revolutionary movements are "the place to look for what God is doing, and the place to begin to understand 'what's up'" (p. 21). During the 1950s, this strategy of God's contemporaneity was "decisively evident in the present situation in the Communist movement" (p. 19). In a letter to John Mackay, Lehmann notes that "the Communist movement forced one concretely to face the revolutionary dynamic of our time, as no other phenomenon did. It is this symptomatic or symbolic role of communism in God's activity that the report underlines."[75] God's act in bringing about the kingdom indicates a missionary "pattern," of which communism afforded the most potent contemporary example.

The reference to communism, given the role it played in opposition to America, allowed the report to distinguish the missionary act from traditional accounts whereby the Christian West sent missionaries to the non-Christian world. God's act encompassed the whole of creation and thus included the West within the purview of missionary activity. Gill notes that "the boundaries of world missions have now coincided. The mission field is coterminous with the world."[76] This severs a hegemonic identification of the authority of the gospel and Western civilization. Following Niebuhr's *Christ and Culture,* the report describes as "idolatry" the attempt to identify Western culture with Christianity ("Why Missions?" p. 25). The church must acknowledge the "truth in the charge that western Christianity has been the tool of imperialism and must beware of any identification between the church and the western democracies, their policies or their cultural patterns."[77] It continues that "there has never been a Christian culture," only "more or less Christianized cultures as well as cultures falling away from Christianity"(p. 25).

75. Paul Lehmann to John A. Mackay, 31 January 1952, Paul L. Lehmann Collection, Special Collections (Princeton Theological Seminary, Box 41.1, Princeton, NJ). Here Lehmann acknowledges a "lack of clarity about the nature and role of the Holy Spirit," and hoped that Willingen would "break new theological ground, at precisely this point."

76. Gill, "Christian Missions: Whence and Wither?" p. 2.

77. Theodore F. Romig, "Minutes of the Meeting of Commission 1 held at Buck Hill Falls on April 28-30," 1951, p. 4, Paul L. Lehmann Collection, Special Collections (Princeton Theological Seminary, Box 41.1, Princeton, NJ).

It is impossible for Christians to "abstract" themselves from the local culture; they bear it wherever they go. Some aspects of Western culture should be promulgated, and others not. Non-Western cultures, likewise, have much to offer the Western church. This global perspective recon-figures the form of the task. Mission was not a geographical movement but the cultivation of an authentic faith — one that would advertise the living truth of the Christian faith to culture and society. Was not the global tur-moil the result of the failure of both the church and Christian nations to act in accordance with the essential precepts of the faith? Communism consti-tuted "a judgment on the Christian church, on the things left undone: pro-tection for the helpless and exploited, food for the hungry, rest and recre-ation for the toil-worn" (p. 23).[78] It equally demanded a response in terms of the "adaptation and purification of democratic traditions and institu-tions commensurate with the factors making for social disintegration" (p. 20). This challenge to the church and to the sociopolitical structures of Western civilization meant that "the missionary movement has passed from the tasks, the problems, and the procedure of an extensive, to those of an intensive cultivation of the field" (p. 2). Mission was the "total life" of the church, "as manifested in each activity, it is a witness to what God has done, will do, and is now doing" (p. 16). These activities include preaching, teach-ing, breaking of bread and prayer, steadfast witness, peacemaking, healing, serving the Lord, suffering, and rejoicing.

A Preliminary Reaction

Rosin notes of *missio Dei* that "the role which the English (American) ex-pression 'God's mission' explicitly or implicitly played at the conference at Willingen was a decisive one for the genesis of this formula."[79] The Trini-tarian grounding of mission originated in this report and undergirds the

---

78. Such language reflects an actual conclusion by David Paton, a China missionary who understood the expulsion to be a direct result of missionary failures and the resulting divine judgment. See David M. Paton, "First Thoughts on the Debacle of Christian Missions in China," *International Review of Mission* 40, no. 4 (1951): 411-20; see also Paton, *Christian Missions and the Judgment of God* (London: SCM, 1953).

79. H. H. Rosin, *'Missio Dei': An Examination of the Origin, Contents and Function of the Term in Protestant Missiological Discussion* (Leiden: Interuniversity Institute for Missiological and Ecumenical Research, Department of Missiology, 1972), p. 23.

later Hoekendijk-led study, *Missionary Structure of the Congregation.*[80] One of the central problems in *missio Dei* theology — that of discerning God's acting in the political, cultural, religious, or social forces — is an immediate consequence of this theological pattern of linking missionary activity to revolutionary movements. The triune God acts in breaking down and building up, and the corresponding missionary act identifies and participates in this act. Reference to the doctrine of the Trinity opens the cultural space as the proper realm of the missionary movement, but, once it is opened, specific reference to the Trinitarian persons and the form of their acting falls away. This helps explain *missio Dei* theology's clear dysfunction — but also its wide usage.

The previously examined divide between the Anglo-American and German positions comes back into focus. For the Continental commentators, the American report's overrealized eschatology stimulated the fear of a return to an activist strain of thinking in which historical progress and the arrival of the kingdom of God were, in some sense, coterminous. As Günther suggests, the report illustrates that "American theology never took part in the radical break between nature and revelation." Such circumspection, however, proved secondary to a greater danger. Reference to the Trinity allowed missions to obviate Barth's undue disjunction of God and creation. Günther continues that "the Americans succeeded in avoiding, by attention to the triune working of God, an unbridgeable dialectic between the Word of God and nature."[81] This link between the doctrine of the Trinity and creation seemingly confirmed what German mission had long argued, and enabled a critical reappropriation of the *völkisch* emphasis that had become identified with National Socialism and repudiated as such after World War II.

This connection between Trinity and culture opened the necessary space for the church and her missionary task. Günther suggests that "the distinction between nature and task, the being and witnessing character of the church are overcome from the inside; already the being of the community is a reflex of the revelation of God, re-*actio* of the *actio* of God and

80. Bosch regards the later direction taken by *missio Dei* to be embryonic in the American report. While the political ramifications undergo development, as to the underlying Trinitarianism, it is more accurate to view the problematic developments in the MSC as in direct continuity with the American report. David J. Bosch, *Witness to the World: The Christian Mission in Theological Perspective* (London: Marshall, Morgan and Scott, 1980), pp. 179-80.

81. Günther, *Von Edinburgh nach Mexico City,* pp. 101, 104.

thus a witness to the living acting God."[82] With the link between history and redemption, while problematic for the Continentals, church became "an event linked into that chain of events through which a gracious Lord is reconciling the world to himself" ("Why Missions?" p. 16). Ontological gravitas accompanied this historicizing of the missionary act. Because God is "a missionary God," the Christian community is a missionary community, and so is the anthropology of the new creation. "The missionary impulse is born with the New Man, because to be a Christian is to be a missionary" (p. 4). With missionary activity the "very character of faith," "*all* Christians are missionaries or they are not Christians," and the church "does not *have* missions, but *is* Mission."[83]

This missionary emphasis, proceeding as it does through the doctrine of the Trinity, secured a common ground for the erstwhile combative Anglo-Americans and Germans. Rosin describes *missio Dei* theology as "the Trojan horse through which the (unassimilated) 'American' vision was fetched into the well-guarded walls of the ecumenical theology of mission."[84] After defending itself against the Anglo-American position, *missio Dei* seemingly confirmed German mission's treatment of *Volkstum* and its link to God's acting in creation through both the law and the gospel. *Missio Dei*, in this way, provides an ecumenically affirmed rubric while suffering from significant internal discord.

82. Günther, *Von Edinburgh nach Mexico City,* p. 104.

83. Gill, "Christian Missions: Whence and Wither?" pp. 4, 7, 8.

84. Rosin, '*Missio Dei,*' p. 26. Hartenstein illustrates well the German fear of the American position in his report on the 1938 IMC Tambaram conference. The American concentration on the kingdom of God supplied Christendom with "a comprehensive password with which to wage the war to realize God's kingdom in all areas of social and political life. What moves our American brothers is an unbroken trust in people, a tough determination and a truly passionate belief that God's reign has to be established on earth at this time." Karl Hartenstein, "Tambaram, wie es arbeitete," in *Das Wunder der Kirche unter den Völkern der Erde: Bericht über Weltmissions-Konferenz in Tambaram,* ed. Martin Schlunk (Stuttgart: Evangelischer Missionsverlag, 1939), pp. 41-42. Quoted by Wilhelm Richebächer, "*Missio Dei:* The Basis of Mission Theology or a Wrong Path?" *International Review of Mission* 92, no. 4 (2003): 603 n. 24.

Willingen, 1952

Hartenstein's Contribution

Hartenstein's original articulation of *missio Dei* occurred eighteen years before Willingen. Did he, during the intervening period, develop an alternate Trinitarian grounding for missions? No. Hartenstein's contribution to the conference's preparatory work, entitled "Missions and Eschatology," recasts his earlier position in line with Oscar Cullmann's eschatology.[85] For Manfred Linz, "no other theology was so determinative on the European continent for the present grounding of mission than that of O. Cullmann's understanding of *Heilsgeschichte*."[86] Hartenstein certainly used Cullmann as reinforcement of his earlier position, saying that it was the "new realization of redemptive-historical thinking" that provided "a new grounding both for our witness and for our act, in the present situation of church and mission within a world of the greatest disruption" ("Zur Neubesinnung," p. 9). *Heilsgeschichte* encapsulates Christ's decisive act in the past, his future action, and present working. This act of Jesus Christ leads to the question of the content "of this interim period between the first and second coming of the Lord" (p. 9).[87] Drawing on Karl Heim's *Jesus der Weltvollender*, Hartenstein offers three answers.[88] First,

85. Karl Hartenstein, "Mission and Eschatology," 1952, International Missionary Council Archives 1910-1961, Microfiche 264007.10 (Geneva: World Council of Churches, 1952). This is an abridged version of his 1951 article, Karl Hartenstein, "Zur Neubesinnung über das Wesen der Mission," in *Deutsche Evangelische Weltmission Jahrbuch 1951*, ed. Walter Freytag (Hamburg: Verlag der Deutschen Evangelischen Missions-Hilfe, 1951). Hereafter quotations from this source will appear in parentheses in the text.

86. Manfred Linz, *Anwalt der Welt: zur Theologie der Mission* (Stuttgart: Kreuz-Verlag, 1964), p. 158. Cullmann remains significant for missiology. Bosch, a student of Cullmann, says that his approach provides the "soundest base for an understanding of the eschatological nature of mission from a postmodern perspective." Bosch, *Transforming Mission*, p. 504. One of the key criticisms Barth makes of Cullmann's *Christ and Time* (1946), however, concerns his relegation of the resurrection to the end of the book, thus giving it no actual eschatological significance, i.e., no significance for determining the contemporary acting of the church (*CD*, III/2, 443).

87. Freytag, too, argued that the Christian community "lives in a time-span between two poles: resurrection and second coming, world reconciliation and world redemption." Freytag, "The Meaning and Purpose of the Christian Mission," p. 158.

88. Karl Heim, *Jesus der Weltvollender: der Glaube an die Versöhnung und Weltverwandlung* (Berlin: Furche, 1937).

this period displays the hidden rule of the resurrected Christ as he builds his community through the power of the Spirit. Hartenstein rejects every position that neglects "the prospect of God's continuous saving action in the present time," for Jesus, sitting at the Father's right hand, "calls and gathers His ecclesia to be His instrument in performing His design of salvation until His Second Coming."[89] Second, the Christian community becomes his instrument, the acting of Christ in history. She is "the visible sign of his invisible presence" ("Zur Neubesinnung," p. 14). Third, "mission is the means by which the ascended Lord makes this interim period into his plan of salvation, through which he gives to this interim period its authentic meaning" (p. 12). Christ, as the ascended one, "is present to his community in the Spirit; the critical and central function of the community is her missionary witness" (p. 15). Traditional approaches to mission retain a certain validity, but they are insufficient when conceived from a salvation history perspective since they exist at a distance from the church. The church has forgotten that "she is a missionary, apostolic church," replacing the missionary acting of Jesus Christ with a "supra-temporal, true doctrine which remains the same for all times" (p. 20). This approach to doctrine "paralyzed the will to do mission, and obscured the meaning of the redemptive-historical character of the interim" (p. 20). Thus, for Hartenstein, it is "the greatest weakness of the church and mission that she no longer sees herself in this redemptive-historical framework, that she is no longer aware that she is to be the instrument of the Lord for the realization of his plan for salvation" (p. 18). Hartenstein's key concern remains that of an apologia for the missionary existence of the Christian community.

With regard to the doctrine of the Trinity and to *missio Dei*, Rosin maintains of Hartenstein that "neither he, nor his friends brought it with them to Willingen as a watchword. The preparatory paper written by him, on 'Mission and Eschatology', does not in any way point in that direction."[90] Nor did any of Hartenstein's preparatory work contain a single ref-

---

89. Hartenstein, "Mission and Eschatology," p. 3.

90. Rosin, '*Missio Dei*,' p. 7. Leading into Willingen, Hartenstein's central concern was that the term *Heilsgeschichte* would "be very difficult for the Anglo-American spirit," since they possessed no "category" to understand it. He recommends that all members of the theological study group read Cullmann's *Christus und die Zeit (Christ and Time)* so that the Anglo-Americans might appreciate the Continentals' main concern. Karl Hartenstein to Erik W. Nielsen, 7 February 1952, International Missionary Council Archives 1910-1961, Mi-

erence to Barth. Rather, according to Günther, Cullmann provided Hartenstein with the kind of eschatological framework that could situate his Pietist core.[91] Contra the received history, while Hartenstein initiated the language of *missio Dei* and developed a profound articulation of the church's missionary nature, he neither mediated Barth to Willingen nor developed a Trinitarian grounding for mission.

"The Missionary Calling of the Church"

This diffidence toward the doctrine of the Trinity continues at Willingen itself. Not a single keynote address, including those delivered by members of the American commission, dealt with the doctrine. Rather, both Paul Minear and John Mackay (an *ex officio* member of the American commission) restated a Christocentric approach. Mackay, for example, maintained that "to be a Christian, to be a missionary, is, in the completest sense 'to adhere to Jesus Christ', to be supremely Christo-centric both in one's theology and in one's behaviour."[92] The Trinitarian absence persists across Willingen's published findings. Only with the final report does some reference to doctrine finally appear.

As a preparatory document, the American report was but one contribution besides those of Hoekendijk, Warren, Freytag, Hartenstein, and the Dutch report. It was left to the "Study Group I," chaired by Russell Chandran and including Hartenstein, Lehmann, and Hoekendijk, to draft the final statement. Following two days of discussion, this group issued a report entitled "The Theological Basis of the Missionary Obligation."[93] Widespread disappointment greeted its publication. Blauw, himself a contributor to the Dutch report, described it as "extremely weak."[94] The report was, in ecumenical parlance, "received but not adopted" and relegated

---

crofiche 264007.3 (Geneva: WCC, 1952). While Cullmann did not figure in the "American" report, he was not ignored. See Arthur C. Cochrane, "Eschatology and Missions," 1951, International Missionary Council Archives 1910-1961, Microfiche 264007.5-6 (Geneva: WCC, 1951).

91. Günther, *Von Edinburgh nach Mexico City,* p. 89.

92. John A. Mackay, "The Great Commission and the Church Today," in *Missions under the Cross,* ed. Goodall, p. 133.

93. Goodall, ed., *Missions under the Cross,* pp. 238-45.

94. Johannes Blauw, "Willingen 1952," *De Heerbaan* 5 (1952): 302.

to "interim" status. Erik Nielsen, in a conciliatory letter to Lehmann, notes his disappointment over the reception of the theological group's report.[95] That Nielsen wrote to Lehmann in particular demonstrates his — and thus the American report's — influence over the interim report's direction.

The absence of detailed minutes and the ecumenical modesty characterizing personal accounts makes it impossible to make a historical reconstruction of the discussion. However, it would seem that the conference feared that an undue link with political movements negated geographical and, by extension, evangelistic concepts of mission. Set within a political framework, "to the ends of the earth" would be interpreted in only imperialist or colonialist terms. In direct negation of the American report, the final conference statement held that "mission involves both geographical extension and also intensive penetration of all spheres of life."[96] The two need not be mutually exclusive.

Lehmann was joined in this battle by Hoekendijk. For Newbigin, their positions were closely related, and together they tried "to swing missionary thinking away from the 'church-centered' model which had dominated it since Tambaram and to speak more of God's work in the secular world."[97] Hoedemaker holds an alternative position: for him, Hoekendijk's ideas "diverged just as widely from the North American report" because it "emphasized the responsibility of the church to be aware of the 'signs of the times', of what God is saying through the events of the day (especially in China)." He attributes this divergence to the "classic issue" of reducing eschatology to political involvement, which so divided the American and Continental positions.

Here, however, Hoedemaker neglects the American report's focus on revolution. He continues that, for Hoekendijk, "the church, usually preferring tradition over revolution and thereby misjudging the character of history, chooses *Volk* rather than *Gesellschaft* (society) as its sociological point of reference." In reaction to the kind of static approaches to culture that enabled compromised *Volk*-based mission theories, Hoekendijk exactly emphasized the pattern of revolution as this militated against the cultural conservatism characteristic of the Christendom church. Such "worldwide

95. Erik W. Nielsen to Paul Lehmann, 15 September 1952, Paul L. Lehmann Collection, Special Collections (Princeton Theological Seminary, Box 41.1, Princeton, NJ).

96. Goodall, ed., *Missions under the Cross*, pp. 240, 191.

97. J. E. Lesslie Newbigin, *Unfinished Agenda: An Autobiography* (Geneva: WCC, 1985), p. 138.

revolutionary ferment provides the opportunity for a missionary church to develop *kerygma, koinonia,* and *diakonia* in an eschatological perspective." Here Hoekendijk "closely associated himself" with the likes of Lehmann, who enabled Hoekendijk to develop "a theological interpretation of the obviously revolutionary character of contemporary history."[98]

It was wrong to speak of revelation's "hiddenness," for if the living history of redemption unfolds as a secret sector within created existence, then this inevitably stimulates a smug superiority by those possessing the hidden knowledge. True missionary activity demands an open appreciation of God's acting in history. This affinity between Lehmann and Hoekendijk reinforces the centrality of creation within the American report, while illustrating that Trinity doctrine was itself of derivative significance.

Newbigin joined a consolidated committee of Hartenstein, Lehmann, and Chandran that was commissioned to produce a final report in one night. Accounts of what occurred are rare. Blaxall's hagiographical rendering says that the report "needed so much 'knocking into shape'" that Newbigin had retired "into solitary labour in the committee room furthest situated from the main hall," only to appear in due time as a "spare, vital figure" with "a paper in his hand which he handed to the chairman with the charming smile which so endears him to everyone." Since he was not privy to the original discussion, the final report appears to have been of Newbigin's own invention. There was sufficient distance between this document and the interim report for the conference "to realize that however excellent it may be it was not a report of the group." However, it did "represent the *general* mind of the conference, and so was adopted as a conference statement."[99]

"The Missionary Calling of the Church" is the first ecumenical expression of the Trinitarian grounding of missionary activity. It begins by declaring that "the missionary movement of which we are a part has its source in the Triune God Himself." The statement then expounds this affirmation in a creedal fashion. God created the world to reflect the "glory of His love." As humanity is "involved in a common alienation from God," however, God sent his Son to redeem lost humanity and his Spirit to gather the body of

98. L. A. Hoedemaker, "The Legacy of J. C. Hoekendijk," *International Bulletin of Missionary Research* 19, no. 4 (1995): 167, 169.

99. A. W. Blaxall, "Willingen, 1952: The Calling of the Church to Mission and Unity," *The Christian Council Quarterly*, no. 34 (1952): 2.

Christ and enable worship of the Father in spirit and truth. These actions of God commit the members of Christ's body "to full participation in His redeeming mission."[100] This leads to one of Willingen's most famous assertions: "There is no participation in Christ without participation in His mission in the world. That by which the Church receives its existence is that by which it is also given its world-mission. 'As the Father hath sent me, even so I send you.'"[101] As the church's origins are in the divine economy, so she lives only by participating in that economy.

The remainder of the statement fails to draw on this preamble, developing in deliberate contrast to the proposed "Trinitarian" connection between historical progress and missions. While the sovereign God "rules the revolutionary forces of history," the Christian church faces "a world in which other faiths of revolutionary power confront us in the full tide of victory." God's rule is sure, but it is "the hidden power of the Cross." The battle is "set between His hidden Kingdom and those evil spiritual forces which lure men on towards false hopes, or bind them down to apathy, indifference and despair."[102] The report retained the priority of redemptive history, while acknowledging the perpetual institutional retreat into safe enclaves. To this end, it affirms that the

> . . . word "witness" cannot possibly mean that the Church stands over against the world, detached from it and regarding it from a position of superior righteousness or security. The Church is in the world, as the Lord of the Church identified Himself wholly with mankind, so must the Church also do. The nearer the Church draws to its Lord the nearer it draws to the world.[103]

100. Goodall, ed., *Missions under the Cross*, p. 189. One might indicate the startling similarity between this and the IMC Jerusalem statement of 1928, which held that "our true and compelling motive lies in the very nature of the God to whom we have given our hearts. Since He is love, His very nature is to share. Christ is the expression in time of the eternal self-giving of the Father." John R. Mott, ed., *The World Mission of Christianity: Messages and Recommendations of the Enlarged Meeting of the International Missionary Council held at Jerusalem, March 24-April 8, 1928* (London: International Missionary Council, 1928), p. 10.

101. Goodall, ed., *Missions under the Cross*, p. 190. This famous statement reflects a question asked by Hoekendijk: Can the church experience fellowship "which is not identical with a participation (= *koinonia*) in Christ's apostolic ministry"? J. C. Hoekendijk, "The Church in Missionary Thinking," *International Review of Mission* 41 (1952): 331.

102. Goodall, ed., *Missions under the Cross*, pp. 188-89.

103. Goodall, ed., *Missions under the Cross*, p. 191.

While this suggests some acquiescence to the core concern of Lehmann and Hoekendijk, sufficient theological resources already existed without the complications introduced by the interim report. For example, von Thadden's keynote address affirms that "a Church under the Cross should be the exact opposite of an introverted and contemplative company. It should be a Church *for* the world. This insight has been given us during the past ten years."[104] This achieved an external orientation for the church by proceeding through, not in distinction to, christology. In other words, it was possible to address christologically the central problem for which a direct connection between history and missions was the proposed solution.

How do we interpret the Trinitarianism articulated at Willingen? For Hoedemaker, "the trinitarian approach advocated in the text must be understood as a modification and reduction of the rejected approaches."[105] This is surely correct. Elsewhere he notes that "the trinitarian terminology of the official Willingen report conceals a contrast between the approach of the American preparatory report (mission is the response to what the triune God is doing in the world) and the more classic salvation-historical approaches."[106] Newbigin, as the statement's chief author, confirms that if the two dominant issues concerned the rejection of church-centrism, and the relationship of "the missionary task to the signs of Christ's present sovereignty in the secular world," these ideas were not incorporated into the final

104. Reinold von Thadden, "The Church under the Cross," in *Missions under the Cross,* ed. Goodall, p. 62. Myriad other examples could be given. Freytag's preparatory contribution noted that the "gathering of the community does not have its purpose in itself," and that since "the Kingdom of God is universal and the expectancy of the final End includes the whole world," restricting the church's activity "to a particular sphere always involves the danger of remaining immobilized at a penultimate stage, of wanting well-attended and powerful churches instead of going forward to meet the Lord." Freytag, "The Meaning and Purpose of the Christian Mission," pp. 159, 161.

105. L. A. Hoedemaker, "Mission and Unity: The Relevance of Hoekendijk's Vision," in *Changing Partnership of Missionary and Ecumenical Movements: Essays in Honour of Marc Spindler,* ed. Leny Lagerwerf, Karel Steenbrink, and F. J. Verstraelen (Leiden-Utrecht: Interuniversity Institute for Missiological and Ecumenical Research, 1995), p. 29. James Scherer says that the final Willingen statement "wavered uncertainly between Trinitarianism, christocentrism, and church-centrism. It appeared mostly to reject any criticism of church-centered missionary thinking." James A. Scherer, *Gospel, Church and Kingdom: Comparative Studies in World Mission Theology* (Minneapolis: Augsburg, 1987), pp. 97-98.

106. L. A. Hoedemaker, "The People of God and the Ends of the Earth," in *Missiology: An Ecumenical Introduction,* ed. F. J. Verstraelen et al. (Grand Rapids: Eerdmans, 1995), p. 165.

statement "in spite of the passionate eloquence of Hoekendijk."[107] Rather, "a substitute document was prepared which, without really coming to grips with these two issues, nevertheless gave a clear affirmation of the basis of the missionary calling of the Church in the being of the Triune God himself."[108] This "substitute document" transcended the impasse of the interim report, a compromise that received the full support of the Willingen members.

The final report says that "some phrases in our report, though they represent what we can with good conscience say together, cover up persistent differences among us."[109] For Günther, this allowed divergent approaches "to stand side by side in a relatively unconnected way."[110] Richebächer, too, holds that the term *missio Dei* "acted as little more than a paper-clip holding together debating positions that had been in serious opposition before and during the conference."[111] The Trinitarianism is a concession — ecumenical damage control. The statement's ambiguity does not detract from its significance: it remains one of the seminal delineations of *missio Dei* theology to which the majority of authors refer. But *missio Dei*'s success results from its capacity to unify discordant positions. Elasticity is a hallmark of the concept, present at its genesis, and a function it continues to fulfill.

Post-Willingen Reception of Missio Dei *Theology*

If the Trinitarian developments at Willingen constitute a Copernican turn for mission theology, this is a judgment of hindsight.[112] Participants under-

---

107. Newbigin, "Mission to Six Continents," p. 179. Reflective of the confusion, Scherer complains that Willingen's Trinitarianism failed to provide a sufficient eschatological account of creation. He expects "a more ultimate expression of the promised transformation of God's creation." Willingen's statement intentionally stepped back from this tendency in the American report. However, the insufficient reference to the doctrine of creation is assumed to be a consequence of Barth's rejection of natural theology. James A. Scherer, "Mission Theology," in *Toward the Twenty-First Century in Christian Mission: Essays in Honor of Gerald H. Anderson,* ed. James M. Phillips and Robert T. Coote (Grand Rapids: Eerdmans, 1993), p. 198.

108. Newbigin, "Mission to Six Continents," p. 179.

109. Goodall, ed., *Missions under the Cross,* p. 244.

110. Wolfgang Günther, "The History and Significance of World Mission Conferences in the 20th Century," *International Review of Mission* 92, no. 4 (2003): 529.

111. Richebächer, "*Missio Dei:* The Basis of Mission Theology or a Wrong Path?" p. 591.

112. Even forty years after Willingen, José Míguez Bonino would make the startling

stood Willingen as having failed in its central task. Goodall, in his official reflection on the conference, lamented that "there did not finally emerge the one inevitable word in which theological clarity and prophetic insight were manifestly conjoined. Nor did there appear the one new directive which might set the world mission of the Church on a surer and swifter road towards its fulfilment."[113] The historical reception of Willingen invalidates this judgment. That it was made, and that it reflected general opinion, confirms the relative insignificance of Trinity doctrine both at Willingen and for some period after.[114]

Lehmann's report on the conference fails to mention the Trinitarian developments, issuing instead a sweeping condemnation of Willingen's final statement.[115] "The failure of the Christian Church in the summer of 1952" was a failure "of prophetic and apostolic nerve" (p. 431). The interim report was submerged, for it "undertook to explore a direct line between missions and history, between evangelism and politics" (p. 434). The problem was twofold. First, the Anglo-Catholics "refused to consider the instrumental character of the Christian mission. Instead, the argument

---

statement that the Trinitarian approach to missions is "a rather forgotten proposal of Willingen 1952," which "has had almost no repercussion in Protestant missiology and in developments with the Commission on World Mission and Evangelism of the WCC." José Míguez Bonino, *Faces of Latin American Protestantism: 1993 Carnahan Lectures,* trans. Eugene L. Stockwell (Grand Rapids: Eerdmans, 1997), pp. 138-39.

113. Norman Goodall, "Willingen — Milestone, not Terminus," in *Missions under the Cross,* ed. Goodall, p. 14. Kraemer, for example, notes "the 'impasse' of mission in the failed attempt at Willingen to reach an agreement over mission theology or a new rationale for mission." Kraemer, "Mission im Wandel der Völkerwelt," p. 294. But Freytag, reflecting on Willingen after the Lutheran World Federation conference held in Hannover just weeks later, says that "looking back to Willingen from Hannover I felt that we had been together much more closely at Willingen — far more than we were aware during Willingen itself. And secondly, Hannover failed in exactly the same place as Willingen: the report of the theological section, to which had been attributed by far the most elaborate preparation, simply stated that one had to desist from giving a report." Quoted in a letter from Freda Dearing to J. W. Decker, 29 August 1952, International Missionary Council Archives 1910-1961, Microfiche 264012.4 (Geneva: WCC, 1952).

114. Examples of this point are legion. For two of the more substantial reviews, see John Beattie, "Willingen, 1952," *International Review of Mission* 41, no. 4 (1952): 433-43; Martin Pörklen, "Der neue Auftrag: Persönliche Eindrücke von der Weltmissions-Konferenz Willingen 1952," *Weltmission heute,* no. 3 (1952): 3-32.

115. Paul Lehmann, "Willingen and Lund: The Church on the Way to Unity," *Theology Today* 9, no. 4 (1953): 431-41. All quotes in this paragraph are from this essay.

was that the Church, as the Body of Christ, is itself the mission, since it belongs to the outgoing activity of the Triune God-head himself" (p. 435). Reference to the Trinity, in other words, became a means of emphasizing the church and her mediatorial role. Second, due to the theological language surrounding National Socialism, the German Lutherans "insisted upon the no less dangerous division of the divine activity in history into two spheres. One could, they contended, see God's judgment in historical events, but not God's redemption" (p. 435). The lessons drawn from the German church's seduction by Nazism's siren call of *Volkstum* disallow any liaison between political movements and divine activity. The resulting "Willingen impasse" smoothed over the fissures raised by Lehmann's report with "an aura of pious hope and pious rhetoric" (p. 434).

Hartenstein's more appreciative account reads as though the conference confirmed his pre-Willingen position. This retrofit was simply done. With the patterned approach to the doctrine of the Trinity established at Willingen, Hartenstein's early depiction of *missio Dei* located in the key "sending" text of John 20:21, satisfied the basic requirement. His assumption of Trinitarian language did not alter his key position. "The sending of the Son into the world is the actual *missio Dei*, which must and will be carried on in obedience by his witnesses to the ends of the earth and to the end of the age."[116] This occurs in the period between "Cross and kingdom, between the first and second coming of the Lord."[117] It is, as such, an eschatological event. "From the '*Missio Dei*' alone comes the '*missio ecclesiae*'. That locates mission in the broadest conceivable framework of salvation history and God's plan of salvation."[118] Hartenstein's premature death weeks after Willingen leaves an open-ended question as to the direction he might have taken, but his conference report does not suggest any development in his thought. Bosch argues the opposite: that Hartenstein used the language of *missio Dei* as a conservative move, "to protect mission against secularization and horizontalization, and to reserve it exclusively for God."[119] This

116. Karl Hartenstein, "Übergang und Neubeginn: Zur Tagung des Internationalen Missionsrats in Willingen," *Zeitwende* 24, no. 4 (1952): 338.

117. Karl Hartenstein, "Theologische Besinnung," in *Mission zwischen Gestern und Morgen*, ed. Walter Freytag (Stuttgart: Evang. Missionsverlag, 1952), p. 56.

118. Hartenstein, "Theologische Besinnung," p. 62.

119. Bosch, *Transforming Mission*, p. 392. For some authors, the significance of Hartenstein's contribution lies simply in his coining the phrase *missio Dei*. Herwig Wagner, for example, notes that, while the American report used the English phrase "God's mission,"

adds a further layer of confusion, because *missio Dei* language now overlay two diametrically opposed positions.

While Willingen was understood to have failed in terms of its theological statement, the hope remained that it had initiated a continuing program of reflection.[120] This never came about. While Vicedom made the phrase *missio Dei* famous, his work followed Willingen's Trinitarianism. Through the 1950s, only Hartenstein's conference summary and Andersen's 1955 work refer to the Trinity as a significant development. Neither the 1957-58 IMC Ghana conference nor the section on "witness" at the 1961 WCC New Delhi conference picks up Willingen's findings.[121] Newbigin, drafter of the Willingen statement, himself took a further decade to reach the conclusion that "a Trinitarian, rather than a purely christological understanding of the missionary task, is more and more necessary."[122] The MSC simply draws on the Trinitarianism of the American report. Given the MSC's identification between *missio Dei* and the 1960s political zeitgeist, reference to *missio Dei* and the Trinitarian grounding of missions fell away in the 1970s. While it remained a popular method for coordinating Christianity with other world religions, only with the question of "mission to the West" associated with Newbigin during the mid-1980s did the concept reemerge with some theological gravitas. When it did, descriptions of the *missio Dei* simply referred back to the Willingen statement, which had, by this time, accrued all the authority proper to an "ecumenical" statement. Despite its acknowledged

---

this did not appear in the Willingen report. It fell to Hartenstein to introduce the Latin version of the term. Wagner, "Hartensteins Beitrag zum Aufbruch in der Missionstheologie 1945-1960," in *Karl Hartenstein: Leben in weltweitem Horizont,* ed. Fritz Lamparter (Bonn: Verlag für Kultur und Wissenschaft, 1995), p. 130.

120. Wilhelm Andersen, *Towards a Theology of Mission: A Study of the Encounter between the Missionary Enterprise and the Church and Its Theology* (London: SCM, 1955), p. 53.

121. Christoph Benn, "The Theology of Mission and the Integration of the International Missionary Council and the World Council of Churches," *International Review of Mission* 76, no. 3 (1987): 397. Gensichen, too, states that "those who had hoped that New Delhi would make some progress in the direction of a clearer trinitarian formulation of the missionary witness were at all events disappointed." Hans-Werner Gensichen, "New Delhi and the World Mission of the Church," *Lutheran World* 9, no. 2 (1962): 139.

122. Newbigin, *Unfinished Agenda,* p. 192. No less an ecumenical authority than Visser 't Hooft "disapproved of its theology" (p. 199). Nevertheless, Newbigin's concern resulted in the 1963 publication of *The Relevance of Trinitarian Doctrine for Today's Mission* and the 1978 publication of *The Open Secret.*

failure, the Willingen statement remains close to a complete definition of *missio Dei*.

The Competing Forms of *Missio Dei* Theology

Missio Dei's ambiguous genealogy produces, in turn, a theological ambiguity. Willingen's Trinitarianism is an incidental development. This does not disqualify the significance of the basic theological move — the missionary act must be located in the triune being of God. It does, however, reveal that the lamented contemporary problems of *missio Dei* inhere within the original form of the concept and stem from its deficient Trinitarianism.

As to the concept's origins, the received connection between Willingen, Hartenstein, and Barth can no longer be sustained. Hartenstein did not bring the doctrine of the Trinity to Willingen. Barth's 1932 essay had no immediate impact on the conference: it was not referred to in any of the preparatory documents, in the findings, or in the aftermath of the conference. Furthermore, Newbigin, as the drafter of the Willingen statement, had no experience with Barth's work.[123] The Trinitarianism developed in the American report in contrast to christology as a way of entreating cultural involvement. God's act became an abstract pattern of breaking down and building up the kingdom in history. While Willingen attempted to redress this theological juxtaposition by placing "missions under the Cross," it retained the underlying procedure of establishing a pattern of God's activity in creation. This "pattern" approach, embodied in the language of "sending," constitutes the Trinitarianism of *missio Dei* and is unquestioningly presupposed by every diverse rendition of that theology. It supplies the single point of unification.

This occurs, however, because Willingen's "compromise" manifests a known theological problem. One final question raised in the conference findings was about whether the missionary obligation of the church was to be "understood primarily as derived from the redemptive purpose and

123. After reading the "incomprehensible" *Römerbrief* during his early theological education, Newbigin set Barth aside until personal contact during the 1950s encouraged him to tackle the *Church Dogmatics,* which he read backwards over the summer of 1974. Newbigin, *Unfinished Agenda,* p. 31; Geoffrey Wainwright, *Lesslie Newbigin: A Theological Life* (Oxford: Oxford University Press, 2000), p. 22.

acts of God or as derived from the nature of God Himself."[124] Günther interprets this question in terms of the options delineated by Hartenstein and Lehmann: Is mission "a task, a functional activity (the redemptive-history/eschatology group), or an answer, a reflex of faith (the American group)?"[125] This (almost accidental) analysis of the problem proves instructive as we turn to a constructive redevelopment of *missio Dei*. The key Trinitarian flaw rests in this breach between who God is in himself and who he is in his economy. Where a Trinitarian grounding of mission should overcome this breach, *missio Dei* trades on it: a perceived gap between God and the world supplies the necessary space for reconstructing the missionary act. In that mission is attempting to achieve what only God can, the result is a distended "missionary" eschatology or ecclesiology.

Once the doctrine of the Trinity provided a "pattern" of God's acting, it became a question of filling in the pattern. The dichotomy between God's act and being produces a corresponding dichotomy in the form of human response. For Johannes Aagaard, "at the bottom of all these problems was and is found the still unresolved ecclesiological question, not as a separate question but as the core question of all questions."[126] This is to be doubted. At Willingen, "all were agreed that the 'mission' is essential to the nature of the Church and not something super-added to it."[127] The church is a missionary community. The main tension centered on defining this missionary nature: Did the pattern of sending proceed from God's *being*, resulting in a missionary act that unfolded in historical process? Or did it proceed from God's *act*, resulting in a missionary act that unfolded in the institutional life of the church? While these positions appear very different, in actuality they trade on the fundamental Trinitarian breach of being and act, with the eschatological approach emphasizing the former and the ecclesiological approach emphasizing the latter. In that *missio Dei* attempts to ground mission in the doctrine of the Trinity, the doctrine attacks any such breach. It does not permit the kinds of activities grounded in natural theology and thus appears not to permit any human action. *Missio Dei*, in other words, eats away at itself. The foundational issue is Trinitarian, and any solution must begin there. It is a problem of God himself.

124. Goodall, ed., *Missions under the Cross*, p. 244.

125. Günther, *Von Edinburgh nach Mexico City*, p. 109.

126. Johannes Aagaard, "Some Main Trends in Modern Protestant Missiology," *Studia Theologica* 19 (1965): 253.

127. Goodall, ed., *Missions under the Cross*, p. 244.

CHAPTER FIVE

The Missionary Connection

Everything that can be said about our participation in the being and work of Jesus Christ, here in the depth as such, properly consists only in this: It lies in the nature of what happens there in God, in the eternal continuation of the reconciliation and revelation accomplished in time, that it, in full reality, also happens here to and in us. . . . Our participation in the being and work of Jesus Christ must not follow as a second thing, but is, as the one thing which must be accomplished, wholly and utterly accomplished in Him.

Karl Barth, *Church Dogmatics*[1]

Introduction

Contra popular perception, *missio Dei*'s decisive flaw resides in its insufficient Trinitarian grounding. From this desiccated root sprouts the range of its contemporary problems. The doctrine of the Trinity distances the missionary act from any accidental grounding. Fulfilling only this critical function, mission's reformulation occurs in some contest with the doctrine. Or the term "Trinity" becomes shorthand for the doctrines of creation and pneumatology in active distinction from christology. A split

1. Barth, *KD* II/1, 176 (my translation); *CD* II/1, 157-58.

forms between God's being and God's particular act, with a second movement apart from the event of reconciliation needed to render this act effective in the present. Such a split is not easily eliminated, because it demarcates the necessary space for the human response and, as such, receives theological ratification. The language of "sending," with its Trinitarian provenance, serves as a formal conduit connecting God and the world. However, its substance draws on competing doctrines of creation that accent either culture or the church.

This chapter begins the constructive rethinking of *missio Dei*. By severing any link with Barth, we can take the opportunity to reformulate the Trinitarian ground of mission using his work. An overwhelming perception exists that Barth and mission are like oil and water; this perception trades on a tacit suspicion that, to a greater or lesser degree, the missionary act demands some liaison with natural theology. Barth's unrelenting rejection of natural theology and avowed affirmation of divine subjectivity produces a position that appears, at best, indifferent toward mission. A certain methodological assumption results: one is restricted to drawing inferences for mission from Barth's thought. This already confirms the supposed distance between mission and theology proper — and does so to detrimental effect. Mission is a second-order reflection; it is not of essential dogmatic import because it does not belong to eternal Christian existence. The claims presented here are of a different order.

No critical debate even intimates the missionary end of Barth's theology. That he emphasizes the category of "witness" is well known. Craig Carter, for example, says that "the key to Barth's ecclesiology is his contention that the sole purpose of the Church is to bear witness to Jesus Christ in this world. The rest of his ecclesiology is an attempt to bring all aspects of this doctrine into harmony with this central insight."[2] While correct, such observations fail to refer to the definite missionary form of Christian witness and community. With this, the concrete substance of Barth's ecclesiology drops away. Theological reasons for this omission prove difficult to trace. Mission is, without doubt, "tacitly suspected as fanatical, intolerant and interfering," but this circumstantial evaluation fails to justify the *theological* lacuna.[3]

---

2. Craig A. Carter, "Karl Barth's Revision of Protestant Ecclesiology," *Perspectives in Religious Studies* 22, no. 1 (1995): 44.

3. See, e.g., Barth's reflection on the problem: "It is painful to have to admit, and it is a

Whatever the reason, the following discussion must first overcome this nonmissionary predilection. Anachronistic definitions prevail. "Mission" refers to those ventures stereotypically characterized as belonging to the nineteenth century. Reference to mission in Barth, following this dominant phenomenological assumption, can be immediately narrowed down to his criticisms of religion or to his articulation of the problem-laden term "vocation."[4] As a consequence of the presumed distance between dogmatic theology and the field of mission, any claim that results from material not allotted to this cordoned missionary purview already strikes a false note. To draw a conclusion such as "God is a missionary God" from his doctrine of God already seems to move beyond the intent of Barth's theology. Specific reference to mission does occur throughout the *Church Dogmatics*, and limiting the discussion to part of one volume distorts its role within the whole. This is not to pretend that mission is some master key, but it is to repudiate any distance between mission and Barth's decisive theological contributions.

The missionary task is not a derivative step of some more essential being of the church, thus Barth's significance for *missio Dei*. His depiction of the Christian community's missionary existence, to be sure, looks very different from traditional missionary apologies. Given his circumspection regarding mediatoral models, it is often held that Barth fails to account for the concrete necessities of both church life and the missionary act. Without some account of her being as a "concrete reality in the world," the church, for Hans Urs von Balthasar, cannot "bear witness to the presence of faith and revelation in the world."[5] Barth's rejection of human mediation, how-

---

serious indictment of our established European churches, that in the main this [devotion to mission] is to be found only in external organizations and the so-called sects, and that in the great churches it is usually encountered only among those who belong to special societies and not in the congregations as such, in which it seems to be tacitly suspected as fanatical, intolerant and interfering" (*CD* III/4, 505; *KD* III/4, 579).

4. This book does not make references to Barth's position on "religion" for one particular reason. It is the popular entrance point for missiologists, and a superficial treatment would potentially encourage a return to the intellectual ruts and binary oppositions that I am trying to challenge in this work. Any constructive rethinking of the subject would require more unsaying than there is space available. For a snapshot of its standard reception, see Henning Wrogemann, *Mission und Religion in der systematischen Theologie der Gegenwart: das Missionsverständnis deutschsprachiger protestantischer Dogmatiker im 20. Jahrhundert* (Göttingen: Vandenhoeck und Ruprecht, 1997), pp. 81-88.

5. Hans Urs von Balthasar, *The Theology of Karl Barth: Exposition and Interpretation*

ever, is a derivative consequence of his rejection of the being-and-act dichotomy within divine ontology. While seemingly necessary for the missionary act, the problem of natural theology is, for Barth, the problem of cleaving God's being in and for himself from his particular movement into the economy. The tension is clear. Christian agency necessitates a gap between God and the world, and yet the presence of this gap destroys the basis of that agency, distorting both the nature of the church and her external act.

This chapter enters the problem through the "point of connection" debate between Barth and Brunner. Brunner formulates his position in light of "missionary experience," drawing on Gutmann, Keyßer, and Knak. The issues surrounding Barth's 1932 mission lecture reemerge — but at this point apparently baptized by dialectical theology. While Barth's rejection of Brunner would seem to constitute a de facto rejection of mission, the missionary act is already impossible if grounded within natural theology, for this undergirds the destructive dichotomy of prior institutional being and derivative missionary function. In other words, the breach between God's being and act determines a community with a corresponding breach. In obviating this dichotomy in divine ontology, Barth obviates it in the corresponding ecclesial ontology. "It lies in the nature of what happens there in God, in the eternal continuation of the reconciliation and revelation accomplished in time, that it, in full reality, also happens here to and in us" (rev., *KD* II/1, 176; *CD* II/1, 157-58). The Christian community is a missionary community because God in himself overcomes the gap between the divine and the human precisely in his being as Father, Son, and Spirit.

The Ground of Mission

The Point of Connection

While popularized in systematic imagination by Brunner, the phrase "point of connection" is not Brunner's coinage.[6] The term's origins and

---

(San Francisco: Ignatius, 1992), p. 245. Von Balthasar continues: "God speaks; but does man really respond with his own word? Barth's own example of the 'reflector lights' on an automobile that reflect back to a motorist, but only when the car in back is shining its own headlights, clearly shows that, for Barth, the creature indeed responds but not really with its own light and word" (p. 393).

6. The following discussion assumes an acquaintance with the material contained in

entrance into systematic theology's vocabulary require clarification, but by the turn of the twentieth century it was common throughout missionary thinking, present in both English and German. Insofar as it is concerned with the relationship between the gospel and a non-Christian context, "point of connection" is a term that has to do with foreign missions. Brunner attributes it precisely to these origins. In an article entitled "Die Bedeutung der missionarischen Erfahrung für die Theologie" (The Significance of Missionary Experience for Theology), he observes the new missionary context of Western society.[7] An emerging secularism and nascent paganism had flooded into the breach created by the collapse of Christendom. "The people of Europe are becoming heathen" (p. 3). The consequent cultural resistance to the gospel explains the surging dogmatic interest in questions of *analogia entis,* natural theology, and the point of connection (p. 8). These are missionary questions and will increase in intensity until the theologian understands this impetus and takes "missionary experience" as the base material for a renewed engagement with Western civilization (p. 8). Western theology must draw on the missionary endeavor with its "tremendous treasure of experience and insight acquired from two hundred years of practice" (p. 7). If the church is not to retreat behind her own walls, she must clear the cultural space for the proclamation of the gospel. The missionary endeavor had accomplished just this in overtly non-Christian contexts by "preaching the gospel to the heathen, teaching their children, engaging in their individual pastoral care, forming communities among them and penetrating the peoples with the spirit of the gospel" (p. 7). A single task was behind this success: the missionary weighed "which mechanisms of the practical life, which orders of the social life, prove themselves to be valuable starting points and bases and which prove to be the opposite" (p. 9).

This insight sets the task for the new missionary context of Western civilization. The "other task" of Western theology, to be set alongside the preaching of the gospel, consists of discerning those cultural practices that

chap. 3 on the relationship between dialectical theology and German missions, and especially on the difference between "a point of contact" and "a point of connection."

7. Emil Brunner, "Die Bedeutung der missionarischen Erfahrung für die Theologie," in *Die deutsche evangelische Heidenmission: Jahrbuch 1933 der vereinigten deutschen Missionskonferenzen* (Hamburg: Selbstverlag der Missionskonferenzen, 1933), p. 3 (in this paragraph, references to this source will appear in parentheses in the text). See also Barth's treatment in *CD* I/1, 25-27.

either promote or derogate the gospel, and then, respectively, encourage or discipline those practices. This means locating "a point of connection" as the point at which the facilitating and disciplining trajectories meet.

Brunner's position here draws on the work of Gutmann and Knak.[8] This point can be extended: as his 1935 introduction to *Natur und Gnade* brings to the fore, Brunner's position shadows that of German mission theory.[9] In identical manner to Knak, his treatment of the "point of connection" begins with a discussion of basic biblical translation. Local languages and prior philosophical assumptions are necessary for the communication of the gospel.[10] "The apostles cannot proclaim their message without the aid of a general logic and grammar, an experience of the world laid down in vocabulary, and without all the words, with their given religious pre-understanding, which were decisive for them."[11] These words gain new meaning when they accompany the entrance of a new message. Indeed, with this process of translation, "a ditch, or even possibly an abyss, is crossed."[12] This "capacity for words," the first element in a point of connection, is illustrated by the principle of the vernacular that underlay the Reformation. To deny this concrete priority of context, by extension, is to deny the mundane activity of biblical interpretation and to run counter to the Reformation.

Whatever remnant of the *imago Dei* remains within fallen humanity, it is in contact with this natural capacity that the church speaks. Proclamation, for it to truly communicate, must connect with an individual's conscience. This is the "center of natural self-understanding," and so any

---

8. Brunner lauds their work for providing base datum for theological reflection, but laments that they attempted the theological interpretation themselves. The clear problems with their position, thus, are not a result of the approach per se, but are consequent upon the inappropriate conclusions drawn from this approach. Brunner, "Die Bedeutung der missionarischen Erfahrung für die Theologie," p. 10.

9. Emil Brunner, *Natur und Gnade: zum Gespräch mit Karl Barth*, 2nd ed. (Tübingen: Mohr, 1935), pp. i-vii. John Baillie translated portions of this in his introduction to Emil Brunner and Karl Barth, *Natural Theology: Comprising 'Nature and Grace' by Professor Dr. Emil Brunner and the Reply 'No!' by Dr. Karl Barth* (London: Centenary Press, 1946), pp. 10-12.

10. Emil Brunner, "Die Frage nach dem 'Anknüpfungspunkt' als Problem der Theologie," *Zwischen den Zeiten* 10 (1932): 505-9.

11. Brunner, "Die Frage nach dem 'Anknüpfungspunkt' als Problem der Theologie," p. 510.

12. Brunner, "Die Frage nach dem 'Anknüpfungspunkt' als Problem der Theologie," p. 508.

"proclamation which does not connect with the conscience misses human beings."[13] As the necessary God-given milieu for shaping human beings and their religious expression, context forms this key receptor for the gospel. Basic to this is the disciplining "intermediary order" of the law, which Paul conceived "as a schoolmaster to bring us unto Christ."[14] Scripture is clear about the reality of a natural, though perverted, knowledge of God among "the heathen." The law, as the given structure of God's creation, shapes the natural conscience in preparation for the gospel by making one aware of one's own responsibility. This responsibility constitutes the second — the disciplining — element of a point of connection. "Everything depends on the demonstration of this responsibility that makes one guilty, and this responsibility depends on the reality of a general revelation in creation, which precedes the revelation of reconciliation in Jesus Christ, and indeed all historical life." Thus, "without hesitation, whoever thinks as a missionary understands the central significance of this connection — stimulating judgment and penitence — with the double revelation in creation."[15] Paul himself, as *the* missionary, demonstrates this to be the case.

This general revelation provides the necessary interpretive framework for the gospel. Truth alone is insufficient. "The Church's proclamation must be *comprehensible* else it is useless, however true its contents."[16] To be effective it must connect with the openings available to it in culture. Given the secular nature of the West, that is, since "the preparatory and maturing effect of the law is wholly absent," there is "no longer any point of contact." Without these preconditions, human beings cannot understand the gospel. This "falling away of the intermediary order" renders the Bible "unintelligible." Brunner regards it as "impossible to rebuild faith on such terrain as to grow forests again on land long cleared. The humus is lacking. No *justitia civilis* and no *theologia naturalis* mean, according to human judgment, no Gospel. One must first make the drunken man sober before one can preach the Gospel to him."[17] Such logic leads to his central conclusion concerning missionary prolegomena:

13. Brunner, "Die Frage nach dem 'Anknüpfungspunkt' als Problem der Theologie," p. 517.

14. Emil Brunner, "Christianity and Reality," pp. 25, International Missionary Council Archives 1910-1961, Microfiche 261134.6 (Geneva: WCC, 1930).

15. Brunner, *Natur und Gnade*, pp. ii-iii.

16. Brunner and Barth, *Natural Theology*, p. 56.

17. Brunner, "Christianity and Reality," p. 25.

[T]he Church fundamentally has a double task in her teaching — the pedagogical in the broad sense, that is, the conservation and cultivation of the cultural humus, the wakening and keeping awake of the human race in its regard for the law, thought, authority and humanity — and, secondly, that which is peculiarly the Church's own — the preaching of the Gospel.[18]

The Western church has to encourage those cultural conditions necessary for the activation of revelation. This Christian apologetic has "a *preparatory* function. Such theological work can indeed be a preparation of the hearing of the Word of God."[19] Of this position, Ustorf concludes: "Brunner still made *culture* . . . the *precondition* for evangelization."[20] With a general revelation the necessary precursor to the gospel, the church's external task became one of civilizing those elements identified by a point of connection. The primary concern of the missionary task is with those contingencies that render the context missionary.

All the necessary authority for such a theological position flows from the practical exigencies of ecclesial existence in the world. This "question of the point of connection is completely understandable and urgent only for those, who as evangelists, as missionaries, as pastor or teachers of religion, take an active part in the church."[21] This, for Brunner, is the defining difference between himself and Barth: "Barth thinks as a churchman for the church; I think rather as a missionary."[22] Disengaged theological speculation will never comprehend the key issue.

---

18. Brunner, "Christianity and Reality," p. 26. The link with German mission theology should be obvious, but to reiterate with a quote from Siegfried Knak: missionary experience teaches "that the preaching of the Cross of Christ can only be properly understood if all sorts of preliminary conditions are first created." Knak, *German Protestant Missionary Work: Its Characteristic Features in Practice and Theory* (New York: International Missionary Council, 1938), p. 22.

19. Brunner and Barth, *Natural Theology*, p. 62 n. 14.

20. Werner Ustorf, *Sailing on the Next Tide: Missions, Missiology, and the Third Reich* (Frankfurt am Main: Peter Lang, 2000), p. 109.

21. Brunner, "Die Frage nach dem 'Anknüpfungspunkt' als Problem der Theologie," p. 529.

22. Emil Brunner, "Toward a Missionary Theology," *Christian Century* 66, no. 27 (1949): 817. Brunner even suggests, in a specific reference to his 1947 Gifford Lectures, published as *Christianity and Civilization*, that his legacy to the "younger generation" is the term "Missionary Theology."

In distinction from Karl Barth . . . my theological thinking was, from the very start, dominated by the endeavor to preach the gospel to "the pagans," i.e. to those outside the Christian Church and to interpret it to the secular mind. The difference between the one who has his eyes fixed on the believers and the missionary who thinks of the non-believers was at the basis of our disputes which began as early as 1917. This was the reason why I was so much interested to find the "Anknüpfungspunkt," the point of contact, between man's mind as such (what theologians call "natural man") and the Word of God. How could I preach them the Gospel if they were not interested, or if they did not understand?[23]

Without dedicated attention to the "point of connection," gospel proclamation withers and theology becomes "exhausted in leathery definitions."[24]

Nothing illustrated Barth's lack of missionary intent better than the role he gave to the Trinity in his prolegomena. "Something" — that is, the gospel — Brunner maintains, cannot be understood apart from the "Someone," that is, the person who hears the message,

> . . . and the removal of this question through the doctrine of the Trinity, i.e. the elimination of this dualism of the Something and the Someone through this thinking — that this Something is not Something but God the Son, and that Someone is God the Holy Spirit — is only an evading of the real question. For that Someone remains *to* whom the Holy Spirit speaks, and that Something remains which is the divine Word.[25]

The doctrine of the Trinity "defends the central faith" and, as such, is properly part of theological discourse, but it "does not belong to the sphere of the church's message."[26] It is a critical doctrine, not one that positively informs Christian existence in the world. Barth's recourse to the Trinity abrogates the faith's true duty. While he may have created an aesthetically pleasing dogmatic package, in that he failed to take the second step of con-

23. Emil Brunner, "A Spiritual Autobiography," *Japan Christian Quarterly* (July 1955): 242.

24. Brunner, "Die Frage nach dem 'Anknüpfungspunkt' als Problem der Theologie," p. 531.

25. Brunner, "Die Bedeutung der missionarischen Erfahrung für die Theologie," p. 8.

26. Emil Brunner, *The Christian Doctrine of God,* trans. Olive Wyon (Philadelphia: Westminster, 1950), p. 206.

necting this message with the world, Barth abandoned those in most desperate need of hearing the gospel. A binary opposition forms. Only a theology concerned with the point of connection provides the necessary mediating step for revelation to encounter humanity.[27] Only careful attention to natural theology constitutes a missionary approach. Barth's account of the Trinity, by contrast, is antimissionary. He is concerned with those already within the church and with the beauty of the Christian message. We return to the complaint of German missions: Barth's position paralyzes the will to do mission.

The Breached God and His Corresponding Community

Barth's notorious vocative *Nein!* renounces the possibility of a natural "point of connection for the redeeming action of God."[28] He denies that any such connection resides in some creaturely capacity as a necessary precondition for revelation. Care must be taken here. It is important that Barth does not deny a point of connection. This is the proper act of the Holy Spirit, and any alternative grounding is "incompatible with the third article of the creed."[29] It is impossible, Barth declares, to "ascribe the event of revelation to God, and yet attribute to humanity the instrument and point of connection for it" (rev., *KD* I/2, 305; *CD* I/2, 280).[30] The issue of a

27. See Trevor A. Hart, *Regarding Karl Barth: Toward a Reading of His Theology* (Downers Grove, IL: InterVarsity, 1999), p. 152.

28. Brunner and Barth, *Natural Theology,* p. 74.

29. Brunner and Barth, *Natural Theology,* p. 121. Some on the missionary side did appreciate the distinction. Schärer wrote in 1944 against those who affirm that "there surely must be a point of connection, that some continuity surely must exist between God and humanity. We answer that: the possibility of contact and of faith lies not in humanity and is not a human presupposition, it lies solely in the reality and effectuality of the Holy Spirit." Hans Schärer, "Die Begründung der Mission in der katholischen und evangelischen Missionswissenschaft," *Theologische Studien* 16 (1944): 42.

30. Barth's treatment of the "unknown God" proves instructive here. He uses Acts 17:22-31 and Paul's sermon on the resurrection of Jesus Christ in complete contrast to the popular position — as proof of the *impossibility* of a "point of connection." Barth notes Paul's "'indignation in the Spirit' at the abundance of idols to be seen in Athens" (*CD* II/1, 121). All the openings suggested by the passage — the Athenians' great religiousness (v. 22), their altar to the "unknown God" (v. 23), and their knowledge of human unity and kinship with God (vv. 26-28) — constitute openings, not because of their piety, but because they indicate a people in desperate need of the gospel. With the focal point of vv. 32 and after, this

point of connection is the issue of natural theology, the essential problem of which is its cleavage of God's *being* from his *act*. Formally stated, "natural theology is the doctrine of humanity with God existing outside God's revelation in Jesus Christ. It works out the knowledge of God that is possible and real on the basis of this independent union with God and its consequences for the whole relationship of God, world, and humanity" (*CD* II/1, 168; *KD* II/1, 189).[31]

There is a knowledge of God — which is already fellowship with God — apart from the event of reconciliation in which God reveals himself. This is not a sterile concern; it includes grave implications for how the church conceives and orders her proper work. Natural theology imposes a breach between God's being and his act, and it asymmetrically orders that breach with an emphasis on God's now universalized being over his particular act. The church in her own life manifests a corresponding breach, determining her own existence with an emphasis on her internal being and apart from her external missionary act. "Natural theology," Barth laments, "is grounded mischievously deep and firm even in the sphere of the Church" (*CD* II/1, 135; *KD* II/1, 149-50). The problem of natural theology is not restricted to questions of God's witness within creation, but it is determinative of how the church understands herself.

The centrality of this breach for the missionary question is illustrated in Barth's essay "Evangelical Theology in the Nineteenth Century."[32] Because

---

hope dissipates as the Athenians receive the message "partly with mockery, partly with boredom" (*CD* II/1, 104). This experience mirrors the speech at Lystra (Acts 14:15-17), that other "attempt at contact" that ended in "open failure" (*CD* II/1, 122). Those things that suggest openness toward the gospel, such as the altar, demonstrate that the Lystrians require that "the true God should be preached to them" (*CD* II/1, 122). The true God does not "live in shrines made by human hands" (v. 24). Barth continues that "we can certainly call what Paul does a 'making contact.' But if we do, we must take into account that the 'point of contact' is not regarded as already present on man's side but as newly instituted in and with the proclamation of the Gospel" (*CD* II/1, 121). Paul "does not argue from within. He argues against them strictly from outside" (*CD* II/1, 123). The "times of human ignorance," previously "overlooked by God," are now over. God's command is for "all people everywhere to repent" (v. 30). It is only as Paul turns his back on the Athenians that a few follow him.

31. Barth further states that "a natural theology which does not strive to be the only master is not a natural theology" (*CD* II/1, 173; *KD* II/1, 195).

32. Karl Barth, "Evangelical Theology in the Nineteenth Century," in *God, Grace and Gospel* (Edinburgh: Oliver and Boyd, 1959), pp. 55-74. In the following quotes from this source, page numbers appear in parentheses in the text.

nineteenth-century theology regarded the confrontation of its own age as its decisive task, "*the* problem of all its problems," Barth subjects this theology to the standards of a missionary apologetic (p. 60). What it was "fundamentally aiming at" can only be "understood against the background of the missionary or evangelical interest characteristic of the whole of Christianity of modern times" (p. 63). Christianity's increasing irrelevance within post-Enlightenment society resulted in this need to connect with its contemporaries. This it "so craved as its first necessity" (p. 63). Such social marginalization prompted a particular missionary response: theology had to "pursue its own theme only within the framework of a generally intelligible view of the totality of things, human, cosmic and divine" (pp. 62-63). It required the translation of the faith into contemporary idiom; it had to become understandable within a given framework. This, Barth continues, "might explain the failure of their missionary task at a deeper level" (p. 64). This missionary desire directed the church away from the act within which God is known toward a general category of being, for it became necessary to "show the possibility of faith within the context and under the conditions of the views of the world which were at the time authoritative for their contemporaries and for themselves also" (p. 63). The motive for this theological task came from a cultural shift that led to designating the context as missionary, that is, a contingent motive, and this context demanded a particular method, that is, a method that would satisfy this contingency.

Operating with these twin assumptions (that relating to the world was the church's primary task and that this occurred by establishing the general possibility of the Christian faith), Barth saw the key theological task as one of identifying the general religious ontic. What is the potentiality "that belonged originally to man as such and was essentially and peculiarly his own" (p. 64)? If this religious ontic provides the point of connection, then the task of witness rests in illustrating the superiority of the Christian version of this ontic. The Christian becomes defined as "that person who is distinguished from others by the *allocation,* the reception, possession, use and enjoyment of the *salvation* given and revealed to the world by God in Jesus Christ" (rev., *KD* IV/3.2, 644-45; *CD* IV/3.2, 561). This, in turn, stimulates a preoccupation with the *beneficia Christi* and with an account of Christian edification based on the cultivation of excellence in these benefits.[33] The benefits identify the Chris-

---

33. For Barth's definition of what constitutes the *beneficia,* see *CD* IV/3.2, 561-62. Barth laments the misuse, typical of the Ritschlian school, of Melanchthon's axiom: "Hoc est

tian ontic as Christian and thus constitute the distinction that manifests the truth of the Christian faith within the general religious ontic. With the "reception, possession, use and enjoyment of the *beneficia Christi*" now "the *only* relevant, essential and important element in the goal of my calling," human connection with God and with the world "consists absolutely and exclusively in my Christian being, possession and capacity, in my experience of salvation" (rev., *KD* IV/3.2, 647; *CD* IV/3.2, 564). The benefits are not themselves at issue. The problem is the reduction of Christian being and witness to the experience of these benefits, and the coordinated limitation of the benefits active in the event of reconciliation to the "dead end" of this passive reception.[34]

Christum cognoscere — beneficia Christi cognoscere" (This is to know Christ — to know the benefits of Christ), which reduces Christ to "a Being from whom certain benefits accrue to man, which have a definite 'value' for him." Karl Barth, *Dogmatics in Outline,* trans. George T. Thomson (New York: Philosophical Library, 1949), p. 70. For a summary of his argument and its implications for mission, see Darrell L. Guder, *The Continuing Conversion of the Church* (Grand Rapids: Eerdmans, 2000), pp. 121-31.

34. Barth's criticisms here are not merely directed against the single problem of cultural Protestantism. This problem results from defining the church without reference to the reason for her existence. Barth says of the marks contained in article VII of the Augsburg Confession that "there can be no doubt that all this is the Church," but notes the "yawning gap" in that it failed to formulate the church in terms of her purpose (*CD* IV/3.2, 766; *KD* IV/3.2, 876). Two issues follow. First, this derogates the missionary act. Barth examines the dominance of Augsburg Confession article VII in "relation to the history of missionary thinking" (*CD* I/2, 640; *KD* I/2, 717). This document derived its particular authority from its presentation to the "emperor and empire," acquiring with this "a modified publicity, the last and necessary call to all humanity had already taken place as wrought by God Himself." This eschatological perspective meant that "the accomplished *confession* is *identical with an accomplished world mission*" (*CD* I/2, 641). It constituted a "kind of an ultimate or penultimate trumpet — loud enough to make all further missions superfluous" (*CD* I/2, 641). In other words, this call to the "true preaching of the word" presumes missionary cessation, i.e., the true location of this preaching occurs within the walls of the church and to the already faithful. Second, the necessary missionary purpose becomes divested into the church. Barth warns that "a terrible misunderstanding threatens. Invocation of God the Father, the spiritual life of Christians and the Christian community, the Christian ethos shaped thereby, is not an end in itself. It is not a wonderful glass-bead game played for its own sake by a company of initiated in a quiet valley with no outward contacts. . . . Even in his resurrection and ascension [Jesus Christ] did not retreat into separation from the world. On the contrary, it was for the world and not himself that he acted and that he still acts" (*ChrL,* pp. 96-97). Accounts of the church that fail on this question of purpose, by contrast, mean that the work of Jesus Christ, "of this divine messenger and ambassador actually ceased in the dead end of the Church as an institution of salvation for those who belong to her" (rev., *KD* IV/3.2, 877; *CD* IV/3.2, 767).

The "holy egoism" that characterizes the evangelistic vocation of the *beneficia* finds a correspondence in the community (*CD* IV/3.2, 767; *KD* IV/3.2, 878). Her orientation to the world consists foremost in an orientation to herself as distinct from the world, with an ever-deeper encouragement of those things that create this distinction.[35] With the distinction fundamental to the witness of the *beneficia Christi* ontic in nature, maturation into the benefits occurs via the negative function of eliminating worldly vestiges and the positive function of growing in *habitus*. Being and witness coincide and produce a particular account of Christian growth as requiring ecclesiastical mechanics. This mode of witness produces a church that is "essentially and decisively, a kind of institute of salvation, the foremost and comprehensive *medium salutis*" (*CD* IV/3.2, 567; *KD* IV/ 3.2, 651).[36] This informs how the church orders the word and sacraments. That the church is a *community* with practices and that these are necessary to Christian existence is not being contested (Heb. 10:25); the problem is one of distinguishing this life from its given purpose, in forming liturgy to serve the perceived witness of the *beneficia Christi* by configuring institutions, offices, government, and practices according to this internal end. This witness of withdrawal renders mediation and *habitus* a necessity.

A third-article correlate proceeds from the cardinal first-article problem: the Spirit is forced into a particular mode of acting. If the basis of the

35. Barth issues this kind of judgment as much against Pietism as against nineteenth-century liberal Protestantism. Of the latter he declares that this church is the "Church of the pious man, the Church of the good man, the Church of the moral man, but, at any rate, the Church of *man*." Barth, "The Christian as Witness," in *God in Action* (Manhasset, NY: Round Table, 1963), p. 135. Of the former, he declares, "Let us improve matters *ourselves!* Let *us* cultivate the Christian *life!* They turned aside from the living God and began to cultivate in a very sincere, very worthy, and very pious manner what we see before us in full bloom: the pious man" (p. 137). Neither the Christian nor the Church is "a goal in itself, an end in itself. . . . Where there is Christianity or a church institution, piety, inner life, going to heaven, which is an end in itself, that is no Christianity, even if it appears in a very strong form. Piety as such — nothing! Christian piety is a life in action in which man serves the purpose of God. Certainly there is such a thing as Christian spiritual life and the life of the Christian in communities, but all pointing to the task of the Church." Barth, "Fragebeantwortung bei der Konferenz der World Student Christian Federation," in *Gespräche, 1959-1962*, ed. Eberhard Busch, *Gesamtausgabe* (Zürich: Theologischer Verlag, 1995), pp. 433-44.

36. This reference to Calvin (*Inst.*, IV.I.I) demonstrates the wider setting of this discussion. Barth does not limit his criticisms to nineteenth-century theology. He observes the same approach in the Reformers' depiction of the church, themselves building on Cyprian, as the "mother of the faithful" (*CD* IV/3.2, 766; *KD* IV/3.2, 876).

connection between the church and the world is this general ontic, then the proper act of the Spirit must be one of ensuring the necessary Christian distinction from this generality. A causal link forms between the act of the Holy Spirit and the growth of the church in her illustrative benefits. This economy of salvation determines the instrumental cooperation of human agency, with the decisive theological question one of relating the action of the Spirit to actions undertaken by the human, most notably those of the word and sacraments.

Evangelistic missions become ancillary within this schema. The lack of reference to the church's original and essential existence for the world, this "striking deficiency in the self-understanding of the Church," helps explain "the pronounced lack of joy in mission, and even unreadiness for it" (*CD* IV/3.2, 767; *KD* IV/3.2, 878).[37] Mission is, of necessity, a derivative activity besides this essential internal occupation. Yet, with the intent behind the *beneficia* missionary, it results in a definite missionary method. This concentric focus of the benefits "is not usually practicable without being completed and accompanied by striving in what seems to be the *opposite*

---

37. The "missionary" nature of the sacraments is well recognized. Stephen Neill says that "the doctrine of the Trinity is not an arid piece of Greek logomachy; it is the only possible form for the expression of the nature of a God whose being can be apprehended by man only as redemptive mission. Both the great sacraments are missionary in their character, both related directly to the gathering of the nations into the Kingdom of God." Neill, *Creative Tension* (London: Edinburgh House, 1959), p. 112. To reiterate, the issue is not with the *beneficia* but with the way the breach in the being and act of the community liturgically codifies the benefits in terms of their possession and without reference to their missionary purpose. By contrast, with baptism as an example, Barth says that in becoming a member of the community through baptism, the individual "does not just come to share her possession, enjoyment and comfort." The individual is "now personally co-responsible for the execution of the missionary command which constitutes the community, of the commission to the outside world which surrounds both her and him on a large scale and a small scale alike. The task of every Christian — not additionally but from the very outset, on every step of the way assigned to him in baptism — is this task as a bearer of the Gospel to the others who stand without" (*CD* IV/4, 200; *KD* IV/4, 220). Eberhard Jüngel, continuing in this vein, states that "if the ontological connection between the man Jesus and all others is the legal basis of the kerygma, then the church, proclamation, baptism and the Lord's supper are grounded in such a way that they necessarily point beyond themselves. They do this in that they point in a definite and direct way to Jesus Christ, but not, so to speak, *back* to him but rather *forward* to him, thus pointing *into* the breadth of humanity beyond the walls of the church. In this, the Christian must always be ready to hear afresh the voice of Jesus Christ." Jüngel, *God's Being Is in Becoming*, trans. John B. Webster (Grand Rapids: Eerdmans, 2001), p. 136.

dimension, i.e., by a centrifugal striving for *expression* and *disclosure*" (rev., *KD* IV/3.2, 654; *CD* IV/3.2, 569). The contingency of the general ontic renders this paradoxical expansionism necessary, for the church must continually make apparent her distinction from the world. The replication of the particular Christian ontic is one of validating its distinction. The "deeply suspect pious egocentricity" of this church results in a wave of evangelical missions, the main task of which is the distribution and implementation of those things that differentiate the church from the world (*CD* IV/3.2, 568; *KD* IV/3.2, 652). This confirms the initiating "pious egocentricity" for it produces a "collective egocentricity" (*CD* IV/3.2, 570; *KD* IV/3.2, 654). Since this act is not the end of Christian being, this method receives no theological attention, and its inherent bias toward imperialism should by now be clear. Missions occur in order to promote the true nonmissionary vocation of celebrating the Christian distinctive within the general religious ontic. This ontic is cultural in nature: that is, it differentiates one way of life from another, and its transmission occurs from one value system to another. Mission exists at a distance from this church: its mode, as one of propagating those cultural elements essential to growth in the true witness of the benefits, confirms the insular nature of Christian being, and it can be jettisoned as nonessential to that being. The act is, as such, doubly threatened. Employing natural theology to create space for the missionary act defines the act in opposition to the proper being of the church and makes its practical mode necessarily propagandistic.[38]

This definition of Christian being and witness contrasts with God's own act in reconciling the world to himself. A significant disproportionality exists between "the self-lessness and self-sacrifice of God and Jesus Christ in which the salvation of the world is realized and revealed, and the self-satisfaction with which Christians are pleased to receive that salvation as the self-serving users of the very different being and action of their Lord!" (rev., *KD* IV/3.2, 651; *CD* IV/3.2, 567). In other words, the primary breach in the being and act of God produces a corresponding breach in the being and act of the community. The Christian lives "in a world of one's own apart

---

38. Bosch, for example, observes that if a community lacks a "missionary dimension and yet becomes involved in a missionary enterprise[,] such a church erects a colossal missionary machine without being in itself missionary. The result is all manner of aberrations: the church imparts its own ghetto mentality to the people it 'reaches'. It engages, not in mission, but in propaganda, reproducing carbon copies of itself." David J. Bosch, "Theological Education in Missionary Perspective," *Missiology* 10, no. 1 (1982): 25.

from Christ, being occupied with one's own concerns and their best satisfaction instead of with the concerns of Christ" (*CD* IV/3.2, 596; *KD* IV/3.2, 683). A "confusing juxtaposition" develops "between the divine gift and the divine task, Gospel and Law, justification and sanctification" (*CD* IV/3.2, 565; *KD* IV/3.2, 648). This juxtaposition is related by way of a tension, with one element often prioritized above the other; however, with the disjunction itself improper, there exists no definite theological criterion for such an ordering. "True" Christian being reduces to participation in the goods mediated by Jesus Christ, with a twofold effect over the nature of the task, which, first, becomes the distribution of the means to these goods, and second, is of derivative significance as not itself one of the goods.

Such an account of Christian being is not defined in terms of fellowship with Jesus Christ. Christ did not himself work to develop culture, nor was he "active only in the sense of pious contemplation" (*CD* III/4, 486; *KD* III/4, 557). His own work was that of doing the work of the Father, proclaiming the kingdom in word and deed. It is the proper work of the Son to witness to the Father (John 5:32), the proper work of the Spirit to witness to the Son (John 15:26; 14:26), while the Father witnesses to its truth (John 1:18; 5:36; 8:18; 17:26). Therefore, witness is internal to the life of God. Fellowship with Jesus Christ requires that the Christian act in correspondence to the nature of his own acting. As Christ exhibits no breach between his being and his act, neither can his community. Christian existence cannot be "an end in itself. As fellowship with Christ, it is in principle and nature a *service*. It is *witness*" (rev., *KD* IV/3.2, 742; *CD* IV/3.2, 648). The benefits are to be celebrated within the community, but "we cannot speak *in abstracto* of the *beneficia Christi*. We must know His *beneficia* in action in order to know Him."[39] The wonderful fruit of the Christian existence "blooms only *in actu*" (rev., *KD* IV/3.2, 707; IV/3.2, 617).[40] Christian being as a living relationship with Jesus Christ cannot differ from the nature of his own life; it takes the form of witness, concretely defined as active missionary service to the world. The benefits confirm Christian calling, prepare the community for the task entrusted to her, and are finally only known as they are active in service to this task of witness.

39. Barth, *Dogmatics in Outline*, p. 70.
40. Barth continues that "the act, however, is not an abstract act of faith, love, and hope to be performed in that inner world, but concretely the act of the Christian in relation to the external world, the act of one's witness."

God Is God and the Creature the Creature

The above depiction of the problem, first, of locating the point of connection and thus the nature of Christian difference within the general religious ontic, and second, of the being and act of the church determined according to this end, is a problem of the first and third articles. The being of God is generally available within the given of nature and apart from his own act in revealing himself, with the Spirit accentuating Christian particularity within this given by cultivating *habitus* through liturgy and practices. Such approaches to Christian witness need not formally deny the central affirmation of "the real prophetic-apostolic witness to God's speaking and acting in the history of Israel and in the history of Jesus Christ" (*CD* II/1, p. 99; *KD* II/1, p. 110). They do, however, establish an independent ordering: on the left "stands independently the reference to humanity in the cosmos: humanity provided with the ability to receive the voice of the cosmos"; and on the right "stands independently the reference to the direct confirmation by God Himself, which is in some sense the result of the direct speaking of the Holy Spirit" (*CD* II/1, 99-100; *KD* II/1, 110).

This is the breach between being and act manifested by natural theology. It is overcome by reestablishing the *diastasis* between God and humanity, for it removes the responsibility to overcome the breach between God and creation from the creature and properly attributes it to God alone. "God is and remains God, and the human is and remains human in this relationship" (rev., *KD* II/1, 265; *CD* II/1, 234). This liberates God to be God, says T. F. Torrance, "in the sheer majesty of his divine nature and in his absolutely unique existence and power, while man, disenchanted of his pretended divinity, could be free at last to be truly and genuinely human."[41] The critical distance established by this *diastasis* is not itself the crucial thing. The accent falls on the properly ordered *relationship* that results from the event of reconciliation. It is a question of the acting God and of the consequential determination of the acting human. With his treatment of the being of the church as *actus purus*, Barth posits the missionary existence of the community as a necessity grounded in who God is.

---

41. Thomas F. Torrance, "The Problem of Natural Theology in the Thought of Karl Barth," *Religious Studies* 6 (1970): 121.

The First Article in Relationship to the Cosmos

The missionary act, it is so argued, requires an account of creation that has some facilitating capacity for the transmission of the gospel. Barth's christological emphasis fails to give full credence to the work of the Father in nature and the Spirit in forming the religious life, and thus denudes the missionary act. Barth affirms the legitimacy of locating "a common basis of communication between the Church and the world, between belief and unbelief — the task of pointing the way which leads from the ignorance to the knowledge of God" (rev., *KD* II/1, 100; *CD* II/1, 91-92). This orientation is basic to the extent that the church cannot "be the church if she is not actively engaged in this work" (*CD* II/1, 92; *KD* II/1, 101). Hence, neither the necessity of the missionary act nor whether human beings must be active in the event of reconciliation is at issue. It is a question of method: Is a general witness to God within creation essential to the missionary act? Or, is recourse to such a general witness detrimental to the human missionary act? *Diastasis* sets the proper order.

In terms of the first article, the being of the church is "*purus* in that it is *divine,* beginning with itself, and comprehensible only from and through itself, thus anthropologically not understandable as a given" (rev., *KD* I/1, 41; *CD* I/1, 41). Because it is fellowship between the divine and the human, it is asymmetrical in nature and, as fellowship, it is not available to possession. The act of communicating this relationship cannot occur apart from its reality, either as though a second step were required to render a potential actual, or as a necessity forced on God or humanity. Missionary motivation and method, as such, must rest in this reality and not in external contingency.

Reconciled existence with God as life framed by the *diastasis* between divine and the human cannot nullify human agency. That God is God is no mere tautology. It is an ordering act, a creating and setting in relationship. "Creation provides the *space* for the story of the covenant of grace" (rev., *KD* III/1, 46; *CD* III/1, 44). Nature is the context of the divine/human relationship. The "epitome of the whole order of *creation*" cannot be "God here and the human there"; it is that "God is the God of the human and the human the human of God" (*CD* IV/3.1, 43; *KD* IV/3.1, 45). The event of reconciliation, as reconciliation, is "the *confirmation* and *restoration* of the order of creation" (*CD* IV/3.1, 43; *KD* IV/3.1, 46). God's act, to be sure, opposes improper claims, but in this act frees the creature to be the creature. God "problematizes and *relativizes* the truth of His creature," and, in so doing, "*integrates* and institutes that truth" (rev., *KD* IV/3.1, 174; *CD* IV/3.1, 153). This relativization and integration occurs because "to relativize means critically to set something in its limited and conditioned place. But it also means *positively* to set it in the *relationship* indicated by the limits of this place" (*CD* IV/3.1, 163; *KD* IV/3.1, 186). Contextualization is not the passive human activity of identifying surroundings and thus living at some distance from them.[42] It is the encounter of *being* contextualized, a "being set in context" and liberation to live within it.[43]

The perceived value of natural theology rests in its sensitivity to the human context. Diverse human expressions of the gospel enlarge our human understanding of who Jesus Christ is.[44] Every language, with all the connection this shares with culture, can communicate the gospel. The gospel speaks to the context and even shapes it. This being the case, a further step follows: that the gospel speaks to culture means that culture provides a pedagogical path for the proclamation of the gospel. Natural theology provides

> . . . a common basis of *conversation* between the Church and the world, between faith and unbelief. This basis is, of course, presumed to be necessary to the existence and activity of the church. What is in mind is the possibility that the proclamation of the Bible and the church, which as such is at once alien to humanity, will "connect" with something which is already familiar. (rev., *KD* II/1, 96; *CD* II/1, 88)

42. Given the common preoccupation with "worldviews" as a means for a missionary point of contact, Barth's sharp reaction against this approach is especially instructive here. The main problem rests in humanity's capacity to remain at a distance from an encounter with God. See *CD* III/2, 6-19, and *CD* IV/3.1, 254-60.

43. See Walter Lowe's helpful discussion of contextualization within the context of an apocalyptic event. Lowe, "Prospects for a Postmodern Christian Theology: Apocalyptic without Reserve," *Modern Theology* 15, no. 1 (1999): 23. The apocalyptic encounter that approaches history from the final form of the *parousia* "is not something which can be seized and handled by us as an instrument or weapon. On the contrary, it seizes and handles us" (*CD* II/1, 637; *KD* II/1, 718).

44. As Newbigin suggests, "the full answer to the question 'Who is Jesus Christ?' can only be given when the fullness of humankind has been gathered into the confession of his name." Until then every confession is partial and provisional. "Christology is Christology *in via*, and the way is a missionary way, the way which the Church must take from the culture of first-century Palestine to all the nations and their cultures, to the ends of the earth and to the end of time." J. E. Lesslie Newbigin, "Christ and the Cultures," *Scottish Journal of Theology* 31, no. 1 (1978): 10.

Two issues are conflated here: first, the necessary importance of nature as the context for the relationship between the divine and the human; second, the responsibility laid over context as the medium for overcoming the divide between God and human beings. In that it cannot bear this second responsibility, natural theology distorts and devalues the human context. This is made clear by its pedagogical implementation. Given that it is a "transitional" path, this natural knowledge is a preliminary stage through which the missionary places the hearer before a decision; it is a childish position beyond which the hearer must move, and from which the missionary has already moved. The pedagogic aim will take place without "the seriousness with which the natural man engages in this pursuit, but with the tolerant superiority of one who understands him but has already seen through the final vanity of his labour" (*CD* II/1, 88; *KD* II/1, 97).

This is a duplicitous act in which the missionary keeps hidden the knowledge toward which she wants her hearers to move. If the missionary were to succeed by this method, then her approach could "finally only reveal to the conversation partner that *she* were *either* deceiving him when she *pretended* to negotiate with him on the ground of common presuppositions, *or even* that she was not engaged with the matter if she *really* did this" (rev., *KD* I/1, 29-30; *CD* I/1, 31). Either the missionary lied or she had failed to engage her own message. Both stances demonstrate to the hearer the missionary's own lack of belief in the message. That this "game" occurs is the "inner contradiction in every form of a 'Christian' natural theology" (*CD* II/1, 94; *KD* II/1, 103).[45] However, the recipient of the message "must not first be deceived by being addressed from his own standpoint, which is the standpoint of unbelief" (*CD* II/1, 92; *KD* II/1, 101).

Christian natural theology, paradoxically, is not finally interested in the actual human context. The Christian community lives with an intentional dislocation from this apparent environment, which is demonstrated, by the reality of God's judgment, to be an "illusionary position and sphere" (*CD* II/1, 171; *KD* II/1, 192). It is precisely because of this that the Christian community proceeds in mission. Human witnesses do not need to condescend to their unbelieving partners. "They do not need any particular art to draw near to them. They are, indeed, already with them.

---

45. As Louth suggests, Barth observes "a sort of religious racism . . . lurking in the position of the Christian natural theologian." Andrew Louth, "Barth and the Problem of Natural Theology," *Downside Review* 87, no. 3 (1969): 272.

For they stand with their witness of faith as poor sinners alongside other poor sinners, and as people called by God alongside fellow human beings called by God. They are not superior to them" (*CD* II/1, 96; *KD* II/1, 105).[46]

With the reality of sin and of reconciliation the basis, an authentic appreciation of indigenous agency and of the space of nature necessitates that "this conversation must in all circumstances be pursued by the Church in full *candour* towards the other partner and therefore with faith as the starting-point" (*CD* II/1, 92; *KD* II/1, 100). The Christian witness must respect her fellow human beings by telling them the truth concerning their context. The actual connection between the Christian community and the world consists in the need for the "natural" person to die. This message of repentance and baptism is the true basis of Christian solidarity with the world. Because the Christian community is as fallen as the community to which she witnesses, she lacks authority over her own faith. Faith enters the conversation "in the simple form of a witness," and this is sufficient (*CD* II/1, 96; *KD* II/1, 105). She does not possess the message, which means that the authority of her proclamation rests not in her own particular expression of the gospel. It is because nature does not serve this connecting function that each context can be converted, that is, can serve the gospel.

In terms of the proper motive for mission, the assumption basic to the point of connection concerns nature's innate capacity to determine humanity's encounter with the gospel. This manifests itself in a concern for Christianity's "relevance" relative to changes in context (thus, the rise in missionary language within the Western church as she is now understood to inhabit a "missionary context"). This is an expressly nontheological assumption (Rom. 3:23). All times are marked by a "radical negation of the

46. See also Karl Barth, *The Epistle to the Romans,* trans. Edwyn C. Hoskyns (London: Oxford University Press, 1968), pp. 100-101; Karl Barth, "Die Theologie und die Mission in der Gegenwart," *Zwischen den Zeiten* 10, no. 3 (1932): 191. This position leads Japanese theologian Yasuo Furuya to ask, "Why has it not been Brunner but rather Barth who has been effectively preaching the Gospel to those outside the Japanese Church and successfully making a point of contact between them and the Word of God?" His answer is that Brunner's "intended apologetics" only sees unbelief in others, "while he is dogmatic and uncritical about his own position." Barth's "unintended apologetics," on the other hand, "is an apologetics which has no intention whatever to prove the superiority of its own faith over against others, either philosophically or historically, because of its serious awareness of its own unbelief which is under exactly the same need of grace as others, and simply bears witness in faith to Jesus Christ." Yasuo Carl Furuya, "Apologetic or Kerygmatic Theology?" *Theology Today* 16, no. 4 (1960): 479-80.

revelation believed in the Church" (*CD* I/1, 28; *KD* I/1, 26). Christian revelation is not part of a general religious possibility. Nature possesses no capacity either to facilitate or to retard human confrontation with the gospel (John 1:11). The vicissitudes of place and time neither establish nor destroy the necessary preconditions for missionary contact. This does not preclude listening to context and its questions as a necessary component of the church's witness, but that examination is not prior to and determinative of that witness. Mission is not a functional contingency because its true form is not response undertaken by the church relative to the determination of context, grounded neither in the fruits of Western civilization nor in reaction to a burgeoning secularism.

The failure to understand that God, as Creator, first acts to set humanity in context has a determinative effect over mission method. The rejection of hegemonic forms of Christian expansion finds positive expression in the contemporary valorization of context — and necessarily so. Conversion to the Christian faith means precisely that: conversion and not proselytism. In that it is a reaction to propagandistic missionary methods, however, this account of context proceeds from the same basis. The substance of the message rests in its cultural appropriation, either as the imposition of civilization or the reification of tradition. First, mission becomes contingent on historical circumstance, that is, the act is not part of the message itself. Second, not being part of the message, mission cannot focus on the message but on those things that ratify the act, that is, on those contingencies that make mission a possibility. Mission, as with theology, must have an alternative basis, "an inner necessity grounded in the matter itself." That is, mission must flow from the gospel and so from who God is in himself as Father, Son, and Spirit (*CD* I/1, 31; *KD* I/1, 30). A true appreciation of creation necessitates rejecting every missionary method that "dissolves the unity of God" into an "abstract consideration of his being" (*CD* II/1, 90; *KD* II/1, 99). God and his act is the only determinative for the missionary existence of the Christian community. Any other basis inevitably leads to propagandistic missionary methods.

The Third Article in Relationship to the Human

If the problem with natural theology's use of the first article consists in an improper account of creation reflective of a primary breach in the being and act of God, then natural theology of the third article stimulates a concomitant breach in the being and act of the Christian community, which lives in correspondence to this "breached" God. Because the task of witness rests in the celebration of the distinctive Christian religious ontic, a direct connection with the Spirit becomes necessary to patch up or add something to innate human capacity. However, the being of the church is *actus*, "free *action*, not a continuously available relationship; grace is an event of *personal address*, not a transmitted material condition" (*CD* I/1, 41; *KD* I/1, 41). The fact that human beings are called to witness is, again, not the issue. The issue is the nature and mode of this witness as it forms in correspondence to this event of personal address.

The Missionary Form as a Transmitted Material Condition

Barth is unwavering: Christ completed, once for all, the act of reconciliation. This emphasis, for some, closes the space of human activity. Manecke, for example, laments that Barth "left no space in the Christ event which can or must be filled by the church."[47] The only opening seems to rest in Barth's minimalist affirmation that Jesus Christ, "in the exercise of His prophetic office (in which He ministers alone), does *not want to remain solitary*" (rev., *KD* IV/3.2, 695; *CD* IV/3.2, 606). The church appears as a secondary thing, ancillary to Jesus' primary work.[48] If he ministers alone, then the church accomplishes nothing in the economy of salvation; it is, by extension, of no *necessary* value. That is, if the church did not act, nothing of substance would change in terms of the fellowship between God and humanity. Barth, in seeming confirmation, says that "the church is not the author, dispenser, or mediator of grace and its revelation. She is

47. Dieter Manecke, *Mission als Zeugendienst: Karl Barths theologische Begründung der Mission im Gegenüber zu den Entwürfen von Walter Holsten, Walter Freytag und Joh. Christiaan Hoekendijk* (Wuppertal: Rolf Brockhaus Verlag, 1972), p. 210.

48. Healy says that "Christianity is thus fundamentally about God's actions for us in Word and Spirit. Only consequently is it about our necessary response and 'cooperation' as God's 'partners.'" Nicholas M. Healy, "Karl Barth's Ecclesiology Reconsidered," *Scottish Journal of Theology* 57, no. 3 (2004): 294. The dominant error with this common position lies in the distance it introduces between Christ's act and the Christian response. The human act does not assist with Christ's act — its establishment is the goal of his act. The Christian community is to be distinguished as a subsequent subject, but is established as a subject in the act of Christ reconciling the world to the Father in the power of the Holy Spirit.

not the subject of the work of salvation, or the word of salvation. She cannot act as such. She cannot strut about as such, as though this were her calling" (rev., *KD* IV/4, 35; *CD* IV/4, 32). God in Christ by the Spirit has already accomplished everything, and "the world would not necessarily be lost if there were no church" (*CD* IV/3.2, 826; *KD* IV/3.2, 946).

A subjective correlate forms alongside this objective aphorism. Given that no causal link exists between the church's activity and the event of reconciliation, the need for any ontological difference between the church and the world dissipates; nor is creating such facility the proper work of the Spirit. Reconciliation's reality destroys the need for any addition to natural creaturely capacities: that is, the act itself establishes the proper relationship between Creator and creature. Only deleterious consequences follow a missionary method located in theologies of *analogia entis, habitus,* and deification. Deification disrupts this relationship and thus disrupts the human act determined by this relationship.[49] The Christian community makes use of a very different being to that of Christ himself, whose own humanity was not deified but maintained without confusion. The same complaint holds for *habitus,* which "comes from *habere,* and therefore denotes possession" (*CD* IV/2, 90; *KD* IV/2, 98). All such approaches approximate "too closely to the quite unbiblical idea of a supernatural qualifying of grace in respect of the believer" (*CD* I/2, 400; *KD* I/2, 440). Faith cannot be "a determination of human action which humans can give to it at will or maintain at will once it is received. On the contrary, it is the gracious address of God to humanity, the free personal presence of Jesus Christ in his activity" (*CD* I/1, 18; *KD* I/1, 17). Faith is not

---

49. Barth is crystal clear: "God becomes human in order that humans may — not become God, but come to God" (*CD* IV/2, 106; *KD* IV/2, 118). Eugene Rogers's erroneous statement that "Barth sees the human response to God primarily . . . in terms of deification" illustrates how nonmissionary depictions of the church struggle to understand the act proper to the human without recourse to deification with its consequent ecclesial forms. Eugene F. Rogers, "The Eclipse of the Spirit in Karl Barth," in *Conversing with Barth,* ed. Mike Higton and John C. McDowell (Aldershot: Ashgate, 2004), p. 176. For a formal account of Barth's denial of deification, see Bruce L. McCormack, "Participation in God, Yes, Deification, No: Two Modern Protestant Responses to an Ancient Question," in *Denkwürdiges Geheimnis: Beiträge zur Gotteslehre, Festschrift für Eberhard Jüngel zum 70. Geburtstag,* ed. Ingolf Ulrich Dalferth, Johannes Fischer, and Hans-Peter Grosshans (Tübingen: Mohr Siebeck, 2004), pp. 347-74. For an excellent study concerning how various conceptions of salvation — including that of deification — inform missionary method and congregational life, see David J. Bosch, "Salvation: A Missiological Perspective," *Ex Auditu* 5 (1989): 139-57.

an act of human control; it is an act of human submission to the prior acting of Jesus Christ.

Understanding faith as the event of this relationship prompts the charge of "occasionalism."[50] Versions of this charge are legion. For Joseph Mangina, "the church is an 'event' for Barth not so much in that he denies its ordinary, historical character, but rather in that he refuses to allow the Spirit's work to be conditioned or qualified by the 'given' nexus of practices in which the church has its identity."[51] Robert Jenson, in a similar

50. The act of witness, it is held, requires some account of development in Christian virtue. Hauerwas, for example, says that Barth "treats the Christian life primarily in terms of events and acts, which, while repeatable, cannot contribute in a theologically significant way to the development of ourselves as men of character." Stanley Hauerwas, *Character and the Christian Life* (San Antonio, TX: Trinity University Press, 1975), p. 173. He has somewhat modified this position, saying that "the oft made criticism of Barth's 'actualism,' which seems to entail an occasionalism (a critique that I did not begin but did my part in continuing), is, I am increasingly convinced, misplaced." Hauerwas, *With the Grain of the Universe: The Church's Witness and Natural Theology* (Grand Rapids: Brazos Press, 2001), p. 188. Even with this caveat, however, a certain understanding of objectivity that presupposes a range of givens is regarded as integral to the church's witness. This absence leads Hauerwas to question whether "Barth's ecclesiology is sufficient to sustain the witness that he thought was intrinsic to Christianity" (*With the Grain*, p. 39). Barth must posit the church with this concrete objectivity lest her witness fail. Healy, while he critiques Hauerwas's position for prioritizing social-philosophical categories over that of divine action, notes that Hauerwas, more than Barth, emphasizes "the necessity and centrality of the church's work in the economy of salvation." Healy, "Karl Barth's Ecclesiology Reconsidered," pp. 296, 287. The problem here is that a church defined with minimal reference to divine action is counted as more productive in the economy of salvation than is Barth's church. Barth does not deny the centrality of the church as a consequence of reconciliation. He denies that this account of given objectivity is the proper human nature and thus task of the church. We have previously examined what effect this has on the Christian community's missionary existence.

51. Joseph L. Mangina, "The Stranger as Sacrament: Karl Barth and the Ethics of Ecclesial Practice," *International Journal of Systematic Theology* 1, no. 3 (1999): 333. It is worth noting here the absence of mission, and the effect of this absence, within discussions of church practices. As Jüngel suggests, while "one of the constitutive marks of the church is to bring the good news of God's freely given grace to *all people*, [this] still awaits ecclesiological reception. And it is perhaps this fundamental ecclesiological defect that again and again threatens to stifle the missionary zeal that has erupted in the church in modern times. Without appropriate theological self-correction, there will always be the danger that *practice* will run aground on the church's inadequate understanding of itself." In other words, without the intention to mission, the occupation with ecclesiastical practice may well stimulate an effect opposite to that desired by its advocates. Eberhard Jüngel, "To Tell the World about

vein, suggests that "the whole web of Spirit-avoidance" that he perceives in the *Church Dogmatics* is due to Barth's "avoidance of the *church*." With the use of the term "church," Jenson has a specific "ecclesiology of *communion*" in mind, one in which "a structured continuing community were identified as the 'objectivity' of the gospel's truth *pro nobis*."[52] The objectivity of the gospel correlates with its subjective appropriation by the human. All such assertions, it must be remembered, seek to encourage the act of Christian witness. Characterizing Christian existence as mere response, it is argued, provides an insufficient foundation within concrete human realities necessary to the operation of witness. "The very notion of witness" requires some account of mediation, defined, if not in causal terms, then "as a means taken up by God" for the proclamation of the gospel.[53]

God: The Task for the Mission of the Church on the Threshold of the Third Millennium," *International Review of Mission* 89, no. 1 (2000): 204.

52. Robert W. Jenson, "You Wonder Where the Spirit Went," *Pro Ecclesia* 2, no. 3 (1993): 302-3. This preoccupation with the internal being of the church gravely denudes the role of mission within dogmatic imagination. Andrew Burgess, for example, observes that "flowing out of the orientation of the gospel to the church as its object, it is very interesting to note that lack of treatment Jenson gives to the church's missionary nature. Given his Lutheran background and the occasional mention that mission receives, perhaps we can assume that he sees eternal proclamation of the gospel as important and necessary, but he offers no significant discussion of it." Burgess, *The Ascension in Karl Barth* (Aldershot: Ashgate, 2004), p. 182. Though Jenson emphasizes the term "witness," describes Christianity as "a missionary faith," and affirms that "the church has a mission: to see to the speaking of the gospel, whether to the world as message of salvation or to God as appeal and praise," explicit development of mission is absent from his account of the church. Robert W. Jenson, *Systematic Theology I: The Triune God* (New York: Oxford University Press, 1997), pp. 35, 11. Jenson stands here merely as a representative example; this omission is the norm not the exception within contemporary dogmatic treatises, though one that is often disguised by the encompassing denotation *systematic*. Barth, by contrast, notes that during the past few centuries "the world-wide mission of the Church was taken up in earnest, the time of a new vision and expectation of the kingdom of God as coming and already come, the time of a new awakening of Christianity to its responsibility to state and society, the time of a new consciousness of its ecumenical existence and mission." This prompts the following conclusion: "These are actualities of Church history which a Church dogmatics cannot overlook" (*CD* IV/1, 527; *KD* IV/1, 588. While one agrees with his sentiment, it would seem that dogmatics can all too easily continue to ignore this "actuality."

53. Kimlyn J. Bender, *Karl Barth's Christological Ecclesiology* (Aldershot: Ashgate, 2005), p. 281. John Thompson, too, says that Barth's position is "vulnerable in his view of witness as a sign or pointer to Christ rather than as a means of grace." Thompson, *Modern Trinitarian Perspectives* (Oxford: Oxford University Press, 1994), p. 75. For a fuller treatment of this type

The imperative derives from the split between the being and act of God and the consequent depiction of the nature of Christian witness. The disjunction of the divine gift from the divine task means that witness is a second step alongside — grounded in and proceeding out of, but not material to — that event. The task, since it does not belong to the event, requires some element external to reconciliation as a means for making witness effective, that is, for making reconciliation actual. Though this secondary breach corresponds to the primary one in God, its very necessity rebounds back on to the doctrine of God, demarcating certain limits for the divine act. The question of divine and human agency becomes a zero-sum game. Colm O'Grady, for example, attributes Barth's aversion to a transmitted material condition to his "preconceived idea of a *solely* divine salvific activity in the economy of salvation."[54] This is, in one sense, accurate. Overcoming the primary breach in the being and act of God renders the need for ontological change in the reconciled human unnecessary. The human lives in fellowship with God as human. It is inaccurate, however, because it assumes that gap as necessary for human action: for the human to do something, God cannot do everything. In this complaint emerges again the binary opposition endemic to *missio Dei*. Overcoming the primary breach in the being and act of God, however, permits a definition of human agency not predicated on this breach.[55] The missionary existence of the community is the form of human fellowship with the divine that corresponds to God's own transition of the gap between the divine and the human in the event of reconciliation.

The Missionary Form as the Event of Personal Address

Barth permits no synergism that posits human agency as a necessary secondary causal force alongside God's own acting. Because there is no disrup-

---

of position, upon which Bender draws, see John Yocum, *Ecclesial Mediation in Karl Barth* (Aldershot: Ashgate, 2004).

54. Colm O'Grady, *The Church in Catholic Theology: Dialogue with Karl Barth* (Washington, DC: Corpus, 1969), p. 338.

55. As Jüngel suggests, human being and the being of the world itself "is something other than the capacity to possess itself." Humanity needs to learn that this is not "a lack (which God must correct)," but is "a distinction which establishes [one's] autonomy and freedom." Eberhard Jüngel, *God as the Mystery of the World: On the Foundation of the Theology of the Crucified One in the Dispute between Theism and Atheism* (Grand Rapids: Eerdmans, 1983), p. 381.

tion between who God is in himself and who he is in the act of reconciliation, no need exists to bridge this illusory gap via a range of connecting or mediating endeavors. No doubt, this threatens many dominant accounts of Christian being and acting with their corresponding ecclesiastical forms. The issue here is how Barth reconceives that action: How does the Christian community exist, not as a materially transmitted condition, but in the form of personal address?

That the human lives in contest with the divine is true, but only prior to the actuality of reconciliation and its eschatological fulfillment. God's gracious act establishes the creature as creature, and in doing so liberates it for its proper work. The truth of reconciliation does not occur at a distance from humanity, requiring a second step to make that reconciliation real. This work is "not an alien happening which passes us by at a greater or lesser distance" (*CD* II/2, 664; *KD* II/2, 716). It does not trump human agency. If it did, if human action were "simply a passive participation" in God's acting in Jesus Christ, then "it is itself a divine action, not a human action evoked by and responsive to God" (*CD* IV/4, 19; *KD* IV/4, 20-21).[56] If this were the case, then the reconciliation of the divine and the human would be mere illusion. Rather, human "participation in the being and work of Jesus Christ must not follow as a second thing, but is, as the one thing which must be accomplished, wholly and utterly accomplished in Him" (rev., *KD* II/1, 176; *CD* II/1, 157-58). The subjective response is ingredient in the objective accomplishment. Webster summarizes the logic this way:

> The perfection of Jesus Christ's work is such that it stands in need of no human or created mediation. Christ's work is characterized by what might be called "inclusive perfection": its completeness is not only its "being finished," but its effective power in renewing human life by bringing about human response to itself. Consequently, the relation of "objective" and "subjective" shifts. The objective is not a complete realm, separate from the subjective and, therefore, standing in need of "translation" into the subjective. Rather, the objective includes the subjective within itself, and is efficacious without reliance on a quasi-independent realm of mediating created agencies.[57]

56. This is the "christomonist solution" (*CD* IV/4, 19; *KD* IV/4, 20). Barth continues that "the *omni*-effectuality of God must not be interpreted as his *sole*-effectuality!" (rev., *KD* IV/4, 20; *CD* IV/4, 22).

57. John B. Webster, *Barth's Ethics of Reconciliation* (Cambridge: Cambridge University

It is because the event of reconciliation is completed as an act of God that the human has an objective place in this event. Jesus' work calls forth "our objective responsibility," and this involves our participation as "we are ourselves its subjects and it is we who are responsible in it" (*CD* II/2, 664; *KD* II/2, 716). Jesus objectively accomplishes the reconciliation of the divine with the human, and, as subjectively appropriated in the Spirit, human beings live in this reconciled relationship.

Accounts of the nature of the human response act predicated on an ontological difference from the world dictate against this human responsibility, for it intrudes on the nature of divine and human fellowship. Faith cannot be a *"habitual having"* since this "would be a possession outside the divine giving and . . . receiving at God's hand" (*CD* III/4, 663; *KD* III/4, 763). If Christian existence were this *habitus,* then the missionary act would be an act of mediating — of handing over — what the community already possesses. The church would be an end in herself, and her act would be external to the relationship the human shares with God. Only as the church is not herself the means is the community able to witness to the means of grace.

> While the creature is wholly the object and recipient of God's grace, it becomes *ipso facto* — not its means (since grace works immediately or not at all), but its witness, herald and proclaimer, thus, in the utter humility of this its spiritual existence, undertaking an *active* function within the history of the covenant, carrying out a sending and a commission, a sending and a commission to its *fellow-creatures.* (rev., *KD* III/3, 74; *CD* III/3, 64-65)

The human does not add to the completed event of reconciliation, but in its completion, the human community lives as it is active in its corresponding movement to the world. "At the very point where the human herself is called to freedom by the will and work of God, we find that she is also summoned, mobilized and enlisted into action in participation in the occurrence of this will and work of God" (*CD* III/4, 481; *KD* III/4, 551). As reconciliation is the establishment of fellowship of the divine with the hu-

---

Press, 1995), pp. 127-28. To continue with Webster, "the 'subjective' aspect of reconciliation — its effectiveness in human knowledge — is a function of itself." Webster, "'Eloquent and Radiant': The Prophetic Office of Christ and the Mission of the Church," in *Barth's Moral Theology: Human Action in Barth's Thought* (Grand Rapids: Eerdmans, 1998), p. 132.

man and the human with the human, reconciliation is a living event actual in history. As this history, the important thing becomes, not deification, but being conformed to the image of God's Son (Rom. 8:29) (*CD* II/2, 424; *KD* II/2, 470). The "point of contact" consists of this adaptation of the human to the work of God, which means conformity to the work of the Son (*CD* I/1, 238; *KD* I/1, 251). Christians receive the determination to be Jesus' witnesses (Acts 1:8), to become "witnesses to the witness" (*CD* II/2, 425; *KD* II/2, 470). The act is material to Jesus' call to fellowship with him; the gift of fellowship as conformity to Christ is a task laid upon the community.

The subjective human response participates in the occurrence of the already complete event of reconciliation as an echo of that act. The creature "*serves* God's self-glorification in the same way as an echoing wall can serve only to repeat and broadcast the voice which the echo 'answers.' But it really does serve it!" (*CD* II/1, 670; *KD* II/1, 756).[58] Precisely as an echo, the Christian community receives a definite form, one that corresponds to Jesus Christ's own declaration of his work. Christ's resurrection and ascension correspond to the completion of his work by "bringing its *meaning* and its *right* and *light*" (rev., *KD* IV/2, 158; *CD* IV/2, 141). These events did not augment his finished work; they add to the event only that Jesus "was to be *seen* and was actually *seen* as the one who He *was* and *is*" (rev., *KD* IV/ 2, 149; *CD* IV/2, 133). They are "the event of His *self-declaration*" (*CD* IV/2, 133; *KD* IV/2, 149).

This declaration of who Jesus Christ is as the light of the world calls forth the corresponding human echo. Christ's community moved immediately toward Israel and the Gentiles "as those who were *authentically* instructed, as those who knew Him *genuinely* and *rightly*, as witnesses, *authorized* by Him, to His history and existence!" (rev., *KD* IV/2, 150; *CD* IV/ 2, 134). The Christian community does not continue Christ's being; she does not extend or augment his history. Jesus Christ's being and work lacks nothing. The only lack is that not all humanity sees him as the word of God. It is the presence of the Spirit that "is still lacking in the world at large," and it is the proper work of the Spirit to impel Jesus Christ's community into the world (*CD* IV/1, 148; *KD* IV/1, 163). The completion of reconciliation establishes this service of witness as true service to the self-

---

58. Barth further states that "the mission of the Church is the task of reflecting, like a mirror, the Kingdom of God — the work of Christ and of the Holy Spirit. To *reflect* it, not to *do* it!" Barth, "Fragebeantwortung bei der Konferenz der World Student Christian Federation," p. 421.

declaration of the risen and ascended Lord, and this declaration is "a sufficient missionary impulse for the disciples and basis of the community" (*CD* IV/1, 318; *KD* IV/1, 351).

The act of the Christian community does not complete Jesus' own act, but it has its own objectivity as is proper to the creature. The awakening and summoning of Christians means "a *positive* alteration of their being below" (*CD* IV/2, 527; *KD* IV/2, 596). With this determination to become a witness, the human is "objectively changed by the event of revelation" (*CD* II/1, 111; *KD* II/1, 122). The prophets and apostles did indeed have "an indispensable mediative task," and it was through their "witness" that Jesus Christ "makes Himself known" (rev., *KD* IV/3.2, 592; *CD* IV/3.2, 515). This is a question of the Spirit, of how human beings become "what they had not been before, witnesses of the great acts of God as they had taken place in Jesus Christ" (*CD* IV/2, 341; *KD* IV/2, 381). This objective function is not dependent on whether a human "regards herself as able or worthy, nor whether she is willing, nor whether she can guarantee specific results" (*CD* IV/3.2, 609; *KD* IV/3.2, 698). It is not a special calling reserved for those of greater moral or spiritual fortitude. Jesus Christ's "missionary charge" applies to the Christian "apart from any inherent capacity" (*CD* III/2, 449; *KD* III/2, 539). The objective effectiveness of this human witness is "in virtue of the special work to which God has at this point determined and engaged it, because it has become the instrument of His work and has been marked off and is used as such" (*CD* II/1, 17; *KD* II/1, 17).[59] "A real witness knows that he has been *made* a witness, and that he is *called* to be a witness."[60] This "being called means being *given a commission*," it means *"existence in the execution of this commission"* (rev., *KD* IV/3.2, 658; *CD* IV/3.2, 573).[61] With this divine commission, "the apostle of Jesus Christ not only can but *must* be a missionary" (*CD* III/2, 607; *KD* III/2, 738). There is no split between the divine gift and the divine task. This objective act is the nature of Christian existence because it is the nature of the living fellowship between the divine and the human.

59. To quote Jüngel, that another object "can be introduced as a mediation of God's being-as-object is certainly not something grounded in the mediating object itself, but in God's making use of it as such." Jüngel, *God's Being Is in Becoming*, pp. 61-62.

60. Barth, "The Christian as Witness," p. 102.

61. These witnesses, to quote Sonderegger, "will betray all their human traits, including their fallibility in their speech, but they cannot do otherwise. They are carried along by the torrent of God's own speech and act." Katherine Sonderegger, "*Et Resurrexit Tertia Die:* Jenson and Barth on Christ's Resurrection," in Higton and McDowell, *Conversing with Barth*, p. 199.

The Missionary End

"Mission" is a term fraught with such baggage that any constructive use of it requires a good deal of ground-clearing. This cloud of prejudice is partially due to the prevailing anachronistic definitions of mission, and partially to the absence of the concept from theological reflection. However, it reflects a deeper problem of the breach in the being and act of God, of which the natural theology is one manifestation. This primary breach produces a corresponding breach in the being and act of the church, with deleterious consequences for accounts of the nature of Christian community and witness. The community becomes one focused in on herself and distinguished from the world — the space that constitutes the event of witness — as she grows in her distinctive version of the general religious ontic. Mission is a derivative and provisional function of this true end, and its act consists of replicating those elements necessary to the nurture of this Christian distinctive. The task becomes a second step alongside some otherwise defined nature of Christian being. As a second step, those contingencies that initiate the act become determinative for its form.

Barth rejects this cleavage in God by reestablishing the *diastasis* between God and humanity. God overcomes this breach in his own being, and the effect is that God and humanity now share a properly ordered fellowship. The opposition is not one of "nature" and "revelation," but one "of human nature uniquely and definitively *exalted* in Jesus Christ, uniquely and definitively placed at the side of God and in fellowship with Him" (rev., *KD* IV/2, 112; *CD* IV/2, 101). The proper human act that corresponds to this exaltation is mission. The church exists only as "a missionary in the world," and "Christian piety is a life in action in which man serves the purpose of God."[62] This task is only wrongly juxtaposed with the nature of the Christian community as a community. It is the very nature of reconciled human community to become conformed to the image of Christ, to become his witness in the definite form of the church's missionary service to the world. This determination of the human act is one in active correspondence to God's very being, and is the beginning point for the reformulation of *missio Dei* theology, to which we now turn.

---

62. Barth, "Fragebeantwortung bei der Konferenz der World Student Christian Federation," p. 433.

CHAPTER SIX

The Trinity Is a Missionary God

If God requires and makes possible that He should be served by the creature, this service itself means that the creature is taken up into the sphere of divine lordship. We have always to remember that God's glory really consists in His self-giving, and that this has its centre and meaning in God's Son, Jesus Christ, and that the name of Jesus Christ stands for the event in which humanity, and in humanity the whole of creation, is awakened and called and enabled to participate in the being of God. . . . [T]he self declaration of God is true and real, which means that God Himself is God in such a way that He wills to have the creature as a creature with Him, that He does not will to be God without it, without claiming it, but also without being personally present to it.

Karl Barth, *Church Dogmatics*[1]

Introduction

The breached God, occasioned by an improper recourse to natural theology, resulted in a corresponding breached community characterized by a prioritized contemplative being and a derivative missionary act. In other words,

---

1. Barth, *CD* II/1, p. 670; *KD* II/1, p. 756. All source and page citations for quotations from Barth's *Church Dogmatics* in this chapter will appear in parentheses in the text.

the problem of the church's connection with the world is foremost a problem of God: of who he is in himself and who he is in his act of creating, reconciling, and redeeming. How does God's being anticipate his becoming, and his becoming declare his being from all eternity? As no breach characterizes the relationship of God's being to his act, so no corresponding breach should determine the life of his community. In the event of reconciliation, the one God sets himself and the creature in a "differentiated fellowship of action" (*CD* IV/3.2, 598; *KD* IV/3.2, 685). While this ordered relationship, by definition, precludes any human assumption of properly divine responsibility, it is one in which the triune God calls forth a corresponding community. This community, as secondary agents of the event of divine and human reconciliation, lives according to that event and thus in a particular commission. This community is, as such, "a missionary community or she is not the Christian community" (rev., *KD* III/4, 578; *CD* III/4, 505).

This chapter begins the positive reconstruction of *missio Dei* theology. The question of the grounding and consequent form of mission is, first, a question of who *God* is in himself. God is a missionary God because his deliberate acting in apostolic movement toward humanity is not a second step alongside — and thus in distinction to — his perfect divine being. In his economy, in his movement for the human, God lives his own eternal life. The missionary message is one of "the Father from whom it proceeds, the Son who fulfils it objectively (for us), and the Holy Spirit who fulfils it subjectively (in us)" (*CD* I/2, 1; *KD* I/2, 1). Everything that can be said concerning the mission of God and the resulting determination of the Christian community is only an outworking of this "one effective action of God" in the twofold form of Jesus Christ and the Holy Spirit (*CD* IV/3.2, 752; *KD* IV/3.2, 861). Second, it is a question of how it is *actual* that this God lives his own proper life in the economy of salvation. Jesus Christ, the mediator between God and humanity, has objectively completed the reconciliation of the world, and he calls humanity to active participation in the fellowship of God's self-humiliation and his exaltation of the human. Third, it is a question of the *accomplishment* of reconciliation. The Spirit acts to secure the human's subjective involvement in God's act, uniting the human with the history that takes place first in God's own life and then in the history of Jesus Christ with us. Participation in this history takes the particular form of a servant. That is, the community accompanies Jesus Christ in his mission as she herself is an apostolic community — shaped to be so by the witness of the Spirit.

God In and For Himself is a Missionary God

The Problem of God

Missio Dei's "Trinitarianism" developed at an express distance from christology. Propagandistic and imperialist missionary methods were regarded as a result of a myopic focus on Jesus Christ. God's sending of his Son and Spirit revealed God's "sending" nature. Reconceiving mission in terms of God's triune being critically distinguished the act from the fallible human work. However, while this offered a theological justification for the missionary act, a question emerged: Was this to be "understood primarily as derived from the redemptive purpose and acts of God or as derived from the nature of God Himself"?[2] Two forms of *missio Dei* developed relative to each side of this distinction. Those who emphasized the "acts of God" tended to go toward the more established patterns of church structures and missions, with the effect that mission became reduced to the action of the church in her mundane practices, especially the Eucharist. Those who emphasized the "nature of God" sought a more direct connection between mission and political involvement.

While the forms differed, however, they were unified by a Trinitarianism formulated according to this fundamental cleavage between God's being and act. With "sending" as the defining term, constructive accounts of every theological stripe focused on the range of mediators sent by God. *Missio Dei* turned to the doctrines of creation, as the universal work of the Father, and to the Spirit's presence in history and culture. Even those who were concerned about safeguarding traditional accounts only succeeded in underscoring the distinction: a *missio Christi* formed alongside the *missio Dei* as a way of informing "those aspects of God's mission which we do know."[3] A pattern of "sending" characterized Christian existence. This gave mission a Trinitarian façade, but its musculature was nurtured by the doctrines of creation and pneumatology.

This tendency to make a dichotomy between the being of God and his act of movement into the world is not peculiar to *missio Dei* theology.

---

2. Norman Goodall, ed., *Missions under the Cross* (London: Edinburgh House, 1953), p. 244.

3. Jacques Matthey, "God's Mission Today: Summary and Conclusions," *International Review of Mission* 92, no. 4 (2003): 581.

Its origins lie in the christological — and consequently the Trinitarian — controversies and the struggle with how God could be one while also being Father, Son, and Spirit. Many of the difficulties derived from first thinking of God's being in general and according to certain given assumptions about the necessary nature of divinity, and then of his triune nature (*CD* II/1, 349; *KD* II/1, 392). The problem for our missionary question lies in how God's being in and for himself became defined in some opposition to his economy. It belongs to the nature of divinity, and thus to God's perfection, that he is not sent.[4] That is, while the economy epistemically reveals God to be three in one, God's *movement* into the economy cannot be itself ontologically determinative. This has consequences for the missionary question, for God becomes properly defined according to certain attributes, such as simplicity and immutability, while his decision to be for the human becomes "not something which belongs to His proper and essential life, but only to His relationship to the world" (*CD* II/2, 79; *KD* II/2, 85).

If it is possible to so define God's true being apart from his economy, then his *coming* in the economy, though it forms as a parallel to God's eternal nature, occurs in contest with his being. Such a position might suggest an ontological "cleft or rift or gulf in God Himself, between His being and essence in Himself and his activity and work as the Reconciler of the world created by Him" (*CD* IV/1, 184; *KD* IV/1, 201). In himself, God remains the almighty Lord, but in his becoming human he lives at some distance from his being. In his act of reconciliation and redemption, it pleased God "to be in discontinuity with Himself, to be against Himself, to set Himself in self-contradiction," to become "God against God" (*CD* IV/1, 184; *KD* IV/1, 201). If this were the case, then "how could He reconcile the world with Himself?" (*CD* IV/1, 185; *KD* IV/1, 202). This is the missionary question: "What value would His deity be to us if — instead of crossing in that deity the very real gulf between Himself and us — He left that deity behind Him in His coming to us, if it came to be outside of Him as He became ours?" (*CD* IV/1, 185; *KD* IV/1, 202).

If God exists *in se* at "an alien distance," then, first, his becoming hu-

4. See, for example, Holmes's critique of Augustine: "All talk of a 'missionary God' would be merely oxymoronic: one who is a missionary, and so is sent by another, is necessarily not Lord of all, and so not God; conversely, it is a necessary perfection of God's being that he is not sent." Stephen R. Holmes, "Trinitarian Missiology: Towards a Theology of God as Missionary," *International Journal of Systematic Theology* 8, no. 1 (2006): 77.

man would be a "self-alienation" of his own being and not a revelation of the one he is. Second, any human participation in the life of God would have to do only with his external life. God's real being would have to be withheld from humanity. Instead, the verity of reconciliation rests in the affirmation that God himself is present in the encounter between the person Jesus Christ and fallen humanity. Grounding mission in the Trinity means grounding his movement into the world in his being from and to all eternity. The transition between who God is *in se* and his act of reconciliation is "*first* a *divine* problem — the problem of God's *own* being," for it is a problem of how "in anticipation His existence includes within itself our existence with Him. How can the one *be* true and the other *become* true?" (rev., *KD* IV/2, 382-83; *CD* IV/2, 342-43). The problem of *missio Dei* is, as such, "a *problem* of God Himself" (*CD* IV/2, 344; *KD* IV/2, 384).

The Triune Economy and the Being of God

Missio Dei, in its use of the Trinity-derived category of "sending," constitutes an attempt to surmount this problem of the connection between God in himself and the world. In one iteration, an immanent connection forms as God's being becomes a universal principle of world history.[5] God's sending nature becomes a messianic pattern to be repeated, and it is evident in movements that work to break down the old creation and build up the new, movements devoted to the principles of humanization and shalom. The church is reduced to a mere postscript in God's acting, ultimately to the detriment of the task of Christian witness. This account of God's economy became detached from the particular act of God in Christ and susceptible to the charge of projection as recourse to divine ontology supplied an inviolate legitimation to a variety of human ideals.

For Matthey, the solution to *missio Dei*'s abstraction of God's triune being is to disavow "any more precise description of inner-trinitarian *pro-*

---

5. Catherine Mowry LaCugna, for example, solves the problem of God by eliminating "the framework that operates with a gap," the framework of the immanent and economic Trinity. She argues that theology should "abandon the self-defeating fixation on 'God *in se.*'" While, due to the emphasis on *koinonia,* her position better remembers church than this version of *missio Dei,* nevertheless, it uses God's economy to construct a "pattern" of his acting in history. The resulting connection is one of an immanentist variety with all the attendant problems. LaCugna, *God for Us: The Trinity and Christian Life* (New York: HarperSanFrancisco, 1993), p. 225.

cessions. . . . Who are we to know the inner life of God?"[6] Matthey is certainly correct that speculative accounts of God's being, developed in abstraction from the economy of salvation, quickly reduce to an uncritical validation of existing culture. But does it follow that humanity cannot know the inner life of God? Is God ultimately unknowable? While enduring theological validity attaches to the hiddenness and mystery of God, this formulation undercuts the missionary enterprise. The gospel is precisely that "God has not withheld Himself from humanity as true being, but that He has given no less than Himself to humanity as the overcoming of their need, and light in their darkness — Himself as Father in His own Son by the Holy Spirit" (*CD* II/1, 261-62; *KD* II/1, 293). This good news is both the basis and content of the missionary task.

Somewhat counterintuitively, the problems of *missio Dei* theology derive from its inattention to God's being. Abstraction occurred because the focus shifted from *God's* being as Father, Son, and Spirit to *being*. Sending became a universal category with the particular sending of Jesus Christ as one, albeit special, occasion within this general activity of God. As Matthey suggests, this occurred as a result of the differentiation between the missions and the processions, for the processions develop as formal abstractions above the economy. The solution moves in an opposite direction to what Matthey proposes. The proper "subject is *God* and not being, or being only as the being of *God*." A revised Trinitarian theology of mission must begin with the identity of the one who lives his own proper life in reconciling the world to himself, and it is in his acting for the redemption of humanity in sending his Son and Spirit that "we have to do with His *being* as *God*" (*CD* II/1, 260, 261; *KD* II/1, 292).

To avoid the kind of abstraction basic to this form of *missio Dei,* we must begin with a theology of God's aseity — of God's existence in and for himself — for this includes a necessary disjunction: God is God, and the human the human. Such a position must be developed in the light of God's own self-declaration of who he is in his economy.[7] For Barth, it was

6. Jacques Matthey, "Reconciliation, *Missio Dei* and the Church's Mission," in *Mission — Violence and Reconciliation: Papers Read at the Biennial Conference of the British and Irish Association for Mission Studies at the University of Edinburgh, June 2003,* ed. Howard Mellor and Timothy Yates (Sheffield, UK: Cliff College Publishing, 2004), pp. 121-22.

7. See John B. Webster, "Life in and of Himself: Reflections on God's Aseity," in *Engaging the Doctrine of God: Contemporary Protestant Perspectives,* ed. Bruce L. McCormack (Grand Rapids: Baker Academic, 2008), p. 108.

"a retrogression when the idea of God's *aseitas* was interpreted, or rather supplanted, by that of *independentia* or *infinitas,* and later by that of the unconditioned or absolute" (*CD* II/1, 303; *KD* II/1, 341).The result, as Colin Gunton notes, was to turn "a positive (that God is fully real in and for himself) into a negative (that God is defined in terms of his opposition to rather than otherness from the world)."[8] If God's life in himself opposed his creation, any consequent connection would contradict his own being. It is necessary to affirm, instead, that in his act of creating, reconciling, and redeeming, God gives himself entirely to humanity.

Aseity, however, does indicate God's otherness from creation as a necessary correlate. This protects against connections of the above immanent variety, for it means that who God is in himself cannot be reduced to his economy.[9] Doing so would make him "humanity's prisoner" (*CD* I/1, 371; *KD* I/1, 391). As the one act of God in the twofold form of Son and Spirit, "God gives Himself, but He does not give Himself away" (*CD* IV/1, 185; *KD* IV/1, 202). God's connection with the world does not present as a zero-sum game, whereby he is present in history only insofar as he limits his being. For the gift to be the gift of his own being, he must remain in his act as he is himself, and this includes his otherness from humanity.[10] Precisely because God does so give himself, his "becoming and being is and remains a determination of *His* existence. It is *His* act, *His* work" (*CD* I/2, 1; *KD* I/2, 1). As the living God, he cannot cease to live in his act; he remains subject in his economy, not surrendering his living being "by translating it into act" (*CD* II/2, 181; *KD* II/2, 199).

God is in himself distinct from his creation. His connection, as such, occurs not via a simple extension, or abrogation, of his being. Nor does his movement in creation result from some contingency external to God's own life as though his being required some addition to become complete. If this were the case, it would not be a free act and, as such, not the full being of God. God's perfection does not require creation. He moves in his

8. Colin E. Gunton, *Act and Being: Towards a Theology of the Divine Attributes* (London: SCM, 2002), p. 20.

9. From this perspective, it is also necessary to resist "Rahner's rule": "The 'economic' Trinity is the 'immanent' Trinity and the 'immanent' Trinity is the 'economic' Trinity." Karl Rahner, *The Trinity,* trans. Joseph Donceel (New York: Crossroad, 1997), p. 22.

10. See Eberhard Busch, "God Is God: The Meaning of a Controversial Formula and the Fundamental Problem of Speaking about God," *Princeton Seminary Bulletin* 7, no. 2 (1986): 99-113.

economy, to quote Jüngel, because he "has *turned* himself *towards* humanity," because "he *is* really *for us*."[11] God's connection with the world is the result of his own deliberate decision to be for humanity, and this decision belongs to God's being distinct from the world.

In terms of the basis of the missionary act, God's decision must find a clear correspondence in the Christian community. Like Israel, the church is "to choose this day whom she will serve" and is "actualized" by this choice (*CD* III/4, 476; *KD* III/4, 545). This choice is basic to the church's being because it "points back and responds to a divine choice, and therefore the human act to a divine" (*CD* III/4, 475; *KD* III/4, 545).[12] The church's turning to the world is constitutive of her being in relationship with God as he is in himself. Failing to act in this corresponding decision constitutes a breach in the relationship. "Israel's declension from its God and His commandments consists concretely in the breach of *fellowship* between its own being and Himself, which means in practice the *breaking* of the *analogy* between its action and that of its God" (*CD* IV/2, 781; *KD* IV/2, 886). The church, as such, cannot become a mere postscript to God's acting, for this is the form of the divine/human fellowship.

Such a position isolates the basis of the missionary act from every con-

---

11. Eberhard Jüngel, *God's Being Is in Becoming*, trans. John B. Webster (Grand Rapids: Eerdmans, 2001), p. 105.

12. Barth is clear, even with this strong conception of humanity choosing God, that there is no possibility of a return to the activism and synergism that bespeaks a collapse of the *diastasis* between God and humanity. "Certainly it is a history between God and humanity. Certainly there takes place within it a twofold human decision. But this decision takes place in such a way as to form, not the second point in an ellipse, but the circumference around the one central point of which it is the repetition and confirmation. If we think of predestination as identical with this history, there is no danger of the activistic understanding leading us astray in the direction of synergism. In this history there is, of course, cooperation between God and humanity, but not of a kind which does not owe its origin entirely to the working of God" (*CD* II/2, 194; *KD* II/2, 214). This critique follows Barth's reaction to Ritschl's description of Christianity as "an ellipse which is determined by two foci." This unstable image resolves itself around the foci closer to general human experience. He states that "the reality of the experience of God's Word no longer rests on itself; it has become an ellipse instead of a circle, and of the poles, the one nearer us and opposite God, is the human being who has the experience" (*CD* I/1, 213; *KD* I/1, 222), quoting Albrecht Ritschl, *The Christian Doctrine of Justification and Reconciliation: The Positive Development of the Doctrine*, trans. Hugh Ross Mackintosh and A. B. Macaulay (Edinburgh: T. & T. Clark, 1900), p. 11. For Barth's reflection on how this image of two foci in an ellipse relates to conceptions of *analogia entis* and human falsehood, see *CD* IV/3.1, 444-45; *KD* IV/3.1, 512-13.

tingency, for "the proclamation of the Church cannot begin with some sort of human need, concern, care, lack, or problem, nor may it take from these its content or direction."[13] If this were the case, then the Christian community would serve God as an independent agent: her own being for the world proceeding out of her own faithfulness and according to her own interpretation of the message entrusted to her. This leads again to an undue identification of the gospel with a culture and the reduction of the missionary act to distributing the structures basic to this culture and out of which Christian witness flows. As God's deliberate turning to the world belongs to his own being, so the church's deliberate turning to the world belongs to her relationship with him. It is not an act an otherwise constituted church may or may not choose to perform.

Triune Immanence and the Act of God

In the second iteration of *missio Dei*, God's connection with the world is through his redemptive act in Jesus Christ, one that the church now serves. While this appears to be a more satisfactory position, it draws on an identical breach between who God is in himself and who he is in reconciling the world to himself. In this case, the deliberate decision of God for the human occurs as a second step, and this establishes a logical and ontological order of being and then act. John Webster, by way of example, posits two movements in the life of God. God's perfection includes his act as "not the first but a second movement of the being of God. The first movement is the eternally mobile repose of the Holy Trinity, the life, peace and love of Father, Son and Spirit." The second corresponding movement occurs when "the fullness of God is the origin and continuing ground of a reality which is *outside* his own life; 'outside', not in the sense of unrelated, but in the sense of having its own integral being as a gift rather than as an extension of God's own being."[14] To protect both the otherness of God and human freedom, creation cannot be a contingent necessity to God. It must be "outside" God.

The problem, which becomes evident with the introduction of mis-

13. Karl Barth, "The Proclamation of God's Free Grace," in *God Here and Now* (New York: Routledge, 2003), p. 37.

14. John B. Webster, *Confessing God: Essays in Christian Dogmatics II* (Edinburgh: T. & T. Clark, 2005), p. 167.

sionary witness as a critical standard, lies in the ambiguity of how the second movement is "not unrelated" to the first.[15] This language of a first and second movement in the life of God tends to be formulated in terms of a logical and consequential order. God's perfection attaches to the first movement in such a way that the second movement proceeds out of the first. For the church, her life becomes oriented to this account of divine perfection, which does not include his movement into the economy as part of that perfection. The church, her life of worship, is defined in terms of God's own "mobile repose," and hence otherness from the world. This has acute consequences for the missionary nature of the church, as indicated by the general absence of mission from dogmatic treatments of God's connection with his creation and from the concomitant ecclesiologies. In other words, one can develop full accounts of the church without reference to her missionary being.

Ecumenically attractive "communion" ecclesiologies located in a social Trinitarianism illustrate the issue well. Such positions have the strength of understanding God's being in terms of act. As Father, Son, and Spirit, "the *nature* of God is communion."[16] The "being of God is a community of energies, of *perichoretic* interaction."[17] The term "act" indicates here the internal relationships of the persons of the Trinity, and it follows

15. This curious avoidance of the missionary question, which, I propose, is indicative of an inadequate description of God's perfection as determined by who he is in his economy, is evident in Webster's otherwise fine work *Barth's Ethics of Reconciliation* (Cambridge: Cambridge University Press, 1995). Webster posits two forms of human action that flow from Barth's doctrine of creation and inform his ethics of reconciliation: prayer and the active life. His primary concern is to demonstrate the prevenience of grace in relation to human response. While "prayer" in this section does not primarily refer to "cultic or liturgical formation of moral dispositions," it nonetheless receives a material form (p. 77). The "active life," by contrast, is used as a negative contrast to a "work ethic" while not itself receiving any material form. The problem is that Barth is himself clear as to the form of the "active life": active participation in the missionary existence of the Christian community (see *CD* III/4, 470-516). Why omit such a description when dealing with the "ethics of reconciliation," especially when Barth understands the so defined "active life" to be "service of the active human life confronting and corresponding to the center of divine action, i.e., the coming of God's kingdom" (*CD* III/4, 485)?

16. John D. Zizioulas, *Being as Communion: Studies in Personhood and the Church* (Crestwood, NY: St. Vladimir's, 1985), p. 134.

17. Colin E. Gunton, "The Church on Earth: The Roots of Community," in *On Being the Church: Essays on the Christian Community*, ed. Colin E. Gunton and Daniel W. Hardy (Edinburgh: T. & T. Clark, 1989), p. 68.

that nothing accrues to God's being in his act of creating. God's life is already active. While his economy of reconciliation is epistemologically significant, it is not ontologically substantive for God's life *in se*. A tacit ordering develops whereby God's immanent life becomes his most basic existence, with this movement in the economy already secondary to this being. God's *in se* Trinitarian being-in-act is a first complete step alongside which God's movement toward the world in creating, reconciling, and redeeming is a second step.

The material effect of this position for *missio Dei* is evident in how communion ecclesiologies posit the nature of the church and her missionary task. The "being of the Church must be rooted in the being of God." She is to reflect "God's eternal being in relationship."[18] Such claims are, of course, correct. The nature of the church, and so how she acts, must indeed correspond to the life of the triune God. However, the problem is that if the nature of God's perfection does not include the second movement into the economy, then the church becomes oriented to a corresponding non-economic perfection. Robert Jenson illustrates this point when he posits the church according to "its own proper entity, in which it is in God's intention antecedent to the gospel."[19] The being of the church is antecedent to God's using it to carry the gospel to the world because God's own life is antecedent to his economy. The *koinonia* basic to the being of the church is defined in terms of a repose for which the second movement into the world is "not unrelated," but does not of itself define the nature of that fellowship.

Two consequences follow. First, as Nicholas Healy suggests, with this inner communion logically and so ontologically prior to the external act, the church's inner life becomes the focal point.[20] Ecclesiastical practices and the nature of worship become theologically directed and liturgically codified to nurture this form of fellowship. Second, as it belongs to God's life to reveal himself as a natural overflow of his prior internal relationships, so the church's witness emerges as a *gestalt* — a natural overflow — of these internal practices and the corresponding *koinonia*. The church's external witness, as such, takes the practical form of an ever-intensifying internal devotion.

18. Gunton, "The Church on Earth," pp. 74, 73.

19. Robert W. Jenson, *Systematic Theology II: The Works of God* (New York: Oxford University Press, 1999), p. 168.

20. Nicholas M. Healy, "Communion Ecclesiology: A Cautionary Note," *Pro Ecclesia* 4, no. 4 (1995): 444.

One could draw a variety of so-called implications for mission from such a position.[21] This is already to indicate its fundamental flaw. Mission becomes the derivative external extension of this primary inward-oriented relationality, and distinguished from the act of worship. The resulting missionary method thus becomes one of transmitting those practices necessary to building up this essentially noneconomic fellowship.[22] Such a claim is easily illustrated by observing the absence of any reference to the missionary act within communion accounts of the church. Indeed, it is not only possible, but normative, to develop full ecclesiologies based on a social account of the Trinity and to omit the missionary act as immaterial to the being of the church.[23] This is not a problem of simple oversight, perhaps surmounted by a remedial inclusion of the missionary act. It is a theological determination consequent on defining God's perfection without giving his coming in the economy any ontological weight. As God's act is a derivative overflow of who he is, so the church's missionary act is a second step alongside her eternal nature.

While it is necessary to distinguish God's immanent life from his economy — precisely for the sake of God's deliberate decision for humanity — this cannot result in an ordering for which the economy becomes a derivative act alongside an otherwise defined being. It is because God's act is free, deliberate, and noncontingent that it is not a second step.

The freedom in which God exists means that He does not need His own being in order to be who He is: because He already *has* His own being

21. The dominant approach within the contemporary theology of mission consists of drawing implications for mission from preexistent theological models that do not themselves treat mission as in any way constitutive. Thus mission obtains theological justification for the act in positions that regard mission as secondary and, *eo ipso,* nonessential.

22. That culture assumes such a status in relation to the doctrine of the Trinity is overt in Robert W. Jenson, "Christian Civilization," in *God, Truth, and Witness: Engaging Stanley Hauerwas,* ed. L. Gregory Jones, Reinhard Hütter, and C. Rosalee Velloso da Silva (Grand Rapids: Brazos, 2005), p. 161.

23. Miroslav Volf, in his acclaimed book *After Our Likeness,* uses a social Trinitarian model to advance a theological method whereby he focuses "mainly inside, at the inner nature of the church," while sidelining "the outside world and the church's mission" to his "peripheral vision." Reference to the Trinity, in other words, does not make it necessary to understand the nature of the church in terms of her movement into the world; instead, it is normative to think of the church in terms of her *koinonia* defined in internal terms. Volf, *After Our Likeness: The Church as the Image of the Trinity* (Grand Rapids: Eerdmans, 1998), p. 7.

and *is* Himself; because nothing can accrue to Him from Himself which He had not or was not already; because, therefore, His being in its self-realization or the actuality of His being answers to no external pressure but is only the affirmation of His own plenitude and a self-realization in freedom. (*CD* II/1, 306; *KD* II/1, 344).

God's movement adds nothing to his eternal glory, and precisely as such it is not to be so distanced from his being that its contemporary operation unfolds as a mechanistic dynamic behind which God has retired, "taking His rest and satisfying Himself again with His own inner life" (*CD* II/2, 182; *KD* II/2, 199).[24] God's *movement* into the economy belongs to his being from all eternity. It is not alongside who God is; rather, it is the very plenitude of God's own life that is capable of including the human in such a way that this inclusion is God's own self-realization. Even if theological accounts posit God's being in active terms such as relationality, these remain unsatisfactory if they do not witness to a God who, in loving freedom, "tied Himself to the universe" (*CD* II/2, 155; *KD* II/2, 169). For *missio Dei,* the coordinated ecclesiological affirmation rests in denying that the church must first *be* before she can *act* in mission. As there is no "contradiction and rift in the being of God," so the *koinonia* of Christian community has to be understood in terms of her own movement for the world (*CD* IV/1, 186; *KD* IV/1, 203). The church is a missionary community because the God she worships is missionary.

The Living God

Missio Dei's binary forms, one located in the being of God (and thus in the external movement of history), the other in the act of God (and thus in the internal life of the church), reflect a contest of the following contrary affirmations: "the assertion of the divinity of a motionless being as the beginning of all things, against the assertion of the divinity of a moved history, static against dynamic, in the final analysis perhaps a quietistic against an activistic view of life" (rev., *KD* II/2, 205-6; *CD* II/2, 187). The resulting gap between God's life *in se* and his existence in relationship to the world re-

---

24. God's self-determination is a living determination, and there is no need to substitute this for "a concept of isolated static being" (*CD* II/2, 184; *KD* II/2, 202).

quires some bridging external to God himself: either the church orients herself and the world to this "quietistic God," or history assumes the role of the "activistic God." The problem, however, lies not in the distinction between God's life *in se* and his movement in the economy, but in an ordering that renders the economy ontologically void. It becomes a question of their proper relationship, and this is itself to be governed by the history of God's fellowship with humanity in Jesus Christ. To foreshadow the following section, "insofar as we recognize the mystery of the divine decision in the *concrete person of Jesus Christ* we contradict the dynamic and activist view; insofar as we understand Jesus Christ as the *decision of the eternally living God* we contradict the static and quietist view" (rev., *KD* II/2, 206; *CD* II/2, 187). In Jesus Christ, God's being is active in determining the human, and the human is passive in this determination. With the divine decision retaining the initiative, the relationship of the active to the passive is indeed asymmetrical, though it does not itself bear ontological weight. Such an asymmetrical relationship satisfies all the theological caveats concerning the need to begin with God as he is in himself and the need to understand this God in terms of his movement into his economy, for this asymmetry gives the relationship a definite character: it is an eloquent living fellowship.

As triune, God's own life is one of the distinction of the Father and Son and of the union of the Father and Son in the Holy Spirit. God's fatherliness is the capacity to "set Himself in relation to everything distinct from Him" (*CD* I/1, 394; *KD* I/1, 414-15). Such is his acting from all eternity. In begetting the Son, the Father does not disqualify the difference between himself and the Son; God is his own opposite (*CD* IV/1, 201; *KD* IV/1, 220).[25] He brings that difference into unity with himself; he is the one God. There is an above and below in God, and this encounter is the fellowship of love shared between the Father and the Son. God's gracious act toward the human occurs not in differentiation to who God is. The Father's act in begetting the Son establishes both the deliberate nature of his turning to humanity and the fact that this act belongs to God's perfect being in and for himself from and to all eternity.

The answer to God's own antithesis is the presence and action of the

---

25. The German term, which I have translated as "opposite," and which the *CD* translates as "counterpart," is *"gegenüber."* A notoriously difficult term to translate, the sense here includes the notion of encounter and determination.

Holy Spirit. The fellowship of the Father's eternal begetting of the Son and the Son's eternal being begotten of the Father are opened up by the proceeding of the Holy Spirit from the Father and Son. It is in the Spirit that "the history, the transition, the mediation and the communication between the Father and the Son take place and are revealed *as such*" (*CD* IV/2, 345; *KD* IV/2, 385). The unity that is God's own life, as such, is the very opposite of "being in and for oneself," of "being enclosed and imprisoned in one's own being" (*CD* IV/1, 202; *KD* IV/1, 220-21). It is a unity of "a first with a second, an above with a below, an origin with a consequence. It is a dynamic not static, a living not dead, unity" (rev., *KD* IV/1, 221; *CD* IV/1, 202). This unity in distinction refers to the "operation," the dynamic quality of a "uniting," a life that is the majestic, glorious, abundant nature of God. God is in himself unity in distinction, and the nature of this unity is expressive. God's life *in se* is a "*history in partnership*" (*CD* IV/2, 345; *KD* IV/2, 385).

The character of this history is not "mute and obscure" (*CD* IV/3.1, 79; *KD* IV/3.1, 87). Such is the way of idolatry. The "true and living God is eloquent and radiant" (*CD* IV/3.1, 79; *KD* IV/3.1, 87). It is not only in his relationship to the world that he is thus. His eloquence and radiance in creation and history belong to his being from all eternity in the distinction of Father and Son in the unity of the Spirit. "God is, from all eternity, in Himself living, i.e. God *is* in that He *acts* from all eternity in His inner relationships as Father, Son and Holy Spirit" (rev., *KD* II/2, 192; *CD* II/2, 175).[26] This livingness is not to be abstracted from the deliberate decision of God's life. "There is no going back behind this act and decision, behind the livingness of God" (rev., *KD* II/1, 305; *CD* II/1, 272). God is distinct from his creation in his own bridging of the gap between himself and creation, for this "history in partnership is the *life of God* before and above all creaturely life" (*CD* IV/2, 345; *KD* IV/2, 385). He is complete in such a way that his becoming is not an ancillary step beside who he is in himself. His apostolic act is his own "superfluity," but not as a second movement (*CD* IV/1, 201; *KD* IV/1, 220). The first and second in the life of God does not proceed as cause and effect as though the partnership shared by the Father and Son were merely "a first and static thing which is then succeeded by the history as a second and dynamic" (*CD* IV/2, 344; *KD* IV/2, 385).

26. As Jüngel suggests, "the ontological location of God's being in becoming is an attempt to *think* theologically in what way God is *the living one*." Jüngel, *God's Being Is in Becoming*, pp. xxv-xxvi.

All of this is to again fall prey to an undue compartmentalization of God's being from his act. "From all eternity God posits His whole majesty (and this is the meaning and purpose of the act of eternal predestination) in his particular relationship to this particular being *over against* Himself. God pledges and commits Himself to be the God of *humanity*" (*CD* II/2, 177; *KD* II/2, 193-94). The Father's act in sending the Son and Spirit into fallen creation is not separate from who God is in himself. God is in himself the answer to the problem of the connection between the divine and the human. "As He bridges the gulf which opens up before us between there and here, before and after, above and below, He is Himself the pledge that it is really bridged" (*CD* IV/2, 345; *KD* IV/2, 385-86). The problem of God's connection with the human and its solution *is* true in God, and because it is true in God, it must *become* true. God is *in se* already being-in-act, but in such a way that his movement into the economy is not incidental to his immanence. God is already "ours in advance" (*CD* I/1, 383; *KD* I/1, 403-4). As opposed to claims that God's perfection precludes his sending, "missionary" describes its very nature. "It is not accidental or external to Him, but *essential* and proper, to declare Himself. He does this as He is God and lives as such" (*CD* IV/3.1, 79-80; *KD* IV/3.1, 87).[27] As the living God, God is a missionary God: in God's self-determination, the apostolic mission properly belongs to the eternal life of God.

The Unity of the One Son

God's Self-Determination

The missionary enterprise originates, not in historical contingencies external to the event of divine/human fellowship, but in the being of God. The answer to the problem of the gap and the bridge is the triune being of God, because it "takes place first in *God Himself*. It is an event in His essence and being and life" (*CD* IV/2, 341; *KD* IV/2, 381). However, this does not yet address how the corresponding human act might participate in this eternal ground. How does God's missionary being *determine* the human act of

27. Jüngel, too, holds that "the self-relatedness of the deity of God takes place in an unsurpassable way in the very selflessness of the incarnation of God. That is the meaning of talk about the humanity of God. It is not a second thing next to the eternal God but rather the event of the deity of God." Eberhard Jüngel, *God as the Mystery of the World*, p. 372.

mission, and how is this act *determined by* the being of God? This question does not depart from the doctrine of God; rather, it is one of how it is actual that God lives his own proper life in the economy of salvation, and, to quote Jüngel, of "the *ground* of humanity's being taken up into the event of God's being."[28] The question of the missionary act is answered in God's self-humiliation and his exaltation of the human.

Natural theology constitutes an improper attempt to bridge the gap between humanity and God, with consequences both for the doctrine of God and for the corresponding nature of the Christian community. A necessary defense against this improper breach of God's being and act rests in the proper distinction of God and humanity, the establishment of God as God and the human as human. In his eternal decision, God determines himself to fellowship with the human, and determines the human to fellowship with himself.

This self-determination is "*primarily* a determination of *divine* essence: not an alteration, but a determination! God does not first elect and determine the human, but first and above all Himself" (rev., *KD* IV/2, 92; *CD* IV/2, 84). God lives in his primal decision, for "there is no height or depth in which God can be God in any other way" (*CD* II/2, 77; *KD* II/2, 82-83). God is Father, Son, and Spirit. No God exists behind this God. Nor does any diminution of God's divinity occur in this decision. Humanity is encountered by the fullness of God in Jesus Christ.

As his *self*-determination, God does not act out of any need. Everything the human might offer God, such as its differentiation from God, "He has also *in Himself* as God, as the original and essential determination of His being and life as *God*" (rev., *KD* IV/1, 220; *CD* IV/1, 201). Far from devaluing the human, this decision constitutes the highest valuation of the human (Heb. 2:6-9). God humbles himself to be the God of the human (Phil. 2:6-11), and this is the glory of God. The Father's sending of the Son in the power of the Spirit is not merely a remedial work for a fallen world. God's act is not out of any contingency, even if that be human sin. His redemptive mission is God's self-declaration of who he is in himself from all eternity. In this determination to be for and with the human, the apostolic mission belongs properly to the eternal life of God. This "election of grace is the whole of the Gospel, the Gospel *in nuce*. It is the very essence of all good news" (*CD* II/2, 13-14; *KD* II/2, 13).

28. Jüngel, *God's Being Is in Becoming*, p. 76.

Significant implications follow for *missio Dei* theology. The particular and living nature of God's decision precludes launching predestination "upon the general stream of world-events in time" (*CD* II/2, 185; *KD* II/2, 203). Reconciliation is complete. As this completion corresponds to the form of God's own eternal perfection, it does not mean the termination of God's decision. The event of election in which the missionary determination of God determines the human missionary correspondence remains the event of election. The differentiated fellowship of action which is God's life from all eternity cannot be reduced down to a "messianic pattern" to be repeated.

Nor does this account of predestination lead to the opposite emphasis whereby God's self-determination is handed over to the church. Predestination is not to be launched "upon the particular stream of the saving events in which world-events as a whole find their meaning and end" (*CD* II/2, 185; *KD* II/2, 203). Because it is a history of God's reconciliation with the *world*, it "is not exhausted in the history of the Christian community and the Christian faith" (*CD* IV/1, 644; *KD* IV/1, 719). God's *encountering* humanity cannot be surpassed.

To put it another way, the dueling orders of God-church-world and God-world-church both fail, for their ordering is based on an improper breach in the life of God. A better epigram of this relationship would be: God — God/human — human. God does not choose between the church and the world: God, in Jesus Christ, chooses humanity. This sets the church in her proper relationship to the world. The human response, as the form of human fellowship with the divine, conforms to God's initiating action. While God remains the acting subject in the divine-human fellowship, the human is also subject by virtue of this relationship as it acts in correspondence to God's decision. Against trends within *missio Dei* to undervalue the Christian community, the human act receives a definite communal form as it becomes obedient to God's own particular apostolic self-determination. With God's decision for the whole of humanity, it is not sufficient for that community to receive her determination in repose. "What Christians have *in and for themselves* in the sharply differentiated *particularity* of their being they have as the bearers and representatives of a specially qualified and emphasized *solidarity* with all other human beings" (*CD* IV/1, 750; *KD* IV/1, 838). Her dignity rests in her active mission to the world, and "it is not idly, but as she *performs* this, that the community exists for the world" (*CD* IV/3.2, 769; *KD* IV/3.2, 879). This particular commission within which the community lives constitutes the differentiating

element between her and the world. As God's holiness forms as his movement into the economy, so the community's holy distance from the world
is her active existence in solidarity with those for whom God has decided.

Actus Purus et Singularis

God's bridging of the gap in himself in his eternal self-determination and
determination of the human means that he, "in the beginning of all His
ways and works, was not alone, and did not work alone: *not without the human*" (rev., *KD* IV/2, 34; *CD* IV/2, 32). This reference to humanity is not
first a reference to humanity in general. "The reality of this eternal being
together of God and humanity is a *concrete* decree. It has as its content one
name and one person" (*CD* II/2, 158; *KD* II/2, 172). Jesus Christ is God's
elect, and, because of that, "*actus purus* is not sufficient as a description of
God; *et singularis* must, at least, be added" (rev., *KD* II/1, 296; *CD* II/1, 264).
Jesus Christ is the "*one* thing which both differentiates and comprehends
the reconciling God above and the reconciled human below" (*CD* IV/1, 122;
KD IV/1, 133-34). In him, the history of God is not a history of the divine
alone. The proper historicity of God's life *in se* cannot be reduced to a
static existence of the divine in isolated repose. "This history, encounter
and decision between God and humanity was in the beginning with God,
and is identical neither with the one nor the other" (*CD* II/2, 185; *KD* II/2,
203). It is a question of the nature of his fellowship and its living unity, and
the hypostatic union of Jesus Christ's two natures is the decisive event of
the ordered participation of the divine and the human.

This unity of the one Son critically negates the improper antagonism
of the active and the passive by setting them in their proper relationship.
First, "in so far as He is *God,* we must obviously — and above all! — ascribe to Him the active determination of electing" (rev., *KD* II/2, 110; *CD*
II/2, 103). God was deliberate in this self-determination before the creation
of the world, and so the activist side of the relationship retains the priority.
Human participation in the divine is a result of the prior reality of divine
participation in human being. Second, "in so far as He is *human,* the passive determination of election is also necessarily proper to Him" (*CD* II/2,
103; *KD* II/2, 110). Jesus Christ is obedient to God's decision and witnesses
to the Father as he acts in correspondence to this decision. In Jesus Christ,
"God stands before the human and the human stands before God, as it is

God's eternal will, and as it is the eternal determination of the human which corresponds to the will of God" (rev., *KD* II/2, 101; *CD* II/2, 94). The missionary movement from God's being to humanity and the corresponding missionary determination of the Christian community is through this "*living* and *active*" mediator (*CD* IV/1, 123; *KD* IV/1, 135).

This twofold movement of divine humiliation and human exaltation in God's eternal decision can be clarified via the Nicene phrase "and became man." The two emphases of this phrase — that the incarnation is a *fact* and an *event* — inform the coordinated question of how God's missionary life *determines* the human act, and of how his missionary community *is determined by* the being of God.[29]

The Incarnation: Et homo factus *est*

The incarnation is a completed fact. "What was God's eternal will has *happened* within time, a *perfectum* once and for all, and it is impossible to go behind or before it, to abstract from it, to act in relation to it as though it had not yet happened: *et homo factus* est" (rev., *KD* IV/2, 48; *CD* IV/2, 45-46). Jesus Christ, in his existence as very God and very human, is the mediator. He is not "a possibility somewhere before us, but an actuality behind us" (rev., *KD* IV/2, 48-49; *CD* IV/2, 46). God's self-humiliation is a reality that cannot be avoided. It confronts humanity in all its complete perfection, establishing the determining order of divine and human participation: the divine retains the intentional priority in the event of participation; the human participates in posing as a participant in something that precedes her.[30]

29. This point is also found in *CD* I/2, 170, where Barth, with respect to a discussion between the Lutheran and Reformed emphases, observes that we can view the incarnation "from the standpoint of the *completed* event, or we may look at it from the standpoint of the completed *event*."

30. Bruce L. McCormack, "Barths grundsätzlicher Chalcedonismus?" *Zeitschrift für dialektische Theologie* 18, no. 2 (2002): 162-64. Throughout this discussion the *KD* uses the phrase "Teilnahme und Teilhabe," which the *CD* translates as "mutual participation." However, when Barth wants to express the idea of mutuality he adds the term "beiderseitig" (mutual) to the phrase "Teilnahme und Teilhabe" (see *KD* IV/2, 78). Thus, "mutuality" is not the intended focus. The proper sense concerns the determining order of the participation: where "Teilnahme" refers to the intentional engagement in participation by the divine, "Teilhabe" refers to the human's participation in the sense of "attendance," an idea Barth will develop with the phrase "tätiges Dabeisein," a "being actively present."

Because the Son of God and the Son of Man live in the unity of the one Son without confusion or separation, both share in this mutual fellowship in a way that is proper to their respective natures. That the divine and the human live a "mutual" relationship "cannot be understood in the sense of 'interchangeable'. The relationship between the two is not reversible" (*CD* IV/2, 70-71; *KD* IV/2, 76). Jesus Christ's humanity is not altered in this relationship. He was not deified by virtue of his divinity, nor did any super-added capacity accrue to his humanity. "If the human essence of Jesus Christ is deified, can He really be the Mediator between God and us?" (*CD* IV/2, 89; *KD* IV/2, 97). Yet, precisely in Jesus Christ's being human, "human essence becomes and is exalted into fellowship with God" (rev., *KD* IV/2, 127; *CD* IV/2, 114). His humanity is established as proper humanity, for it is as fully human that the fact of the incarnation already indicates the reality of this true fellowship between God and the human. Due to the uniqueness and perfection of the hypostatic union, this union is "*established* and will *not* cease" (rev., *KD* IV/2, 112; *CD* IV/2, 101). True humanity is located in Jesus Christ and is thus determined to fellowship with God. It is a promise of the determination of all humanity.

The asymmetry of this divine-human fellowship precludes any static connection apart from this active encounter. The exaltation of the human in the event of reconciliation, "since it consists in participation in the being of God[,] can only come from *God*" (*CD* IV/1, 8-9; *KD* IV/1, 7). That God in his self-determination aims at human participation in his divine being is not at issue.[31] God "receives us through His Son into *His* fellow-

---

31. This is, to be sure, an eschatological statement, a subject I will examine in the next chapter. However, we must take care with statements such as the following from Bruce McCormack: "Barth never speaks directly of a participation in God *in this world* with respect to anyone other than Jesus Christ." Bruce L. McCormack, "Participation in God, Yes, Deification, No: Two Modern Protestant Responses to an Ancient Question," in *Denkwürdiges Geheimnis: Beiträge zur Gotteslehre, Festschrift für Eberhard Jüngel zum 70. Geburtstag*, ed. Ingolf Ulrich Dalferth, Johannes Fischer, and Hans-Peter Grosshans (Tübingen: Mohr Siebeck, 2004), p. 359. This, on the one hand, is not materially incorrect: only Jesus Christ, as both divine and human, directly participates in the being of the Trinity. "The event of reconciliation proclaimed in the resurrection of Jesus Christ . . . can and will always be found and known in Him . . . but for the time being it will be found and known only in Him" (*CD* IV/1, 730; *KD* IV/1, 815). On the other hand, it fails to take account of the eschatological reality of such an affirmation, one that characterizes not only the entire existence of the Christian community but of the entire world. For McCormack, human "participation in God belongs to our eschatological future, a future whose arrival will

ship with *Himself*" (*CD* II/1, 275; *KD* II/1, 309). With this, the whole of creation is "awakened and called and enabled to participate in the being of God" (*CD* II/1, 670; *KD* II/1, 756). While *"true* and *real,"* however, human participation in God's triune self-knowledge is *"indirect* participation" (*CD* II/1, 59; *KD* II/1, 64). Only as humans participate in Jesus Christ's own humanity do they participate in the life of God. This "direct participation in *Jesus Christ*" occurs "only in *discipleship,* only in the life of obedience as a member of His *community*" (*CD* III/3, 257; *KD* III/3, 291). It obtains a definite form that corresponds to Jesus Christ's own humanity, which, as it is exalted to live in fellowship with God, to quote Bruce McCormack, "consists in this: "that He actively conforms Himself to the history of God's self-humiliation and, in doing so, *is made a vehicle of it.*"[32] As Jesus Christ was himself both fully God and fully human, there is "qualitatively different determination" of his human essence. Human beings who live in rec-

---

mean the end of history" (p. 359). He continues that "defenders of the older metaphysics will find in the historical and relational account of participation in God . . . too little in the way of present realization" (p. 374). In other words, McCormack's emphatic *"in this world"* impacts the subjective appropriation of the objective reconciliation accomplished in Jesus Christ. A defense against this potential misconception requires an account of what action is undertaken in this world, and there is a firm actualist reason for asserting that human beings do participate in God's being here and now. Such a statement needs obvious qualification to avoid the danger of any undue ontological conflation. If God's being is a being in becoming, however, and if human beings become active subjects in the act in which God reveals himself, it follows that, in this function, human beings must share some fellowship with the being of God. This finds confirmation in a statement such as the following from Barth: the creature is "responsible before God, and thus has a share in the Work of God and therefore in God Himself — a creaturely share in a creaturely manner, but nevertheless a real share" (*CD* III/2, 177; *KD* III/2, 211). Because God's being is a being-in-becoming, McCormack's acknowledgment that "our existence is brought into a relation of correspondence to our true essence in Him and the split between them overcome," does not require the qualification "even if only actualistically," for, as triune, God's being is "actualistic" (p. 360). Actualist accounts require a concrete exposition of the human act corresponding to the act in which God reveals himself, and, with Barth's conception of the Christian community's missionary existence, his work contains a thick account of this event. McCormack's necessary caveats are all achieved by reference to the language of calling, located, as it is, within the doctrine of election and calling's objective de jure reality and subjective de facto possibility. Recognizing human participation in God's being via active participation in the missionary existence of the Christian community retains all the necessary admonitions against deification while granting the historical reality of Barth's language of "awaken," "call," and "participation."

32. McCormack, "Barths grundsätzlicher Chalcedonismus?" p. 165.

onciled fellowship with God do not become a vehicle of God's grace in the same way; they do not themselves become "little Christs."[33]

Nevertheless, as fellowship is a living relationship of God's determination and the human's response, so Jesus Christ's "human essence determined in this way is in fact the same as ours" (*CD* IV/2, 89; *KD* IV/2, 98). Participation in Jesus Christ's act of response is the direct form of human participation in him, following his sending into the world proclaiming the coming and present kingdom of God. The "*ontological* connection" between the human Jesus and human being, and between the "active" and the "prospective" Christian, takes this particular form: in the New Testament, "the gathering and upbuilding of the *community* of those who acknowledge Jesus Christ is depicted as a *necessity* grounded in Himself," and "this community is sent out and entrusted with the task of *mission* in the world, again with a *necessity* grounded in Himself. Jesus Christ would not be who He is if He lacked His community, and if this community lacked, or was even capable of lacking, a missionary character" (rev., *KD* IV/2, 305; *CD* IV/2, 275). The immediate and differentiated ontological connection between Jesus Christ and his community takes the necessary form of the missionary existence of the community.

This determination to proclamatory service does not demand a super-added capacity: the human being is not altered in this service. Indeed, the opposite is true. "As God exists for the world in His divine way, and Jesus Christ in His divine-human, so the Christian community exists for it in her own purely human way" (rev., *KD* IV/3.2, 899; *CD* IV/3.2, 786). It is a determination proper to human life in its asymmetrical fellowship with the divine: God claims and the human responds. The Christian does not become a "co-creator, co-savior, co-ruler and so a kind of co-god, but merely that her creaturely acting at her place, and within her limits, might

---

33. Paul T. Nimmo, as an illustration of this point, says that "the fullness of the Chalcedonian definition cannot therefore be arrogated by the Christian, because the union it describes is and remains extrinsic to the believer — it is an alien and forensic union even as it determines the Christian's true existence." Nimmo, "Karl Barth and the *concursus Dei* — A Chalcedonianism Too Far?" *International Journal of Systematic Theology* 9, no. 1 (2007): 67. The Christian never shares an immediate determination of the divine, as is true of Jesus Christ. In Barth's words, the "*unio personalis* of Jesus Christ is itself alone the true *unio mystica*" (*CD* IV/2, 57; *KD* IV/2, 61-62). However, this does not preclude the objective determination of the Christian community in which she is made subject in God's own act and thus is necessarily active in missionary existence.

be shaped into an acting that corresponds to the divine acting" (rev., *KD* III/4, 552; *CD* III/4, 482). The distinction between Jesus Christ and his community remains as a "strict and indissoluble distinction of position and functions" (*CD* IV/3.1, 279; *KD* IV/3.1, 321-22). The mutuality remains irreversible. Yet the "real difference" between Jesus Christ and his community does not translate into a "rigid *either-or* between His being and action and the being and action of the community" (*CD* IV/3.1, 206-7; *KD* IV/3.1, 236). He can represent his community to the Father, and his community can represent him to the world. The totality of redemptive history is a history of this dynamic differentiation in unity, where human beings are also present as active subjects in the history of Jesus Christ. A failure to understand this "direct connection" constitutes a failure to understand his "whole being and work" (*CD* IV/3.1, 279; *KD* IV/3.1, 322). This connection exists as a result of his perfect work and in his coordinated giving of the Holy Spirit. Because reconciliation takes place as a completed event, it cannot be a history of the divine and the human in isolation. It is an action in which the divine takes up dwelling in the human, and the human participates in the fullness of the divine.

The living history of this ordered ontological connection takes a missionary form. "Opposite the Lord Jesus, absolutely subordinate to Him, but distinct from Him, there is another element in the reality of His revelation: *an apostolate,* human beings, commissioned, authorized and empowered by Him to witness, whose human word can be accepted by all kinds of people as proclamation of the 'wonderful works of God.'" (rev., *KD* I/1, 477; *CD* I/1, 455). The sending of the community is not an act external to Jesus Christ's own being sent; the community does not take up Christ's lordship. Her sending is an act that is the form of human reconciliation with God in the asymmetrical character of a correspondence to God's own act. What the human "may be for God is inwardly and inseparably connected to what God is for her: with her deliverance, her employment; with her faith in the promise of God, her responsibility for its wider proclamation; with her blessedness, her obedience in His service and commission as a witness to God's graceful election" (rev., *KD* II/2, 458; *CD* II/2, 414).

No separation occurs whereby the Christian exists in relationship to God in a way that differs from the way in which God exists for the human. This is to posit the event of reconciliation apart from God's act. Instead, Christian calling is a "matter of the common *action* of the Lord and His servant which derives from and corresponds to their common being. It is thus a matter of the *self-proclamation* of Jesus Christ and of the confirmatory *witness* of Christians" (*CD* IV/3.2, 651; *KD* IV/3.2, 746).[34] In the same way that Jesus Christ "learnt obedience" (Heb. 5:8-9), his community is to conform to the image of the Son becoming vehicles of the Word. This common action is the nature of the living fellowship of the divine and the human.

All of this is to confirm two elements of *missio Dei* theology that are often set in opposition: the community, in her necessary movement to the world, exists in immediate connection with Jesus Christ. The first affirmation is the basis of the second, and to hold them apart is to erode both. This locates the Christian community's particular "sending" in relationship to other possible "sendings" in creation. The presence of the Father in the act of the Son and Spirit precludes any easy identification of "sending" with the person of Jesus Christ to the extent that the church takes over his mission, or to the extent that his mission subsumes the church. "Her sending is not a repetition; it is also not an extension or a continuation of His sending. His own sending does not cease in that He sends her. Nor does His sending disappear in her sending. His sending remains her free and independent presupposition. Her sending is simply ordered (on a lower level!) in relation to His" (rev., *KD* IV/3.2, 878; *CD* IV/3.2, 768). Jesus Christ does not, with his ascension, transfer his lordship over to the Christian community, becoming a means or predicate of her missionary "sending." Neither does Jesus Christ's acting in the world negate the proper task of the Christian community, so that her own sending merges with the flux of history. "As the Father sends" refers to his capacity to bring that which is different into unity with himself while affirming that distinction.[35]

34. The two points being made here — first, that this relationship determines the human into his or her true humanity, and second, that this takes a particular missionary form due to the ontological connection with Jesus Christ — are confirmed by the following statement: human beings are elected "to participate in the grace of the one who elects them: to participation in His creatureliness (which is already grace) and to participation in His Sonship (which is grace in a preeminent manner)" (rev., *KD* II/2, 130; *CD* II/2, 121).

35. In this act of the Father with respect to the human, "there remains a genuine *antithesis* that is not obscured or resolved by admixture or transference, either by divine influence or infusion. There is still a genuine *encounter,* and therefore a genuine meeting" (*CD* III/3, 136-37; *KD* III/3, 154). This reference to the *concursus Dei* renders "the flight into synergism" unnecessary, because the action of the Father by the Word and Spirit establishes "the individual being and life and activity of the *creature*" (*CD* III/3, 144; *KD* III/3, 63). God's acting in reconciliation and redemption establishes — and does not overrule — his human opposite.

In the same way, a proper unity and distinction characterizes the "historically interconnected event" of the sending of Jesus Christ and that of his community (*CD* IV/3.2, 768; *KD* IV/3.2, 879).

> Jesus Christ is sent in order *to precede* His community on the way into the world. She is sent in order *to follow* Him on the same way. That is, and remains, two different aspects. The origin of His and her sending, however, is — and this makes them comparable — *one: the same* God, who as the Father sends Him, and also sends her through Him, His Son. Also, the goal of His and her sending is — this again makes them comparable — *one:* He and she are both sent into the *world*. This, very generally, means that they are directed to the world and exist for the world. (rev., *KD* IV/3.2, 879; *CD* IV/3.2, 768)

That the sending of Jesus Christ and of Christian community is and remains two different movements means that the community, in her being sent, does not receive an immediate ontological initiation into the Trinitarian sendings that are the life of God. The "direct" sending of the community by Jesus Christ constitutes an ontological connection with the determination of Jesus Christ's own humanity, and, by this, constitutes an "indirect" participation in the history in partnership that is God's triune life.

The enduring truth of *missio Dei* theology rests in shifting the ground of mission from historical accident and human whim to the being of the Trinity. It failed in the movement from this missionary being to the human act. The relationship between divine and human agency remained clouded, with either divine agency disqualifying the human or human agency usurping the divine. In this first part of the answer, the completed fact of the incarnation establishes the formal relationship between God and humanity. Human beings do participate in the being of God, but in a differentiated fellowship of action established by the actuality of the incarnation. This participation is the material determination of the corresponding human missionary act.

The uniqueness of the hypostatic union and the asymmetrical nature of divine and human fellowship ensure the necessary distinction between missions and every historical accident. No direct connection forms between the missionary being of God and the Christian community. Only through the humanity of Jesus Christ does the community live in her missionary determination. Thus stated, this commission does not become an act the community may choose to undertake or neglect; rather, it is the very nature of the living fellowship of the divine and the human. In Jesus Christ, the human act of mission is grounded in the being of God. The Christian community remains, as recipient of this gift, contingent upon the act of God, and so must be active in supplicant movement following the trail of Jesus Christ under the compulsion of the Spirit. The missionary act, as a properly human response, is one of receiving, but it is a receiving in an active corresponding evangelistic movement.

The Incarnation: Et homo *factus* est

Alongside this perfect, once-for-all establishment of the divine and human relationship, it is necessary for us "to keep the *event* character of this fact before our eyes: the act of God, in which it is a fact, and without which it could not be, is — accomplished. But in that it is completed in the occurrence of an *act* of God, it is a being which does not cease as such to be a becoming: *et homo* factus *est*" (rev., *KD* IV/2, 49; *CD* IV/2, 46). The asymmetrical divine and human relationship does not produce a process of active cause and static effect. As a fellowship, this relationship is not

> . . . a matter of two different and successive actions, but of a single action in which each of the two elements is related to the other and can be known and understood only in this relationship: the going out of God only as it aims at the coming in of the human; the coming in of the human only as the reach and outworking of the going out of God; and the whole in its original and proper form only as the being and history of the one Jesus Christ. (*CD* IV/2, 21; *KD* IV/2, 21)

This is the living movement of election from all eternity: it is the union of the one Son. Understanding the relationship of the human with the divine as an act that is a becoming precludes depicting that relationship as a transmitted material condition. Even in Jesus Christ there is "no (direct or indirect) identification, but an effective *confrontation* of the divine essence with the human and so the human with the divine, and thus *the* determination of the one in relation to the other without altering its essence in this event of *confrontation*" (rev., *KD* IV/2, 96; *CD* IV/2, 87-88). Jesus Christ's completion of reconciliation established the new creation as a historical reality, but this reality cannot be conceived of apart from the event in which it is actual. That is, unlike the approach that understands *missio Dei* as the unfolding process of breaking down and building up, because it is an act of God, the event of the incarnation retains its eschatological force. The completed reconciliation of the world is an event: it takes place.

This event character means that the fact of divine-human fellowship takes the form of a living history whose subject is Jesus Christ. The incarnation is "an *actuality,* as an *operatio* between God and the human, fulfilled in Jesus Christ as a union of God with the human" (*CD* IV/2, 105; *KD* IV/2, 116). History characterizes the nature of the divine-human commerce, which is not identical with the one or the other, but which is ordered with God giving and the human receiving. This mutual correspondence is not "a mere being together. . . . It is a *being,* but a being in a *history*" (*CD* IV/1, 126; *KD* IV/1, 138). The divine and human natures of Jesus Christ were, from the first, actual in God. The one Son is the "strictest, total union" of the divine and human natures (*CD* IV/2, 87; *KD* IV/2, 95). As such, they were being-in-becoming. The person of Jesus Christ "is a union in which there can be neither mixture nor change, division nor separation. The being of Jesus Christ consists in this union. 'Union'? To say this is already to suggest an act or movement" (*CD* IV/2, 109; *KD* IV/2, 121). McCormack argues that "we would do better to think of the hypostatic union in actualistic terms as a *uniting,* rather than as a completed action, a union."[36] It is a uniting, a history, because it is a living decision, an event of

---

36. McCormack, "Participation in God," p. 355. Torrance, as an illustration of this principle, says that it is "one of the most pressing needs of theology to have the hypostatic union restated much more in terms of the mission of Christ." Thomas F. Torrance, "The Atonement and the Oneness of the Church," *Scottish Journal of Theology* 7, no. 3 (1954): 246. The hypostatic union, Torrance continues, was not simply a moment when the divine and human became of one substance in Mary's womb. It did not only provide a framework for reconciliation. Rather, the hypostatic union was a dynamic expression of Christ's existence, an ongoing and unfolding dynamic. Christ learnt obedience by this struggle, the Cross being its final and ultimate achievement. "Reconciliation is not something added to hypostatic union so much as the hypostatic union itself at work in expiation and atonement" (p. 247). George Hunsinger also holds that "the incarnation, the meeting of two natures in Christ, is what occurred as he enacted his saving history. Although his deity and his humanity were actual from the very outset (*conceptus de Spiritu Sancto!*) their union was never essentially static. It was a state of being in the process of becoming." Hunsinger, "Karl Barth's Christology: Its Basic Chalcedonian Character," in *Disruptive Grace: Studies in the Theology of Karl Barth* (Grand Rapids: Eerdmans, 2000), p. 141.

self-determination. "The Word of God is not to be understood as history first and then and as such as decision too. It is to be understood primarily and basically as decision and then and as such as history too" (*CD* I/1, 156; *KD* I/1, 162). There is no secondary step of derivative act alongside prior being; the act of determination is the basis and manner of its outworking.

As the history of Jesus Christ, this uniting does not reduce to a principle. It retains its particularity, and, along with that, its proclamatory character. The life of Jesus "unquestionably belongs to a definite time. It has happened. But, in so far as it has happened as *this* history, the act of *God,* it has not ceased to be history and therefore to *happen*" (*CD* IV/2, 107; *KD* IV/2, 119). As the *history* of the living Lord Jesus Christ, it is active as past, present, and future. As a history of the *living* Lord Jesus Christ, it receives its character from his resurrection and ascension: it is a declarative history proclaiming who Jesus Christ is from all eternity (Rom. 1:4). This is the first form of the *parousia,* "*that time* in which the birth, life and death of Jesus Christ once and for all occurred, and *that time* in which his resurrection first revealed this as history!" (rev., *KD* IV/2, 119; *CD* IV/2, 107). Jesus Christ's history declares its own meaning, and, by extension, human participation in this history takes a corresponding declarative form.

The *parousia* now occurs in a second form as the interim impartation of the Holy Spirit. It happens here and now as "the reconciliation of the world with God," and thus includes "the being of the Church in the world" (*CD* IV/2, 107; *KD* IV/2, 118). It is both a past reality and a future that comes upon the Christian community, drawing her beyond herself. Yet this event is not exhausted in its present reality. It is, third, "also future — the event which lies completely and wholly in front of us, which has not yet happened, but which simply comes upon us" (*CD* II/1, 262; *KD* II/1, 294). The present act of the *parousia* awaits in hope the definitive return of Jesus Christ. This futurity "happens without detriment to its historical completeness and its full contemporaneity. On the contrary, it is in its historical completeness and its full contemporaneity that it is truly future" (*CD* II/1, 262; *KD* II/1, 294).

I will develop the concrete effect this threefold form of the *parousia* has over the missionary existence of the Christian community in the next chapter. Let it suffice to say here that, as the event character of the fact of the incarnation is this declarative history, so the act of declaration and witness is not limited to a particular segment of linear time. Witness is the nature of the Son's relationship with the Father (John 14:10), the Father's relationship to the Son (John 5:32), the Spirit's relationship to the Son (John 15:26), the Son's relationship to his disciples (Acts 26:16-18), and the disciples' relationship to the Son (Rev. 7:9-10). Witness is not something beyond which the community will move in the *eschaton*. It is the very nature of the *eschaton,* for it is the very nature of the history that is the human fellowship with the divine.

A formal answer to the question of how the human missionary act is *determined by* the being of God lies in the nature of this living history. As the earthly-historical form of his existence, the "relationship of the being of Jesus Christ to that of His community is not static nor immobile, but *mobile* and *dynamic,* and therefore *historical*" (*CD* IV/3.2, 759; *KD* IV/3.2, 868). Because it is historical, that is, an event of divine-human encounter, it is not something that occurs "when the being is involved in changes or different modes of behaviour intrinsic to itself" (*CD* III/2, 158; *KD* III/2, 189). Missionary existence is not a "duty," if we understand that word to mean an otherwise true motivation implemented according to the resources of contingent human capacity. This ground too easily submits to an imperialist mode. Mission becomes derivative of a preexisting institution, and its necessity relative to the social, cultural, political, and economic capital of that institution. By contrast, the history of a being begins when "its circular movement is broken from without by a movement *towards it* and the corresponding movement *from it,* when it is transcended from without so that it must and can transcend itself outwards" (*CD* III/2, 158; *KD* III/2, 18). The history of the Christian community corresponds to the asymmetrical fellowship of God's election of the human and the human's response — to God's own history. "The history inaugurated by God becomes humanity's own subjective history" (*CD* III/2, 176; *KD* III/2, 210). When God encounters humanity and "determines its being in the nature proper to it," this being is "compelled and enabled" to transcend its self-occupation and enter Jesus Christ's history (*CD* III/2, 158; *KD* III/2, 189). The form of this transcendence is not abstract. In the Spirit, God's Word

> ... goes out also to us humans, not returning to Him empty but with the booty or increase of our faith and knowledge and obedience, and not remaining with Him on its return but constantly going out again to us to bring back new gains, and thus establishing communication between Him and us and initiating a history of mutual giving and receiving. (*CD* IV/3.1, 421; *KD* IV/3.1, 485-86)

This language, for many interpreters, again brings Barth close to deification. As will become clear, however, the self-transcendence that is proper human participation in the history of God's self-determination takes the objective form of the missionary act. Any reference to mediation, at this point, intrudes on the proper differentiated fellowship of action that is the Christian's union with Christ: the community is not an end in herself satisfied with the benefits she has received.[37] As history, the receptive stance of human being is not a static stance. The fact and event of the incarnation means, first, that the missionary act of the Christian community remains contingent on the prior act of God, and second, that this contingency itself demands corresponding movement. The community transcends her closed history by her impulsion into the world following Jesus Christ in the power of the Spirit.

The Witness of the Spirit

God's movement into his redemptive economy, while a deliberate act, is not an ancillary second step alongside an otherwise defined perfection. The attribute "missionary" narrates the very nature of God's perfection. The problem of the gap between the divine and the human is overcome for all eternity in the Father's begetting of the Son in the unity of the Spirit. God is a living God. Humanity participates in this missionary being of God through active participation in the history of Jesus Christ in the same unity of the Spirit. Jesus has completed once for all the reconciliation of the world, but, as with the nature of God's perfection, this completion is a history that takes place. This leads to the third question of the *accomplishment* of this event in the human sphere. This question does not "leave the circle of our consideration of the being and essence and activity of God. It is within this circle, within the doctrine of God, that the question arises" (*CD* II/2, 510; *KD* II/2, 566). If the objective accomplishment of the Son

37. Colin Gunton says that, "if the Church is to be the Church in the post-Constantinian age, she must renew her sense of her (passively constituted) *calling* to be a particular people serving a universal end. . . . Only by a turning away, enabled by the Lord who is the electing Spirit, from the self-absorption of those who have lost their sense of direction to an orientation to the promised reconciliation of all things in Christ can this happen." Gunton, "Election and Ecclesiology in the Post-Constantinian Church," *Scottish Journal of Theology* 53, no. 2 (2000): 226.

consists in establishing this living history of fellowship between the divine and the human, this subsection concerns the subjective accomplishment of the Holy Spirit — the nature of human participation in that history (*CD* I/1, 453; *KD* I/1, 475).[38]

As to what "God wants *from* the human," reference to the "the divine election is, in the last resort, the determination of the human — her determination to this service, this commission, this office of witness" (*CD* II/2, 510; *KD* II/2, 565). This is the proper work of the Spirit, for it is only by the power of the Spirit that the community becomes and is a witness to Jesus Christ to the whole world (Acts 1:8). By the Spirit, the history of the incarnation speaks to the human, and the human enters that history, being "empowered, but also summoned and constrained, to pass it on" (*CD* IV/2, 126; *KD* IV/2, 141). Without the Spirit, by contrast, "there is no Christian, no community, no Christian word, no Christian act!" (rev., *KD* IV/2, 357; *CD* IV/2, 319).

Because, in the event of the incarnation, the reconciliation of the world is an already established fact, the human response "has no creative but only a *cognitive* character. It does not alter anything" (*CD* IV/1, 751; *KD* IV/1, 839). It is precisely because the human act does not, nor has to, alter anything that it can attest the reality that has already taken place, and this reality is the basis of the missionary act. Since no gap exists between God's being and his act, the proper human act requires no ontological addition to either the individual or the community to bridge that gap. Faith as a human is a confession in that it is "simply the *confirmation* of a change which has already taken place, the change in the whole human situation which took place in the death of Jesus Christ and was revealed in His resurrection" (*CD* IV/1, 751; *KD* IV/1, 839-40). The knowledge of God frees humanity to be truly human and to live in fellowship with God as truly human.

The resulting missionary objection might be parsed as such: much of the traditional justification for missions, and the concomitant methodology, has been predicated on a gap between the act of God in Christ and the absence of this act within the world. Mission transitions this gap, facilitat-

---

38. Barth continues that "the very common Pauline formula 'ἐν πνεύματι' describes the human's thinking, acting, and speaking as taking place in participation in God's revelation. It is an exact subjective correlate of 'ἐν Χριστῷ,' which denotes the same thing objectively" (*CD* I/1, 453; *KD* I/1, 476).

ing the confession of those who previously did not know the good news of the gospel; mission is thus in some way basic to the occurrence of reconciliation. Wolfhart Pannenberg, based on the ongoing "apostolic ministry" of 2 Corinthians 5:19, asks: "Do we not have to regard not merely God's reconciling act but also its human acceptance as constitutive of the event?"[39] Because this ministry is not yet complete, it follows that reconciliation cannot yet be complete. It is complete for those who have come to believe, but not for the world. Positing reconciliation as an act of God alone seems to deny this apostolic ministry, denuding the human role in reconciliation and, by implication, its present actuality. For Werner Krusche, too, characterizing the difference between the church and the world in terms of a mere "cognitive head-start" undoes the essential missionary motivation; for, if everyone is already reconciled to God, then "all are beyond danger because there is no judgment."[40] Furthermore, without conversion conferring an "ontic otherness," the role of the church becomes devalued: she ceases to be the one institution responsible for cultivating and maintaining this otherness.[41]

In a similar way, Nicholas Healy suggests that, by reducing "Christianity to a matter of knowledge," Barth "unwittingly encourages its appropriation and domestication within a non-Christian framework."[42] The difference between the church and the world is treated, and thus rejected by those to whom the church witnesses, as mere worldview. "By ruling out a sociohistorically concrete treatment of the (real) church Barth thus proscribes the development of a set of institutions that could contribute to a distinctive Christian ethos." Christian witness requires an "empirical dis-

39. Wolfhart Pannenberg, *Systematic Theology* (Grand Rapids: Eerdmans, 1994), 2:415.

40. Werner Krusche, "Parish Structure — A Hindrance to Mission? A Survey and Evaluation of the Ecumenical Discussion on the Structures of the Missionary Congregation," in *Sources for Change: Searching for Flexible Church Structures*, ed. Herbert T. Neve (Geneva: World Council of Churches, 1968), pp. 61, 82. Waldron Scott, for example, finds Barth's approach on reconciliation detrimental, for it forgets that "the heathen *are* lost: world evangelization is therefore a matter of utmost urgency." Scott, *Karl Barth's Theology of Mission* (Downers Grove, IL: InterVarsity, 1978), p. 29. For L. Leland Mebust, the objectionable element in Barth's theology for mission is his "description of an objective being of man in Christ established prior to and outside man's actual encounter with the gospel." Mebust, "Barth on Mission," *Dialogue* 20 (1981): 19.

41. Krusche, "Parish Structure — A Hindrance to Mission?" p. 60.

42. Nicholas M. Healy, "The Logic of Karl Barth's Ecclesiology: Analysis, Assessment, and Proposed Modifications," *Modern Theology* 10, no. 3 (1994): 265.

tinctiveness" and "the effective socialization of church members through sets of distinctively Christian institutions and practices."[43] This socialization establishes a holy distance from the world, and the community witnesses to the truth of reconciliation by living this difference. In other words, this affirmation of the "completion of reconciliation" is the basis of *missio Dei's* reduction of the church to a mere postscript alongside God's acting.

The basic assumptions framing this position should be familiar by now. The possibility of Christian witness is presumed to be located in some ontological or ethical difference between the church and the world. This demands the peculiar arrangement of the church and mission in which the cultivation of Christ's benefits are treated as the Christian end and the church's true purpose, and their communication secondary to their reception. The missionary act is made necessary due to the world's ignorance of God, but it is necessary only to the point of belief. Once reconciliation has occurred, believers are no longer subject to this missionary act. Mission is not itself a component in the life of reconciliation. Insofar as this arrangement is deemed "necessary" for human agency, the completion of reconciliation discounts concrete human activity. This leads to the conclusion that positing the human response to reconciliation in noetic terms, to expand the complaint of German missions, paralyzes the will to *do* mission and to *be* the church.

Given the critical function of the doctrine of the Trinity within *missio Dei*, it is necessary to address the apparently totalizing nature of God's act and the consequences for the human response. This is a question of the Spirit, for he is the "power of the transition, mediation, communication and history which take place first in the life of God Himself and then consequently in our life, in the relationship of the man Jesus to us" (*CD* IV/2, 347; *KD* IV/2, 388). Indeed, the precipitating "problem of God" derives from the Spirit's creation of human witnesses. In Jesus Christ, there exists from all eternity the living fecund fellowship of the divine and the human. The indirect human participation in the missionary being of the Trinity occurs with the direct participation of the Christian community in the history of Jesus Christ. However, this direct participation is only a work of the presence and action of the Holy Spirit, who "*guarantees* the human what he cannot guarantee himself, his personal *participation in revelation*" (*CD*

---

43. Healy, "The Logic of Barth's Ecclesiology," pp. 264-65.

I/1, 453; *KD* I/1, 475). The necessary relationship between the Creator and the creature is not something that can be assured by the creature. "*God creates it* by His own presence in the creature and therefore as a relationship of Himself to Himself. The Spirit of God is God in His freedom to be present to the creature, and therefore to create this relation, and therefore to be the life of the creature" (*CD* I/1, 450; *KD* I/1, 473). The Spirit can act this way because he is "the One who constitutes and guarantees the unity of the *totus Christus*, i.e., of Jesus Christ in the heights and in the depths, in His transcendence and in His immanence" (*CD* IV/3.2, 760; *KD* IV/3.1, 870). Following the Chalcedonian formula, the Spirit does not identify, intermingle, merge, or change one into the other, but rather binds the divine and the human, that which seems to be "necessarily and irresistibly divergent," into a true unity (*CD* IV/3.2, 761; *KD* IV/3.1, 871). This bringing and holding together consists of "the transition of the self-witness of Jesus Christ into Church history, into the history of individual lives, into world history" (*CD* IV/2, 131; *KD* IV/2, 146). The human being is drawn into that unifying which is the history of God's own self-knowledge.

This work, in that it proceeds from the side of the subjective realization in the human in this objective reality of reconciliation, is not materially different from the act of God's self-humiliation and the exaltation of the human. The Spirit's work does not entail an "independent content," or a "new instruction, illumination and stimulation" of human beings that extends or completes God's self-revelation in Jesus Christ. The Spirit's bringing human community into unity with the history of Jesus Christ takes a definite form. "Subjective revelation can be only the repetition, the impress, the sealing of objective revelation upon us" (*CD* I/2, 239; *KD* I/2, 261).

The rush of Pentecost is the rush to proclaim in every tongue so that all may hear. This identification of the Spirit with the Word prevents any undue conflation of this Spirit with the Christian community, or with a universal spirit present in creation, culture, and history. Though these approaches have often been treated as basic to missionary methods, a direct link between the Spirit and the Word serves an equally positive missionary function by resisting every attempt to impose a second step between Jesus Christ's act and the community's response of witness. The Spirit conforms the community to the image of Christ. Any departure from the proclamatory existence lived by Jesus Christ himself constitutes a departure from the Spirit. As the community of the Spirit, her life is a purposeful one constituted by a missionary commission.

Active Participation in the Divine Work

Eternal life is the knowledge of the one God and of Jesus Christ, whom he sent (John 17:3). With eternal life the gift of reconciliation, human knowledge of God "is act, is active participation in the movement of knowledge which comes from God and returns to God" (rev., *KD* III/2, 214; *CD* III/2, 179). As the work of the Spirit, such movement cannot result in a mute being. The action of God aims at bringing in the human who "is summoned to action, being made a *subject* by this summons of the object. A self-quiescent being would not be the being which knows God and acts in responsibility before God, i.e., it would not be the human being, any more than a self-quiescent being could possibly be the divine being" (*CD* III/2, 176; *KD* III/2, 210). What happens to the human in the event of reconciliation takes the form of enlistment in the history that is God's own life. Though this precludes all ontological aggrandizement, it demands subjective and objective accomplishment. God's command calls the human to "*transcend* oneself" (rev., *KD* III/4, 542; *CD* III/4, 473). Life in the knowledge of God means the exaltation of the human: the movement from below *to above*. This means conforming to the image of the Son, becoming obedient to God as he is.[44]

A potential confusion arises in this language of transcendence. "We are talking about the *sanctification* of human life and not, along with all the heathens and fanatics, about its divinization. But in the sanctification of human life we are necessarily dealing with the restoration of a correspondence of human action to divine" (rev., *KD* III/4, 543; *CD* III/4, 474). This means, negatively, that the active knowledge of God cannot be occupied with preserving, cherishing, or protecting existence. It does not permit the individual "the kind of preoccupation with God, fellow human beings and the environment which in the last resort means only a more intensive preoccupation with herself and enjoyment of herself." Nor can there be any "hasty equation" of the self-transcendence of the Christian with the transportation of the individual "into the absolute" as though one could "participate in the transcendence of God and even act as the transcendent God." It is precisely "the naked 'living man', the *homo incurvatus*

---

44. "God will be known as the One He is. But precisely as the One He is, He acts. It is as the One who acts, however, that He will be known. And to know him as the One who acts means to become obedient to Him" (*CD* II/1, 26; *KD* II/1, 27).

in se," who needs "to be unrolled and opened up, to be called out of his impossible isolation and self-absorption by the command of God" (*CD* III/4, 473; *KD* III/4, 542).

The missionary message of the Christian community cannot consist in calling human beings to an increasingly more self-centered life, an *ecclesia incurvatus in se*. The transcendence of the human consists of opening humans and their communities beyond their closed histories to combine them in the particular history of Jesus Christ. This history entails a visible differentiation from the world, for the fellowship of action that is human life with God results in a corresponding difference from other people. This is not the result of the techniques of socialization; it is a result of their particular calling, one that gives a determined direction and concrete meaning. Ontological difference is not the basis of Christian witness alongside which the missionary task is a secondary step. The objective difference that is the Christian witness is the movement of the church into the world.

Part of the confusion with the missionary nature of Christian calling arises, for Barth, in "the mediaeval overestimation of the *vita contemplativa* of meditation, prayer, and worship in a state of absolute obedience" and the coordinated reduction of the *vita activa* to "less perfect states" (*CD* III/4, 473; *KD* III/4, 542).[45] The resulting vision of the perfection expected by God's command consisted of a monastic type of "rest," or "the rather dubious activity of peaceful contemplation" (Barth, *CD* III/4, 474; *KD* III/4, 543). He follows the Reformers in rejecting this evaluation of the serene and aristocratic life as the zenith of Christian existence, alongside which the remainder of human work is substandard and provisional. The *vita contemplativa* was, as such, "a degenerate and pseudo-Christian form" (*CD* III/4, 474; *KD* III/4, 543). However, Barth does not go all the way with the Reformers. While he affirms their depiction of the *vita activa* as "an equal obligation upon all," the Reformers' failure lay in forming an immediate relationship between vocation and secular work (*CD* III/4, 474; *KD* III/4, 543). Such a relationship sanctified the achievements of this work, one consequence of which is evident in positing Western civilization as an illustration of the truth of the Christian life.

45. For a helpful background discussion of how "κλῆσις" became reduced to peculiar vocations, see Gregory Alan Robertson, "'Vivit! Regnat! Triumphat!' The Prophetic Office of Jesus Christ, the Christian life, and the Mission of the Church in Karl Barth's *Church Dogmatics* IV/3" (Th.D. dissertation, Wycliffe College and the University of Toronto, 2003), pp. 259-62.

Quoting Brunner, Barth asks: "Is it really 'from the Bible that Europe draws her highest ideal of the value of all work which helps to create a civilization,' and therefore her superiority, today rapidly diminishing, over other continents?"(*CD* III/4, 472; *KD* III/4, 540).[46] This economic and political superiority supplied the necessary difference between the Christian faith and other faiths. With this difference the supposed essential basis of Christian witness, missionary work consisted of working for this difference, that is, bringing civilization, as a necessary precondition for the gospel message, to non-Western cultures. Christian calling collapses into historical accident — the white man's burden — with the consequences for the missionary task all too evident. While the Christian "calling" is an equal obligation on all, this obligation must itself correspond to divine acting. This gives it a missionary form, "objectively the *expansion* of the reality and truth of Jesus Christ" (*CD* IV/4, 97; *KD* IV/4, 106).

As the human is brought by the act of the Spirit into the history of Jesus Christ, so this history determines the form of the human response. The problem of God is overcome because God in himself from all eternity has an above and a below. This is not God being at disunity with himself, but is the very nature of his living unity. Even as the Creator, God can "become worldly, making His own both its form, the *forma servi,* and also its cause; and all without giving up His own form, the *forma Dei,* and His own glory, but adopting the form and cause of the human into the most perfect communion with His own, accepting solidarity with the world" (*CD* IV/1, 187; *KD* IV/1, 204). As the history of God includes his taking the "form of a servant," service characterizes the human response. Since God, in Jesus Christ, has become a brother to humanity, and made humanity children of God, human beings cannot assume the posture of passive neutrality. Service is the objective character of obedient human action, for to serve means "to choose God, to the exclusion of neutrality and of another Lord" (*CD* III/4, 475; *KD* III/4, 544). This means following Jesus Christ's own "way of service," his "total service" in relation to the world (*CD* III/4, 477; *KD* III/4, 546). In becoming his disciple, the human is "*claimed* for the continuation of the divine work to which she owes her freedom" (rev., *KD* III/4, 552; *CD* III/4, 482). The strong language of "continuation" can be used here:

---

46. The internal quote is from Emil Brunner, *Das Gebot und die Ordnungen: Entwurf einer protestantisch-theologischen Ethik* (Tübingen: J.C.B. Mohr, 1932), p. 372.

[W]hen service is rendered, two very different active subjects are obviously at work together in different ways, with a clear differentiation of function. The One is the *Lord*, who quite apart from the superiority of His person is also superior in the fact that in the common work it is wholly and utterly a matter of *His* cause. The other is the *servant*, who quite apart from the littleness of his person is also subordinate in the fact that in his participation in the common work it can only be a matter of renouncing his own cause and treating that of the Lord as though it were his, or rather of really making it his own. (*CD* IV/3.2, 601; *KD* IV/3.2, 689-90)

The completion of reconciliation is the basis of human participation in that event.[47] Humanity is exalted by acting in correspondence to divine humiliation. "Sanctification means exaltation, but because it is exaltation in fellowship with the One who came to serve it is exaltation to the lowliness in which He served and still serves, and rules as He serves" (*CD* IV/2, 691; *KD* IV/2, 782).[48] As Jesus Christ's own life took a missionary form (Heb. 3:1), so the human "apostolate is the active participation of the members of Christ in His unction, His Messianic office" (*CD* II/2, 432; *KD* II/2, 478) This lowliness is the missionary charge of doing what Jesus does, not as a consequence of one's own will, but because Jesus has chosen human beings for this purpose. Their lives are one of "*witnesses, messengers, ambassadors* and *heralds*" to the "comprehensive and radical alteration of the human situation, of the whole situation of the world" (rev., *KD* III/4, 558; *CD* III/4, 487). The disciples do not bring about this alteration. Nevertheless, God claims servants to continue in the divine work. This missionary witness is the singular task of the Christian community, and "no other task is so urgent as that of spreading this news on earth, of making it known to all people that all may conform to it, of publishing it indeed to every creature" (*CD* III/4, 487; *KD* III/4, 558). Jesus Christ is a story to be told and not a system to be described (*CD* II/2, 188; *KD* II/2, 206). The Christian community cannot confuse her task with the whole of the gos-

47. Webster says that human "agency is neither identical with, nor in competition with, the action of God, but in correspondence with God's activity, subordinate to that activity and in that very subordination enjoying its genuine substance." Webster, *Barth's Ethics of Reconciliation*, p. 167.

48. Barth continues that "exalted into fellowship with Jesus Christ each Christian as such is set in the lowliness of His service" (*CD* IV/2, 693; *KD* IV/2, 785).

pel, and her mission cannot consist in transplanting her own story. Yet, by telling Jesus Christ's story, entering the world in the power of the Spirit, the missionary community becomes part of that story and participates in Christ's history. According to Eberhard Jüngel, the Christian community corresponds to the humanity of God "only by *constantly telling the story anew*."[49] Telling the story refers to the particular history of Jesus Christ and thus constantly refers back to this history, and because of that, to the history of the people of God, the history of Israel and the coming Kingdom. Though the task is simple, as it is human participation in the history of Jesus Christ, the spreading of the news is so "gigantic" that "no less capacity is required than that which must be granted and continually confirmed by God, by Jesus, and by the Holy Spirit" (*CD* III/4, 487; *KD* III/4, 558). Drawing on John 20:21, Barth confirms that "the apostolate consists of this sharing in Jesus' own mission" (*CD* II/2, 432; *KD* II/2, 4). Such is the role of the human in the event of reconciliation. As the human is responsible before God, so she "has a share in the Work of God and therefore in God Himself — a creaturely share in a creaturely manner, but nevertheless a real share" (*CD* III/2, 177; *KD* III/2, 211). To be sure, Jesus Christ is the true witness, and his disciples are witnesses at second hand. However, this is the nature of their relationship, such that "the intimate and necessary connection between Him as the Head and the community as His body would obviously snap if she [the community] tried to exist otherwise than in this imitative and serving participation in His mission to the world" (rev., *KD* IV/3.2, 906; *CD* IV/3.2, 792). All of this reinforces Willingen's axiom: "There is no participation in Christ without participation in His mission in the world."[50]

The Determination of the Whole Community

The meaning and direction of Christian life in the Spirit consist in the active — not merely passive — share in the loving kindness of God, with the determination to open up and direct the whole world to this loving kindness. This is the subjective and objective accomplishment of the human's knowing God in the event of reconciliation, and its "first and decisive *con-*

49. Jüngel, *God as the Mystery of the World,* p. 304.
50. Goodall, *Missions under the Cross,* p. 190.

cretion" is "the human being's direct or indirect *cooperation* in the fulfillment of the task of the *Christian community*" (rev., *KD* III/4, 553-54; *CD*
III/4, 483). That the community is so stressed is a consequence of marrying
the Reformers' emphasis on the *vita activa* as an equal obligation on all
with the ecclesial locus of the medieval *vita contemplativa*. The active life is
one of being the covenant partner with God. First, since the covenant is the
internal basis of creation, this life applies to the whole of creation. It is not
possible for the community to withdraw into a sacred sphere of its own
making. Second, as a covenant partner with God, the individual must live
as a responsible member of the Christian community. Restricting the true
form of creaturely life to "one of the smallest human minorities" may appear to be "intolerably narrow, extremely presumptuous and even alien
and impractical" (*CD* III/4, 483; *KD* III/4, 554).[51] Because the act of human
freedom is "the entry of the human being into the service of this confrontation," however, this "must first and decisively take place in her relationship to the *centre* of this action and therefore in her relationship to *Jesus
Christ*" (*CD* III/4, 486; *KD* III/4, 556-57). The active life of the individual is
necessarily one of active participation in the commission of the Christian
community.

With the circle of election coincidental with that of Jesus Christ's
community, two common distinctions dissipate: that of the living Christians versus dead ones, and that of the clergy versus the laity. The community is not comprised of

> . . . two ranks: on the one side an institutionally and once-for-all privi-
> leged circle which is responsible for the whole and represents it; and on
> the other a class which is finally deprived of this privilege and can and
> should leave it to the other group to act responsibly and representatively
> in matters of the community's mission! (*CD* IV/3.2, 782; *KD* IV/3.2, 895)

The passivity demanded of the Christian is one of active service in fellowship with God, not one defined with respect to ecclesial offices and in the
reception of a "service." No one is ever "off duty" (*CD* III/4, 490; *KD* III/4,
561). Nor can individuals hand this responsibility over to institutional
structures. No one is permitted to participate in the "historical life of the

---

51. The obverse, for Barth, is that any departure from the church is also a departure
from election in Jesus Christ — thus, *extra ecclesiam nulla salus* (see *CD* II/2, 197; *KD* II/2,
217; see also *CD* IV/2, 622; *KD* IV/2, 704).

community . . . only by way of a bare theoretical and abstract churchliness" (rev., *KD* IV/1, 730; *CD* IV/1, 654). Christian membership is not a voluntary personal choice that may, at some time in the future, result in taking account of that membership. "The discharge of witness" Jesus Christ committed to his church is not "left to the good pleasure of her members" (*CD* I/2, 693; *KD* I/2, 776). None is "debarred" from God's grace, and so "none may regard themselves as not adapted to and therefore dispensed from participation in her sending to the world" (*CD* IV/3.2, 782; *KD* IV/3.2, 895). As participation in the history of Jesus Christ is the form of human reconciliation with the divine, withdrawing from this sending constitutes withdrawing from the fellowship of the Spirit and the grace of Jesus Christ and the love of God.

While the community "is not divided by this organization into an active and a passive part," there are specific callings and gifts, particular vocations (rev., *KD* III/4, 561; *CD* III/4, 490).[52] The community is not "a barracks, nor can her members be the uniformed inhabitants, nor can their activity be the execution of a well-drilled manoeuver" (*CD* IV/3.2, 856; *KD* IV/3.2, 981). Missionary existence is not an imposed duty begrudgingly performed according to precise and intractable guidelines. The Spirit does not create uniformity. As the triune God lives "not with an undifferentiated, lifeless and motionless unity," so the community lives "in correspondence with the being and life of God" with this same richness characterizing her life (*CD* IV/3.2, 854; *KD* IV/3.2, 980). True human witness to this God means that the attestation of his gospel "cannot possibly become the uniform and monotonous function of a collective" (*CD* IV/3.2, 801; *KD* IV/3.2, 916), Differentiation is proper to the community's life as a result of the different endowments, including a "fluid distinction" between those with a more *direct* or *indirect* role in her mission (*CD* IV/3.2, 783; *KD* IV/ 3.2, 895). Such differentiation cannot result in a division in the service of witness rendered by the community. Should such a division develop, it can be overcome with "the spontaneous reorientation of the Church outwards instead of inwards, to the world instead of herself" (*CD* IV/3.1, 35; *KD* IV/ 3.1, 36-37). Again, the focus on offices and a mediatory mode of witness is a

52. Barth says that "all those baptized as Christians are *eo ipso* consecrated, ordained and dedicated to the ministry of the Church. They cannot be consecrated, ordained, or dedicated a second, third, or fourth time without devaluation of their baptism" (*CD* IV/4, 201; *KD* IV/4, 221).

consequence of a theological failing with respect to mission. Those who are obedient to the community's "*mission* to the world" realize that in the "removal of the *inner* frontier we have an intimation and preparation for the crossing of the *outer*, and therefore an indication to the Church to take up her *prophetic* office" (*CD* IV/3.1, 35; *KD* IV/3.1, 37). Since reconciliation has the character of revelation, this apostolic criterion demands a living community differentiated in action — not in service.

Nor can the community privatize her assets by employing third party contractors. "The community herself and as such is the acting subject also in foreign missions — or she is not the Christian community" (rev., *KD* IV/3.2, 1003; *CD* IV/3.2, 875).[53] Missionary societies may continue to be necessary, but only as representations of the missionary community. "The community is not to be released even apparently from the comprehensive missionary obligation laid upon her" (rev., *KD* IV/3.2, 1003; *CD* IV/3.2, 875). This missionary calling is true for everyone within the community. "Each individual is responsible for her actually being a missionary community" (*CD* III/4, 505; *KD* III/4, 578). This responsibility does not result from a general satisfaction with the contemporary state of Christian piety, whereby mission is that act of passing a particular form of Christianity, specific to a time and a place, "to their own families and people as though it were a kind of inherited characteristic" (rev., *KD* III/4, 578; *CD* III/4, 505). Neither does this responsibility proceed from a general dissatisfaction with the divorce between Christian ideals and the contemporary practice of the gospel within a particular society, nor from a longing to communicate the gospel beyond these social boundaries. These motivations configure mission as a reaction to a secondary contingent concern and thus place it at one step removed from proper Christian existence. The true motivation for mission resides at a more basic level, centering on

---

53. Such an affirmation is more than mere rhetoric; it has solid historical grounding. While the church cannot forsake her responsibility to the particular vocation of missions, church history demonstrates that the gospel has not been spread primarily via those occupying missionary offices. As Newbigin observes, "the first witnesses to the gospel in Antioch were not missionaries but refugees. And so it has happened over and over again and so it continues to happen. 'Unreached peoples' are reached and cultural frontiers are crossed by refugees, fugitives, famine-stricken villagers, conscripted soldiers, traders, professional workers, and many others." J. E. Lesslie Newbigin, "Cross-Currents in Ecumenical and Evangelical Understandings of Mission," *International Bulletin of Missionary Research* 6, no. 4 (1982): 150.

"whether individual Christians actually know, and whether they are putting this knowledge into practice, that, at base and in truth, every Christian is a missionary" (rev., *KD* III/4, 578-79; *CD* III/4, 505). Not every Christian will be called to a peculiar missionary vocation, but mission characterizes the whole of Christian existence. As Barth suggests, "Remember: every Christian is a missionary, a recruiting officer for new witnesses! That she is this constitutes the knowledge and orientation without which our communities cannot be missionary communities, and, in point of fact, cannot be truly Christian communities at all" (rev., *KD* III/4, 579; *CD* III/4, 505). This is the proper end of the formal location of mission in the doctrine of the Trinity. The resulting missionary form of the Christian community is the subject of the next chapter.

CHAPTER SEVEN

The Calling of Witness

We now rejoice in the positive aspect that, in due subordination and relativity, the statement: *"I am,"* must undoubtedly *follow* the affirmation: *"God is."*

That [the person] *is,* and is therefore *obedient,* means that the statement "I *am*" must be interpreted by the further statement: "I *will."* We have already explained this to mean: "I am *present,"* namely, present in that process of knowledge which has its origin and goal in God. If we explain it further by means of the statement: "I *will,"* we are emphasizing that human existence, and thus this "being present," is not something passive, but rather an "active being present." The human is purely receptive in the movement from God to us. But one is also purely spontaneous in the movement to God there. One is not merely a partial function in a moving whole. One is altogether not only a function. Here is God, but here, over against God and in relation to God, the human is also *subject.*

Karl Barth, Church Dogmatics[1]

Discovering the, by no means self-evident, fundamental presuppositions was my concern, and in that process finally the insight thrust itself upon me: all along the line, "the confession before humanity"

---

1. Rev. Barth, *KD* III/2, 213, 214-15; *CD* III/2, 179, 180.

does not stand on the periphery, but — grounded as it is in the work of the living Jesus Christ Himself — belongs to the centre of the Christian life in the Christian community. Yes, the problem of witness determines whether or not the Christian is a Christian, and the Christian community the Christian community.

Karl Barth, *Church Dogmatics*[2]

Introduction

God's apostolic movement into the world is not a second step alongside who he actually is in and for himself. With the Father's begetting of the Son in the unity in the Spirit, a first and a second belongs to God's life from all and to eternity. The gap between God's being and his act, basic to *missio Dei* theology, is demonstrated to be false at the outset. He overcomes the distance between himself and the human in his own free self-humiliation and in the corresponding gracious exaltation of the human. He is already "ours in advance" (*CD* I/1, 383; *KD* I/1, 404). God the Father "sends" the Son and the Spirit from all eternity in the distinction and unity that is his own perfect life. God the Son, the Mediator between the divine and the human, objectively completes the event of reconciliation. God the Holy Spirit guarantees the human's participation in reconciliation by bringing about the transition of Jesus Christ's self-declaration into the subjective history of those who are called to active participation in his mission. This one action of God in twofold form has both this objective and subjective side, for it is a "divine act and offer and also an active human participation in it: the unique history of Jesus Christ; but enclosed and exemplified in this the history of many other people of many other ages" (*CD* IV/1, 643; *KD* IV/1, 719). It only remains to develop what is involved for these other human histories to become and be active participants in the divine act of reconciliation. This is the focus of this chapter: the *subjective realization* of reconciliation.

The following develops the material form of human participation in the missionary history of God via three sections. First, as his acting toward the world is not a derivative function alongside some otherwise defined

2. Rev. Barth, *KD* IV/3.1, vii-viii; *CD* IV/3.1, xi-xii.

being, so we cannot reintroduce this gap when outlining the missionary community's concrete form. The active being of the community exists in immediate relationship to the living Lord Jesus Christ in the exercise of his prophetic office. Second, one reason for mission's theological marginalization rests in the assumption that the act is a provisional phenomenon not characteristic of the *eschaton;* in other words, mission is conceived in overt distinction to the eternal life of divine-human fellowship. To affirm that God is a missionary God is already to render this disjunction untenable, but this eschatological question is further developed with respect to life in the promise of the Spirit. Third, living in the promise of the Spirit gives the community a definite visible form: she is an apostolic community. Even in her life of worship, the community exists in active movement toward the world. Apart from this movement, she is only apparently the body of Christ, having withdrawn herself from the sphere of his and the Spirit's presence.

Jesus Christ's Prophetic Existence

The Effect of Prophetic Provisionality

One central problem with *missio Dei* theology was in its seeming inability to furnish practical forms for the missionary act once it had become a divine attribute. This inability was a result of a split between God's life in and for himself and his life in the economy. Without this deleterious predicate split, it is now possible to readdress the question of the Christian community's practical form, which corresponds to the nature of divine-human fellowship. In so doing, care must be taken not to reintroduce a second step between God's act and the response of the community. One cannot formulate missionary practice by reducing Jesus Christ to a template, developing it as an "immediate copy of His divine-human appearance" albeit "on a reduced scale and in shadowy outline" (*CD* IV/3.1, 277; *KD* IV/3.1, 319).[3] With such an approach, "there yawns a deep cleft" be-

---

3. This reflection on the concrete form of missionary activity must not make the "mistake of using the theological and specifically the christological statements which we ourselves can and should make to fill up the space in which only the living Jesus Christ in His *self-revelation* can affirm" (*CD* IV/3.1, 285; *KD* IV/3.1, 329). Webster understands such statements to mean that "it would be a considerable misreading to interpret Barth as developing

tween Jesus Christ as himself the word and the ongoing proclamation of this word (*CD* IV/3.1, 277; *KD* IV/3.1, 319). The reappearance of the gap undoes the positive missionary determination of the community by locating mission again within human faithfulness and historical accident. One has here shifted the focus from God's acting in Jesus Christ by the Holy Spirit to an abstract determination of the human consequent upon this action. Jesus Christ's act renders mission a possibility that is then fulfilled according to human capacity. The definite form of the community's life must develop as a "real and genuine *continuity* of this Word, and therefore of a *real presence* of the prophecy of Jesus Christ" (*CD* IV/3.1, 277; *KD* IV/3.1, 320). This basis must be kept at the fore throughout.

This necessary continuity means that developing specific patterns of missionary action is a properly theological task. This stands in contrast to the prevalent assumption within dogmatic theology that the community's missionary determination emerges as a practical implication of some deeper theological focus. The primary dogmatic concern, it is assumed, is with the dynamic of God's humiliation and the human's exaltation. Mission is a derivative concern informed by these ultimate questions. This is not simply a formal problem of theological method; it is of material significance both for the nature of Christian existence and for the substance of theology.

The contemporary confusion over the interrelationship between the three parts of the doctrine of reconciliation as it appears in Barth's *Church Dogmatics* illustrates the problem well. What is the proper coordination and, perhaps, relative priority of Jesus Christ's priestly office and justification, his kingly office and sanctification, and his prophetic office and calling? Gregory Robertson observes that, while it is generally acknowledged that those three constitute a formal unity, actual treatments exhibit a myopic focus only on the interaction between justification and sanctification.[4]

---

the prophetic office as a kind of theological rationale for the modern church's missionary movement to the world." John B. Webster, "'Eloquent and Radiant': The Prophetic Office of Christ and the Mission of the Church," in *Barth's Moral Theology: Human Action in Barth's Thought* (Grand Rapids: Eerdmans, 1998), p. 133. Webster is certainly correct if by "theological rationale" he means some form of validation that, once given, sets mission on a mechanistic path. This is to predicate the act on a split between Jesus' prophetic action and that of his community. Insofar as the concrete form of the human community corresponds to Jesus Christ's living presence in the power of the Spirit, however, an account of his prophetic office precisely constitutes a theological rationale for the community's missionary existence.

4. Gregory Alan Robertson, "'Vivit! Regnat! Triumphat!' The Prophetic Office of Jesus

This seemingly innocuous methodological move occasions significant consequences for our missionary question. George Hunsinger, as a representative example, holds that "justification and sanctification are primarily conceived . . . as the objective aspects of salvation to which [calling] is the corresponding existential aspect."[5] Though necessary, even imperative, this existential aspect is not of itself materially significant for reconciliation's theological substantiation. The formal interrelation and theological substance of justification and sanctification has been established prior to the event of calling, which follows as the relative outworking of these already complete principles. This prompts the following conclusion by Hunsinger:

> [W]itness is seen as penultimate, and eternal life as the ultimate, form of fellowship. Witness as a matter of declaring, and eternal life as one of enjoying, the salvation accomplished in and by Jesus Christ. Witness consists of fellowship with Jesus Christ in his prophetic work; eternal life, of fellowship with him in his royal work.[6]

I will examine whether missionary witness is properly set in contrast to *eternal* life. Clearly, the particular missionary act of proclaiming the coming kingdom and calling humanity to repentance is a provisional event. Universal mission is an expression of the community's future hope. When this interim period has "run its course," then the "existence and mission of the community" will have served its purpose (*CD* III/2, 489; *KD* III/ 2, 587). The problem develops when, due to the provisionality of this particular missionary form, the overarching category of witness becomes contrasted with some more ultimate form of fellowship. The act of witness becomes of derivative interest alongside the materially intact dynamic of divine humiliation and human exaltation. This is partly the result of defining "mission" according to the phenomenon rather than the theological substance — a cardinal abrogation of basic theological method — and this approach is not theologically benign. As the kingly office assumes priority over the prophetic office, so the nature of sanctification forms in distinction to the calling of witness.

Christ, the Christian life, and the Mission of the Church in Karl Barth's Church Dogmatics IV/3" (Th.D. diss., Wycliffe College and the University of Toronto, 2003), p. 258 n. 50.

5. George Hunsinger, *How to Read Karl Barth: The Shape of His Theology* (New York: Oxford University Press, 1991), p. 155.

6. Hunsinger, *How to Read Karl Barth,* p. 181.

Barth himself bears some responsibility for this confusion. His own position develops through the *Church Dogmatics*. Early on he posits "the prophetic office at the first (Galilean) stage, the priestly at the second (the passion) and the kingly at the third (exaltation)" (*CD* II/2, 431; *KD* II/2, 478). Later he attributes this variety of position to "a lack of clarity concerning the inner relationship of the *revelation* of Jesus Christ and His *work*" (*CD* IV/3.1, 15; *KD* IV/3.1, 14). It reflects the "preponderant tendency to understand the relationship of the three mediatorial functions *e ratione executionis*, that is, as that of different stages in the course of the history of Jesus, and therefore in a historical framework" (*CD* IV/3.1, 15; *KD* IV/3.1, 14). Understanding the offices within this framework obscures the living unity of Jesus Christ's history. Each formalized stage built toward a climax with regard to which the earlier stage became of only relative importance. Attention focused especially on the kingly and priestly offices, with the prophetic office "put in the shade by their superior light as in a sense provisional" and, thus, could not "receive the justice due to it" (*CD* IV/3.1, 15; *KD* IV/3.1, 14-15). As itself the lowest rung, the corresponding missionary form of Christian existence was a provisional form beside the more final forms of fellowship with the divine. Barth links the late discovery within Protestantism of the "Christian duty of mission" with this deficient attention given to the prophetic office (*CD* IV/3.1, 305; *KD* IV/3.1, 352).

The Superfluity of the Resurrection

Conceiving these three offices in terms of Jesus Christ's own history precludes a sequential interpretation because his life is the outworking of the history of God's humiliation and the exaltation of the human. That is, the offices are to be framed according to the hypostatic union: the priestly office develops from the perspective of the true God humiliated for humanity; the kingly office develops from the perspective of true humanity elevated into God. These two offices, in other words, constitute the living history of fellowship of the one Jesus Christ, and are, as such, complete: nothing further can be added to this encounter, nor do the two resolve into a third thing. In truth, the prophetic office does not constitute a "further development of our material knowledge of the event of reconciliation" (*CD* IV/3.1, 7; *KD* IV/3.1, 6). However, since this is the case, the prophetic office develops from the perspective of this divine-human encounter "in its *unity* and *completeness,* the viewing of Jesus Christ Himself, in whom the two lines cross" (*CD* IV/1, 136; *KD* IV/1, 149). The completion of this exhaustive encounter of the divine and the human cannot be understood apart from its definite character, apart from the reality of its "outreaching, embracing and comprehensive character" (*CD* IV/3.1, 279; *KD* IV/3.1, 322). That is, accounts of the divine-human fellowship that fail to refer to the particular historical form of missionary witness are reduced to mere abstractions. Jesus Christ's life is not merely a possibility, but it is the actuality of God in relationship to humans, and it takes a particular form: as both God and man, Jesus Christ is the true witness. Barth describes this third christological aspect as

> . . . at once the simplest and the highest. It is the source of the two first, and it comprehends them both. As the God who humbles Himself and therefore reconciles human being with Himself, and as the human exalted by God and therefore reconciled with Him, as the One who is very *God* and very *human* in this concrete sense, Jesus Christ Himself is *one.* (*CD* IV/1, 135; *KD* IV/1, 148)

The simplicity and oneness of the prophetic office is no mere formal unity, some abstracted epistemological indicator incidental to the eternal divine and human fellowship. The prophetic office is the "simplest" because it is the actuality of God's own living eloquence, the expressive living history that belongs to his being from and to all eternity. Jesus Christ is the true witness because God is in and for himself the true witness.

As the prophetic office describes the oneness of this event, so it describes the nature of its perfection. It is Jesus Christ's resurrection from the dead with power by the Spirit of holiness that reveals God's own majesty to take this form, declaring the Son of David to be the Son of God (Rom. 1:3-4). With his resurrection, "His being and action as very God and very human emerged from the concealment of His particular existence as an inclusive being and action enfolding the world" (*CD* IV/3.1, 283; *KD* IV/3.1, 327). It reveals God's missionary nature, for God reveals his active determination to be for the human, that is, it points back to the "absolutely *prevenient* 'history' which as the *opus Trinitatis internum ad extra* is in God Himself the eternal beginning of all His way and works" (*CD* IV/3.2, 484; *KD* IV/3.2, 556). God is in and for himself complete from all eternity. Nothing adds to this completion. Nothing accrues to God's being in his movement into the economy, for he already has an above and below within himself. It belongs to the very nature of God's perfection that it takes this economic form of witness: God is a missionary God. As such, in what takes place when human beings become witnesses of God, "in what takes place between the human Jesus and ourselves when we may become and be Christians, *God Himself lives* — not a life foreign to Him, but the life which is most proper to Him" (rev., *KD* IV/2, 382; *CD* IV/2, 342). Given this perfect superfluity of God's life, any account that abstracts from his declarative becoming has substituted a dead idol for the living God. Such a caution includes the refusal to accord the corresponding human act of witness any material status in the event of reconciliation, for it constitutes a denial of the reality of God's own life.

As it belongs to God's own being to be complete in this inclusive way, so the event of reconciliation is complete in like manner. God's perfection is as proclamatory to eternity as it is from eternity. God's living eloquence is declared in the living unity of the Son. "Where God is present as active Subject; where He lives, as is the case in the life of Jesus Christ, life is not just possibly or secondarily but definitely and primarily declaration, and therefore light, truth, Word and glory" (*CD* IV/3.1, 79; *KD* IV/3.1, 87). It is the nature of this divine and human fellowship to overflow, not as a second step, but as the reality of its own perfection. As reconciliation "takes place in its perfection, and with no need of supplement, it also expresses, discloses, mediates and reveals itself" (*CD* IV/3.1, 8; *KD* IV/3.1, 6). The corresponding missionary form is no idle implication formulated alongside an otherwise defined substance of reconciliation. "The real goal and end of the resurrection of Jesus and its attestation was His going out into the *world,* into *all the world*" (*CD* IV/3.1, 303; *KD* IV/3.1, 350). The oneness of this event includes its movement from particularity to universality, its movement from Easter to the final form of the *parousia.* This does not direct the community to her own resources, but it liberates her to "fulfill her duty of mission in the knowledge that her Lord has long since preceded her with *His* Word in His resurrection, and that He is always well *ahead* of her, so that in this respect, too, she has only to follow Him" (*CD* IV/3.1, 305; *KD* IV/3.1, 351, 352). This is the basis of the missionary existence of the community, the active form of human participation in the encounter of divine-human fellowship. All that follows concerning the missionary nature of Christian being is merely a reflection of what it means for God to be a *missionary* God and thus for Jesus Christ to be the *living* Lord.

Reconciliation as Revelation

Jesus Christ's resurrection from the dead, the sending of the Spirit, and the spilling of his community out onto the streets proclaiming his name to the ends of the earth and of time reveal the nature of God's own perfection in and for himself. Mission, as the completion of reconciliation, is the prophet Jesus Christ acting in the power of the Spirit. He is "alone the acting and directing subject (both offering and offered) of the reasonable service of God" (*CD* II/2, 715; *KD* II/2, 799). No one else, not even the community in her corresponding missionary existence, accomplishes this for him. In Jesus Christ, the differentiated fellowship of the divine and the human is already an accomplished reality. Such statements, critics assume, severely limit or perhaps even disqualify the human missionary response.[7] Jesus Christ's prophetic work and the human act, however, are not binary opposites; mission as the event of Jesus Christ's own self-declaration is the basis of the missionary existence of the Christian community.

As God is a missionary God, so "revelation is reconciliation, as certainly as it is God Himself: God with us; God beside us, and chiefly and decisively, God for us."[8] Reconciliation is God giving himself freely to the human, and with this, to quote Webster, "revelation is purposive."[9] God does not simply make himself known in his economy, but he overcomes the gap between himself and those who would live in enmity with him. Reconciliation is itself the expansive reality of God's being, and so its accomplishment is "not locked in itself, but a moving out, a communicative occurrence. It does not become an event in any other way than that it also expresses, discloses and mediates itself" (rev., *KD* IV/3.1, 7; *CD* IV/3.1, 8). Precisely as such, reconciliation cannot mean that Jesus Christ remains aloof from those in need and alone in its occurrence. If this were the case,

---

7. Manecke, for example, says that Barth's "understanding of mission is more a reference to God's action . . . than it is to an effectual activity of his community that brings about the eschatological turning point (God through us)." Dieter Manecke, *Mission als Zeugendienst: Karl Barths theologische Begründung der Mission im Gegenüber zu den Entwürfen von Walter Holsten, Walter Freytag und Joh. Christiaan Hoekendijk* (Wuppertal, Germany: Rolf Brockhaus Verlag, 1972), p. 193.

8. Karl Barth, *God in Action,* trans. Elmer G. Homrighausen and Karl J. Ernst (Manhasset, NY: Round Table, 1963), p. 17.

9. John B. Webster, *Holy Scripture: A Dogmatic Sketch* (Cambridge: Cambridge University Press, 2003), p. 16.

then it would declare the reconciliation of humans to be false. Precisely in its reality, reconciliation constitutes a "summons to conscious, intelligent, living, grateful, willing and active participation in its occurrence" (*CD* IV/3.2, 8; *KD* IV/3.2, 6). As the Christian is drawn into the sphere of Jesus Christ's own history and it becomes her own objective experience, it is Christ's good will to give human beings, for all their imperfection, the opportunity "under the promise of the Spirit to participate in reconciliation as an active subject, namely, as a recipient and bearer of the Word of reconciliation" (*CD* IV/3.1, 392-93; *KD* IV/3.1, 453). With reconciliation's reality constituting the given possibility of participation in revelation, the human response cannot be any more than that of a witness. The Christian can only "participate in a repetition in which she has nothing of her own to utter or express or produce, but can only discharge the debt of response to what comes upon her in this encounter" (*CD* IV/3.1, 45; *KD* IV/3.1, 48). The Christian cannot evade the determination to this service. It is not a task that the Christian may or may not choose to undertake, for it belongs to the living nature of reconciliation itself. Failure to undertake this task indicates the absence to the living history of divine and human fellowship. As Jesus Christ liberates human beings to this relationship, he liberates them to become active subjects in service to his own prophetic work.

Missionary activity receives a definite form: it is active participation in reconciled and reconciling communities.[10] As a reality, reconciliation per-

---

10. An important tension emerges, through this discussion, between the individual and the community. Migliore suggests that Barth might have better emphasized the communal character of Christian existence by placing "the paragraphs on the Holy Spirit and the Christian community (§62, 67, 72) *prior* to rather than *after* the paragraphs on justification, sanctification, and vocation (§61, 66, 71). Barth himself indicated both in writing and in conversation that it would have been possible and even desirable to do this." Daniel L. Migliore, "*Participatio Christi*: The Central Theme of Barth's Doctrine of Sanctification," *Zeitschrift für Dialektische Theologie* 18, no. 3 (2002): 304. The contemporary concern with ecclesiastical practices, with the potential socializing function of the Christian community, makes this an important suggestion. Might the lack commentators perceive here in Barth be overcome by emphasizing the necessity of the community?

First, as previously examined, it is clear that, for Barth, one can be a Christian only as he or she actively participates in the commission of the Christian community. Participation in this task is not voluntary, but is the result of the Christian's election in Jesus Christ. "There is no *vocatio*, and therefore no *unio cum Christo*, which does not as such lead directly into the communion of saints, i.e., the *communio vocatorum*" (*CD* IV/3.2, 682; *KD* IV/3.2, 781). By linking election and calling, Barth notes that "if he is in the community, he is a κλητός. If he is not a κλητός, he is not in the community" (*CD* IV/3.2, 525; *KD* IV/3.2, 604).

mits no abstraction of the kind associated with *missio Dei* theology. Reconciliation as revelation reinforces the importance of the Christian community as a *community*, a living fellowship. Such fellowship, however, cannot itself be conceived in static terms, as an inward orientation occupied with reconciling relationships. Jesus Christ's prophetic work does not "only end in a blind alley" of Christian self-satisfaction (*CD* IV/3.1, 18; *KD* IV/3.1, 17). "Reconciliation, generally and as such, does not merely take place for itself in a special sphere closed off by the resistance and contradiction which it encounters. On the contrary, it takes place as it establishes Christian knowledge in the world and in and among the people who are reconciled in its oc-

---

This focus on the community in relationship to the individual is also necessary as protection against any conception of a private Christianity that consists in the enjoyment of the benefits that accrue to the individual. To emphasize the necessarily communal form of Christianity is to emphasize the nature of Christianity as public confession, and indeed the mode of that confession. If reconciliation has the character of revelation, then the visible presence of a community living in this reconciliation itself has the character of revelation. Witness, thus, is not the action of an individual in isolation, but an action of the community as she lives according to the promise of reconciliation. To be a witness means to actively participate in the task given the community in her founding charter.

Second, while the *form* of Christian existence is necessarily communal, the focus on the individual in relation to the community plays a vital role with regard to the missionary *intention* of this community. On the one hand, this tension helps offset the potential abuses that arise when Christianity becomes identified with a nation, state, people, group, or culture. "There are no predestined families and no predestined nations — even the Israelite nation is simply the first (transitory!) form of the community! — nor is there a predestined humanity. There are only predestined (predestined in Jesus Christ, and through the community!) *people*." (rev., *KD* II/2, 344; *CD* II/2, 313). The missionary task is not based in manifest destiny, technological, political, economic, or cultural superiority, nor is it grounded in any form of historical accident. This same problem, on the other hand, can be considered from the perspective of the static — or passively receptive — form the church can take if and when the gospel becomes domesticated. Barth, for example, laments that "even in the sphere of Christendom there are many who belong sociologically, by name and baptism, but do not belong at all in practice, being blind and deaf heathen" (*CD* IV/3.1, 119; *KD* IV/3.1, 133). Belonging to the community takes a definite, active form. In summary, "the Christian community as such and all her members exist under the promise of grace. The *fulfillment* of this promise, however, may not be flatly equated with the existence of the Christian community; we cannot simply say that the grace of this liberation belongs to all her members in virtue of their adherence to this collective and without their needing specifically to request, receive and exercise it" (*CD* IV/3.2, 781; *KD* IV/3.2, 894). Thus, it is as individuals continually receive and engage in their calling that the community takes place, and the form of this taking place is that of missionary existence.

currence" (*CD* IV/3.1, 214; *KD* IV/3.1, 245).[11] Reconciliation's reality means movement out in its dynamic to those estranged from God. Apart from any personal benefits that accrued to the disciples, the reality of resurrection came to them in the form of the "*missionary command:* 'Go you into *all the world*'! It was for this that the Resurrected one appeared" (rev., *KD* IV/3.1, 350; *CD* IV/3.1, 303). The nature of human reconciliation with God and with one another must itself correspond to the nature of God's self-revelation, that is, the community exists in her service of witness to the world. Reconciliation is an event, a determination, a sending, a task, a commission, a mission. Jesus Christ speaks to his called people with the "intention and commission that it for its part should speak to the *world,* that it should be His messenger within it" (*CD* IV/3.1, 18; *KD* IV/3.1, 17). The life of the community takes on the character of revelation, "of the *word* of God demanding expression" (*CD* IV/3.1, 38; *KD* IV/3.1, 40). She is thus revelatory in her movement into the world, for the fact of reconciliation includes within it the certain call to the whole of humanity.

The two affirmations of the direct act of Jesus Christ in his prophetic office and of no secondary step between mission and the nature of Christian existence are, as such, mutually defining. The whole being and action of the Christian community rests on this single declaration: Jesus Christ is risen, he is risen indeed. The community's own particular form cannot be any different from the content of this revelation. The reality of reconciliation is a life of active participation in Jesus Christ's own mission by the power of the Spirit.

Life in the Promise of the Spirit

With his resurrection from the dead, "Jesus is victor!" However, we must remember that the "is" at the center of this phrase is "*dynamic* rather than static" — it "conceals a drama" (*CD* IV/3.1, 165; *KD* IV/3.1, 188). The Chris-

---

11. From the perspective of *missio Dei,* locating this discussion within the doctrine of reconciliation overcomes a significant lacuna in the concept's development. As Matthey suggests, "reconciliation was not absent from WCC mission conferences and documents, but was not highlighted in particular." Jacques Matthey, "Reconciliation, *Missio Dei* and the Church's Mission," in *Mission — Violence and Reconciliation: Papers Read at the Biennial Conference of the British and Irish Association for Mission Studies at the University of Edinburgh, June 2003,* ed. Howard Mellor and Timothy Yates (Sheffield, UK: Cliff College Publishing, 2004), p. 114.

tian now lives within a *"dynamic teleology,"* one in which the light has already attained victory and is still wrestling toward it, and in which the darkness has already lost and is still in active resistance (*CD* IV/3.1, 168; *KD* IV/3.1, 192). God "has spoken His final Word, but He has not yet finished speaking it. The last hour has struck, but it is still striking" (*CD* IV/1, 736-37; *KD* IV/1, 823). God gives humanity this space because he does not want his final word to be spoken "until He has first heard a *human response* to it, a *human* Yes" (*CD* IV/1, 737; *KD* IV/1, 809). God intends the reconciliation of the world, and this, of necessity, includes the free human response.

Life in the promise of the Spirit is a life lived within this eschatological drama, as the one event of the *parousia* in three different forms: the Easter event, the interim period of the impartation of the Spirit, and the final return. Since it is already real, one cannot limit its eschatological truth to the final stage of the *parousia*. As Jesus Christ's three offices are not relative according to a historical framework, so the reality of the *parousia* "is not more in one case or less in another. It is the one thing taking place in different ways" (*CD* IV/3.1, 293; *KD* IV/3.1, 338). He is not absent, abandoning his mission to the Christian community. Now is the time of Jesus Christ's "effective presence" (*CD* IV/3.1, 292; *KD* IV/3.1, 337). As ascended to the right hand of the Father, Jesus is "remote from earthly history and the Christianity which exists in it. He is unattainably superior to it" (rev., *KD* IV/2, 737; *CD* IV/2, 652). Controlled by neither history nor his community, he remains sovereign in relationship to both.

Because Jesus Christ lives, however, he is not restricted to the right hand of the Father. As God is not in himself "the prisoner of His own height and distance," so Jesus Christ comprehends and controls these antitheses (*CD* IV/2, 653; *KD* IV/2, 738). As the Mediator between God and humanity, Jesus Christ does not "exist merely for Himself and to that extent concentrically" (*CD* IV/3.2, 548; *KD* IV/3.2, 629). In the "supreme expression of Himself, He *also* exists *eccentrically,* i.e., in and with the realization of the existence of these humans" (*CD* IV/3.2, 548; *KD* IV/3.2, 629). He overcomes the gap between the "there and then" and the "here and now" in the promise of the Holy Spirit. The Spirit is not an intermediary force between Jesus Christ and those he calls. Jesus Christ is present and active as the true witness in the form of the Spirit, and the community is "healthy in proportion as she gives free course to the Spirit" (*CD* IV/2, 321; *KD* IV/2, 359). The Spirit is the power by which Jesus Christ encloses the history of those called by him into his history.

The *parousia* determines the whole of human existence.[12] It is a *total* event, for the reality it declares is not merely one possible future awaiting actualization, but is already actual and becoming fulfilled. It is a *definite* event, for God's judgment spoken in the resurrection of Jesus Christ includes the final judgment within it, and this directs the human response. It is a *universal* event, for it takes an expressly missionary form. "The *necessity* of Christian mission is grounded in the Easter event: a Christianity without a mission to all would not at all be Christianity, for it would reveal itself as not at all deriving from this event, and as not at all gathered and upbuilt by Jesus Christ who is resurrected from the dead for all" (rev., *KD* IV/3.1, 351; *CD* IV/3.1, 304). With the existence of the community grounded in this universalism, along with her "first-born *right*," a "first-born *duty* is imposed: her *missionary* duty" (rev., *KD* IV/3.1, 350; *CD* IV/3.1, 303). No arrogance can accompany the imposition of this duty. It is one of "unqualified participation in the cause of God and therefore in the cause of the world and humanity" (*CD* IV/3.1, 248; *KD* IV/3.1, 285). Nor, given the abundant joy characterizing God's own self-determination, does this participation take the form of "a compulsory law which must be kept but with at least the mental reservation that in some depth of one's existence one can still be a camp-follower and therefore a spectator of the good Lord and other people and finally oneself" (*CD* IV/3.1, 248; *KD* IV/3.1, 285).[13] Mission is not a duty one can choose to fulfill. Any failure to live as a witness directs the community back to her own strength as though the act depended on frenetic human activity. The community is "not Atlas bearing the burden of the whole world on her shoulders"(*CD* IV/3.1, 115; *KD* IV/3.1, 129). Her sending into the world does not become the means of salvation as though Easter needed to be repeated. The battle has been won, and the work of the community consists of hurrying after Jesus Christ's own prophetic work. Only the action of the Spirit opens the community to live in and with this eschatological reality. The Spirit is the "summoning power of the divine promise, which points the community beyond herself, which

12. For the following threefold characterization as total, definite, and universal, see *CD* IV/3.1, 301-7; *KD* IV/3.1, 348-54.

13. Newbigin likewise observes that "we have regarded witness as a demand laid upon us instead of seeing it as a gift promised to us. We have made the missionary imperative into a law, a heavy burden laid upon the conscience of Christians, whereas the New Testament sees it as a gracious gift, as . . . a spin-off from Pentecost." J. E. Lesslie Newbigin, "Context and Conversion," *International Review of Mission* 68, no. 3 (1979): 308.

calls her to transcend herself and in that way to be in truth the community of God — in truth, i.e., as she bears *witness* to the truth known within her, as she knows herself to be charged with this witness and *sent out* to establish it" (*CD* IV/1, 152; *KD* IV/1, 168). The life of community is thus basic, but only as an expansive reality. As not herself the means of salvation, the community lives in the promise of the Spirit, that is, the community proclaims the coming kingdom of God as the future of creation and this marks her as "a missionary community" (*CD* IV/1, 152-53; *KD* IV/1, 168).

Human Being in Jesus Christ

Even if this argument is sufficient to establish mission as the form of Christian existence that corresponds to the universalism of the Easter event, it remains common to accord that act only provisional significance. While mission might be necessary now, it does not belong in eternity. Moltmann, reflecting the received position, holds that apostolicity is "not an eschatological term, but a term related to the *eschaton,* because it is not a characteristic of the *eschaton* itself."[14] Apostolicity hereby becomes juxtaposed to "eternal life," and, by extension, the missionary act relegated to penultimate status and remote beside some other ultimate form of divine-human fellowship. If this were the case, then the experience of reconciliation now (and thus of God's self-revelation) would not be actual fellowship with God but a provisional form awaiting a more final and potentially different reality. We now live in hope in an interim period where the "already" includes a "not yet." Yet, if apostolicity is not a component in the community's future reconciliation, then the kingdom is not the structuring reality of contemporary Christian existence. This kind of eschatological docetism is to be repudiated, for with the resurrection the disciples were liberated for "eternal life and therefore for service in this life" (*CD* IV/3.1, 303; *KD* IV/3.1, 349). The eternal form of fellowship human beings share with God takes place here and now as the act of missionary service.

On the question of what happens to the human in the event of eternal life, two problems that are reflective of the two sides of the eschatological tension present themselves. First, it is necessary not to revert to pagan no-

14. Jürgen Moltmann, *The Church in the Power of the Spirit: A Contribution to Messianic Ecclesiology* (Minneapolis: Fortress, 1993), p. 357.

tions of divinity. God is no "supreme being with neither life, nor activity, nor history, in a neutrality which can never be moved or affected by anything, a being with which the human can ultimately be united only in rest or in some kind of passive enjoyment or adoring contemplation" (*CD* IV/1, 112; *KD* IV/1, 122). Such notions reintroduce a stark division between God's being and his act, and they bespeak a static form of Christian existence now. As eternal life is the knowledge of God (John 17:3), so the promise of eternal life given to humanity corresponds to the history of God's own being. Given the nature of God's own self-determination, this form of fellowship "must consist in a being with God as this active ruler which encounters the human person" (rev., *KD* IV/1, 122; *CD* IV/1, 112). Eternal life is the human living in service to God. Second, the problem of synergism reemerges. The *telos* of justification and sanctification is that the human might become "the *partner* of God and live as such" (*CD* IV/1, 113; *KD* IV/1, 123). Such participation in the cause of God is the true goal of the human. Synergism is the problem of prematurely ascribing this immediate relationship of service to "the human at a place where it does not — not yet! — belong to them" (rev., *KD* IV/1, 123; *CD* IV/1, 113). When this occurs, humans claim a responsibility that is properly God's own. In other words, the two problems of a static or an overactive life reflect an improper coordination of the present in relation to the future. On the one hand, an improper future expectation determines present acting in a direction different from the nature of the living God's own eternal existence. On the other hand, a future reality is improperly usurped by the present. Eternal life must be active after the nature of the differentiated fellowship of action that is the divine-human fellowship. Though that fellowship takes a provisional form now, given reconciliation's completion, it remains true even in that provisionality. While it is fulfilled, the *nature* of this fellowship does not change with the *eschaton*.

Given the eschatological location, orientation, and determination of the Christian community, eternal life reflects no clean demarcation between the present and the future. The divine promise is actual now only in Jesus Christ. For humans, it is a future occurrence for which the community awaits in hope. Insofar as the divine promise is already actual in Jesus Christ, the community already has to do with her future in God. Nor is this reality limited to the sphere of the church's acting. Because the future of salvation is present in its fullness in the Easter event, this determination belongs to all of creation. "What '*will be*' there and then in the *eschaton* is in visibility that which really *is* here and now in virtue of the reconciling action of God, which constitutes the controlling sense to temporal history" (*CD* IV/3.2, 489; *KD* IV/3.2, 562). The concrete determination of the Christian community's existence in hope is itself a function of this future's reality. Because the promise of God is true, its contemporary reality is undone if it is understood "'eschatologically,' *and therefore* (provisionally at least) unrealistically, instead of in reverse as supremely realistically, *and therefore,* and in this sense, 'eschatologically'" (rev., *KD* IV/3.2, 562; *CD* IV/3.2, 489).[15]

Easter is the hope of the whole world, and it is precisely as such that the community is commissioned to live as witnesses to this promise. In other words, the differentiating element between the church and the world is that as the Spirit awakens human beings to faith "they do not merely live *under* the promise, which could be said of all humanity, but *in* and *with* and *by* the promise. They seize, apprehend, relate themselves appropriately to it, and therefore in their present life already live as future humans" (rev., *KD* IV/1, 131; *CD* IV/1, 120). The holy distinction of this life is the result, not of the prolonged conferment of a *habitus,* but of the particular missionary determination of Christian hope. As Christian calling is being seized by the promise of God, any failure to live according to this commission is to live as one who does not belong to this future, as one who has no hope.

In terms of the current question concerning the provisional status of the missionary act relative to eternal life, the present reality of this hope constitutes a *"biblical universalism"* (rev., *KD* IV/3.2, 562; *CD* IV/3.2, 488).[16] Such is the basis of the missionary commission. The very universalism mission serves is the nature of the *eschaton.* It is the impetus by which community exists. If mission were terminal, then the act itself would declare the unreality of the universalism in which it is located. That which is to come would be "a second reality distinct from a supposed first reality here and now, and therefore necessarily exposed to suspicion of being merely ideal and therefore unreal" (*CD* IV/3.2, 489; *KD* IV/3.2, 562). One can hear, in this eschatological perspective, echoes of the suggested modalism that developed when God's deliberate decision for the world formed as a second step beside who he is in and for himself. Life in hope

---

15. Because eschatology is "the other world in this world, the incorruptible within the corruptible, eternal life in temporal, divine in human," the church is "the eschatological fact *par excellence*" (*CD* IV/3.1, 321; *KD* IV/3.1, 370).

16. Again, it is necessary to emphasize that the universalism in question is not that of *apokatastasis* or a de facto universal reconciliation.

means dedication to the service of God, which is the nature of human fellowship with the divine, of human participation in the history of God.
Failure to live this way demonstrates the unreality of the hope and thus
bears false witness to the reality of Jesus Christ's lordship over the world.
The missionary form is wrongly contrasted with eternal life; it is the form
that life takes in the promise of the Spirit as the community actively participates in Jesus Christ's prophetic office.

Christian Calling

Christians are those who "apprehend not only the justification and sanctification of the human, but also, in Jesus Christ, their *calling* to *eternal life*"
(rev., *KD* IV/1, 124; *CD* IV/1, 114). Eternal life is fellowship between the human and God in which the human serves God and fellow humanity. Christian calling is the "teleological setting in the kingdom of God," and it takes
the "form of *mission* in relation to the community" (*CD* IV/1, 527; *KD* IV/1,
588).[17] Calling is not to a "special Christian existence," as though the exercise of the missionary commission might only apply to certain individuals
(*CD* IV/3.2, 524; *KD* IV/3.2, 602). Nor is calling an initial stage beyond
which the Christian moves. Insofar as the prophetic office expresses the
oneness of the event of reconciliation, what befalls the Christian in being
called "is not a partial work" alongside which there is a "variously described organization of a progressive alteration of the human" (*CD* IV/3.2,
508; *KD* IV/3.2, 583-84). Sanctification is not a further step that completes
Christian calling. Calling is for the purpose of becoming and being a
Christian, "a *homo christianus*" (*CD* IV/3.2, 521; *KD* IV/3.2, 599). There is

17. This treatment replaces the language of "vocation," used through the *Church Dogmatics,* with that of "calling." Barth himself laments that, through church history, the trajectory of "vocation" began to bear "a desperate resemblance to the monologue of the Christian concerning one's faith" (*CD* IV/3.2, 497; *KD* IV/3.2, 572). This leads back to the blind
alley of the church curved in upon herself, with "calling" limited to specially ordained Christians. To reinforce his point concerning the purpose of the benefits of Christ as equipping
one for a task, Barth engages in a truly remarkable extended examination of every calling
narrative within Scripture (see *CD* IV/3.2, 577-92; *KD* IV/3.2, 662-78). From this he concludes that, where Scripture "refers to the status *gratiae et salutis* of the called one," it is always in the context of the "commissioning and sending of the called one, and sees him set in
a function to be exercised between God and other human beings, between God and the
world" (*CD* IV/3.2, 592; *KD* IV/3.2, 679).

no second step alongside Christian being and this commission, as though being conveyed a potentiality beside which the commission constituted its fulfillment. "Each elect individual is as such a *messenger* of God. This is one's service and commission. It is for this purpose that one may represent and portray the glory and grace of God. One is sent. One is an *apostle*" (*CD* II/2, 415; *KD* II/2, 458). An individual is a Christian only insofar as one is obedient to this calling.[18]

Again, the point needs to be emphasized: while calling is now manifested in this provisional missionary commission, it is itself the nature of fellowship with God and thus the ultimate human end of eternal life. The nature of this fellowship and its contemporary form might be further examined using the phrase *unio cum Christo*. Like the superfluity of the divine and human fellowship in Jesus Christ, "the embracing concept of 'calling' describes a *history*: the history of the Christian in connection with that of Jesus Christ Himself as engaged in His prophetic work" (rev., *KD* IV/3.2, 760; *CD* IV/3.2, 663). Because calling means union with Jesus Christ, it indicates neither the disappearance nor the identification of Jesus Christ with the community awakened by the Spirit. For the human,

---

18. As Bosch suggests, for Barth "a withdrawal from mission thus signifies a withdrawal from grace rather than from duty. The true Christian cannot not-witness." David J. Bosch, *Witness to the World: The Christian Mission in Theological Perspective* (London: Marshall, Morgan and Scott, 1980), p. 168. Barth notes how such a position strikes at the heart of "the Christian world and western man" (*CD* IV/3.2, 523; *KD* IV/3.2, 601). Might it not be argued that the real "validity of calling is the special basis of a particular form of Christianity and not as the indispensable basis or *conditio sine qua non* of Christian existence as such" (*CD* IV/3.2, 522)? Such an objection Barth understands as related to the phenomenon of Christendom, the presupposed "practical occurrence between civilization, culture and political power on the one side and the Church on the other" (*CD* IV/3.2, 524). This greater or lesser identification stimulated a definition of Christian being that consisted of sharing in the "determination of Western humanity naturally passed on with one's mother's milk and the water of baptism" (*CD* IV/3.2, 523). "All that is needed is to have, not a new, but a given and present attachment, implicitly and secondarily to Jesus Christ, but explicitly and primarily to a family, nation, culture and civilization" (*CD* IV/3.2, 522). Calling became a secondary step in addition to this automatic listing on the church rolls and so ceased to be determinative of Christian being. It became an offense for Christians with a special calling to demand an active form of Christian life from those called by virtue of being born. Those with a special Christian calling "must not give the impression either tacitly or vocally that the Christian as such, and so *every* Christian, in every time and under every horizon, can become and be a Christian *only* by calling. The assertion must never be made that those who are not called cannot be Christians" (rev., *KD* IV/3.2, 601; *CD* IV/3.2, 522-23).

the ordering of this fellowship might be described as one of *active passivity.*[19] As this is true of Jesus Christ himself, these terms should not be interpreted in light of simple interhuman relationships.[20] The Christian's union with Christ is participation in his own history and thus corresponds to the ordering that belongs to God's own life of fellowship. It reflects the

> ... twofold *differentiation* of that mutual participation in and sharing of the divine and the human natures of Jesus Christ: The *character* of the two moments of this event, for all their reciprocity, are different — in the one, as the essence of the Son of God, it is wholly a *giving*, and in the other, exalted to existence and reality only through and in Him, is wholly a *receiving.* (rev., *KD* IV/2, 78; *CD* IV/2, 72)

19. Barth's position, as Wiedenmann suggests, coincidentally relativizes and activates the human missionary act: "relativizing: because in the long run it is God, who works everything alone; activation: because it is, nevertheless, service to that Word of God which continually desires to be active." Ludwig Wiedenmann, *Mission und Eschatologie: Eine Analyse der neueren deutschen evangelischen Missionstheologie* (Paderborn, Germany: Verlag Bonifacius-Druckerei, 1965), p. 66. Webster makes a very similar assertion, declaring that Barth both "relativizes and establishes the activity of Christian witness. 'Relativizes,' because it asserts the entire adequacy of Jesus' own self-declaration; 'establishes', because the willed form of that self-declaration includes its echo in human declaration." Webster, "Eloquent and Radiant," p. 144. Webster also uses the phrase "active passivity" with regard to the reading of Scripture, which is a "human activity whose substance lies in its reference to and self-renunciation before the presence and action of God." Webster, *Holy Scripture*, p. 72.

20. Passivity is not itself alien to the life of God. As Jüngel suggests, "on the basis of Barth's inference from God's being revealed to his 'inner' being, we shall have to understand, *in* God himself, too, God's 'being-in-act' which corresponds to the passion of the Son of God, as in a certain sense a *passive* being — passive in the sense of obedience. This passivity of obedience in God is also the highest form of activity in so far as it is *affirmed* passivity. It belongs 'to the inner *life* of God that there should take place within it obedience.'" Eberhard Jüngel, *God's Being Is in Becoming*, trans. John B. Webster (Grand Rapids: Eerdmans, 2001), pp. 100-101. Nor should the human's passivity with respect to God be understood as of a kind with how it appears with respect to fellow humans. For Tanner, "[p]assivity with respect to God does not conform to any simple contrast with activity since one might be passive or active on the plane of created reality, in dependence upon, as the passive recipient of, God's gifts; simple passivity with respect to God tells you nothing either way. Or to make the point a little differently, a simple contrast between activity and passivity will not do for creatures' relations with God because no matter how active one is as a creature, one is never anything other than the recipient of God's active grace — God remains active over all." Kathryn E. Tanner, *Jesus, Humanity and the Trinity: A Brief Systematic Theology* (Edinburgh: T. & T. Clark, 2001), p. 4.

Passivity or receptivity is the proper mode of human activity with respect to the activity of God, not a preliminary provisional stage in the expectation of a different form of fellowship. It is itself an ingredient in the event of reconciliation. Creatureliness is established, not abolished, by reconciliation, and the passivity that properly characterizes the human relationship to the divine cannot be disqualified with the final *eschaton*. While in the future of eternal life this service of God may be actively undertaken, it still occurs according to the asymmetrical ordering of giving and receiving.

This union of Jesus Christ and the Christian "would not be complete if their relationship were actualized only from above downwards and not also from below upwards, if it were not reciprocal" (*CD* IV/3.2, 543; *KD* IV/3.2, 624-25). As Jesus Christ is not today idle, so Christians cannot be idle as spectators remotely reflecting on their own reconciliation. At no stage is the Christian's *being* as a child of God "empty; it does not have to be accidentally or arbitrarily filled out. It is not idle; it does not have to become active" (*CD* IV/3.2, 533; *KD* IV/3.2, 613). The promise and goal of calling is that human beings might become and be children of God. This is a properly human life. No ontological change occurs. Rather, to be a child of the Father includes the reception of "the fatherly characteristics, determination, commission, and practical *mode of life*" (*CD* IV/3.2, 534; *KD* IV/3.2, 613). The Christian receives the declarative mode of life that corresponds to God's own living being. God's children, from the very outset, have

> . . . a definite *function* which is committed to them, a definite *action* which they are commissioned to perform. Their nature is fashioned and characterized by the fatherly basis and origin of their existence. If only in analogy to the existence of Jesus Christ, yet very really in this analogy they, too, as the children of God exist in repetition, confirmation and revelation not only of the manner but also of the will and act of God as the One from whom they derive. (*CD* IV/3.2, 533; *KD* IV/3.2, 613)

The Christian is called to be the herald of God. Participating in this event places humans in "actual fellowship with Jesus Christ, namely, in the service of His prophecy, in the *ministerium Verbi divini* of the Word of reconciliation, and therefore in the service of God and their fellow human beings" (*CD* IV/3.2, 482; *KD* IV/3.2, 554). The act of the child of God corresponds to Jesus Christ's own mission, and so it corresponds to God's own self-determination. Its character as a "service" differentiates "cooperation" from synergism (*CD* IV/3.2, 601; *KD* IV/3.2, 688).[21] As a service, "the action, work or activity of Christ unconditionally precedes that of the human called by Him, the Christian, and that of the latter must follow" (*CD* IV/3.2, 597-98; *KD* IV/3.2, 685). Service indicates two active subjects with a differentiation of function united in a single cause. It indicates what is common to these two subjects: the service of God participating in Jesus Christ's mission to the world by the power of the Spirit. In that it is an active work in correspondence to the livingness of Jesus Christ, it is itself fecund in subjective and objective accomplishment within its proper limits as a human work. As God has reconciled the world to himself, so he has entrusted the message of reconciliation to his community (2 Cor. 5:18-19). As the future of the human is the *cooperation* of service with God, so this commission to serve Jesus Christ's prophetic word "is the *centre* of their existence" (*CD* IV/3.2, 574; *KD* IV/3.2, 659).

With their baptism, Christians become consecrated to this commission, and every other element of their human life becomes secondary and subordinate. The prophetic office and the corresponding historical form of witness is not to be relegated to only provisional status alongside some

---

21. At this point a materially determinative confusion develops in the English translation. Where the *KD* says, "es ist schlicht der Begriff des Dienstes," the *CD* says, "this is quite simply the term 'service' or 'ministry'" (*CD* IV/3.2, 601; *KD* IV/3.2, 689). The problem created by the introduction of these two terms, by which "ministry" comes to define "service," as is especially evident in §72.4, "*Der Dienst der Gemeinde.*" Translated as "Ministry of the Community," this misses the basic point that calling and the fellowship with Jesus Christ in service to his prophetic office is the form of Christian existence and true for every member of the community. It tacitly — but seriously — fails to account for affirmations such as the following: Canon law "must avoid the fatal word 'office' and replace it by '*service*,' which can be applied to *all* Christians. . . . [T]rue canon law will have to be all the more vigilant against practical clericalism: against every distinction between the active and the inactive (or passive) Church" (*CD* IV/2, 694; *KD* IV/2, 787). Witness, now linked with the clerical ministry, becomes evacuated of its material missionary content. Lifted from its context in the life of each Christian, it becomes an overarching interpretive principle that generally directs the actions of the institutional church. While one should not overstate the effect of translation issues, the charge that Barth's ecclesiology lacks concretion is understandable from this perspective. On the one hand, with this mistranslation it appears that Barth supports the standard framework of an institutional church, while, on the other, he fails to populate that church with the standard inner mediatorial workings of the sacraments and clergy. This problematic translation, in other words, permits interpreters to think within established categories and attempt to align Barth with these categories, rather than to incorporate this material development of the community's concrete missionary form.

fuller end. As a being under the "verdict" and "direction" of God — under justification and sanctification — the Christian lives in this "promise." This takes the form of Christian calling and it is "*more* than calling into a state of justification and sanctification" (*CD* IV/1, 109; *KD* IV/1, 118). It has a necessarily expressive form: if one is not a witness, one is not a Christian, and if the Christian community is not a missionary community, she is not a Christian community. This stark conclusion occurs for, if one is not a witness, then one is not living in that dynamic encounter and unity of justification and sanctification.

Apostolic Community

"We come here to the test: whether the Christian community believes in Jesus Christ, or in a synthesis which allegedly interprets and explains history and so which artificially bridges the threatening abyss" (rev., *KD* IV/3.2, 821; *CD* IV/3.2, 718). Given the naturalism that traditionally characterized its method, mission is itself often considered exemplary of this kind of synthesis. Now, because mission is not a second step alongside some more proper Christian being, the charge turns on its head. The improper synthesis is the church building herself up as the true end of the Christian faith, thereby positing herself as the means for transitioning the gap between God and history. Instead, the Christian community is called to live within God's own transitioning of the gap, to live within her missionary existence in active obedience to reconciliation's reality. The test of belief is the community's actual apostolic existence. Apostolicity is the community's proper *nota ecclesiae,* her "external characteristic the absence of which is impossible for the actual community of Jesus Christ" (rev., *KD* IV/3.2, 883; *CD* IV/3.2, 771-72). This commission does not refer back to any human longing, need, or power. Mission is not a contingency located in historical accident, either as a result of the positive benefits of Western civilization or out of a perceived need that is a result of the Christian community's social marginalization. It does not proceed from within the human. The divine gift of fellowship necessarily becomes a task, one that comes wholly and most astonishingly upon the community so that she is without alternative.[22] The Christian "has no option but to sprint into the breach

22. With the terms "gift" *(Gabe)* and "task" *(Aufgabe),* Barth is making a wordplay that

between Jesus Christ, whom it is given her to know, and those to whom it is not yet given to know Him, showing them by her existence that what she expects is really before them too" (rev., *KD* IV/3.2, 1071; *CD* IV/3.2, 933). This is living according to the universalism of the Easter event.

Apostolicity, foremost, refers to the community's intimate ground in Scripture — and the necessity of remaining in this ground. Interpreting this concern for the word and its proclamation in the normative terms of a pronouncement within the community's walls fails to satisfy this apostolic condition. A community of the word is a community engaged in the movement that engaged the apostles, for this was the nature of their own discipleship to the word. It was such because such is the nature of Jesus Christ's own identity. Following David Demson's instructive exposition, "the gospel story makes constant reference to Jesus' obedience to his mission. This emphasis indicates that the center of Jesus' person is not in himself but in relation to the events of his life and the persons he encountered."[23] The immediate connection between the reading of apostolic Scripture and participation in the act of the apostolate is that Jesus did not first act for human beings and only then choose — as a second step he might not otherwise have taken — human beings to proclaim this message. Rather, the appointing, calling, and commissioning of his apostles is an "ingredient in Jesus' identity," that is, it is basic to his obedience and thus his fellowship with the Father.[24]

The story of who Jesus Christ is cannot be told apart from his relationship to those he called and their subsequent history. Indeed, the power of his life is demonstrated in his capacity to form human witnesses. Calling is the necessary predicate of apostolic sending. Because Christ remains active in the event of calling, the capacity to proclaim the reconciliation of the world occurs only as the disciples are upheld by Jesus Christ. His presence is "explicitly promised to their mission, and to their persons in *their*

---

is lost in the English. And, as John Webster suggests, "Apostolicity is a matter of *being accosted* by a mandate from outside. It is a Christological-pneumatological concept, and only by derivation is it ecclesiological. Apostolicity is the church's standing beneath the imperious directive: 'Go.'" Webster, *Holy Scripture*, p. 51.

23. David E. Demson, *Hans Frei and Karl Barth: Different Ways of Reading Scripture* (Grand Rapids: Eerdmans, 1997), p. ix. There is only minimal space to develop this insight. See Demson's further treatment in "The Stages of the Gospel Story," in *Hans Frei and Karl Barth*, pp. 1-23.

24. Demson, *Hans Frei and Karl Barth*, p. x.

mission."[25] Nor is his calling of the twelve the end of Christ's power. Though "first bestowed on the apostles, [it] is the power by which many (or all) others are drawn into the apostolate," for it is the power of Jesus Christ's own presence.[26] The apostolic authority of Scripture consists of the power to include other histories in the history of Jesus Christ's own apostolate.

A vital distinction, of course, exists between the "twelve" and the general apostolate of the Christian community. They alone are Jesus Christ's "direct witnesses, they belong together with Him in a unique and special way, with Peter at their head in all his weakness" (*CD* IV/1, 718; *KD* IV/1, 802). Alongside this, the "message, activity and life of the Christian Church" bears an *"indirect witness"* (*CD* IV/3.1, 96; *KD* IV/3.1, 107). The importance of the twelve rests in their original and foundational witness preserved as Scripture, to which the general apostolate does not contribute. Yet it belongs to the truth of this original witness that "what took place between the apostles and the first three and five thousand in Jerusalem can take place again and has, in fact, taken place again" (*CD* IV/1, 717; *KD* IV/1, 801). In other words, the distinction lies in the foundational significance of their *firsthand* witness for the church, not in the *function* of witness itself. It is due to the particularity of the apostles that this general succession of their function is a reality; it is because of their witness that the community can and must witness.

The church exists "by the ongoing work and word of the apostles" and so "by doing what the apostles did and are still doing" (*CD* II/2, 431; *KD* II/2, 477). Living within the community grounded in the witness of the apostles means to share in their own commissioning, for it is only by moving in accordance with the apostles that the community reads and understands Scripture. For the individual, this means enlisting in the community's cause, taking part in her history and in the definite movement that engaged the apostles. As for the community, she must not understand her life to be one of an institution or set of relationships whose missionary task is "only an immediate or more distant deduction from the *gift* of her being and existence" (rev., *KD* IV/3.2, 900-901; *CD* IV/3.2, 787). As Jesus Christ's own identity includes the event of calling, upbuilding, and sending, so he did not live for himself, nor was his life an

25. Demson, *Hans Frei and Karl Barth*, p. 22.
26. Demson, *Hans Frei and Karl Barth*, p. 60.

end in itself. Likewise for the apostles, "their discipleship, apostolate, authority, power and mission was not an end in itself. From first to last . . . it was absolutely a matter of their *service,* their ministry as *heralds*" (*CD* IV/ 1, 724; *KD* IV/1, 809). They attached no importance to their own activity. Their movement into the world consisted of pointing beyond themselves. In the same way, the apostolic community "can never in any respect be an end in herself but, following the existence of the apostles, she exists only as she exercises the ministry of a herald" (*CD* IV/1, 724; *KD* IV/1, 809). The nature of this ministry, because it consists of active participation in Jesus Christ's own mission, is both concrete and particular. Its form replicates the fellowship shared by Jesus Christ and his apostles. Precisely as such, contemporary discipleship cannot be content with merely "reproducing the pictures" of earlier disciples; the living Lord is not "confined as it were to the sequence of His previous encounters" (*CD* IV/2, 552; *KD* IV/ 2, 625). The community's correspondence to the witness of the apostles is always new because the necessary particularities of place and time are not merely passive realities that come upon the community, but are encountered in apostolic movement. There is no doubt that such a task for natural human communities involves vulnerability and uncertainty. Yet, as Jesus Christ's own life was not one of *con*-centricity, but of *ec*-centricity, existence, so the community is the community of the living Lord Jesus Christ to the extent that she lives *ec*-centrically (*CD* IV/3.2, 548; *KD* IV/ 3.2, 629). She "exists as she actively reaches beyond herself into the world" (*CD* IV/3.2, 779; *KD* IV/3.2, 892).

Such missionary existence is not a second step, and thus a commission the community might give herself, but a determination and commission given with her being. To put it differently, the community "does not exist *before* her commission and later acquire it. Nor does she exist *apart* from it, so that there can be no question whether or not she might have to execute it" (*CD* IV/3.2, 795; *KD* IV/3.2, 910). Jesus Christ's obedience to the one who sent him consists of his obedience to his mission. Likewise the obedience of the church consists of her obedience to the one who sent her and thus to his mission. Her essential direction is "outwards to mission, to the world, because she is not merely based upon the apostolate but is identical with it" (*CD* II/2, 430-31; *KD* II/2, 477). The Christian community is identical to the apostolate because she is a people called by Jesus Christ in the power of the Spirit for the fulfillment of the specific commission to witness to the reconciliation of the world in him. She "cannot cease to exist in the work and word of the apostolate without self-surrender or self-betrayal" (*CD* II/2, 431; *KD* II/2, 477).

The Apostolic Visibility of the Community

Grounded in Scripture, the apostolic act constitutes the being of the community. If the community fails to live her life of missionary service, which is the nature of her fellowship with God, then she does not live in the Spirit and cannot be Jesus Christ's community. This counterintuitive link between a concentration on ecclesiastical institutions and the community's possible "unreality" raises questions of her proper "visibility." Healy, for example, believes that accounts of the Christian community must begin with "the concrete, the human history that is constitutive of the church, rather than from some abstract theological notion such as an ecclesiological 'event.'"[27] Part of the difficulty rests in the assumed distillation of mission from church that underlies much of the contemporary discussion. The theological relativization of mission as a temporal and thus provisional and thus unreal act leads in a twofold direction: first, "visibility" is defined in nonmissionary terms, being something that foremost resides in ecclesiastical institutions as they embody the true Christian end; second, the all-too-visible nature of the missionary task is itself suspected as peripheral to the nature of the church. In other words, what counts as "the human history that is constitutive of the church" already presumes a great deal of theological determination. Accounts of the community's visibility are to be governed by the purpose that visibility serves. As Webster suggests, "the issue is not whether the church is *visible,* but rather, what *kind* of visible," and apostolicity is the determining criterion.[28]

Since apostolicity is the concrete determination of the church, a distinction forms between the "apparent" and the "actual" church. Such a distinction should not be understood as eschewing the community's necessary

27. Nicholas M. Healy, "The Logic of Karl Barth's Ecclesiology: Analysis, Assessment, and Proposed Modifications," *Modern Theology* 10, no. 3 (1994): 266. Healy has, more recently, distanced himself from such a position. However, it remains of interest because of the number of interpreters who have developed this point.

28. John B. Webster, "The Visible Attests the Invisible," in *The Community of the Word: Toward an Evangelical Ecclesiology,* ed. Mark Husbands and Daniel B. Trier (Downers Grove, IL: InterVarsity, 2005), p. 100.

institutional character; this only feeds the improper church-vs.-mission dichotomy that I have repudiated. "Apparent" refers here to a conception of witness predicated on the ethical realization of certain anthropological givens, and the resulting preoccupation with the church's internal life and the concomitant orienting of Christian practices. "Visibility" rests in the holy distance that the church establishes between herself and her local culture via the ever greater exhibition of her religious distinctive. Against this, orientation to its own end is itself the world's orientation. The world does not need to be "confirmed and strengthened by another variation of its own way, but to be pointed beyond it in unambiguous practice" (*CD* IV/3.2, 779; *KD* IV/3.2, 891). This important reference to practice indicates, first, that Barth expects a positive form of human action, but, second, that this positive form does not render the community the object and end of that practice. To the extent that visibility rests in the church as an end, "it is the phenomenon of the mere semblance of a Church, and it is only this semblance, and not the real Church" (rev., *KD* IV/2, 698; *CD* IV/2, 617).[29]

The limiting of Christian witness to a nonmissionary account of ecclesial existence emerged as a key concern within mission theology during the mid-twentieth century. It struggled with what Krusche called "the Church's loss of actuality," a factor attributed to the church's "insular existence which is concerned only with herself and her own problems."[30] During the 1930s, the missionary call for the "church to be the church" reflected a twofold need. First, the boundaries between the church and Western societies had blended to such an extent that the church's pronouncements had lost their prophetic edge, their capacity to forestall World War I and the range of tragedies typifying the early twentieth century. She had to establish a critical distance from the social authorities and would accomplish this by better attending to those distinctive aspects of her own life. Second, the church had to maintain a closer identification between cross-cultural missions and the life of the congregation. Only in this way might the perceived connection between missionary societies and the

---

29. "Woe to the community if *what she is* is directly identical with what she is as generally visible, or if she accepts her concrete historical form as her being, equating herself with it and trying to exist in it abstractly!" (rev., *KD* IV/1, 734; *CD* IV/1, 657).

30. Werner Krusche, "Parish Structure — A Hindrance to Mission? A Survey and Evaluation of the Ecumenical Discussion on the Structures of the Missionary Congregation," in *Sources for Change: Searching for Flexible Church Structures*, ed. Herbert T. Neve (Geneva: WCC, 1968), p. 52.

colonialist endeavor be severed. Though the phrase retains its contemporary significance through the work of John Howard Yoder and Stanley Hauerwas, mission thinking soon rejected this "ecclesiocentrism" because of the evident suppression of mission within Western ecclesiologies. Or, to quote Newbigin, the problem, as illustrated by the need for volunteer societies, was "that the very forms of congregational life were a major hindrance to the Church's evangelism."[31] The focus on the church's own life turned the church inward, and the greater liaison between mission and this nonmissionary ecclesial form had a detrimental effect on actual missionary activity.

The charge of propaganda issued against missions concerned the way in which particular forms of the gospel had become identified as the whole of the gospel — its normative expression. Missionary activity consisted of the replication of these partial forms. Missions were sent by churches to establish churches. Because the goal of Christian existence was defined in inward terms and because this goal was dependent on the proper operation of ecclesiastical structures, the structures themselves accompanied the message as a necessary component. The naturalism that so hampered the missionary endeavor simply reflected the naturalism that was endemic to the prevailing ecclesiologies. Cross-cultural movement alerted the Western church to the problem: the very Western character of the church was revealed to be such in a non-Western setting. The logic seemed simple: if the church did not engage in evangelistic movement across cultures, in the "search for converts," then the specter of propaganda would not appear.[32] However, the basic problem lay not in this movement, and attributing it to this movement only succeeded in reinvigorating the precipitating cause. The external movement became forsaken for a more intensified internal focus that only further emphasized particular cultural forms and their necessary replication. It is the dichotomy between church and mission that underlies the problem of propaganda. A proper theological solution demands that the Christian community live her missionary existence, breaking loose from an improper naturalism by referring to her apostolic uni-

31. J. E. Lesslie Newbigin, "Which Way for 'Faith and Order'?" in *What Unity Implies: Six Essays After Uppsala*, ed. Reinhard Groscurth (Geneva: WCC, 1969), pp. 116-17.

32. See Robert Jenson's treatment as illustrative of this kind of attitude, all the while hinting that the mission theorists did not understand the activity as itself "an integral event of the kingdom's advent." Jenson, *The Triune Identity: God According to the Gospel* (Philadelphia: Fortress, 1982), p. 29.

versalism, that is, by entering other histories in the knowledge of the reconciliation of the world.

Mission opposes propaganda. As mission proceeds from the very being of God and aims at his kingdom, the church constitutes neither the beginning nor the end of mission. She "has no cause of her own which she must represent, for which she must make propaganda" (rev., *KD* IV/3.2, 950; *CD* IV/3.2, 830). One characteristic sin that continually threatens the church rests in the attempt to "represent herself rather than the sanctification which has taken place in Jesus Christ; of trying to forget that her existence is provisional, and that she can exist only as she points beyond herself" (*CD* IV/2, 622-23; *KD* IV/2, 704). Choosing this improper self-representation — failure to live under the promise that "you shall be my witnesses" — is choosing to live under the illusion of an "immediate relationship to the direct, absolute and material authority of God, Christ and the Holy Spirit" (*CD* I/2, 544-45; *KD* I/2, 606).

This improper immediacy is to conceive of the church as the means for overcoming the gap between God and the world, with consequences for, among other things, how the Spirit is understood in relation to the acting community. Living thus consists of forgetting the "uniqueness of revelation and with it . . . the prophetic-apostolic situation" (*CD* I/2, 545; *KD* I/2, 606). The missionary concern fades, to be replaced by an account of institutional growth. If the Christian should so "retreat into an island of inwardness," it means the "renunciation of one's service of witness and, thus, of Christian existence, the principle of which is this service of witness" (rev., *KD* IV/3.2, 706; *CD* IV/3.2, 616-17).

This renunciation itself takes a particular form, for the community may still claim to witness both in word and deed. The proclamation of the apparent church softens into "a dull impartation which says everything and nothing, proclaiming a supposed but not a real salvation" (*CD* IV/3.2, 813; *KD* IV/3.2, 931). While her life may exhibit all the necessary markers of biblical content and ecclesiastical tradition, when the community should call for decision, her speech "will come to a halt and become an inarticulate mumbling of pious words" (*CD* IV/3.2, 814; *KD* IV/3.2, 932). By striving for greater relevance within surrounding society, this community "plunges her witness more truly and deeply into the sphere of the impartation of general, neutral and blunted truths" (*CD* IV/3.2, 824; *KD* IV/3.2, 943). Visibility of this kind is simply the ghastly specter of an entity no longer serving the purpose it was created to serve, but one that prolongs its existence by relying on the longevity natural to institutions.[33] In so renouncing her life of witness, the community denies her calling and, as such, her life in Christ. There is no neutrality with respect to the cause of God: either one lives in active missionary fellowship with God, or one removes oneself from this fellowship.

Visible givens may serve human falsehood as much as witness to the reality of reconciliation.[34] They are themselves subject to the event character of reconciliation, being adjudged according to the critical standard of the community's missionary existence. No room exists for any binary opposition of a historically complex visible community and a pristine invisible ideal, aloof from any potential contamination. The real being of the community does not consist of her being "an unknown magnitude to countless thousands," as though "her invisibility were essential and her visibility non-essential or 'accidental'" (*CD* IV/3.2, 723; *KD* IV/3.2, 827). Such a position reinserts a second step between the gospel and its public proclamation. Because she is a missionary community, visibility is essential to the community; she is "to be a magnitude which may be known by all" (*CD* IV/3.2, 723; *KD* IV/3.2, 827). The apostolic visibility of the community is the proper visibility of the Spirit.

To propose that the community is "spiritually" visible is not to relegate Christian reality to some distant transcendent sphere; it is to confirm

---

33. Wilhelm Anderson, reflecting on the findings of Willingen 1952, says of the many parishes that live without reference to the missionary activity of the church, and of the "so-called Churchmanship among us which is entirely satisfied with itself as it is," that "a Church without missionary activity can indeed for a period retain its form as a stiff and lifeless corpse, but the process of putrefaction will in time inevitably set in." Andersen, *Towards a Theology of Mission: A Study of the Encounter between the Missionary Enterprise and the Church and Its Theology* (London: SCM, 1955), pp. 54-55.

34. In his discussion of human falsehood, Barth highlights three resisting elements in the human: first, ignoring God by being consumed with the exigencies of daily affairs; second, through the creation of worldviews, and so by positioning oneself at a remote distance in order to view the world; and third, by pretending to abandon the opposition to the gospel. This religious experience is like "a grey mist of puffed up mediocrity, of pathetic tedium and of important unimportance." It is politely taking one's seat in the pew, "cheerfully to don the vestment and mount the pulpit, zealously to make Christian gestures and movements, soberly to produce theology, and in this way, consciously participating in the confession of Jesus Christ, radically to ensure that His prophetic work is halted, that it can do no more injury to itself, let alone to the world." In this way, visible givens can serve human falsehood and run counter to the gospel (*CD* IV/3.1, 258-59; *KD* IV/3.1, 298-90).

its reality within the historical process. It is as she lives in active participation in Jesus Christ's own mission by the power of the Spirit that she is a visible community. (Part of the problem of missionary conversion and the creation of communities is precisely that it is an all-too-visible reality, offensive within secular and often even seminary contexts.) Her spiritual reality is directly proportional to the concrete visibility of her being. Yet, because God remains subject in his self-revelation, and because the community is an apostolic community, "*what she is,* the *character,* the *truth* of her existence in time and space, is not a matter of a general but a very special visibility" (*CD* IV/1, 654; *KD* IV/1, 731). Her visible existence is easily confused with religious propaganda, power politics, or the general functioning of a social club, even to the extent of the community confusing her own visibility in these ways. "*Her* true invisible being, and therefore *her* real distance from and superiority to the world, is that she is elected and called to be a people *alongside* and *with* Jesus Christ and with a share in His self-declaration" (rev., *KD* IV/3.2, 835; *CD* IV/3.2, 729). The community's holy distance from the world rests in the active participation in Jesus Christ's mission to the world.

This missionary existence is the power of the Holy Spirit, liberating the apostolic nature of the community to emerge out of churchly institution, tradition, and habit. Again, the key point is not a negative one; invisibility is wrongly contrasted with visibility. Missionary visibility attests the not-yet generally visible reality of the reconciliation of the whole world. Nor is visibility a real concern, because "where the Holy Spirit is at work the step to visibility is unavoidable" (rev., *KD* IV/1, 735; *CD* IV/1, 658). Since the mystery that is the basis of the community is her active life of fellowship with the missionary God, "her most inward being has an irresistible impulse towards that which is without, her most proper being towards that which is alien" (*CD* IV/3.2, 789; *KD* IV/3.2, 903).[35] This impulse from invis-

---

35. John Webster, explicating this point, says that "if the church is what it is because of the gospel, then its life and activities will betray an 'ecstatic' character. That is to say, the definitive activities of the church are those that most clearly betray the fact that the origin, maintenance and perfection of its life lie beyond itself, in the work and word of God which the gospel proclaims. The church's true being is located outside itself. It exists by virtue of God's decision and calling; it is nourished and sustained by the ever-fresh gift of the Holy Spirit; its goal lies in the definitive self-manifestation of the Lord Jesus at his appearing." John B. Webster, "The Church as Witnessing Community," *Scottish Bulletin of Evangelical Theology* 21, no. 1 (2003): 29.

ibility to visibility is one of particularity to universality, which is characteristic of the Christian community's missionary movement from Easter to the final definite revelation of Jesus Christ as Lord. It is the concrete visibility of the community's eschatological existence as she is impelled by the Holy Spirit.

The Necessary Humanity of the Community

The material heart of the locating of mission within God's self-determination and the corresponding determination of the Christian community is this:

> First and supremely it is God who exists for the world. And since the community of Jesus Christ exists first and supremely for God, she has no option but in her own manner and place to exist for the world. How else could she exist for God? The centre around which she moves eccentrically is not, then, simply the world as such, but the world for which God is. For God is who He is, not *in abstracto* nor without relationship, but as God for the world! (*CD* IV/3.2, 762; *KD* IV/3.2, 872)

God's overcoming of the above and below in his own life from and to all eternity means that the community cannot live in fellowship with him without standing at the side of those in affliction. As God has not associated himself with the world in the manner of "idle co-existence," so the community cannot engage the world in "a sincere but inactive participation" (*CD* IV/3.2, 777; *KD* IV/3.2, 889). Her solidarity with the world means full and active commitment to and engagement with it. This precludes any passive identification, as though service to the world consists in the main of an internally orientated life with all the attendant accounts of growth in faith. Jesus Christ's community is "holy in her openness to the street and even the alley" (*CD* IV/1, 725; *KD* IV/1, 809).[36] Missionary movement toward the world is a form of Christian solidarity with the world and the distinguishing element between the church and the world turned in upon itself.

36. Barth continues about the Christian community that "in her deepest and most proper tendency she is not churchly, but worldly — the Church with open doors and great windows, behind which she does better not to close herself in upon herself again by putting in pious stained-glass windows."

To serve God is to live in service to the world, and "the community cannot exist in the world without calling people out of it, without inviting them to participate in His work" (*CD* III/4, 504; *KD* III/4, 577). As the community exists in this missionary correspondence to God's own life, she has no need to search for "a point of contact, a connection link, because the connection has long since been established. It is, however, the task of a Christian witness to call to mind this connection."[37] With the completion of reconciliation, God has called the whole world to fellowship with himself. The solidarity of the church with those in affliction is expressed in a concern, not with "an as yet actual, but with *an already* virtual or potential Christian, with a *christianus designatus,* with a *christianus in spe*" (rev., *KD* IV/3.2, 927; *CD* IV/3.2, 810). As Jesus Christ does not will to remain alone, so "a Christian cannot be willing to remain alone."[38] The community holds no position of superiority, for she, too, exists only under and by the same call of Jesus Christ.[39] The community must proclaim the gospel, believing in its truth and with the intention of winning converts. She cannot leave "Christians in hope" at peace, nor allow any neutrality in response to her witness. She must be "a most disturbing fellow-human," giving "the impression of unfitting and culpable intolerance" (*CD* IV/3.2, 495-96; *KD* IV/3.2, 568).

The Christian community possesses no control over the number of her members, and, given the decline in membership experienced at the end of Christendom, the numbers and political-cultural influence of the community may continue to fall away. Her proper responsibility is to sow seeds; it is God who brings the increase. Recognizing this prompts a somewhat counterintuitive conclusion. If the church were able to control her numbers, then the possibility exists that she might refine her message for the most congenial match. She would speak first and loudest to those who appear closest morally, culturally, or intellectually to what is considered to

37. Karl Barth, "The Christian as Witness," in *God in Action* (Manhasset, NY: Round Table, 1963), pp. 130-31.

38. Karl Barth, "Fragebeantwortung bei der Konferenz der World Student Christian Federation," in *Gespräche, 1959-1962,* ed. Eberhard Busch (Zürich: Theologischer Verlag, 1995), p. 435.

39. "It is in relationship to [Jesus Christ] that Christians and non-Christians, in all their differences, are what they are: human beings who have their calling only before them on the one hand — and human beings who have it behind and before them, on the other" (rev., *KD* IV/3.2, 571; *CD* IV/3.2, 497).

be a "good Christian." However, because it is God alone who calls, and because his call stands before every human being, an open possibility exists that even those avowed enemies of the gospel among every class, nation, and tribe might respond to that call. "There is none who might not be destined to find in Jesus of Nazareth his Master" (*CD* III/4, 504; *KD* III/4, 577-78).[40] With this universal possibility, the community must live as fishers of men and women. Calling is an objective commission that constitutes the being of the community, witnessing to the fact of the reconciliation of the world as it is now the community's own subjective reality.

Insofar as the community is this "living *redemptive happening* which takes place," she is "savingly necessary" (*CD* IV/2, 621; *KD* IV/2, 703). Any failing in this missionary solidarity with those in the world is a sign of the community's "own most radical disorder and most dangerous aberration" (*CD* IV/3.2, 825; *KD* IV/3.2, 945). It is in the context of his thick description of the missionary solidarity with the world that Barth gives his infamous threefold affirmation: "(1) The world would be lost without Jesus Christ, without His work and Word. (2) The world would not necessarily be lost if there were no church. (3) The church would be lost if she did not have her counterpart in the world" (rev., *KD* IV/3.2, 946; *CD* IV/3.2, 826). Many interpret this statement as a devaluation of the Christian community. But such interpretations proceed out of the dominant disjunction of the church's *being* from her missionary *act* (which I have been repudiating).[41] In other words, Barth's point is not to deny the church but to indicate its necessarily missionary form apart from which she is not the actual community of the living Lord Jesus Christ.

The world would be lost without Jesus Christ because he alone was sent by the Father in the power of the Spirit to complete the reconciliation of the world. It is Jesus Christ, in the exercise of his prophetic office, who "mediates" this knowledge to the world. As the community's missionary calling is not a second thing, so the event of Jesus Christ's prophetic calling is "an event in which the community participates, not in the form of an autonomous endeavor but rather through her serving participation in His action" (rev., *KD* IV/3.2, 946; *CD* IV/3.2, 826). It is be-

---

40. For Jesus Christ, in the exercise of his prophetic office, "neither the militant godlessness of the outer periphery of the community, nor the intricate heathenism of the inner, is an insurmountable barrier" (*CD* IV/3.1, 121; *KD* IV/3.1, 136).

41. As one example of many, see Stanley Hauerwas, *With the Grain of the Universe: The Church's Witness and Natural Theology* (Grand Rapids: Brazos, 2001), p. 193.

cause the world would be lost without Jesus Christ that the community is a missionary community; the second and third points flow as correlates of this one statement.

Negatively expressed, the world would not be lost if there were no church, because it is Jesus, not the church, who saves the world. However, Barth's concern here is expressly with the church and the *purity of her task*. It constitutes a warning that the community cannot neglect her counterpart in the world. Should she do so, the world would become for her "only an incidental and basically accidental or arbitrary or contingent determination of her own existence. She is no longer prepared to stand or fall with it. Her positive actualization also becomes optional" (*CD* IV/3.2, 825; *KD* IV/3.2, 945). Neglecting the world threatens the very being of the community. Her existence in service to the gospel becomes a secondary task that she may or may not undertake. In doing this, the community makes herself greater than her Lord and comes to rely on her own power as the means for salvation. She cannot assume this inhuman stance of patronizing superiority in relation to her counterpart in the world. Any reification of the church and her practices that forms Christian witness after the mode of propaganda constitutes a denuding of the "actual" community. The existence of the community is missionary service to the gospel, not an occasion for propaganda.

Positively expressed, the church would be lost if she did not have her counterpart in the world, because she has the definite and necessary form as a missionary community. The community "depends absolutely and inescapably upon her co-existence with the rest of humanity," because her "existence finds not merely its meaning, but its very basis and possibility singularly and alone in her mission, her service, her witness, her commission and therefore her positive relation to those who are without. She stands or falls with this relation to them" (rev., *KD* IV/3.2, 946; *CD* IV/3.2, 826). This task is her holiness in the world, the one task the world cannot do for itself. The community "lives and has her being in virtue of this special origin and by having and discharging her special task. No other people has either this origin or this task."[42] This is her special responsibility, her calling, the form of her active service in fellowship with God. In serving God, the community serves the world.

---

42. Barth, *The Christian Life*, p. 133.

Christian Fellowship

This account of apostolic solidarity precludes any ecclesiastical docetism that would overlook the spiritual visibility of the Christian community. The church's missionary existence includes definite human activities, but existing in this movement means that "the principle of necessary repetition and renewal, and not a law of stability, is the law of spiritual growth and continuity of our life" (*CD* II/2, 647; *KD* II/2, 721). The ecstatic movement outwards in reconciliation, encountering other histories and particularities, drives the community back into its apostolic calling. Some find such an account unconvincing for it seemingly lacks an adequate account of Christian growth.[43] Rethinking edification according to the criterion of apostolic existence certainly applies a critical edge to certain prevailing definitions, themselves concerned with the nature of Christian witness. Such accounts, based in the *beneficia Christi*, define growth as enlarging the capacity for and possession of Christian being. This evolutionary approach directs attention "abstractly to the reflection of this act of God and Christ in the *human,* to one's Christian experiences and states" (*CD* IV/3.2, 507; *KD* IV/3.2, 583). To the extent that the Christian is "engrossed in herself, rotating about herself and seeking to assert and develop herself, she alienates herself from what makes her a Christian" (*CD* IV/3.2, 652; *KD* IV/ 3.2, 747).

The oneness of the event of reconciliation prohibits viewing the historical reality and inward upbuilding of the Christian community — justification and sanctification — as ends in themselves. There is no *ordo salutis* through which the Christian must progress and in which calling plays a minor role.[44] Apostolicity is itself the determining criterion of Christian edification. It is the proper work of the Spirit to gather and

43. Rowan Williams, for example, while affirming that "Barth's Trinitarian scheme is indeed tightly interwoven with the whole conception of life," laments his "lack of concern with human growth, human diversity, and human freedom of response." Williams, "Barth on the Triune God," in *Karl Barth: Studies of His Theological Method,* ed. S. W. Sykes (Oxford: Clarendon, 1979), pp. 191-92.

44. An example of this order, Barth notes, is "(1) calling to the Church; (2) illumination; (3) conversion; (4) regeneration; (5) justification; (6) mystical union with the triune God; (7) renewal or sanctification; (8) confirmation and preservation in faith and holiness; and (9) eschatological translation into a state of eternal glory" (*CD* IV/3.2, 505; *KD* IV/3.2, 581). With calling merely the first rung on this developmental ladder, one dispenses with it quickly.

upbuild and send the community in service to Jesus Christ. That is, the Spirit draws the community beyond herself, and by definition, this work cannot "merely lead to the blind alley of a new qualification, enhancement, deepening and enrichment of this being of the community as such" (*CD* IV/3.2, 764; *KD* IV/3.2, 874). Any such limitation of Christian growth to this inward sphere immediately wreaks havoc over her proper external movement. As Jesus Christ's own obedience is evident in his obedience to his mission, so a lack of outward orientation reveals the disobedience of the community.

Active movement into the world edifies the active inner discipleship of the Christian community. The more faithfully the community attests Jesus Christ's own activity, the more definitely she grows in the faith, simply because reconciliation and its dynamic is the gift of eternal life. Calling as active participation in Jesus Christ's prophetic office is the living form of Christian growth. It is a temporal and historical process but is, nonetheless, a "*single* and *total* occurrence" in relation to the Christian (*CD* IV/3.2, 505; *KD* IV/3.2, 580). Edification is necessary as an ingredient in the event of calling itself. Every moment of edification occurs "but only in the course of her commission — only in an implicit and explicit outward movement to the world" (*CD* IV/1, 724; *KD* IV/1, 809). This does not render the life of the community null.

> If her inward service is not to become an institution for private satisfaction in concert, or a work of sterile inbreeding, she must accept the priority of her sending into the world, of her task in relation to those without. Yet for the sake of the execution of this task, in order that the *missionary* community may be the *living* and *authentic Christian* community which is able and willing to execute it, her witness must also be directed inward to her own members. (*CD* IV/3.2, 833; *KD* IV/3.2, 954)

The missionary being of the community is not one of abstract extension. The community is unhealthy if she seeks only to grow "horizontally, directed at securing the greatest possible number of members," for this internal orientation stimulates a form of mission that occurs as "propaganda on behalf of her own spatial expansion" (rev., *KD* IV/2, 731; *CD* IV/2, 646). When the community properly witnesses to her Lord and the universal nature of the kingdom, extensive growth will follow as a necessary byproduct, but creating Christians for the sake of creating Christians is not the end of the faith (*CD* IV/3.2, 839; *KD* IV/3.2, 961).[45] The dichotomy of church from mission whereby the life of the community is defined apart from her secondary movement into the world no longer holds. Missionary existence requires an *intensive* growth, for it is a life of fellowship that corresponds to the nature of God's own living history. Fellowship is an action in service of a common unity. It is a work in the power of the Holy Spirit, and it "takes place as this divine and human work is *in operation:* in movement from its origins, in which it is already complete, toward its goal, in which its completion will become manifest" (rev., *KD* IV/2, 725; *CD* IV/2, 641).

This intensive growth, as such, cannot be confused with an internal focus. The dynamic movement of the church into the world characterizes

---

45. Recognizing this commission as the form of Christian fellowship with God during this interim period helps overcome a coordinated complaint from von Balthasar and Newbigin. Von Balthasar suggests that "dialectical theology is expressly designed as a theology of a journeying People of God who are merely on their way to God but not there: a *theologia viatorum.*" Hans Urs von Balthasar, *The Theology of Karl Barth: Exposition and Interpretation* (San Francisco: Ignatius, 1992), p. 79. Barth certainly holds that the Christian is called "in order that he himself may be one who calls within the world" (*CD* II/2, 418; *KD* II/2, 463). "The goal of missions is not to convert the heathen in the sense of bringing them to a personal enjoyment of their salvation." Personal salvation consists of the fact that "supremely and decisively one becomes a witness in the world" (*CD* IV/3.2, 876; *KD* IV/3.2, 1004). This again reflects Barth's concern that Christian experience of the *beneficia Christi* does not constitute the Christian end, but serves the true end of active fellowship. However, insofar as Barth does develop his thinking according to this missionary end, Newbigin's concern is of special interest. In the context of his reaction against Hoekendijk's reduction of the church/mission dichotomy to mission alone, Newbigin says that "precisely because the Church is here and now a real foretaste of heaven, she can be the witness and instrument of the kingdom of heaven. It is precisely because she is not merely instrumental that she can be instrumental. This is not a merely theoretical matter, but one of real practical importance. There is a kind of missionary zeal which is forever seeking to win more proselytes but which does not spring from and lead back into a quality of life which seems intrinsically worth having in itself. If we answer the question, 'Why should I become a Christian?' simply by saying 'In order to make Christians,' we are involved in an infinite regress. The question, 'To what end?' cannot be simply postponed to the *eschaton.*" J. E. Lesslie Newbigin, *The Household of God: Lectures on the Nature of the Church* (London: SCM, 1953), pp. 147-48. This problem results from treating the missionary existence of the Christian community as secondary, something alongside a more proper form of existence that is restricted to the *eschaton,* for it forms as a provisional existence awaiting the revelation of the full fellowship with God. To reinforce Barth's point, the Christian's life in hope is eschatological because it is now real and so true, and the community is precisely a community on the way due to the nature of God's own perfection.

her internal nature: she is a gathering and self-gathering community. "We have a plurality of people, gathered by the proclamation of the Gospel for the *purpose* of proclaiming it in the world. These people need to be brought together, to be constituted, established and maintained as a *common being* — one people capable of unanimous action" (*CD* IV/2, 635; *KD* IV/2, 718). The perfection of reconciliation in its missionary push to universality means that upbuilding takes the form of integrating people into the community. Renewal occurs "as the listeners themselves become 'apostolic' and, as new disciples, begin to proclaim the good news."[46] Christian fellowship is eschatological in nature. The active movement from Easter to the final *parousia* is material to defining the nature of that fellowship and to the practices basic to its cultivation.

This calling to fellowship cannot result in any cleavage of the community's activities, as though one element of her life better reflected this fellowship when compared to another. Worship is paramount in the life of this integrating community as the place where it "becomes a concrete *event* at a specific time and place" (*CD* IV/2, 639; *KD* IV/2, 719). Because God is a missionary God, worship as a term for the community's life is wrongly contrasted to mission and the external orientation of the community.[47] The Christian community

> . . . can never exist intermittently, nor does she ever exist only partially, as the sent community, but always and in all her functions she is either leaping out or on the point of leaping out to those to whom she is sent. In every respect, even in what seems to be purely inner activity like prayer and the liturgy and the cure of souls and biblical exegesis and theology, her activity is always *ad extra*. She is always directed *extra muros*. (*CD* IV/3.2, 780; *KD* IV/3.2, 892)

Framing worship according to this immediate external orientation appears at such odds with current practice that the practicalities of this position may be questioned. It must be said, however, that what seemingly consti-

46. Karl Barth, "An Exegetical Study of Matthew 28: 16-20," in *The Theology of Christian Mission*, ed. Gerald H. Anderson (Nashville: Abingdon, 1961), p. 63.

47. Holmes suggests: "If God is properly described as 'missionary' . . . he can only be worshipped by a missionary church." Stephen R. Holmes, "Trinitarian Missiology: Towards a Theology of God as Missionary," *International Journal of Systematic Theology* 8, no. 1 (2006): 89.

tutes worship and the practices basic to Christian edification are circumscribed by conceiving them without reference to the missionary act.[48] Yoder makes much the same point in his listing of five apostolic practices, all of which involve both divine and human agency, but "do not fall within what ordinarily is called 'worship,' even less 'liturgy.'"[49] To put it another way, one reason for the difficulties in rethinking missionary practices is due to the intractability of settled liturgical form. Basic to reformulating missionary practice is developing an identification between the outgoing nature of the gospel and the life of the community. Yet authoritative definitions of worship continue to exclude missionary practice as basic to the life of the community. In this vicious circle, the legitimate complaints laid against propagandistic mission method reverberate through worship methods. Worship in Spirit and in truth, by contrast, places the community under Scripture and so in apostolic movement, orienting her to the presence of Jesus Christ and calling her to obedience. Invocation becomes an obligation laid on all Christians, for the community exists only by the action of God. This prayerful fellowship of solidarity with the world constitutes maturation in the Christian life. Only as Christians engage in the calling of active participation in the missionary community, do they mature in discipleship. An "essentially missionary" church is not an "immature, but mature, church" (rev., *KD* IV/4, xii; *CD* IV/4, xi).

Concrete Freedom

The community called in God's reconciliation of the world exists in the movement of reconciliation to those who would live as enemies of God. Every aspect of Christian existence is to be defined in the light of this movement, for it is the nature of God's own history. God liberates the human by the Spirit to participate in Jesus Christ's mission. This forces the community in a movement of "self-transcendence" beyond her own enclosed history and so beyond the comfort of her apparent forms. Guided

48. See, for example, David Demson's criticisms of Reinhard Hütter and the absence of mission as a practice of the church. David E. Demson, "'Church Practices': Sacraments of Invocations? Hütter's Proposal in Light of Barth's," *Toronto Journal of Theology* 18, no. 1 (2002): 79-99.

49. John Howard Yoder, "Sacrament as Social Process: Christ the Transformer of Culture," in *The Royal Priesthood: Essays Ecclesiological and Ecumenical,* by John Howard Yoder, ed. Michael Cartwright (Grand Rapids: Eerdmans, 1994), p. 364.

by her freedom, the community must develop forms necessary to her humanity. The only limiting criterion is that of her witness. Thus, while institutions are a necessary part of church life, what she "has to do must not be determined by her institutions; her institutions must be determined by what she has to do" (*CD* III/4, 489; *KD* III/4, 560). Particular institutional forms develop in accordance with a community's commission.

The freedom of God is a positive event. The community is liberated from every element within history that threatens to impede her witness, but this freedom *from* consists of the being liberated *to* live her proper calling.[50] Christian freedom is purposeful. It is not liberation to religious neutrality, nor to an open possibility of acting should one feel so inclined. God's freedom does not hover in the background like an attentive butler awaiting the faintest wave of the hand. This freedom is a liberation that is only possessed as it is "*lived out* and *exercised* in that act of responsibility before God" (*CD* III/2, 196; *KD* III/2, 233). That responsibility consists of active service to the *causa Dei*. As the community possesses no given capacity to reveal, so she is free with respect to those things apparently constitutive of her own being. The community "builds herself up for the sake of her sending and in relation to it. In her knowledge of her sending, she will do this seriously and really, precisely in her freedom from herself granted her in that knowledge" (rev., *KD* IV/1, 809; *CD* IV/1, 725). The community is liberated from every natural given to organize her own form with respect to her witness.

The community is free, for example, in terms of her language. In that she serves the world and not her own message, the community is "*dependent* on the world" (*CD* IV/3.2, 735; *KD* IV/3.2, 841). The community must speak into the world in such a way that the world can see that the gospel applies also to it. She cannot speak past or over it, nor approach it with a manipulative intent, only to formulate strategies for how best to declare and explain the gospel. Nor must the community approach the world in only a partial engagement, in a way that the message ultimately remains the church's to control. In other words, one must "pray with them in German and not in translated Latin."[51] This includes an aggressive repudia-

---

50. This is not an abstract concern. See Newbigin, "Recent Thinking on Christian Beliefs: VIII. Mission and Missions," *The Expository Times* 88, no. 9 (1977): 261.

51. Karl Barth, "The Proclamation of God's Free Grace," in *God Here and Now* (New York: Routledge, 2003), p. 44.

tion of any sacred language that makes the church a mediatorial step —
not because participation in the community is voluntary and so unnecessary, but because the necessity of a sacred language shifts the focus from
the proper object of Christian witness to the community herself. If the
community acts in this way, she remains at an aloof distance from the
world, denying her basic solidarity with it.

The community is also free with regard to her communal structures.
Since apostolicity is the decisive criterion of the church's being, she has the
"*freedom* to adopt her own form, i.e., the form corresponding to her calling and commission, in the sphere of general human possibilities" (*CD* IV/
3.2, 741; *KD* IV/3.2, 848). The only standard is that "her invisible essence
must always be made visible in the fact that she is a *confessing* and *missionary* Church which leaves those around in no doubt as to whom or what she
has to represent among them" (*CD* IV/3.2, 742; *KD* IV/3.2, 849). No sociological form is of itself either more sacred or profane. One can make such
an affirmation because the missionary nature of the church bespeaks a
community of both Jew and Gentile, a community for which the dividing
wall of partition has been removed (Eph. 2:14). It belongs to the community's

> . . . wonderful freedom to recruit across the frontiers of nations, states
> and other natural or historical unions and societies, not removing the
> distinctions or boundaries but transcending them, not identifying her-
> self with any but being one and the same *ecclesia una catholica* in all, ex-
> isting within them as a universal people, indeed as *the* universal people.
> (*CD* IV/3.2, 741; *KD* IV/3.2, 848)

No culture is normative for the expression of the gospel. As an expressly
missionary freedom, it is the very opposite of propaganda. This both validates and relativizes particular cultural forms: validates because every culture can communicate the word; relativizes because these forms are directed to serve this message and must recognize that every culture is
capable of hearing the word.[52] The proclamation of the word, in other
words, is wrongly contrasted with the safeguarding of local cultures. The
very basis of proclamation resides in the claim that there is no distinction
between Jew and Greek. Following the logic of Romans 10:12-15, the same

---

52. For a developed treatment of this position, see Lamin O. Sanneh, *Translating the
Message: The Missionary Impact on Culture* (Maryknoll, NY: Orbis, 1989).

Lord of all is generous to all who call on him, but how can each call on God if they have not heard? How can they hear if no one proclaims? How can one proclaim if one is not sent? The fact that the gospel is for all, that it is a free cross-cultural community, mandates its proclamation.

With this radical account of the community's freedom, ecclesial continuity no longer exists in mere institutional longevity or in the transmission of even profound confessions, liturgy, dress, hierarchies, and so forth. This is not to suggest that this position lacks an account of such continuity. Indeed, it reinforces the locating of continuity within apostolicity. Andrew Walls illustrates the point well, and Barth provides the entrance point in his affirmation that "in and with the 'handing over' of Jesus which occurred on Good Friday morning, the founding of the church as a church of the Jews *and of the Gentiles,* and so as a *missionary* church, took place" (rev., *KD* IV/2, 291; *CD* IV/2, 263). To summarize the logic of Walls's argument: with the decision of the Jerusalem Council in Acts 15, cultural diversity became understood as a cornerstone affirmation of the gospel. The church is a missionary church, not a cultural church. These Gentile believers were already part of Israel by virtue of their belief in Jesus Christ; they did not require the accompanying markers of the law, nor any other cultic or purity signifiers. Conversion, not proselytism, became the *modus operandi* of Christian expansion, with the effect that Christianity, throughout its history, has not maintained a single cultural or geographical center.[53] It expands in "serial" fashion, growing and then withering in its heartland. Every "threatened eclipse of Christianity was averted by its cross-cultural diffusion. Crossing cultural boundaries has been the life blood of historic Christianity."[54]

Such is the basis of the church's continuity. The above linguistic and

---

53. Lesslie Newbigin provides a biting example of this phenomenon. Upon his retirement from the Church of South India, Newbigin and his wife, Helen, took the opportunity to drive from India to England. Each Sunday they stopped to worship at a local church. "Cappadocia, once the nursery of Christian theology, was the only place in our whole trip where we had to have our Sunday worship by ourselves, for there was no other Christian to be found." They "explored the ancient cave churches with their vivid wall paintings and tried to come to terms with the fact that a great and living church can be destroyed." J. E. Lesslie Newbigin, *Unfinished Agenda: An Autobiography* (Geneva: WCC, 1985), p. 241.

54. Andrew F. Walls, "Christianity in the Non-Western World: A Study in the Serial Nature of Christian Expansion," in *The Cross-Cultural Process in Christian History: Studies in the Transmission and Appropriation of Faith* (Maryknoll, NY: Orbis, 2002), p. 32.

cultural freedoms belong to the very nature of the gospel: the gospel *must* be translated and proclaimed across the range of natural boundaries. "Christian faith must go on being translated, must continuously enter into vernacular culture and interact with it, or it withers and fades."[55] This indicates the meekness of the community and reinforces the basic position that she exists in the fulfillment of her commission. The proper object of her faith is not in her apparent visibility, which may reduce the church to a particular cultural form, but Jesus Christ, whom she serves, for only in his flesh are the two groups made one. She serves him by following him into the world under the compulsion of the Spirit, and, in this movement, becomes and is visible. This is the continuity that belongs to the community as she exists in service to the gospel.

Living in Service to God, She Is Sent in Service to the World

In correspondence to the God who lives in his active determination for the human, the community lives in her corresponding determination for God and thus for the world. Her sending is not a general activity, a matter of some nonspecific encounter with the world. It has a definite form, consisting of that singular activity that "corresponds to her commission, of that for which she is empowered by the One who gives it" (*CD* IV/3.2, 779; *KD* IV/3.2, 892). Mission, which is "the sending or sending out to the nations to attest the Gospel," is the "very root of the existence and therefore of the whole service of the community" (*CD* IV/3.2, 872; *KD* IV/3.2, 981). Concrete, active, intentional missionary existence is no second step alongside fellowship with God. It is not a task the community may or may not choose to perform. If the community abandons her task, she ceases to be the Christian community, for she is then guilty of withdrawing from the history of God's own fellowship. Mission occurs when God encounters humanity, calling, upbuilding, and sending his community in the humanity proper to her, compelling and enabling her by the Spirit to transcend her self-occupation and to participate in Jesus Christ's prophetic work. This is calling to eternal life. Announcing the kingdom of God is the community's great and simple commission, her *"opus proprium"* (rev., *KD* III/4, 579; *CD* III/4, 506). The gospel is good news, and it cannot be understood except as

55. Walls, "Christianity in the Non-Western World," p. 29.

the good news for all humanity. It is a word that goes forth, and the community lives as she is swept up in this torrent. She is to joyously proclaim the reconciliation of the world without any restraint, urging all to believe in Jesus Christ and repent, for the kingdom of God is near and already with us. "The community is as such a missionary community, or she is not the Christian community" (rev., *KD* III/4, 578; *CD* III/4, 504-5). She is missionary by her very nature because the God she serves is missionary.

CHAPTER EIGHT

Missio Dei *Revisited*

In this respect we may think of the diastole cycle of the heart which, in order to pump blood through the whole organism, certainly *returns* in the systole — however, to return there, it must first *go out* again in the renewed diastole. In this relationship of outward and inward action, the service of the community will be and remain the true service of God, and so the true service of *humanity.* Little needs to be said about how seldom this relationship between her outer and her inner service has been correctly perceived, understood, and achieved by Christianity in our hemisphere up even to the present day. It is to be hoped that the existence and example of the so-called "young" churches in Asia and Africa can lead her into a new awareness of this, provided that the latter do not too quickly become "old" with their service reduced to a decisive inward, with only an occasional outward, orientation!

Karl Barth, *Church Dogmatics*[1]

The Problem of *Missio Dei*

We can now propose a constructive redefinition of *missio Dei*. The exercise in historical clarification, which constituted the first part of this work,

1. Barth, *KD* IV/3.2, 954 (my translation); *CD* IV/3.2, 833.

served the wider dogmatic purpose of positing the concept's deficient Trinitarian basis. In popular perception, *missio Dei* places mission within the being of the triune God. While true, it only used the doctrine to distance the act from the politically compromised forms that Western missions took during the late nineteenth century. "God's mission" transcended every particular instance, and, with this critical intent, reference to the Trinity failed to detail any alternative missionary forms. This seeming inability to develop any concrete missionary practices was attributed to dialectical theology and its supposed binary opposition of the divine and the human: God accomplishes everything, the human nothing. However, that attribution had a pernicious effect on the development of *missio Dei* theology, for it disguised the concept's actual grounding within the doctrine of creation. "Sending" provided a Trinitarian façade for a universal principle guiding creation, and God's mission became a pattern of breaking down and building up with the church a mere postscript alongside this historical progress. A genealogical schema developed whereby this later account, linked to the political zeitgeist of the 1960s, became contrasted with an original and orthodox Trinitarian position. No such pristine account exists. While the resulting forms may look different, every approach to *missio Dei* draws on an identically flawed Trinitarianism, that is, the missionary act is predicated on a cleavage of God's being from his act.

Missio Dei Revisited

The Living God

The problems endemic to *missio Dei* must not submerge the theological legitimacy of grounding missions in the being of the triune God. If missions occur only because of the resources attendant to a particular civilization, or to a perceived need prompted by diminishing membership numbers or the Christian presence within a wider society, then mission is a contingent enterprise. As a contingency, it can only be a derivative function of a pre-existing institution, a defensive response to a threatening circumstance and so tasked with maintaining that prior institution. If the missionary act does not belong to the matter itself, that is, to the triune God in reconciling the world to himself, then it is a naturalism to be expunged from the life of the church.

Traditional accounts of *missio Dei* abstracted God's "essence" from his particular act via the category of "sending." God's act in Jesus Christ by the Holy Spirit became a particular instance within his universal sending economy. "Sending" became more determinative for God's own life than for his movement into the world, functioning as an external criterion of truth that connects God's life and his creation. However, these problems are not an inevitable consequence of *missio Dei*'s key methodological move. Instead, the fact that they highlight the dichotomy between church and mission, and the concomitant difficulty with forming a connection between the church and the world, corresponds to a dichotomy within God himself. God moves into his economy as a second step alongside — and thus in distinction to — his already complete being. The problem of how human beings can witness to God is a problem of God, and it is answered because the witness of God is first God himself in his eternal life of fellowship from and to all eternity.

God is a missionary God because he has determined himself to be for and with the human. The plenitude of the Father begetting the Son in the unity of the Spirit means that an "above" and "below" in an outward-turning history belongs to the one God's perfect life. The Father's begetting the Son is a deliberate act, not a second step alongside who God is in and for himself, but the determination of his own life. This act belongs to God's life from and to all eternity, for it is the nature of his perfect splendor that he is this *living* God. It is not possible to go behind this act. Fellowship is the nature of God's life. But neither can this "livingness" be considered in abstraction, as though it were a mere quality of God's existence. In the Spirit, the deliberate perfection of God's fellowship exists as a declarative history, and it cannot be understood apart from its particular movement into the economy. We cannot go behind God's apostolic mission in Jesus Christ by the power of the Holy Spirit to find the pristine noneconomic God. It is the nature of his glorious majesty that his being already anticipates his movement into the economy before the creation of the world. God in himself bridges the gap between the above and the below and gives himself to the human as the guarantor that it is so bridged.

The resurrection reveals the Son of man to be the Son of God from all eternity; it reveals his declarative perfection from all eternity. The knowledge of God is a differentiated fellowship of action in which the antithesis between God and humanity is not resolved into a bland third thing. It is a living encounter in the history of the one Son, a uniting in which there is neither confusion nor separation, but genuine meeting. Given that this fellowship belongs to God's own life from eternity, neither the divine nor the human can be considered in isolation. While this fellowship of the divine and human in Jesus Christ is exhaustive, it has a definite character. Jesus Christ is the true witness. That is, the unity of this fellowship is expressive, and it cannot be understood apart from this outward encompassing movement. Reconciliation's perfection corresponds to the nature of God's own perfection. Even in its completion, it is impossible for God to retire behind his act into an isolated and static being. He lives his own perfect life, that is, "in Himself God is rest, but this fact does not exclude but includes the fact that His being is *decision*" (*CD* II/2, 175; *KD* II/2, 192). Likewise, the declaration of his eternal being in the resurrection finds a corresponding expression in the Risen One's concrete commission to go into all the world. Such a command is not incidental to God's own self-declaration, but is the very nature of the kingdom. The reality of the *parousia* is what gives it its missionary character.

The perfection of God's being does not supply a merely formal framework for thinking about mission; his completion of reconciliation does not establish a general pattern that is then taken up by a range of mediating agencies. God's "livingness" does not direct the human to one's own being apart from the action of God in Christ by the Spirit. In that God has given his very self to humanity in overcoming darkness, sin, and death, human beings cannot apprehend him in any other way than as the living God. Reconciliation is the reality of a living relationship in which the divine and the human each act in a manner proper to their natures. Because his acting for the human is not a second step beside his own life, God does not cease to act in relationship to the human in the twofold form of Jesus Christ's objective completion and the Spirit's subjective accomplishment of reconciliation.

Jesus Christ lives and is active in the exercise of his prophetic office, and this includes within itself the subjective and objective accomplishment of his community. Jesus Christ's life is a "*self-multiplying* history" that "evokes its own reflection in the world" (*CD* IV/3.2, 212; *KD* IV/3.2, 242). It opens up the histories of many other peoples in many other ages from their circular movement and directs them toward the *parousia,* and thus toward the active service of Jesus Christ's own history. This is not merely being together with Jesus Christ, but an active living history, a fellowship within which they become subsequent subjects. Jesus Christ's identity rests in his obedience to his mission. His calling, upbuilding, and sending of his apostles is not an incidental event within the occurrence of reconciliation. It is an ingredient within his ministry of the word. Human beings participate in Jesus Christ's own humanity by conforming to his mission. Apostolicity is the concrete criterion of the church's visible service to God and humanity.

The act of the Spirit in subjectively realizing reconciliation in the human takes the form of impelling the community into the world, following after her Lord. Discipleship to Jesus Christ is both appropriation to him and "the corresponding expropriation, life of and by the Holy Spirit" (*CD* IV/3.2, 549; *KD* IV/3.2, 630). No added capacity accrues to the human in the event of reconciliation: one is simply reconciled as a human. The relationship of the divine to the human in this event is mutual and asymmetrical. Both parties act in accordance with their respective natures: God gives and the human receives. This proper human passivity in relation to God — a being determined — takes an active form. In the knowledge of God there is real objective change: God calls human beings to become his witnesses. It is life under, with, and by the promise of the Spirit, in which the Christian community is conformed and conforms to the realism of Easter. Only as she follows this leading is she the Christian community. In that God's life is a glorious event, the objective human act that corresponds to God's own livingness is the community's missionary movement into the whole world. The mission of God, in other words, includes the response of the community as an immediate consequence of the perfection of his act. The Christian community is necessarily a missionary community because this expressive existence in intentional movement for the world is the nature of the very divine and human fellowship that belongs to God's own being from and to all eternity. The Christian community is a missionary community, for, if she is not, then she is not the community of God's reconciliation.

The Orientation to the Kingdom of God

The community lives in the press toward the total, definite, and universal visibility of the return of Jesus Christ. The resurrection is the visibility of the new creation, and the Christian community is called to live within this future reality. She exists here and now as human beings determined by the promise of this Spirit, and takes the concrete form of liberation for missionary service. Due to the interim nature of this period, the service proper to eternal life has a provisional form. The missionary act, however, because it is service to God, cannot simply be relegated to a penultimate status alongside some other form of fellowship. Calling here and now is not a provisional stage through which Christian life progresses to fuller states, as though sanctification were properly distinguished from missionary service. Though the community waits in hope for the fullness of reconciliation, the nature of reconciliation is fulfilled in its reality. As God is a missionary God, this life of fellowship cannot cease or alter with the *eschaton*. The active life of service in which God as ruler encounters the human is the nature of eternal life. Life in hope means dedication to the service of God, which is the Christian's promised future. Failure to live this way demonstrates the unreality of the hope, and thus it bears false witness to the reality of Jesus Christ's lordship over the world. Missionary action is the reality of hope.

Active participation in the missionary existence of the Christian community is the concrete form human fellowship with God takes here and now. The community neither completes nor replicates Jesus Christ's own acting. She presupposes it, living under and by its reality, subject to the ordering of the differentiated fellowship of action, which is her unity with Jesus Christ in the Spirit. This permits a real and direct continuity between the *missio Dei* and the mission of the church. Participating in Jesus Christ's history by the power of the Spirit means that the community is called by him to cooperate in his prophetic work, and, indeed, she achieves results with him even if not herself effecting them. This is the promise of her existence: a real identity given by God and ensured by the Spirit between Jesus Christ and his community. From this position, Barth declares that "Jesus Christ is the community" (*CD* IV/2, 655; *KD* IV/2, 741). Given that Jesus Christ is "Himself the kingdom of God," so the "kingdom of God is the community" (*CD* IV/2, 656; *KD* IV/2, 742). The *missio Dei* is the *missio ecclesiae*. Due to the asymmetrical nature of the divine and human fellowship, these statements cannot be reversed: "The community is not Jesus Christ" (*CD* IV/2, 655; *KD* IV/2, 741). The *missio ecclesiae* is not the *missio Dei*. Mission cannot be something the community possesses, for it is not the community in isolation. It is this living fellowship in which the divine retains the initiative and the community lives in response. This ordered identity means that the community must be active by the Spirit in following her Lord into the world.

Nor should this continuity between the *missio Dei* and the *missio ecclesiae* be understood as prioritizing the action of the church in its relationship with the world. God's mission is borne by neither the church nor the world, but by his own living action with respect to his creation. The Christian community is the result of and exists within God's call, which means that she exists in service to this mission. The community's solidarity with the world rests in this de jure calling of all creation to God; the distinction from the world is the de facto living with, in, and by the promise the Spirit, living according to hope of the kingdom. This distinction is not a given that belongs to the community's life; but the gift of her life is a commission to participate in God's mission to the world, and she lives as she is conformed and conforms to his mission. At every stage, the concrete form of the Christian community is that of the missionary community intentionally moving into the world proclaiming the kingdom of God. No ontological change is required. The opposite is true. Accounts of mediation for which witness resides in some ontological difference from the world are inimical to the missionary act in a twofold way. First, if an ontological difference from the world is the necessary predicate of the community's witness, how might the world know that the message applied also to it? Missionary fellowship is the form human reconciliation with the divine takes here and now, and it is necessary that this occurs in its full humanity, for both those already living under the promise and those under God's de jure call, showing them that this fellowship is for human beings and thus also for them. Second, as the act comes to depend on the Christian's and the community's own capacity, so the attention falls on the being of the Christian and away from the world. The world becomes of only incidental importance, and the actual missionary movement into the world is only an optional and contingent determination of the community's existence. This neglect of the world to which she is sent in service indicates the community's own most severe aberration.

The Missionary Community

God's act in reconciling the world to himself is not a second step alongside his being in and for himself. The superfluity of his act in bringing humanity, as humanity, into fellowship with himself reveals the declarative perfection of his being from and to all eternity. As there is no breach in the being and act of God, so there can be no breach in the being and act of his community. The Christian community is a missionary community, or she is not the Christian community. This language of mission is not idle. Given the temptation for the community to curve in upon herself, mission directs the form of witness. "Witness" does not reduce to the internal life of the church; the community is not an end in herself. The test is whether the community believes in Easter or a synthesis in which the church claims for herself a direct and immediate and thus final connection with God. As the community under Scripture, it is an apostolic community that reads the text in obedience to the movement of the apostles and thus in the presence of Jesus Christ and by the power of the Spirit. The community's mediative task is one of intentional movement into the world, forsaking all those things that may appear to be her safeguard. God exists for the world, and if the community is to exist for God, then she has to exist for the world. "As the community *called out from* the world, she is emphatically *called out to* it. And the genuineness precisely of that 'being called out from' stands or falls with the fact that there is no interruption between it and the 'being called out to' which infallibly follows, that is, that her 'being set off from the world' and her 'being turned toward the world' take place in one single movement" (rev., *KD* IV/3.2, 874; *CD* IV/3.2, 764 [1 Cor. 5:9-10]). This solidarity with the world is the nature of her holiness, for no other people has been given this task. She may not privatize this task by siphoning it off to independent contractors. She does not exist before or apart from this commission. It is given with her being.

This does not establish missionary activity as an independent supposition, but it does give mission a definite form. Because the subjective aspect of reconciliation is a function of reconciliation's objective reality, and because this subjective reality takes the form of active participation in the missionary community, the visibility of the new creation in history is precisely that of the reconciled community as she moves into the world under the impulsion of the Spirit. She is the community of Jesus Christ's reconciliation, and her commission necessarily takes this community form. His community lives as a reconciled and reconciling community; indeed, the community is a fellowship. However, this receives precise definition from the nature of reconciliation, which takes place as the active knowledge of Jesus Christ is established in the world.

Christian fellowship is the fellowship of a body broken. It is not a settled culture but is one in which the dividing wall of partition has been destroyed (Eph. 2:14). In creating the one new humanity in his own body through the cross, Jesus Christ is our peace. This community of Jew and Gentile, of the new creation, is the missionary community. Jesus Christ's gift of peace is his breathing of his Spirit upon his community and her sending out into the world (John 20:19-23). The only standard is that she is visible as a missionary community, one that leaves no doubt as to the one she serves. As the community of God's reconciliation, the Christian community is a declarative fellowship: she is such only as she moves toward those who would be God's enemies in the knowledge, love, and power of reconciliation's reality. This movement applies to the community life of worship, for as a missionary, God can only be worshiped in a missionary fashion. These institutions are responsible for orienting the community to this form of declarative fellowship.

While it has this definite task, however, *missio Dei* cannot delineate a set of programmatic forms. Its very nature as community of Jew and Gentile precludes such an approach. Such an affirmation is wrongly understood if it is treated as abstracting mission, that is, rendering it nonhistorical and impractical. The missionary act is a living history, not a program. The charge of propaganda may result from the confusion of the world with regard to the church's motivation, or it may be an instance of the world's active resistance to the gospel, but it may equally be true. As the community moves across natural boundaries, the naturalism that limits her missionary witness becomes apparent. Cross-cultural movement unveils how a particular community domesticates the gospel, how a community considers her necessary particular expression to be normative for the whole. Missionary methods often fall prey to this trap, because it is the constant temptation for the community to settle in this way rather than be the body broken open with the press toward the final *parousia* and the universal revelation of the kingdom of God. The response to this temptation cannot rest in a mere self-satisfactory defense of that community's particular naturalisms. While it is properly and necessarily expressed in culturally and historically particular forms, it cannot be limited to these forms. Since creation possesses no inherent capacity to facilitate or retard the communication of the gospel, the community is totally free with regard to the particular forms the community's witness takes in the world, not with regard to her definite service of witness. In other words, within the limits established by the divine and human fellowship, the community is free as she exercises her freedom; that is, missionary forms develop through the process of intentional engaged movement into the world.

The community, grounded in Easter and impelled by the impartation of the Spirit to the universal declaration of the kingdom, must offer an answer to the question "Who is Jesus Christ?" This, as Newbigin suggests, is only answered in the end as the whole of creation confesses his name.[2] Until then, every confession is partial and provisional. Mission drives toward the fullness of this confession, for it necessarily includes learning from the histories encompassed by Jesus Christ's own history. The community learns what new forms of obedience the Spirit requires only as she presses to a fuller understanding of the kingdom. As Jesus Christ learned obedience through the things that he suffered (Heb. 5:8), so his community learns obedience through her prophetic calling into the world for which God is. In dogmatic parlance, the church exists only as *ecclesia semper reformanda*. The evangelistic act "means the unavoidable, necessary act of the continued reformation and renovation of the Church herself, and of Christians themselves, because there is never a *complete* Christian, a *complete* Church, a *complete* Christianity."[3] To claim such static "completion" is to live again under the illusion of an immediate connection with God, forgetting the nature of apostolic reality. The superfluity of reconciliation is true also of the life of the Christian community. Edification must be understood in terms of this overcoming of the domestication of the gospel by way of integration, by way of calling those outside the community to active participation in his mission to the world, by way of reconciliation. This is part of the living history of the divine and human fellowship as the missionary community moves from the origins in which she is already complete to the visibility in which her completion will be manifest.

Joy

Definite actions commend themselves at this point: in that a revised *missio Dei* concerns, first, the doctrine of the Trinity, and second, the nature of

2. J. E. Lesslie Newbigin, "Christ and the Cultures," *Scottish Journal of Theology* 31, no. 1 (1978): 10.

3. Karl Barth, "Fragebeantwortung bei der Konferenz der World Student Christian Federation," in *Gespräche, 1959-1962*, ed. Eberhard Busch (Zürich: Theologischer Verlag, 1995), p. 434.

the community that lives in fellowship with this God — not arising as a second question alongside who God is in and for himself, but within that question — mission is necessarily, and must become, a central concern of dogmatic theology. Approaching theological treatises with an interest in the missionary purpose of the church reveals an egregious blind spot. With few exceptions, mission is absent from the all-encompassing theological "system." Mission, it would seem, is unessential when articulating the fundamentals of the Christian faith. The problem here is not simply one of failing to treat one particular ecclesiastical practice. It indicates an omission that is deleterious to the whole dogmatic task: many of the contemporary challenges with theology stem from the absence of mission as a theological category. How it is possible to read the New Testament without reference to the missionary outpouring of the resurrection and Pentecost is a curio difficult to reconcile with even a basic reading of Scripture.[4] To conceive of Christian witness primarily in terms internal to the life of the community has material consequences for, as representative examples, pneumatology, baptism and the Lord's Supper, liturgy, homiletics, and ethics — and thus for the nature of Christian worship. In that it expresses a fundamental dichotomy of mission from church, reference to natural theology becomes a necessary correlate for the church's connection to the world. In short, the absence of mission has deleterious consequences for the doctrine of God.

There are, however, equally significant and immediate practical consequences. If the community is Christian only insofar as she is missionary, if the missionary act is the concrete form of divine and human fellowship here and now, then the lack of reference to mission at every level of the teaching ministry of the church is a frightful abrogation of theological responsibility. If it is possible for a ministry candidate to progress through academic training — as much within a seminary as a secular university — without any dogmatic attention given to the purpose for which the Christian community exists, then this indicates the community's own radical disorder. Jesus Christ's call for the community to be his witnesses cannot be relegated to some derivative status. Because mission is located in the doctrine of the Trinity, it must again return to theological curricula, must

---

4. As a single example, see Jaroslav Pelikan, *The Acts of the Apostles* (Grand Rapids: Brazos, 2005). Somehow, this notable Christian scholar managed to construct an exegetical text with reference to such loci as angelology, but without a concern for the missionary act.

become central to the teaching ministry of the local congregation, and must inform liturgical practice.[5] The entire community is to hear of the commission of her being and the declarative nature of Christian fellowship, to repent and intentionally move into the world developing missionary forms as she learns the obedience required by the Spirit.

In that missionary existence is the nature of divine and human fellowship, it cannot be remotely stimulated, the result of some external manipulation. The Christian commission it is not a given potential that awaits fulfillment, nor a second step alongside a fuller Christian end, but the immediate calling of Jesus Christ under the impulsion of the Spirit. "A forced Christian is not a Christian" (*CD* IV/3.2, 529; *KD* IV/3.2, 608). Such complaints, at a political level, are clear; however, this admonition applies to coercion of any form, including that conducted on those within the church. For Newbigin, it includes preaching that encourages an ever-deepening obsession with the *beneficia Christi* and the constant refrain of "for me," and with the coordinated encouragement of the fear of eternal punishment. This direct appeal "to the lowest of human emotions, selfishness and fear" cannot be the message of missionary proclamation.[6] Mission appears again as a forced obligation rather than as the kinetic outpouring characteristic of Pentecost.

Joy is the wellspring of the missionary act. It is an involuntary cry that results from finding that pearl of great price. As Webster suggests, the basis of the community's missionary existence is as the "primitive response to Jesus' presence and proclamation: 'They were all amazed' (Mark 1:27)."[7] This dissonance of delight, this excitement of praise, leaves aside apparent givens for a vulnerable existence in the world without a place to lay one's head. The proper posture of the Christian community is as a supplicant, listening to her Lord, and praying for the Spirit, that is, assuming the pose of the apostles in and with the realism and promise of Easter. Witness, fellowship, and joy are of a piece (1 John 1:1-5). Mission is the abundant fellowship of active participation in the very glory that is the life of God from and to all

5. For an instructive treatment of the fundamental issues, including a 1982 lament for the reduction of the theology of mission to "world Christianity," see David J. Bosch, "Theological Education in Missionary Perspective," *Missiology* 10, no. 1 (1982): 13-34.

6. J. E. Lesslie Newbigin, "Cross-Currents in Ecumenical and Evangelical Understandings of Mission," *International Bulletin of Missionary Research* 6, no. 4 (1982): 151.

7. John B. Webster, "The Church as Witnessing Community," *Scottish Bulletin of Evangelical Theology* 21, no. 1 (2003): 29.

eternity. It is life in the community of reconciliation moving out in solidarity with the world in the active knowledge that God died for it, too. It is the response of doxology as we follow the Spirit's lead as captives in the train of the living glorious Lord, the lamb that was slain.

Bibliography

Aagaard, Anna Marie. "Missio Dei in katholischer Sicht." *Evangelische Theologie* 34 (1974): 420-33.

———. "Missiones Dei: A Contribution to the Discussion on the Concept of Mission." In *The Gospel and the Ambiguity of the Church*, edited by Vilmos Vajta, pp. 68-91. Philadelphia: Fortress, 1974.

Aagaard, Johannes. "Church — What Is Your Mission Today?" *Spirituality in East and West*, no. 15 (2002).

———. "Church, What Is Your Mission? — Today." *Update* 3, no. 3/4 (1979): 6-12.

———. "Mission After Uppsala 1968." In *Crucial Issues in Mission Today*, edited by Gerald H. Anderson and Thomas F. Stransky, pp. 13-21. New York: Paulist, 1974.

———. "Some Main Trends in Modern Protestant Missiology." *Studia Theologica* 19 (1965): 238-56.

———. "Trends in Missiological Thinking during the Sixties." *International Review of Mission* 62, no. 1 (1973): 8-25.

Andersen, Wilhelm. *Das wirkende Wort: Theologische Berichte über die Vollversammlung des Lutherischen Weltbundes Hannover 1952*. Munich: Evangelischer Presseverband für Bayern, 1953.

———. "Dr. Kraemer's Contribution to the Understanding of the Nature of Revelation." *International Review of Mission* 46, no. 4 (1957): 361-71.

———. "Further Toward a Theology of Mission." In *The Theology of the Christian Mission*, edited by Gerald H. Anderson, pp. 300-313. Nashville: Abingdon, 1961.

———. *Towards a Theology of Mission: A Study of the Encounter between the Missionary Enterprise and the Church and Its Theology*. London: SCM, 1955.

Aquinas, Thomas. *Summa Theologica*. Translated by the Fathers of the English Dominican Province. 5 vols. Westminster, MD: Christian Classics, 1981.

Aring, Paul Gerhard. *Kirche als Ereignis: ein Beitrag zur Neuorientierung der Missionstheologie*. Neukirchen-Vluyn: Neukirchener Verlag, 1971.

Augustine. *De Trinitate.* Translated by Edmund Hill. Vol. 1/5. Brooklyn: New City, 1991.

Ayres, Lewis. "The Fundamental Grammar of Augustine's Trinitarian Theology." In *Augustine and His Critics: Essays in Honour of Gerald Bonner,* edited by Gerald Bonner, Robert Dodaro, and George Lawless, pp. 51-76. London: Routledge, 2000.

———. *Nicaea and Its Legacy: An Approach to Fourth-Century Trinitarian Theology.* Oxford: Oxford University, 2004.

Balthasar, Hans Urs von. *The Theology of Karl Barth: Exposition and Interpretation.* San Francisco: Ignatius, 1992.

Balz, Heinrich. "Berliner Missionstheologie und Karl Barth: Aneignung und Widerspruch." In *450 Jahre Evangelische Theologie in Berlin,* edited by Gerhard Besier and Christof Gestrich, pp. 419-38. Göttingen: Vandenhoeck und Ruprecht, 1989.

Barnes, Michel René. "Augustine in Contemporary Trinitarian Theology." *Theological Studies* 56 (1995): 237-50.

———. "Rereading Augustine's Theology of the Trinity." In *The Trinity: An Interdisciplinary Symposium on the Trinity,* edited by Stephen T. Davis, Daniel Kendall, and Gerald O'Collins, pp. 145-76. Oxford: Oxford University Press, 1999.

———. "The Visible Christ and the Invisible Trinity: MT. 5:8 in Augustine's Trinitarian Theology of 400." *Modern Theology* 19, no. 3 (2003): 229-355.

Barth, Karl. "The Christian as Witness." In *God in Action,* pp. 94-143. Manhasset, NY: Round Table, 1963.

———. *The Church Dogmatics.* 4 vols. Edinburgh: T. & T. Clark, 1956-69, 1975.

———. *Dogmatics in Outline.* Translated by George T. Thomson. New York: Philosophical Library, 1949.

———. *The Epistle to the Romans.* Translated by Edwyn C. Hoskyns. London: Oxford University Press, 1968.

———. "Evangelical Theology in the Nineteenth Century." In *God, Grace and Gospel,* pp. 55-74. Edinburgh: Oliver and Boyd, 1959.

———. "Evangelische Missionskunde." In *Vorträge und kleinere Arbeiten II: 1909-1914,* edited by Hans-Anton Drewes and Hinrich Stovestandt, pp. 59-70. Zürich: Theologischer Verlag, 1910.

———. "An Exegetical Study of Matthew 28: 16-20." In *The Theology of Christian Mission,* edited by Gerald H. Anderson, pp. 55-71. Nashville: Abingdon, 1961.

———. "Fragebeantwortung bei der Konferenz der World Student Christian Federation." In *Gespräche, 1959-1962,* edited by Eberhard Busch, pp. 421-36. Zürich: Theologischer Verlag, 1995.

———. "Gespräche mit Methodistenpredigern, 1961." In *Gespräche, 1959-1962,* edited by Eberhard Busch, pp. 169-204. Zürich: Theologischer Verlag, 1995.

———. *God in Action.* Translated by Elmer G. Homrighausen and Karl J. Ernst. Manhasset, NY: Round Table, 1963.

———. "Die Not der evangelischen Kirche." *Zwischen den Zeiten* 9, no. 2 (1931): 89-122.

———. "The Proclamation of God's Free Grace." In *God Here and Now,* pp. 34-54. New York: Routledge, 2003.

―――. "Questions which 'Christianity' must face." *The Student World* 25, no. 1 (1932): 93-100.

―――. "Die Theologie und die Mission in der Gegenwart." *Zwischen den Zeiten* 10, no. 3 (1932): 189-215.

Barth, Markus. "What Is the Gospel?" *International Review of Mission* 53, no. 4 (1964): 441-48.

Bassham, Rodger C. "Mission Theology: 1948-1975." *Occasional Bulletin of Missionary Research* 4, no. 2 (1980): 52-58.

Bavinck, J. H. "Theology and Mission." *Free University Quarterly* 8 (1962): 59-66.

Beattie, John. "Willingen, 1952." *International Review of Mission* 41, no. 4 (1952): 433-43.

Bender, Kimlyn J. *Karl Barth's Christological Ecclesiology.* Aldershot, UK: Ashgate, 2005.

Benn, Christoph. "The Theology of Mission and the Integration of the International Missionary Council and the World Council of Churches." *International Review of Mission* 76, no. 3 (1987): 380-402.

Berkouwer, G. C. *Studies in Dogmatics: The Church.* Translated by James E. Davison. Grand Rapids: Eerdmans, 1976.

Bethge, Eberhard, and Victoria Barnett. *Dietrich Bonhoeffer: A Biography.* Rev. ed. Minneapolis: Fortress, 2000.

Bevans, Stephen B. "Ecclesiology Since Vatican II: From a Church with a Mission to a Missionary Church." *Verbum SVD* 46, no. 1 (2005): 27-56.

Bevans, Stephen B., and Roger P. Schroeder. *Constants in Context: A Theology of Mission for Today.* Maryknoll, NY: Orbis, 2004.

Beyerhaus, Peter, and Henry Lefever. *The Responsible Church and the Foreign Mission.* Grand Rapids: Eerdmans, 1964.

Blauw, Johannes. *The Missionary Nature of the Church: A Survey of the Biblical Theology of Mission.* New York: McGraw-Hill, 1962.

―――. "Willingen 1952." *De Heerbaan* 5 (1952): 296-309.

Blaxall, A. W. "Willingen, 1952: The Calling of the Church to Mission and Unity." *The Christian Council Quarterly*, no. 34 (1952): 1-3.

Bloesch, Donald G. *The Evangelical Renaissance.* Grand Rapids: Eerdmans, 1973.

Bolt, John, and Richard A. Muller. "Does the Church Today Need a New 'Mission Paradigm'?" *Calvin Theological Journal* 31 (1996): 196-208.

Bosch, David J. "Mission in Biblical Perspective: A Review Essay." *International Review of Mission* 74 (1985): 531-38.

―――. "Salvation: A Missiological Perspective." *Ex Auditu* 5 (1989): 139-57.

―――. "Systematic Theology and Mission: The Voice of an Early Pioneer." *Theologia Evangelica* 5, no. 3 (1972): 165-89.

―――. "Theological Education in Missionary Perspective." *Missiology* 10, no. 1 (1982): 13-34.

―――. *Transforming Mission: Paradigm Shifts in Theology of Mission.* Maryknoll, NY: Orbis, 1991.

―――. *Witness to the World: The Christian Mission in Theological Perspective.* London: Marshall, Morgan and Scott, 1980.

Bibliography

Braaten, Carl E. "The Triune God: The Source and Model of Christian Unity and Mission." *Missiology* 18, no. 4 (1990): 415-27.

Brachmann, W. "Theologie der Krisis und Mission." *Zeitschrift für Missionskunde und Religionswissenschaft* 45, no. 10 (1930): 289-309.

———. "Theologie der Krisis und Mission: Theorie und Praxis." *Zeitschrift für Missionskunde und Religionswissenschaft* 46, no. 1 (1931): 30-32.

Brunner, Emil. "Die andere Aufgabe der Theologie." *Zwischen den Zeiten* 7 (1929): 255-76.

———. "Die Bedeutung der missionarischen Erfahrung für die Theologie." In *Die deutsche evangelische Heidenmission: Jahrbuch 1933 der vereinigten deutschen Missionskonferenzen,* pp. 3-11. Hamburg: Selbstverlag der Missionskonferenzen, 1933.

———. *The Christian Doctrine of God.* Translated by Olive Wyon. Philadelphia: Westminster, 1950.

———. "Die Frage nach dem 'Anknüpfungspunkt' als Problem der Theologie." *Zwischen den Zeiten* 10 (1932): 505-32.

———. *Das Gebot und die Ordnungen: Entwurf einer protestantisch-theologischen Ethik.* Tübingen: J.C.B. Mohr, 1932.

———. *Natur und Gnade: zum Gespräch mit Karl Barth.* 2nd ed. Tübingen: Mohr, 1935.

———. "Toward a Missionary Theology." *Christian Century* 66, no. 27 (1949): 816-18.

———. *The Word and the World.* London: SCM, 1931.

Brunner, Emil, and Karl Barth. *Natural Theology: Comprising 'Nature and Grace' by Professor Dr. Emil Brunner and the Reply 'No!' by Dr. Karl Barth.* London: Centenary Press, 1946.

Burgess, Andrew R. *The Ascension in Karl Barth.* Aldershot, UK: Ashgate, 2004.

Busch, Eberhard. "God Is God: The Meaning of a Controversial Formula and the Fundamental Problem of Speaking about God." *Princeton Seminary Bulletin* 7, no. 2 (1986): 99-113.

———. *Karl Barth: His Life from Letters and Autobiographical Texts.* Grand Rapids: Eerdmans, 1994.

Carter, Craig A. "Karl Barth's Revision of Protestant Ecclesiology." *Perspectives in Religious Studies* 22, no. 1 (1995): 35-44.

Coffele, Gianfranco. "De Lubac and the Theological Foundation of the Missions." *Communio* 23 (1996): 757-75.

Cox, Harvey G. *God's Revolution and Man's Responsibility.* Valley Forge, PA: Judson, 1965.

Crouch, Andy. "The Mission of the Trinity: An Interview with Simon Chan." *Christianity Today* 51, no. 6 (2007): 48-51.

Davis, John Merle, ed. *The Authority of the Faith.* Edited by John Merle Davis and Kenneth G. Grubb. 7 vols. Vol. 1, The Madras Series. London: International Missionary Council, 1939.

De Jong, Johannes Marie. "Ist Barth überholt?" In *Theologie zwischen Gestern und Morgen: Interpretationen und Anfragen zum Werk Karl Barths,* edited by Wilhelm Dantine and Kurt Lüthi, pp. 38-67. Munich: Chr. Kaiser Verlag, 1968.

Demson, David E. "'Church Practices': Sacraments of Invocations? Hütter's Proposal in Light of Barth's." *Toronto Journal of Theology* 18, no. 1 (2002): 79-99.

————. *Hans Frei and Karl Barth: Different Ways of Reading Scripture.* Grand Rapids: Eerdmans, 1997.

Devaranne, T. "Theologie der Krisis und Mission: Theorie und Praxis." *Zeitschrift für Missionskunde und Religionswissenschaft* 46, no. 1 (1931): 24-30.

DuBose, Francis M. *God Who Sends: A Fresh Quest for Biblical Mission.* Nashville: Broadman, 1983.

Du Roy, Olivier. *L'Intelligence de la foi en la Trinité selon saint Augustin.* Paris: Études augustiniennes, 1966.

Dürr, Johannes. "Die Reinigung der Missionsmotive." *Evangelisches Missions-Magazin* 95 (1951): 2-10.

————. "Kirche, Mission und Reich Gottes." *Evangelisches Missions-Magazin* 97 (1953): 133-44.

————. "Sendung: einige Fragen und Erwägungen." *Evangelisches Missions-Magazin* 98 (1954): 146-52.

Engelsviken, Tormod. "Convergence or Divergence? The Relationship between Recent Ecumenical and Evangelical Mission Documents." *Swedish Missiological Themes* 89, no. 2 (2001): 197-220.

————. "*Missio Dei:* The Understanding and Misunderstanding of a Theological Concept in European Churches and Missiology." *International Review of Mission* 92, no. 4 (2003): 481-97.

Eusebius of Caesarea. *The Proof of the Gospel: Being the Demonstratio Evangelica of Eusebius of Caesarea.* Translated by W. J. Ferrar. 2 vols. Vol. 1. Grand Rapids: Baker, 1981.

Flannery, Austin. *Vatican Council II: The Conciliar and Post Conciliar Documents.* Rev. ed. Vol. 1. Northport, NY: Costello, 1996.

Flett, John G. "From Jerusalem to Oxford: Mission as the Foundation and Goal of Ecumenical Social Thought." *International Bulletin of Missionary Research* 27, no. 1 (2003): 17-22.

Forsyth, P. T. "The Greatest Creditors The Greatest Debtors." In *Missions in State and Church: Sermons and Addresses,* pp. 249-74. New York: A. C. Armstrong and Son, 1908.

Freytag, Walter. "Changes in the Patterns of Western Missions." In *The Ghana Assembly of the International Missionary Council, 28th December, 1957 to 8th January, 1958: Selected papers, with an Essay on the Role of the I.M.C.,* edited by Ronald Kenneth Orchard, pp. 138-47. London: Edinburgh House, 1958.

————. "Karl Hartenstein zum Gedenken." *Evangelische Missions Zeitschrift* 10, no. 1 (1953): 1-5.

————. "The Meaning and Purpose of the Christian Mission." *International Review of Mission* 39, no. 2 (1950): 153-61.

————. "Mitglied im Deutschen Evangelischen Missionsrat und Missionstag und bei den Tagungen der Ökumene." In *Karl Hartenstein: ein Leben für Kirche und Mis-*

sion, edited by Wolfgang Metzger, pp. 293-311. Stuttgart: Evangelischer Missionsverlag, 1953.

Frick, Heinrich. *Die evangelische Mission: Ursprung, Geschichte, Ziel.* Bonn: K. Schroeder, 1922.

———. "Is a Conviction of the Superiority of His Message Essential to the Missionary?" *International Review of Mission* 15, no. 4 (1926): 625-46.

Furuya, Yasuo Carl. "Apologetic or Kerygmatic Theology?" *Theology Today* 16, no. 4 (1960): 471-80.

Gairdner, W. H. T. *Echoes from Edinburgh, 1910: An Account and Interpretation of the World Missionary Conference.* New York: Fleming Revell, 1910.

Gass, W. *Geschichte der protestantischen Dogmatik: in ihrem Zusammenhange mit Theologie überhaupt.* 4 vols. Vol. 2. Berlin: G. Reimer, 1854.

Gensichen, Hans-Werner. "Evangelisieren und Zivilisieren: Motive deutscher protestantischer Mission in der imperialistischen Epoche." *Zeitschrift für Missionswissenschaft und Religionswissenschaft* 67, no. 4 (1983): 257-69.

———. "German Protestant Missions." In *Missionary Ideologies in the Imperialist Era, 1880-1920,* edited by Torben Christensen and William R. Hutchison, pp. 181-90. Århus, Denmark: Aros, 1982.

———. "New Delhi and the World Mission of the Church." *Lutheran World* 9, no. 2 (1962): 133-43.

———. "Schütz, Paul." In *Biographical Dictionary of Christian Missions,* edited by Gerald H. Anderson, p. 605. Grand Rapids: Eerdmans, 1998.

———. "Zur Orient- und Missionserfahrung von Paul Schütz." *Zeitschrift für Missionswissenschaft und Religionswissenschaft* 77, no. 2 (1993): 152-59.

"Go Forth in Peace: Orthodox Perspectives on Mission." In *New Directions in Mission and Evangelism 1: Basic Statements 1974-1991,* edited by James A. Scherer and Stephen B. Bevans, pp. 203-31. Maryknoll, NY: Orbis, 1992.

Gogarten, Friedrich. "Schöpfung und Volkstum: Vortrag, gehalten auf der Berliner Missionswoche, am 3. Oktober 1932." *Zwischen den Zeiten* 10 (1932): 481-504.

Goodall, Norman. "First Principles." *International Review of Mission* 39, no. 3 (1950): 257-62.

———, ed. *Missions under the Cross.* London: Edinburgh House, 1953.

———. "Willingen — Milestone, not Terminus." In *Missions under the Cross,* edited by Norman Goodall, pp. 9-23. London: Edinburgh House, 1953.

Grenz, Stanley J. *Rediscovering the Triune God: The Trinity in Contemporary Theology.* Minneapolis: Fortress, 2004.

Guder, Darrell L. *The Continuing Conversion of the Church.* Grand Rapids: Eerdmans, 2000.

Günther, Wolfgang. "Gott selbst treibt Mission: Das Modell der 'Missio Dei.'" In *Plädoyer für Mission: Beiträge zum Verständnis von Mission heute,* edited by Klaus Schäfer, pp. 56-63. Hamburg: Evangelische Missionswerk in Deutschland, 1998.

———. "The History and Significance of World Mission Conferences in the 20th Century." *International Review of Mission* 92, no. 4 (2003): 521-37.

————. *Von Edinburgh nach Mexico City: die ekklesiologischen Bemühungen der Weltmissionskonferenzen, 1910-1963.* Stuttgart: Evangelischer Missionsverlag, 1970.

Gunton, Colin E. *Act and Being: Towards a Theology of the Divine Attributes.* London: SCM, 2002.

————. "The Church on Earth: The Roots of Community." In *On Being the Church: Essays on the Christian Community,* edited by Colin E. Gunton and Daniel W. Hardy, pp. 48-80. Edinburgh: T. & T. Clark, 1989.

————. "The Community of the Church in Communion with God." In *The Church in the Reformed Tradition: Discussion Papers Prepared by a Working Party of the European Committee,* edited by Colin E. Gunton, Réamonn Páraic, and Alan P. F. Sell, pp. 38-41. Geneva: WARC, 1995.

————. "Election and Ecclesiology in the Post-Constantinian Church." *Scottish Journal of Theology* 53, no. 2 (2000): 212-27.

————. *The One, the Three, and the Many: God, Creation, and the Culture of Modernity.* Cambridge: Cambridge University Press, 1993.

————. *The Promise of Trinitarian Theology.* 2nd ed. London: T. & T. Clark, 2003.

Gutmann, Bruno. *Gemeindeaufbau aus dem Evangelium: Grundsätzliches für Mission und Heimatkirche.* Leipzig: Evangelische Lutherisch Mission, 1925.

Hart, John W. *Karl Barth vs. Emil Brunner: The Formation and Dissolution of a Theological Alliance, 1916-1936.* New York: Peter Lang, 2001.

Hart, Trevor A. *Regarding Karl Barth: Toward a Reading of His Theology.* Downers Grove, IL: InterVarsity, 1999.

Hartenstein, Karl. "Adaptation or Revolution." *The Student World* 28, no. 4 (1935): 308-27.

————. "Botschafter an Christi Statt." In *Botschafter an Christi Statt: von Wesen und Werk deutscher Missionsarbeit,* edited by Martin Schlunk, pp. 1-17. Gütersloh: Bertelsmann, 1932.

————. "Der Beitrag der Theologie zu den missionarischen Problemen der Gegenwart." *Evangelische Missions-Magazin* 82 (1938): 69-83.

————. "Krisis der Mission?" *Die Furche* 17 (1931): 201-7.

————. *Die Mission als theologisches Problem: Beiträge zum grundsätzlichen Verständnis der Mission.* Berlin: Furche Verlag, 1932.

————. "Mission und die kulturelle Frage: Anpassung oder Umbruch." *Evangelisches Missions-Magazin* 79 (1935): 350-67.

————. "The Outlook for German Missions." *World Dominion* 13 (1953): 158-64.

————. "Tambaram, wie es arbeitete." In *Das Wunder der Kirche unter den Völkern der Erde: Bericht über Weltmissions-Konferenz in Tambaram,* edited by Martin Schlunk, pp. 37-45. Stuttgart: Evangelischer Missionsverlag, 1939.

————. "Theologische Besinnung." In *Mission zwischen Gestern und Morgen,* edited by Walter Freytag, pp. 51-72. Stuttgart: Evang. Missionsverlag, 1952.

————. "The Theology of the Word and Missions." *International Review of Mission* 20, no. 2 (1931): 210-27.

————. "Die trinitarische Verkündigung in der Welt der Religionen." In *Die deutsche evangelische Heidenmission: Jahrbuch der vereinigten deutschen Missionskonferenzen*, pp. 3-13. Selbstverlag der Missionskonferenzen, 1939.

—————. "Übergang und Neubeginn: Zur Tagung des Internationalen Missionsrats in Willingen." *Zeitwende* 24, no. 4 (1952): 334-45.

—————. "Versuch einer missionarischen Ethik." *Evangelisches Missions-Magazin* 79 (1935): 1-10, 33-44, 65-72.

—————. *Warum Mission? Eine Antwort an die deutsche evangelische Jugend.* Vol. 4, *Mission und Gemeinde: Das Zeugnis der Mission in der Kirche der Gegenwart.* Stuttgart: Evang. Missionsverlag, 1935.

—————. "Was haben wir von Tambaram zu lernen?" In *Das Wunder der Kirche unter den Völkern der Erde: Bericht über Weltmissions-Konferenz in Tambaram,* edited by Martin Schlunk, pp. 193-203. Stuttgart: Evangelischer Missionsverlag, 1939.

—————. "Was hat die Theologie Karl Barths der Mission zu sagen?" *Zwischen den Zeiten* 6 (1928): 59-83.

—————. "Wozu nötigt die Finanzlage der Mission." *Evangelisches Missions-Magazin* 79 (1934): 217-29.

—————. "Zur Neubesinnung über das Wesen der Mission." In *Deutsche Evangelische Weltmission Jahrbuch 1951,* edited by Walter Freytag, pp. 5-24. Hamburg: Verlag der Deutschen Evangelischen Missions-Hilfe, 1951.

Harvey, John D. "Mission in Jesus' Teaching." In *Mission in the New Testament: An Evangelical Approach,* edited by William J. Larkin and Joel F. Williams, pp. 30-49. Maryknoll, NY: Orbis, 1998.

Hassing, Per. "Bruno Gutmann of Kilimanjaro: Setting the Record Straight." *Missiology* 7, no. 4 (1979): 423-33.

Hauerwas, Stanley. *Character and the Christian Life.* San Antonio, TX: Trinity University Press, 1975.

—————. *The Peaceable Kingdom: A Primer in Christian Ethics.* Notre Dame, IN: University of Notre Dame, 1983.

—————. *With the Grain of the Universe: The Church's Witness and Natural Theology.* Grand Rapids: Brazos, 2001.

—————. "Worship, Evangelism, Ethics: On Eliminating the 'And.'" In *A Better Hope: Resources for a Church Confronting Capitalism, Democracy, and Postmodernity,* pp. 155-61. Grand Rapids: Brazos, 2000.

Healy, Nicholas M. "Communion Ecclesiology: A Cautionary Note." *Pro Ecclesia* 4, no. 4 (1995): 442-53.

—————. "Karl Barth's Ecclesiology Reconsidered." *Scottish Journal of Theology* 57, no. 3 (2004): 287-99.

—————. "The Logic of Karl Barth's Ecclesiology: Analysis, Assessment, and Proposed Modifications." *Modern Theology* 10, no. 3 (1994): 253-70.

Heim, Karl. *Jesus der Weltvollender: der Glaube an die Versöhnung und Weltverwandlung.* Berlin: Furche, 1937.

—————. "Die Tagung des erweiterten internationalen Missionsrats in Jerusalem." *Evangelisches Missions-Magazin* 72 (1928): 161-64.

Helmreich, Ernst Christian. *The German Churches Under Hitler: Background, Struggle, and Epilogue.* Detroit: Wayne State University Press, 1979.

Hendrix, Scott H. *Recultivating the Vineyard: The Reformation Agendas of Christianization.* Louisville: Westminster/John Knox, 2004.

Hermann, Söhnen, and Markus Hartenstein. "Der Lebensgang." In *Karl Hartenstein: ein Leben für Kirche und Mission,* edited by Wolfgang Metzger, pp. 9-99. Stuttgart: Evangelischer Missionsverlag, 1953.

Hoedemaker, L. A. "The Legacy of J. C. Hoekendijk." *International Bulletin of Missionary Research* 19, no. 4 (1995): 166-70.

———. "Mission and Unity: The Relevance of Hoekendijk's Vision." In *Changing Partnership of Missionary and Ecumenical Movements: Essays in Honour of Marc Spindler,* edited by Leny Lagerwerf, Karel Steenbrink, and F. J. Verstraelen, pp. 26-35. Leiden-Utrecht: Interuniversity Institute for Missiological and Ecumenical Research, 1995.

———. "Mission, Unity and Eschaton: A Triadic Relation." *Reformed World* 50, no. 4 (2000): 173-82.

———. "The People of God and the Ends of the Earth." In *Missiology: An Ecumenical Introduction,* edited by F. J. Verstraelen, A. Camps, L. A. Hoedemaker, and M. R. Spindler, pp. 157-71. Grand Rapids: Eerdmans, 1995.

———."Die Welt als Theologisches Problem: Kritischer Rückblick auf die Niederländische Theologie des Apostolates." *Zeitschrift für Dialektische Theologie* 2, no. 1 (2004): 9-20.

———. "Hendrik Kraemer 1888-1965: Biblical Realism Applied to Mission." In *Mission Legacies: Biographical Studies of Leaders of the Modern Missionary Movement,* edited by Gerald H. Anderson, Robert T. Coote, Norman A. Horner, and James M. Phillips. Maryknoll, NY: Orbis Books, 1994.

Hoekendijk, J. C. "The Call to Evangelism." *International Review of Mission* 39 (1950): 162-75.

———. "The Church in Missionary Thinking." *International Review of Mission* 41 (1952): 324-36.

———. "Feier der Befreiung: Was ist Mission?" In *Kontexte 4,* edited by H. J. Schultz, pp. 124-31. Stuttgart, Berlin, 1967.

———. *Kirche und Volk in der deutschen Missionswissenschaft.* Munich: Chr. Kaiser Verlag, 1967.

———. "Notes on the Meaning of Mission(-ary)." In *Planning for Mission: Working Papers on the New Quest for Missionary Communities,* edited by Thomas Wieser, pp. 37-48. New York: U.S. Conference for the World Council of Churches, 1966.

Hoffmeyer, John F. "The Missional Trinity." *Dialog* 40, no. 2 (2001): 108-11.

Holmes, Stephen R. "Trinitarian Missiology: Towards a Theology of God as Missionary." *International Journal of Systematic Theology* 8, no. 1 (2006): 72-90.

Hunsinger, George. *How to Read Karl Barth: The Shape of His Theology.* New York: Oxford University Press, 1991.

———. "Karl Barth's Christology: Its Basic Chalcedonian Character." In *Disruptive*

Grace: Studies in the Theology of Karl Barth, pp. 131-47. Grand Rapids: Eerdmans, 2000.

Hutchison, William R. "American Missionary Ideologies: 'Activism' as Theory, Practice and Stereotype." In *Continuity and Discontinuity in Church History,* edited by F. Forrester Church and Timothy George, pp. 351-62. Leiden: Brill, 1979.

———. *Errand to the World: American Protestant Thought and Foreign Missions.* Chicago: University of Chicago Press, 1987.

Hütter, Reinhard. "The Church as 'Public': Dogma, Practices and the Holy Spirit." *Pro Ecclesia* 3, no. 3 (1994): 334-61.

Jacob, Siegfried. *Das Problem der Anknüpfung für das Wort Gottes in der deutschen evangelischen Missionsliteratur der Nachkriegszeit.* Gütersloh: C. Bertelsmann, 1935.

Jäger, Karl. "Die Neubesinnung der evangelischen Mission auf ihre Motive, Methoden und Ziele." *Evangelische Missions-Magazin* 77 (1933): 202-18.

Jäschke, Ernst. "Bruno Gutmann 1876-1966: Building on Clan, Neighborhood and Age Groups." In *Mission Legacies: Biographical Studies of Leaders of the Modern Missionary Movement,* edited by Gerald H. Anderson, Robert T. Coote, Norman A. Horner, and James M. Phillips, pp. 173-80. Maryknoll, NY: Orbis, 1994.

———. *Bruno Gutmann, His Life, His Thought, and His Work: An Early Attempt at a Theology in an African Context.* Erlangen: Verlag der Evangelische Lutheran Mission 1985.

Jenson, Robert W. "Catechesis for Our Time." In *Marks of the Body of Christ,* edited by Carl E. Braaten and Robert W. Jenson, pp. 137-49. Grand Rapids: Eerdmans, 1999.

———. "Christian Civilization." In *God, Truth, and Witness: Engaging Stanley Hauerwas,* edited by L. Gregory Jones, Reinhard Hütter, and C. Rosalee Velloso da Silva, pp. 153-63. Grand Rapids: Brazos, 2005.

———. *Systematic Theology I: The Triune God.* New York: Oxford University Press, 1997.

———. *Systematic Theology II: The Works of God.* New York: Oxford University Press, 1999.

———. *The Triune Identity: God According to the Gospel.* Philadelphia: Fortress, 1982.

———. "You Wonder Where the Spirit Went." *Pro Ecclesia* 2, no. 3 (1993): 296-304.

Jongeneel, Jan A. B. "Anknüpfungspunkt." In *Die Religion in Geschichte und Gegenwart: Handwörterbuch für Theologie und Religionswissenschaft,* edited by Hans Dieter Betz, Don S. Browning, Bernd Janowski, and Eberhard Jüngel, pp. 507-8. Tübingen: Mohr Siebeck, 1998.

Jüngel, Eberhard. *God's Being Is in Becoming.* Translated by John B. Webster. Grand Rapids: Eerdmans, 2001.

———. *God as the Mystery of the World: On the Foundation of the Theology of the Crucified One in the Dispute between Theism and Atheism.* Grand Rapids: Eerdmans, 1983.

———. "To Tell the World about God: The Task for the Mission of the Church on the Threshold of the Third Millennium." *International Review of Mission* 89, no. 1 (2000): 203-16.

Bibliography

Kähler, Martin. *Schriften zu Christologie und Mission: Gesamtausgabe der Schriften zur Mission.* Edited by Heinzgünter Frohnes. Munich: Chr. Kaiser Verlag, 1971.

Keller, Adolf. *Karl Barth and Christian Unity: The Influence of the Barthian Movement upon the Churches of the World.* Translated by Werner Petersmann and Manfred Manrodt. New York: Macmillan, 1933.

Killus, Dorothea R. "Mission und Heilsgeschichte nach Hartenstein." In *Karl Hartenstein: Leben in weltweitem Horizont,* edited by Fritz Lamparter, pp. 112-27. Bonn: Verlag für Kultur und Wissenschaft, 1995.

Kirk, J. Andrew. "Missio Dei; Missio Ecclesiae." In *Contemporary Issues in Mission,* edited by J. Andrew Kirk, pp. 1-16. Birmingham: Selly Oak Colleges, 1994.

————. *What Is Mission? Theological Explorations.* London: Darton, Longman and Todd, 1999.

Knak, Siegfried. "The Characteristics of German Evangelical Missions in Theory and Practice." In *Evangelism,* edited by John Merle Davis and Kenneth G. Grubb, pp. 289-356. New York: International Missionary Council, 1939.

————. *German Protestant Missionary Work: Its Characteristic Features in Practice and Theory.* New York: International Missionary Council, 1938.

————. "Die Mission und die Theologie in der Gegenwart." *Zwischen den Zeiten* 10, no. 4 (1932): 331-55.

————. "Mission und Kirche im Dritten Reich." In *Das Buch der deutschen Weltmission,* edited by Julius Richter, pp. 240-44. Gotha: Leopold Klotz Verlag, 1935.

————. "Missionsmotive und Missionsmethode unter der Fragestellung der dialektischen Theologie." In *Botschafter an Christi Statt: von Wesen und Werk deutscher Missionsarbeit,* edited by Martin Schlunk, pp. 58-80. Gütersloh: Bertelsmann, 1932.

————. "Ökumenischer Dienst in der Missionswissenschaft." In *Theologia Viatorum II: Jahrbuch der Kirchlichen Hochschule Berlin,* edited by Walter Delius, pp. 156-74. Berlin: Walter De Gruyter, 1950.

————. "Totalitätsanspruch des Staates und der Totalitätsanspruch Gottes an die Völker." *Neue Allgemeine Missions-Zeitschrift* 10, no. 12 (1933): 401-21.

————. *Zwischen Nil und Tafelbai: eine Studie über Evangelium, Volkstum und Zivilisation, am Beispiel der Missionsprobleme unter den Bantu.* Berlin: Heimatdienst-Verlag, 1931.

Köberle, Adolf. "Die Neubesinnung auf den Missionsgedanken in der Theologie der Gegenwart." *Neue Allgemeine Missions-Zeitschrift* 7, no. 11-12 (1930): 321-32, 353-68.

Kraemer, Hendrik. *The Christian Message in a non-Christian World.* London: Harper and Brothers, 1938.

————. "Mission im Wandel der Völkerwelt." In *Der Auftrag der Kirche in der modernen Welt: Festgabe zum siebzigsten Geburtstag von Emil Brunner,* edited by Peter Vogelsanger, pp. 291-307. Zürich: Zwingli Verlag, 1959.

————. *Religion and the Christian Faith.* Philadelphia: Westminster, 1956.

Kramm, Thomas. *Analyse und Bewährung theologischer Modelle zur Begründung der Mission.* Aachen: Missio Aktuell Verlag, 1979.

Krüger, Erich. *Wesen und Aufgabe der Missionstheologie.* Wuppertal-Barmen: Verlag der Rheinischen Missions-Gesellschaft, 1960.

Krusche, Werner. "Parish Structure — A Hindrance to Mission? A Survey and Evaluation of the Ecumenical Discussion on the Structures of the Missionary Congregation." In *Sources for Change: Searching for Flexible Church Structures,* edited by Herbert T. Neve, pp. 51-100. Geneva: World Council of Churches, 1968.

Kuzmiè, Rhys. "*Beruf* and *Berufung* in Karl Barth's *Church Dogmatics:* Toward a Subversive Klesiology." *International Journal of Systematic Theology* 7, no. 3 (2005): 262-78.

LaCugna, Catherine Mowry. *God for Us: The Trinity and Christian life.* San Francisco: HarperSanFrancisco, 1993.

Lehmann, Paul. "The Missionary Obligation of the Church." *Theology Today* 9, no. 1 (1952): 20-38.

———. "Willingen and Lund: The Church on the Way to Unity." *Theology Today* 9, no. 4 (1953): 431-41.

Linz, Manfred. *Anwalt der Welt: zur Theologie der Mission.* Stuttgart: Kreuz-Verlag, 1964.

Linning, Per. "Expanding Mission." *Lutheran World* 16, no. 4 (1969): 351-53.

Louth, Andrew. "Barth and the Problem of Natural Theology." *Downside Review* 87, no. 3 (1969): 268-77.

Lowe, Walter. "Prospects for a Postmodern Christian Theology: Apocalyptic without Reserve." *Modern Theology* 15, no. 1 (1999): 17-24.

Lubac, Henri de. *Theology in History.* Translated by Anne Englund Nash. San Francisco: Ignatius, 1996.

Mackay, John A. *Ecumenics: The Science of the Church Universal.* Englewood Cliffs, NJ: Prentice-Hall, 1964.

———. "The Great Commission and the Church Today." In *Missions under the Cross,* edited by Norman Goodall, pp. 129-41. London: Edinburgh House, 1953.

Manecke, Dieter. *Mission als Zeugendienst: Karl Barths theologische Begründung der Mission im Gegenüber zu den Entwürfen von Walter Holsten, Walter Freytag und Joh. Christiaan Hoekendijk.* Wuppertal: Rolf Brockhaus Verlag, 1972.

Mangina, Joseph L. "The Stranger as Sacrament: Karl Barth and the Ethics of Ecclesial Practice." *International Journal of Systematic Theology* 1, no. 3 (1999): 321-39.

Margull, Hans Jochen. "Sammlung und Sendung: Zur Frage von Kirche und Mission." *Evangelische Missions-Zeitschrift* 16, no. 3 (1959): 65-75.

Marx, Walter. "Mission und dialektische Theologie: Mission und Volkstum." *Neue Allgemeine Missions-Zeitschrift* 10, no. 7 (1933): 225-35.

Matthey, Jacques. "God's Mission Today: Summary and Conclusions." *International Review of Mission* 92, no. 4 (2003): 579-87.

———. "Missiology in the World Council of Churches: Update." *International Review of Mission* 90, no. 4 (2001): 427-43.

———. "Mission als anstößiges Wesensmerkmal der Kirche." *Zeitschrift für Mission* 28, no. 3 (2002): 221-39.

Bibliography

————. "Reconciliation, *Missio Dei* and the Church's Mission." In *Mission — Violence and Reconciliation: Papers Read at the Biennial Conference of the British and Irish Association for Mission Studies at the University of Edinburgh, June 2003*, edited by Howard Mellor and Timothy Yates, pp. 113-37. Sheffield, UK: Cliff College Publishing, 2004.

McCormack, Bruce L. "Barths grundsätzlicher Chalcedonismus?" *Zeitschrift für dialektische Theologie* 18, no. 2 (2002): 138-73.

————. "Participation in God, Yes, Deification, No: Two Modern Protestant Responses to an Ancient Question." In *Denkwürdiges Geheimnis: Beiträge zur Gotteslehre, Festschrift für Eberhard Jüngel zum 70. Geburtstag*, edited by Ingolf Ulrich Dalferth, Johannes Fischer, and Hans-Peter Grosshans, pp. 347-74. Tübingen: Mohr Siebeck, 2004.

Mebust, J. Leland. "Barth on Mission." *Dialogue* 20 (1981): 15-19.

Migliore, Daniel L. "*Participatio Christi:* The Central Theme of Barth's Doctrine of Sanctification." *Zeitschrift für Dialektische Theologie* 18, no. 3 (2002): 286-307.

Míguez Bonino, José. *Faces of Latin American Protestantism: 1993 Carnahan Lectures.* Translated by Eugene L. Stockwell. Grand Rapids: Eerdmans, 1997.

Milbank, John. *Theology and Social Theory: Beyond Secular Reason.* Cambridge, MA: Blackwell, 1990.

"Mission and Evangelism in Unity Today." *International Review of Mission* 88, no. 1/2 (1999): 109-27.

Moltmann, Jürgen. *The Church in the Power of the Spirit: A Contribution to Messianic Ecclesiology.* Minneapolis: Fortress, 1993.

Mott, John R., ed. *The World Mission of Christianity: Messages and Recommendations of the Enlarged Meeting of the International Missionary Council held at Jerusalem, March 24-April 8, 1928.* London: International Missionary Council, 1928.

Neill, Stephen. *Colonialism and Christian Missions.* New York: McGraw-Hill, 1966.

————. *Creative Tension.* London: Edinburgh House, 1959.

————. *The Unfinished Task.* London: Edinburgh House, 1957.

Newbigin, J. E. Lesslie. "Christ and the Cultures." *Scottish Journal of Theology* 31, no. 1 (1978): 1-22.

————. *Come Holy Spirit — Renew the Whole Creation.* Birmingham, UK: Selly Oak Colleges, 1990.

————. "Context and Conversion." *International Review of Mission* 68, no. 3 (1979): 301-12.

————. "Cross-Currents in Ecumenical and Evangelical Understandings of Mission." *International Bulletin of Missionary Research* 6, no. 4 (1982): 146-51.

————. *The Household of God: Lectures on the Nature of the Church.* London: SCM, 1953.

————. "Integration — Some Personal Reflections 1981." *International Review of Mission* 70, no. 4 (1981): 247-55.

————. "Mission to Six Continents." In *The Ecumenical Advance: A History of the Ecu-*

menical Movement, 1948-1968, edited by Harold E. Fey, pp. 171-97. London: SPCK, 1970.

———. *One Body, One Gospel, One World: The Christian Mission Today.* London: International Missionary Council, 1958.

———. "Recent Thinking on Christian Beliefs: VIII. Mission and Missions." *The Expository Times* 88, no. 9 (1977): 260-64.

———. "Reply to Konrad Raiser." *International Bulletin of Missionary Research* 18, no. 2 (1994): 51-52.

———. *Unfinished Agenda: An Autobiography.* Geneva: World Council of Churches, 1985.

———. "Which Way for 'Faith and Order'?" In *What Unity Implies: Six Essays After Uppsala,* edited by Reinhard Groscurth, pp. 115-32. Geneva: World Council of Churches, 1969.

Niebuhr, H. Richard. "An Attempt at a Theological Analysis of Missionary Motivation." *Occasional Bulletin of Missionary Research* 14, no. 1 (1963): 1-6.

———. *Christ and Culture.* New York: Harper, 1951.

———. "The Doctrine of the Trinity and the Unity of the Church." *Theology Today* 3, no. 3 (1946): 371-84.

Niebuhr, Reinhold. "Our World's Denial of God." *Intercollegian* 44 (1927): 127-30.

Nimmo, Paul T. "Karl Barth and the *concursus Dei* — A Chalcedonianism Too Far?" *International Journal of Systematic Theology* 9, no. 1 (2007): 58-72.

O'Grady, Colm. *The Church in Catholic Theology: Dialogue with Karl Barth.* Washington, DC: Corpus, 1969.

Öberg, Ingemar. *Luther and World Mission: A Historical and Systematic Study.* Translated by Dean Apel. St. Louis: Concordia, 2007.

Oberman, Heiko Augustinus, Adolf Martin Ritter, and Hans-Walter Krumwiede. *Kirchen- und Theologiegeschichte in Quellen.* Vol. IV/2. Neukirchen-Vluyn: Neukirchener Verlag, 1977.

Pachuau, Lalsangkima. "Missiology in a Pluralistic World: The Place of Mission Study in Theological Education." *International Review of Mission* 89, no. 4 (2000): 539-55.

Pannenberg, Wolfhart. *Systematic Theology II.* Grand Rapids: Eerdmans, 1994.

Paton, David M. *Christian Missions and the Judgment of God.* London: SCM, 1953.

———. "First Thoughts on the Debacle of Christian Missions in China." *International Review of Mission* 40, no. 4 (1951): 411-20.

Phillip, T. V. "Ecumenical Discussion on the Relation between Church and Mission from 1938-1952." In *A Vision for Man: Essays on Faith, Theology and Society,* edited by Samuel Amirtham, pp. 206-20. Madras: Christian Literature Society, 1978.

———. *Edinburgh to Salvador: Twentieth Century Ecumenical Missiology: A Historical Study of the Ecumenical Discussions on Mission.* Delhi: CSS and ISPCK, 1999.

Pierard, Richard V. "*Völkisch* Thought and Christian Missions in Early Twentieth Century Germany." In *Essays in Religious Studies for Andrew Walls,* edited by James Thrower, pp. 138-49. Aberdeen: Department of Religious Studies, University of Aberdeen, 1986.

Piper, John. *Let the Nations Be Glad! The Supremacy of God in Missions.* 2nd ed. Grand Rapids: Baker Academic, 2003.

Poewe, Karla. "Liberalism, German Missionaries, and National Socialism." In *Mission und Macht im Wandel politischer Orientierungen,* edited by Ulrich van der Heyden and Holger Stoecker, pp. 633-62. Stuttgart: Franz Steiner Verlag, 2005.

―――. "The Spell of National Socialism: The Berlin Mission's Opposition to, and Compromise with, the *Völkisch* Movement and National Socialism: Knak, Braun, Weichert." In *Mission und Gewalt,* edited by Ulrich van der Heyden, Jürgen Becher, and Holger Stoecker, pp. 267-90. Stuttgart: Franz Steiner Verlag, 2000.

Pörklen, Martin. "Der neue Auftrag: Persönliche Eindrücke von der Weltmissions-Konferenz Willingen 1952." *Weltmission heute,* no. 3 (1952): 3-32.

Quick, Oliver Chase. "The Jerusalem Meeting and the Christian Message." *International Review of Mission* 17, no. 4 (1928): 445-54.

Rahner, Karl. *The Trinity.* Translated by Joseph Donceel. New York: Crossroad, 1997.

Rennstich, Karl. "Hartenstein als Direktor der Basler Mission." In *Karl Hartenstein: Leben in weltweitem Horizont,* edited by Fritz Lamparter, pp. 39-56. Bonn: Verlag für Kultur und Wissenschaft, 1995.

Rétif, André. "Trinité et Mission d'après Bérulle." *Neue Zeitschrift für Missionswissenschaft* 13 (1957): 1-8.

Richebächer, Wilhelm. "Editorial." *International Review of Mission* 92, no. 4 (2003): 463-67.

―――. "*Missio Dei:* The Basis of Mission Theology or a Wrong Path?" *International Review of Mission* 92, no. 4 (2003): 588-605.

Richter, Julius. "Mission: Evangelische Mission." In *Die Religion in Geschichte und Gegenwart: Handwörterbuch im gemeinverständlicher Darstellung,* edited by Hermann Gunkel and Leopold Zscharnack, pp. 41-47. Tübingen: J. C. B. Mohr, 1930.

Richter, Martin. "Dialektische Theologie und Mission." *Allgemeine Missions-Zeitschrift* 5 (1928): 228-41.

Ritschl, Albrecht. *The Christian Doctrine of Justification and Reconciliation: The Positive Development of the Doctrine.* Translated by Hugh Ross Mackintosh and A. B. Macaulay. Edinburgh: T. & T. Clark, 1900.

Robertson, Gregory Alan. "'Vivit! Regnat! Triumphat!' The Prophetic Office of Jesus Christ, the Christian life, and the Mission of the Church in Karl Barth's *Church Dogmatics* IV/3." Th.D. diss., Wycliffe College and the University of Toronto, 2003.

Rogers, Eugene F. "The Eclipse of the Spirit in Karl Barth." In *Conversing with Barth,* edited by Mike Higton and John C. McDowell, pp. 173-90. Aldershot, UK: Ashgate, 2004.

Rosin, H. H. *'Missio Dei': An Examination of the Origin, Contents and Function of the Term in Protestant Missiological Discussion.* Leiden: Interuniversity Institute for Missiological and Ecumenical Research, Department of Missiology, 1972.

Rossel, Jacques. "From a Theology of Crisis to a Theology of Revolution? Karl Barth, Mission and Missions." *Ecumenical Review* 21, no. 2 (1969): 204-15.

Bibliography

Rütti, Ludwig. *Zur Theologie der Mission: kritische Analysen und neue Orientierungen.* Munich: Chr. Kaiser Verlag, 1972.

Sanneh, Lamin O. "The Horizontal and the Vertical in Mission: An African Perspective." *International Bulletin of Missionary Research* 7, no. 4 (1983): 165-71.

———. *Translating the Message: The Missionary Impact on Culture.* Maryknoll, NY: Orbis, 1989.

Schärer, Hans. "Die Begründung der Mission in der katholischen und evangelischen Missionswissenschaft." *Theologische Studien* 16 (1944): 3-43.

Scherer, James A. "Church, Kingdom and *Missio Dei:* Lutheran and Orthodox Corrections to Recent Ecumenical Mission Theology." In *The Good News of the Kingdom: Mission Theology for the Third Millennium,* edited by Charles van Engen, Dean S. Gilliland, Paul Everett Pierson, and Arthur F. Glasser, pp. 82-88. Maryknoll, NY: Orbis, 1993.

———. *Gospel, Church and Kingdom: Comparative Studies in World Mission Theology.* Minneapolis: Augsburg, 1987.

———. "The Lutheran Missionary Idea in Historical Perspective." In . . . *That the Gospel may be Sincerely Preached throughout the World: A Lutheran Perspective on Mission and Evangelism in the 20th Century,* edited by James A. Scherer, pp. 1-29. Stuttgart: Kreuz Verlag, 1982.

———. "Mission Theology." In *Toward the Twenty-First Century in Christian Mission: Essays in Honor of Gerald H. Anderson,* edited by James M. Phillips and Robert T. Coote. Grand Rapids: Eerdmans, 1993.

Schick, E. "Wortverkündigung — Bekenntnis — Zeugnis." *Evangelisches Missions-Magazin* 77 (1933): 68-74, 130-34.

Schleiermacher, Friedrich D. E. *On Religion: Speeches to Its Cultured Despisers.* Cambridge: Cambridge University Press, 1996.

———. *Schriften.* Edited by Andreas Arndt. Frankfurt am Main: Deutscher Klassiker Verlag, 1996.

Schlunk, Martin. "Die Mission im Feuer der Kritik." *Neue Allgemeine Missions-Zeitschrift* 10, no. 8 (1933): 257-70.

———. "German Missionary Literature Since 1939." *International Review of Mission* 30, no. 4 (1941): 546-51.

———. "Theology and Missions in Germany in Recent Years." *International Review of Mission* 27, no. 3 (1938): 464-65.

Schreiter, Robert J. "Epilogue: Mission in the Third Millennium." In *Mission in the Third Millennium,* edited by Robert J. Schreiter, pp. 149-61. Maryknoll, NY: Orbis, 2001.

Schütz, Paul. "Heidnisch und Christlich: Versuch einer Bestimmung der Begriffe vom Menschen her." *Orient und Occident* 2 (1929): 3-28.

———. "Der politisch religiöse Synkretismus und seine Entstehung aus dem Geist der Renaissance." *Orient und Occident* 5 (1930): 1-19.

———. *Zwischen Nil und Kaukasus: ein Reisebericht zur religionspolitischen Lage im Orient.* Munich: Chr. Kaiser Verlag, 1930.

Schwarz, Gerold. "Karl Hartenstein 1894-1954: Missions with a Focus on 'The End.'" In *Mission Legacies: Biographical Studies of Leaders of the Modern Missionary Movement,* edited by Gerald H. Anderson, Robert T. Coote, Norman A. Horner, and James M. Phillips, pp. 591-601. Maryknoll, NY: Orbis, 1994.

———. *Mission, Gemeinde und Ökumene in der Theologie Karl Hartensteins.* Stuttgart: Calwer Verlag, 1980.

Scott, Waldron. *Karl Barth's Theology of Mission.* Downers Grove, IL: InterVarsity, 1978.

"Section II of the Fourth Assembly of the WCC, Uppsala, 1968." *Ecumenical Review* 21, no. 4 (1969): 362-72.

Shenk, Wilbert R. "The Mission Dynamic." In *Mission in Bold Humility: David Bosch's Work Considered,* edited by W. A. Saayman and J. J. Kritzinger, pp. 83-93. Maryknoll, NY: Orbis, 1996.

———. *Write the Vision: The Church Renewed.* Valley Forge, PA: Trinity Press International, 1995.

Shepherd, Jack F. "The Missionary Objective: Total World Evangelization." In *Protestant Crosscurrents in Mission: The Ecumenical-Conservative Encounter,* edited by Norman A. Horner, pp. 108-36. Nashville: Abingdon, 1968.

Simon, G. "Die gegenwärtige theologische Kritik an der Mission." *Jahrbuch der Theologischen Schule Bethel* 3 (1932): 167-209.

Smith, Eugene L. "A Response to *Ad Gentes.*" In *The Documents of Vatican II,* edited by Walter M. Abbott. New York: Crossroad, 1989.

Sonderegger, Katherine. "*Et Resurrexit Tertia Die:* Jenson and Barth on Christ's Resurrection." In *Conversing with Barth,* edited by Mike Higton and John C. McDowell, pp. 191-213. Aldershot, UK: Ashgate, 2004.

Spiller, Vsevolod. "Missionary Aims and the Russian Orthodox Church." *International Review of Mission* 52, no. 2 (1963): 195-203.

Stanley, Brian. *The Bible and the Flag: Protestant Missions and British Imperialism in the Nineteenth and Twentieth Centuries.* Leicester: Apollos, 1990.

Suess, Paulo. "*Missio Dei* and the Project of Jesus: The Poor and the 'Other' as Mediators of the Kingdom of God and Protagonists of the Churches." *International Review of Mission* 92, no. 4 (2003): 550-59.

Sumner, George R. *The First and the Last: The Claim of Jesus Christ and the Claims of Other Religious Traditions.* Grand Rapids: Eerdmans, 2004.

Sundermeier, Theo. "Theology of Mission." In *Dictionary of Mission: Theology, History, Perspectives,* edited by Karl Müller, Theo Sundermeier, Stephen B. Bevans, and Richard H. Bliese, pp. 429-51. Maryknoll, NY: Orbis, 1997.

Tanner, Kathryn E. *Jesus, Humanity and the Trinity: A Brief Systematic Theology.* Edinburgh: T. & T. Clark, 2001.

Tanner, Mary. "Ecumenical Theology." In *The Modern Theologians: An Introduction to Christian Theology since 1918,* edited by David Ford and Rachel Muers, pp. 556-71. Malden, MA: Blackwell, 2005.

Thompson, John. *Modern Trinitarian Perspectives.* Oxford: Oxford University Press, 1994.

Tilgner, Wolfgang. *Volksnomostheologie und Schöpfungsglaube: ein Beitrag zur Geschichte des Kirchenkampfes.* Edited by Kurt Dietrich Schmidt. Vol. 16, Arbeiten zur Geschichte des Kirchenkampfes. Göttingen: Vandenhoeck und Ruprecht, 1966.

Torrance, Thomas F. "The Atonement and the Oneness of the Church." *Scottish Journal of Theology* 7, no. 3 (1954): 245-69.

———. "The Problem of Natural Theology in the Thought of Karl Barth." *Religious Studies* 6 (1970): 121-35.

Ustorf, Werner. "Anti-Americanism in German Missiology." *Mission Studies* 6, no. 1 (1989): 23-34.

———. "The Documents that Reappeared: The Minute-Books of Council and Federation of German Protestant Missions 1924-1949." In *Mission Matters,* edited by Lynne Price, Juan Sepúlveda, and Graeme Smith, pp. 63-82. Frankfurt am Main: Peter Lang, 1997.

———. *Sailing on the Next Tide: Missions, Missiology, and the Third Reich.* Frankfurt am Main: Peter Lang, 2000.

———. "'Survival of the Fittest': German Protestant Missions, Nazism and Neocolonialism, 1933-1945." *Journal of Religion in Africa* 28, no. 1 (1988): 93-114.

Verkuyl, Johannes. "The Kingdom of God as the Goal of the Missio Dei." *International Review of Mission* 68 (1979): 168-75.

Vernier, J. "La théologie de Barth et les Missions." *Le Monde non chrétien* 1 (1931): 79-90.

Vicedom, Georg F. *Missio Dei: Einführung in eine Theologie der Mission.* Munich: Chr. Kaiser Verlag, 1958.

Visser 't Hooft, W. A. "Karl Barth and the Ecumenical Movement." *Ecumenical Review* 32, no. 2 (1980): 129-51.

Visser 't Hooft, W. A., and Joseph H. Oldham. *The Church and Its Function in Society.* Chicago: Willett, Clark, 1937.

Volf, Miroslav. *After Our Likeness: The Church as the Image of the Trinity.* Grand Rapids: Eerdmans, 1998.

von Thadden, Reinold. "The Church under the Cross." In *Missions under the Cross,* edited by Norman Goodall, pp. 46-63. London: Edinburgh House, 1953.

Wagner, Herwig. "Hartensteins Beitrag zum Aufbruch in der Missionstheologie 1945-1960." In *Karl Hartenstein: Leben in weltweitem Horizont,* edited by Fritz Lamparter, pp. 128-40. Bonn: Verlag für Kultur und Wissenschaft, 1995.

Wainwright, Geoffrey. *Lesslie Newbigin: A Theological Life.* Oxford: Oxford University Press, 2000.

Walls, Andrew F. "Christianity in the Non-Western World: A Study in the Serial Nature of Christian Expansion." In *The Cross-Cultural Process in Christian History: Studies in the Transmission and Appropriation of Faith,* pp. 27-48. Maryknoll, NY: Orbis, 2002.

———. "Missionary Societies and the Fortunate Subversion of the Church." In *The Missionary Movement in Christian History: Studies in the Transmission of Faith,* pp. 241-54. Maryknoll, NY: Orbis, 1996.

Warneck, Gustav. *Evangelische Missionslehre: ein missionstheoretischer Versuch.* 2nd ed. Vol. 3.2. Gotha: Friedrich Andreas Perthes, 1905.

———."Die moderne Weltevangelismus-theorie." *Allgemeine Missions-Zeitschrift* 24 (1897): 305-25.

———. "The Mutual Relations of Evangelical Missionary Societies to One Another." In *Report of the Centenary Conference on the Protestant Missions of the World, London, 1888,* edited by James Johnston, pp. 431-37. London: James Nisbet, 1888.

———. *Outline of a History of Protestant Missions from the Reformation to the Present Time.* Edited by George Robson. 3rd ed. New York: Fleming Revell, 1906.

———. "Thoughts on the Missionary Century." *Missionary Review of the World* 23, no. 6 (1900): 413-17.

Warren, Max A. *Challenge and Response: Six Studies in Missionary Opportunity.* New York: Morehouse-Barlow Co., 1959.

———. "The Christian Mission and the Cross." In *Missions under the Cross,* edited by Norman Goodall, pp. 24-45. London: Edinburgh House, 1953.

Webster, John B. *Barth's Ethics of Reconciliation.* Cambridge: Cambridge University Press, 1995.

———. "The Church as Witnessing Community." *Scottish Bulletin of Evangelical Theology* 21, no. 1 (2003): 21-33.

———. *Confessing God: Essays in Christian Dogmatics II.* Edinburgh: T. & T. Clark, 2005.

———. "'Eloquent and Radiant': The Prophetic Office of Christ and the Mission of the Church." In *Barth's Moral Theology: Human Action in Barth's Thought,* pp. 125-50. Grand Rapids: Eerdmans, 1998.

———. *Holy Scripture: A Dogmatic Sketch.* Cambridge: Cambridge University Press, 2003.

———. "Life in and of Himself: Reflections on God's Aseity." In *Engaging the Doctrine of God: Contemporary Protestant Perspectives,* edited by Bruce L. McCormack, pp. 107-24. Grand Rapids: Baker Academic, 2008.

———. "The Visible Attests the Invisible." In *The Community of the Word: Toward an Evangelical Ecclesiology,* edited by Mark Husbands and Daniel B. Trier, pp. 96-113. Downers Grove, IL: InterVarsity, 2005.

"Why Missions? Report of Commission I on the Biblical and Theological Basis of Missions." In *Paul L. Lehmann Collection, Special Collections, Princeton Theological Seminary,* edited by Paul Lehmann, 35. Princeton, NJ: Committee on Research in Foreign Missions of the Division of Foreign Missions and the Central Department of Research and Survey, The National Council of the Churches of Christ in the USA, 1952.

Wickeri, Philip L. "Mission from the Margins: The *Missio Dei* in the Crisis of World Christianity." *International Review of Mission* 93, no. 2 (2004): 182-98.

Wiedenmann, Ludwig. *Mission und Eschatologie: Eine Analyse der neueren deutschen evangelischen Missionstheologie.* Paderborn: Verlag Bonifacius-Druckerei, 1965.

Wieser, Thomas, ed. *Planning for Mission: Working Papers on the New Quest for Mission-*

ary Communities. New York: U.S. Conference for the World Council of Churches, 1966.

Williams, Daniel H. "Constantine, Nicaea and the 'Fall' of the Church." In *Christian Origins: Theology, Rhetoric, and Community,* edited by Lewis Ayres and Gareth Jones, pp. 117-36. London: Routledge, 1998.

Williams, Rowan. *Arius: Heresy and Tradition*. rev. ed. Grand Rapids: Eerdmans, 2002.

———. "Barth on the Triune God." In *Karl Barth: Studies of His Theological Method,* edited by S. W. Sykes. Oxford: Clarendon, 1979.

Winter, J. C. *Bruno Gutmann, 1876-1966: A German Approach to Social Anthropology.* Oxford: Clarendon, 1979.

Witschi, Hermann. *Geschichte der Basler Mission 1920-1940.* Vol. 5. Basel: Basileia Verlag, 1970.

World Council of Churches Department on Studies in Evangelism. *The Church for Others, and the Church for the World: A Quest for Structures for Missionary Congregations.* Geneva: World Council of Churches, 1967.

———. *A Theological Reflection on the Work of Evangelism.* Geneva: World Council of Churches, 1963.

Wright, Christopher J. H. *The Mission of God.* Downers Grove, IL: InterVarsity, 2006.

Wrogemann, Henning. *Mission und Religion in der systematischen Theologie der Gegenwart: das Missionsverständnis deutschsprachiger protestantischer Dogmatiker im 20. Jahrhundert.* Göttingen: Vandenhoeck und Ruprecht, 1997.

Yates, Timothy. *Christian Mission in the Twentieth Century.* Cambridge: Cambridge University Press, 1994.

Yocum, John. *Ecclesial Mediation in Karl Barth.* Aldershot, UK: Ashgate, 2004.

Yoder, John Howard. "Let the Church Be the Church." In *The Royal Priesthood: Essays Ecclesiological and Ecumenical,* by John Howard Yoder, edited by Michael Cartwright, pp. 168-80. Grand Rapids: Eerdmans, 1994.

———. "The Otherness of the Church." *The Mennonite Quarterly Review* 35, no. 4 (1961): 286-96.

———. *The Politics of Jesus: Vicit Agnus Noster.* 2nd ed. Grand Rapids: Eerdmans, 1994.

———. "Sacrament as Social Process: Christ the Transformer of Culture." In *The Royal Priesthood: Essays Ecclesiological and Ecumenical,* by John Howard Yoder, edited by Michael Cartwright, pp. 359-73. Grand Rapids: Eerdmans, 1994.

Zizioulas, John D. *Being as Communion: Studies in Personhood and the Church.* Crestwood, NY: St. Vladimir's Seminary Press, 1985.

Index

Aagaard, Anna Marie, 36, 38-39, 42
Aagaard, Johannes, 40, 47, 162; on
  Barth's missiology, 14, 15-16, 17; on
  church and mission, 73; on *missio
  Dei*, 11, 48-49; on political theology,
  56
Accommodationism, 81, 86
Activism: Hutchison on, 82; and mis-
  sion, 108-9, 208-9; Schütz on, 94-95
Ad Gentes, 61
Analogia entis, 1, 167, 187
Andersen, Wilhelm: on Barth, 14; on
  christocentrism, 143-44; on *missio
  Dei*, 6-7, 44, 51; on mission as
  parachurch enterprise, 61-62; on
  Trinity and missionary task, 160
Anglo-Americanism, 81, 86; and expul-
  sion from China, 136-137; and Ger-
  man mission, 118-20, 148; Gutmann
  on, 99; Knak's rejection of, 121; and
  missionary task, 110-11
Anknüpfungspunkt. See Point of contact
Apologetics, 133-36, 170; *missio Dei* as,
  123, 132
Apostles: and apostolicity of church,
  264-65; sending of, 37
Apostolate: and calling, 258; and Christian existence, 254-57; and church,

262-66; and ecclesial continuity, 283;
  and evangelism, 69; and incarnation,
  219; and mission, 52-53; and participation in God's works, 234-35; and
  visibility of church, 266-72
Aquinas, Thomas, 19n.70
Aring, Paul, 38, 59-60, 71
Arius, 18
Atonement, 43-44, 57. *See also* Reconciliation
Augustine: on knowledge of God, 20-
  24; and neo-Cappadocians, 28-29; on
  sending of Son, 19
Authority: Hartenstein on, 132; in mission, 136; and point of connection,
  170
Ayres, Lewis, 22, 23

Baptism, 261
Barnes, Michel René, 22
Barth, Karl: on being and act of God,
  173-79; on call to mission, 134-35;
  christocentrism of, 142-45; as church-
  man, 170; on divine aseity, 201-3; and
  Gutmann, 99; and Hartenstein, 125-
  30; on International Missionary
  Council (Jerusalem), 85; and *missio
  Dei*, 11-17, 144, 161; and mission, 30-

319

Gutmann, 103; on mission strategy, 91

Krusche, Werner, 58, 228, 267

LaCugna, Catherine Mowry, 20

Language, 281-82

Law, 88, 169

Lehmann, Paul: on history of missions, 145-46; and International Missionary Council, 123-24, 152, 158-59; and "Missionary Calling of the Church," 154-57; on mission method, 153-54; on mission obligation, 138-40, 162

Liberalism, 81-83

Linz, Manfred, 150

Loving-kindness (of God), 235-36

Lutheranism, 110-11

Mackay, John, 152

Manecke, Dieter, 43

Mangina, Joseph, 188

Margull, Hans Jochen, 44

Marx, Walter, 88

Matthey, Jacque: on church and world, 54-55, 56-57; on *missio Dei,* 8, 9, 49, 50, 73-74, 200-201

Mbiti, John, 100

McCormack, Bruce, 217, 223

Medical missions, 98

Meditation, 232

Methodists, 68

Milbank, John, 25

Minear, Paul, 152

Missio Christi, 198

Missio Dei: as apologia, 123; and Barth, 11-17, 144; and church, 53-57; competing forms of, 161-62; and divine agency, 38-40; and Economic Trinity, 200-204; and election, 213-14; and eschatology, 242, 254-57; and Great Commission, 141; and Hartenstein, 124, 130-36; and immanence of God, 204-8; and incarnation, 220-26; and International Missionary Conference,

150-52, 157-61; and joy, 295-98; and kingdom of God, 50-53, 290-92; and living God, 208-11, 287-90; and *missio ecclesiae,* 73-74; and "Missionary Calling of the Church," 157; and missionary form, 242-45; and the origins of, 11-17, 126-27; and priority of mission, 75-76; problem of, 35-36, 76-77, 286-87; as problem of God, 4-10, 198-200; reconstruction of, 197; and reduction of church, 229; and "Theology and Mission in the Present Situation," 78, 106-7, 120-22; and Trinity, 17-18, 41, 47-50, 163-66; and "Why Missions?" 147-49. *See also* Mission

Missio ecclesiae, 73-74

Missiology: and Anglo-American liberalism, 81-83; and being and act of God, 173-79; and International Missionary Council, 157-58; and orders of creation, 78-79

Mission: act of, 181-85, 290-91; Barth on, 31-34, 107-9, 110-11, 164-66; and *beneficia Christi,* 174-78; and church, 3-4, 53-57, 61-65, 73-74, 283-84; and colonialism, 51-52; criticisms of, 4-5; and culture, 52, 147; as derivative act, 207-8; determination of, 235-39; dialectical critique of, 86; as divine act, 37, 211-14; end of, 195; and eschatology, 254-57; form of, 186-90, 190-94, 242-45, 249-51, 282; of God, 73-74; and *habitus,* 24; Hartenstein on, 125-26; and history, 47, 145-46; as human act, 211-14; and incarnation, 225-26; judgment as impetus for, 58-59; and loving-kindness of God, 235-36; methodology of, 27-29; motive for, 107-9, 184-85; and National Socialism, 101-5; necessity of, 253-54, 262-63; need for, 59-61; neglect of, 30-31; and orders of creation, 79, 88; participation in, 235; postcolonial concept of, 8-9; priority of, 75; and propaganda,